THE LAW AND PRACTICE OF THE UNITED NATIONS

LEGAL ASPECTS OF
INTERNATIONAL ORGANIZATION

VOLUME 42

The titles published in this series are listed at the end of this volume.

The Law and Practice of the United Nations

Third Revised Edition

by

Benedetto Conforti

MARTINUS NIJHOFF PUBLISHERS
LEIDEN / BOSTON

A C.I.P. Catalogue record for this book is available from the Library of Congress.

Printed on acid-free paper.

ISBN 90-04-14309-2
© 2005 Koninklijke Brill NV, Leiden, The Netherlands.

Koninklijke Brill NV incorporates the imprints Brill Academic Publishers, Martinus Nijhoff Publishers and VSP.

http://www.brill.nl

Printed and bound in The Netherlands.

PREFACE

This volume is the up-to-date English version of the fifth Italian edition of a textbook on the United Nations which was first published in 1971 by CEDAM (Padua).

The book aims to provide a comprehensive legal analysis of problems concerning membership, the structure of U.N. organs, their functions and their acts taking into consideration the text of the Charter, its historical origins, and, particularly, the practice of the organs. Developments in United Nations practice subsequent to 1971 have obviously been taken into account. As a general working criterion, the more recent practice has been added to the pre-existing one, rather than substituting it, even when past practice may appear to be obsolete. Indeed, one of the aims of the book is to trace the "story" of the United Nations from its birth precisely through an analysis of the practice. Moreover, since the Charter has never undergone any substantive modifications, one cannot exclude that what may appear to be old and obsolete today could become of current interest in the future. For this reason the examination of former practice will sooner or later become useful to anyone seeking to interpret the Charter. For instance, in 1975 the United States proposed the admission of the two Vietnams, which were separate countries at that time, and of the two Koreas, under the "package" technique. Thus the well-known 1948 advisory opinion of the International Court of Justice on the "package" proposed by the Soviet Union for collective admission in the 40s and 50s again became timely, despite its having appeared obsolete.

In my own view a legal analysis which is free of dogmatism and firmly linked to practice can describe the role played by the United Nations in the past and at present better than many lengthy and inconclusive political or sociological studies.

The book is very much focused on the Charter as it stands while it only marginally deals with reforms that might be introduced, such as those concerning the structure of the Security Council and the General Assembly. Indeed, it is difficult to foresee radical reforms, giving the U.N. an entirely new shape. This is particularly true with regard to endowing the Organization with the force and efficacy that would be needed for the maintenance of peace and security. Recent events have clearly shown how unfeasible such an endowment would be.

I am indebted to Carlo Focarelli, Massimo Iovane and Angelo Labella for the help provided in the preparation of the manuscript and to Susan Fisher Francioni for the first English draft.

November 1995

* * *

In the second edition of the English version no radical changes have been made, no radical changes having taken place in the structure and the activity of the United Nations. However, some new elements in practice, such as the power of the Security Council to provide for the civil administrations of territories (Kosovo, East Timor) have been taken into account.

Despite the discouraging scenario offered by the international community to-day, the author still belongs to an irreducible group of individuals who believe in the rule of law as opposed to the "real politik", in the need for strengthening the UN system as opposed to the unilateral actions of powerful States, and in a genuine and universal fight for peace and security.

I am grateful to Rachael Young for the help with the revision of the English text.

March 2000

* * *

The third edition of the book, although all parts of it have been up-dated, is mainly focused on the practice of the Security Council. In particular the action of the Security Council under Chapter VII has been taken into account. The legal literature on Chapter VII has grown enormously in recent times, so that it is difficult to select what actually needs to be read. The legal aspects of the action or the inaction of the Security Council have even been discussed by ordinary people with regard to the war against Iraq. The importance of the role of the United Nations has become a leit-motiv of all debates on international politics. Consequently, the opinion often held in the past, according to which it was useless to deal with the legal aspects of the United Nations activity, can be considered as obsolete

I am deeply indebted to Angelo Labella, research fellow of the University of Naples, for help in selecting the bibliography, and to Rachael Kondak, barrister in London, for the review of the English text.

September 2004

B.C.

TABLE OF CONTENTS

INTRODUCTION

CHAPTER ONE
THE MEMBERSHIP

Section I
Acquisition of Membership Status

Section II
Modifications in Membership Status

CHAPTER TWO
THE ORGANS

Section I
The Security Council

Section II
The General Assembly

Section III
The Secretariat

Section III
Maintenance of the Peace: The Functions of the General Assembly

Section IV
Maintenance of the Peace: The Functions of the Secretary-General

Section V
Maintenance of the Peace and Regional Organizations

Section VI
Economic Co-operation and Action for Development

Section VII
The Protection of Human Rights

Section VIII
De-colonization and Self-Determination of Peoples

Section IX
Registration of Treaties

Section X
The Judicial Functions

Section XI
Financing the Organization

CHAPTER FOUR
THE ACTS

ABBREVIATIONS

Documents[*]

CIJ, Memoires	Cour Internationale de Justice, Memoires, plaidoiries et documents
CIJ, Recueil	Cour Internationale de Justice, Recueil des arrets, avis consultatifs et ordonnances
CPIJ, Recueil	Cour Permanente de Justice Internationale, Recueil des arrets (o Recueil des avis consultatifs)
ESCOR	Economic and Social Council Official Records
GAOR	General Assembly Official Records
ILC Yearbook	International Law Commission Yearbook
SCOR	Security Council Official Records
SC Rep.	Repertoire of the Practice of the Security Council
U.N.C.I.O.	United Nations Conference on International Organization
U.N.L.S.	United Nations Legislative Series
UN Rep.	Repertory of the Practice of the United Nations Organs
U.N.T.S.	United Nations Treaty Series

Periodicals

ADeI	Annuario de derecho internacional
ADI	Annuario di diritto internazionale
AF	Annuaire français de droit international
Afr J	African Journal of International Law
AJ	American Journal of International Law
Austr Y	Australian Yeabookof international law
AV	Archiv des Völkerrechts
Bruns'Z	Zeitschrift für ausländisches öffentliches Recht und Völkerrecht
BYB	British Yearbook of International Law
CI	La Comunità internazionale
CS	Comunicazioni e studi dell'Istituto di diritto internazionale e straniero dell'Università di Milano

---

[*] UN Documents are usually quoted according to official acronyms. Sources of General Assembly and Security Council resolutions are not quoted since they can be easily found.

CYIL	The Canadian Yearbook of International Law (Annuaire canadien de droit international)
DI	Diritto internazionale
EJIL	European Journal of International Law
GYIL	German Yearbook of International Law
HILJ	Harvard International Law Journal
HLR	Harvard Law review
ICLQ	The International and Comparative Law Quarterly
IJIL	Indian Journal of International Law
ILM	International Legal Materials
Int. Org.	International Organization
Int PK	International Peacekeeping
IYIL	The Italian Yearbook of International Law
LJIL	Leiden Journal of International law
JapAIL	Japanese Annual of International Law
NILR	Netherlands International Law Review
NYIL	Netherlands Yearbook of International Law
NUCM	ONU, Cronique mensuelle, or ONU, Cronique
RBDI	Revue belge de droit international
RC	Recueil des cours de l'Académie de droit international
RDI	Rivista di diritto internazionale
ReD	Revista espanola de derecho internacional
REgDI	Revue egyptienne de droit international
RGDIP	Revue générale de droit international public
RHDI	Revue hellénique de droit international
SAYB	South African Yearbook of International Law
Schw.Z	Schweizer Zeitschrift für internationales und europäisches Recht
T	Transactions of the Grotius Society
UNJY	United Nations Juridical Yearbook
UNMC	United Nations Monthly Chronicle, or UN Chronicle
Virg.JIL	Virginia Journal of International Law
ZöR	Österreichische Zeitschrift für öffentliches Recht
ZöRV	Österreichische Zeitschrift für öffentliches Recht und Völkerrecht

GENERAL BIBLIOGRAPHY

SCHÜKING-WEHBERG, *Die Satzung des Völkerbundes*, Berlin, 1924.

RAY, *Commentaire du Pacte de la société des Nation*, Paris, 1930.

KOPELMANAS, *L'Organisation des Nations Unies*, Vol. I, *L'Organisation constitutionnelle de l'ONU*, Paris, 1947.

EVATT, *The United Nations*, London, 1948.

ROSS, *Costitution of the United Nations (Analysis of Statement and Functions)*, Copenaghen, 1950.

BENTWICH and MARTIN, *A Commentary on the Charter of the United Nations*, London, 1951.

KELSEN, *The Law of the United Nations*, New York, 1951.

PERASSI, *L'ordinamento delle Nazioni Unite*, Padua, 1953.

COHEN, *The United Nations: Constitutional Developments, Growth and Possibilities*, Cambridge (Mass.), 1961.

BAILEY, *The United Nations: A Short Political Guide*, New York, 1965.

PADELFORD and GOODRICH (ed.), *The United Nations in the Balance (Accomplishments and Prospects)*, New York, 1965.

FALK and MENDLOVITZ (eds.), *The Strategy of World Order*, Vol. III: *The United Nations*, New York, 1966.

ROSS, *The United Nations: Peace and Progress*, Totowa (N.J), 1966.

WATERS, *The United Nations (International Organization and Administration)*, New York,1967.

WÜNSCHE, *Die Vereinten Nationen*, Berlin, 1967.

GREGG and BARKUN (eds.), *The United Nations System and its Functions. Selected Readings*, Princeton (N.J.), 1968.

COYLE and GOLDBERG, *The United Nations and how it Works*, New York-London, 1969.

GOODRICH-HAMBRO-SIMONS, *Charter of the United Nations, Commentary and Documents*, New York, 1969.

JENKS, *The World beyond the Charter in Historical Perspective*, London, 1969.

TUNG, *International Organization under the United Nations System*, New York, 1969.

GIBBONS and MORICAN, *The League of Nations and UNO*, London, 1970.

VIRALLY, *L'Organisation mondiale*, Paris, 1972.

ELMANDJRA, *The United Nations System. An Analysis*, London, 1973.

UDINA, *L'Organizzazione delle Nazioni Unite (Introduzione e testi annotati)*, Padua, 1973.

EDMONDS, *The United Nations. Successes and Failures*, Indianapolis-New York, 1974.

GOODRICH, *The United Nations in a Changing World*, New York-London, 1974.

HÜFNER and NAUMANN, *Das System der Vereinten Nationen. Eine Einführung*, Dusseldorf, 1974.

MEDINA ORTEGA, *La Organizacion de las Naciones Unidas, Su estructura y funciones*, Madrid, 1974.

NICHOLAS, *The United Nations as a Political Institution*, London, 1975.

ZIEGER, *Die Vereinten Nationen*, Hannover, 1976.

WOLFRUM-PRILL-BRÜCKNER (eds.), *Handbuch Vereinten Nationen*, München, 1977.

HALDERMAN, *The Political Role of the United Nations: Advancing the World Community*, New York, 1981.

LUARD, *A History of the United Nations. Volume I: The Years of Western Domination, 1945-1955*, New York, 1982.

GHEBALI, *La crise du système des Nations Unies*, Paris, 1986.

RAMCHARAN, *Keeping Faith with the United Nations*, Dordrecht, 1987.

YODER, *The Evolution of the United Nations*, New York, 1989.

BARNABY (ed.), *Building a more Democratic United Nations*, London, 1991.

COT and PELLET (eds.), *La Charte des Nations Unies (Commentaire article par article)*, Paris, 1991.

SIMMA (ed.), *Charta der Vereinten Nationen (Kommentar)*, München, 1991.

CHAUMONT, *L'Organisation des Nations Unies*, Paris, 1992.

MÜLLER, *The Reform of the United Nations*, vols. 2, New York, 1992.

SCHERMERS and BLOKKER, *International Institutional Law*, The Hague, 1995.

GLASSNER, *The United Nations at work,* Westport Ct, 1998.

MARCHISIO, *L'ONU. Il diritto delle Nazioni Unite*, Bologna, 2000.

SIMMA (ed.), *The Charter of the United Nations: A Commentary*, 2nd ed., Oxford, 2002.

Volger, *A Concise Enciclopedia of the United Nations*, The Hague, 2002.

Mestre-Lafay, L'Organisation des Nations Unies, 17th ed., Paris, 2003.

INTRODUCTION

1. Origins of the United Nations Charter.

BIBLIOGRAPHY: GUGGENHEIM, *L'organisation de la société internazionale*, Neuchatel, 1944, p. 155 ff.; AGO, *L'organizzazione internazionale dalla Società delle Nazioni alle Nazioni Unite*, in *CI*, 1946, p. 5 ff.; McKINNON-WOOD, *The Dissolution of the League of Nations*, in *BYB*, 1946, p. 317 ff.; KOPELMANAS, *L'Organisation des Nations Unies, I. L'Organisation constitutionelle des Nations Unies*, Paris, 1947, p. 10 ff.; MURRAY, *From the League to UN*, London, 1948, p. 65 ff.; MYRES, *Liquidation of League of Nations Functions*, in *AJ*, 1948, p. 320; EAGLETON, *International Government*, New York, 1957, p. 288 ff.; RUSSEL, *A History of United Nations Charter*, Washington, 1958; MARIN, *Reflexiones sobre la Conferencia de San Francisco y la Carta de las Naciones Unidas*, in *ONU: Ano XL*, Madrid, 1987, p. 33 ff.; HILDERBRAND, *Dumbarton Oaks:The Origins of The UN and the Search for Postwar Security*, Chapel Hill, 1990; DRAKIDS, *La Charte de l'Atlantique 1941: La Déclaration des Nations Unies 1942*, Besançon, 1995; HOOPES and BRINKLEY, *Franklin D. Roosevelt and the Creation of the UN*, New Haven, 1997.

A) *From the Atlantic Charter to the San Francisco Conference.*

The term United Nations was adopted during the Second World War by the States who were fighting against the Axis Powers. In a solemn declaration signed in Washington D.C. on January 11, 1942, these nations, besides undertaking to direct every effort toward the enemy's defeat and agreeing not to sign a separate peace or armistice, accepted the principles laid down by President Roosevelt and Prime Minister Churchill in the 1942 Atlantic Charter. The Charter did not envisage the establishment of an organization or association of States which could replace the League of Nations; however, it did indicate the necessity of creating a collective security system after the war capable of discouraging aggression (para. 8) and of establishing strong co-operation between the States in economic and social matters (para. 5). Collective security and co-operation in economic and social matters are today the fundamental aims of the United Nations Organization (or, in official terminology, the United Nations).

Para. 8 of the Atlantic Charter reads as follows: "They [the United States and Great Britain] believe that all of the nations of the world, for realistic as well as spiritual reasons, must come to the abandonment of the use of force. Since no future peace can be maintained if land, sea or air armaments continue to be employed by nations which threaten, or may threaten, aggression outside of their frontiers, they believe, pending the establishment of a wider and permanent system of general security, that the disarmament of such nations is essential". Para. 5 states that the United States and Great Britain "desire to bring about the fullest collaboration between all nations in the economic field with the object of securing, for all, improved labor standards, economic advancement and social security".
     The United Nations Declaration was signed by twenty-six governments, some of them in exile. Another twenty-one governments subsequently adhered to it.

It was only at the Moscow Conference, in October 1943, that the establishment of an international organization similar to the League of Nations was officially envisaged. The Declaration of the Four Nations who participated in the Conference (the United States, the Soviet Union, Great Britain and China) recognised: "the necessity of establishing at the earliest practicable date a general international organization, based on the principle of the sovereign equality of all peace-loving States and open to membership by all such States, large and small, for the maintenance of international peace and security".
     Between the end of August and the beginning of October 1944 the same four governments that had taken part in the Moscow Conference met in Dumbarton Oaks, near Washington D.C., to lay down the foundations of the future world organization. In the meantime the United States Department of State had undertaken a series of studies, investigations and even public opinion polls in the preparation of its draft. The other three governments also presented drafts of their own, although with less ambitious procedures.
     The Dumbarton Oaks "proposals", published at the close of the meetings, already contained all of what are the essential aspects of the U.N. today.
     The proposals confirmed that the purposes of the Organization were to maintain international peace and security, to develop friendly relations among nations, to promote co-operation in economic and social matters. The structure of the new body was to be based on the model of the Covenant of the League of Nations. It was stated that the basic organs would be the same four organs of the League: the Assembly (consisting of all the Member States), the Council (made up of a limited number of States, with permanent seats given to the Great Powers), the Secretariat, headed by a Secretary-General, and the Court of Justice. The Dumbarton Oaks proposals presented, by contrast, quite noteworthy differences with the League of Nations Covenant as far as the functions and powers of the organs were concerned. First of all, the Assembly

(to become the General Assembly) remained the only organ with general competence, while the Council (to become the Security Council), which in the Covenant had had the same power as the Assembly, was given the exclusive task of maintaining international peace and security. Further, the powers of the Council were considerably widened. The proposals laid down in detail the measures to be adopted in the case of aggression or threat of aggression that can be found in Articles 39 and following of the UN Charter. Next to the General Assembly, but in a secondary position ("under the authority") with respect to it, the proposals placed an organ specifically devoted to the development of co-operation in social matters: the Economic and Social Council. Another important difference with the League of Nations Covenant concerned the voting system, as it was proposed that the Assembly and the Economic and Social Council decide by majority rather than by unanimity.

The Dumbarton Oaks proposals can be found in U.N.C.I.O., vol. 3, p. 1 ff. (English text) and vol. 4, p. 1 ff. (French text). Together with the acts of the following San Francisco Conference, they form, for purposes of interpretation, the "preparatory works" of the UN Charter.

The Dumbarton Oaks proposals established that the Security Council would be made up of 11 members: five of them, at that time the so-called Great Powers (the United States, Great Britain, the USSR, China and France), would be permanent members; the other six would be elected by the General Assembly for a two-year period. On the contrary, nothing regarding the voting system in the Council was agreed upon at Dumbarton Oaks. The problem was then discussed by Churchill, Roosevelt and Stalin at the Yalta Conference in February 1945. It was here that the rule, eventually to become Article 27 of the UN Charter, took shape; by it each of the five permanent members were provided with the famous veto power, that is, the possibility to block, with a negative vote, the adoption of any decision by the Council that was not of a merely procedural nature. The rule, in fact, is called the "Yalta formula".

The three powers participating in the Yalta meeting decided to hold a United Nations Conference in San Francisco on April 25, 1945 with the task of drawing up the Charter of the new world Organization "along the lines proposed... at Dumbarton Oaks". France and China were invited to be considered "Sponsoring Governments" at the Conference. France, while agreeing to participate, refused to accept this title; China accepted it.

B) *The San Francisco Conference, the entry into force of the Charter, and present United Nations membership.*

Fifty States took part in the San Francisco Conference. In addition to those countries which had already signed the United Nations Declaration, Argentina and Denmark and two of the Republics belonging to the Soviet Union, the Ukraine and Byelorussia, were invited. Although Poland had signed the declaration, it did not participate in the preparatory works since at the time it had two rival governments (one pro-West and one pro-USSR) and the Great Powers were not able to agree on which government to invite. When the Communist regime had prevailed after the Conference was over, Poland was treated as a participating State and thus considered one of the original members of the Organization.

Byelorussia and the Ukraine, which figure as original members of the United Nations, certainly could not have been considered, at the time of the San Francisco Conference, as real States under international law, as they were not independent. Their participation in the San Francisco preparatory works and their membership in the United Nations had been decided at Yalta for political reasons: to increase the weight of the Soviet Union, both in the Conference (the only other participating Communist State was Yugoslavia) and in the future Organization. In short, the USSR was thus attributed three votes instead of one in the Conference and then in the General Assembly (where, under Article 18, para. 1, of the Charter, every member has one vote). Today, following the break up of the Soviet Union at the end of 1991, Byelorussia (now called Belarus) and the Ukraine are independent and sovereign, as are the other States created by the dissolution.

Another two of the countries participating in the Conference were not exactly States under international law. India was then a British dominion and the Philippines was a protectorate of the United States. However, in these two cases the countries were nearing independence (obtained by India in 1947 and by the Philippines in July of 1946).

The following States participated in the San Francisco Conference: Argentina, Australia, Belgium, Bolivia, Brazil, Byelorussia, Canada, Chile, China, Columbia, Costa Rica, Cuba, Czechoslovakia, Denmark, the Dominican Republic, Ecuador, Egypt, El Salvador, Ethiopia, France, Great Britain, Greece, Guatemala, Haiti, Honduras, India, Iran, Iraq, Lebanon, Liberia, Luxembourg, Mexico, the Netherlands, New Zealand, Nicaragua, Norway, Panama, Paraguay, Peru, the Philippines, Saudi Arabia, Syria, Turkey, the Ukraine, the Union of South Africa, the United States, Uruguay, the USSR, Venezuela and Yugoslavia.

The proceedings of the Conference are published in United Nations Conference on International Organization (U.N.C.I.O.), London-New York, 1945, 19 volumes and indexes.

The San Francisco Conference took place between April 25 and June 26, 1945. Even a cursory glance at the preparatory works can reveal how dominant was the role played by the Great Powers in the Conference. One might say that the Charter was born in a certain sense as a constitution granted (*octroyée*). The basic outline sketched at Dumbarton Oaks was presented as unchangeable. Although the Conference could decide by majority (two-thirds) on the wording of the individual articles, the participants knew that any substantial change in the Dumbarton Oaks proposals would have resulted in the rejection by the Great Powers, or by some of them, of the new Organization, and that it would have then been useless to proceed with its founding. However, many other matters were discussed and numerous provisions were added at San Francisco, including some important ones. These were often adopted at the initiative of middle-sized or small States. Some examples are the provisions concerning colonies (the declaration regarding non-self-governing territories contained in Article 73 of the Charter, the provisions establishing the Trusteeship Council, placed, as was the Economic and Social Council, under the authority of the Assembly), Article 51 of the Charter on the right of self-defence, the rules, drawn from the Covenant of the League of Nations, concerning the registration of treaties, the prevalence of the Charter over any other international agreement, the privileges and immunities of Secretariat officials within the domestic legal systems of the Member States, and so on. By contrast, the few attempts made to even partially modify the "lines" laid down at Dumbarton Oaks, the few attempts aimed at avoiding that the efficacy of the new Organization, would rest largely on the will and agreement of the Great Powers and, in the final analysis, would depend on their unfettered free choice, ended in failure. It is enough to mention the opposition to the drafts that tended to invest the International Court of Justice with some kind of review power over the legality of the acts of the Organization, thus giving it the binding power to interpret the Charter (see U.N.C.I.O., vol. 13, p. 633, p. 645) or at least the provisions of Article 2, para. 7, of the Charter regarding domestic jurisdiction (*ivi.*, vol. 6, p. 113, p. 509); or the vain attempts to obtain from the Great Powers, if not changes, at least an authentic interpretation of the Yalta formula (see § 1 A), so as to dissipate the doubts which the application of this formula would certainly have given rise to and which it has indeed given rise to.

At the request of the other States, the four Sponsoring Powers issued a Statement, later also subscribed to by France, in order to "clarify" the Yalta formula (Article 27, paras. 2 and 3 of the Charter), and especially to clarify when a Security Council decision should be considered to be of a procedural nature, and therefore, under the formula, not subject to the veto and when it should be considered substantial. Actually, the Statement (published in U.N.C.I.O., vol. 11, p. 711 ff.), being the result of a compromise, is almost more obscure than the formula. On this point, see § 23. The Soviet Union stood out in defending the prerogatives of the Great Powers and in its distrust of the Organization. At the Yalta meeting, only with great difficulty had it been convinced to exclude the possibility of the veto on procedural questions. For a long time after the UN. had been set up, the USSR's conduct within the Organization reflected the same recalcitrant attitude. It hardly needs to be pointed out that the Soviet attitude at San Francisco (and also afterwards) is to be explained in view of its ideological isolation at the time.

At the end of the Conference, the Charter as a whole was unanimously approved and signed by all the participating States. Under Article 110, para. 3, it was to enter into force when it had been ratified by the five permanent members of the Security Council and by a majority of the other signatory States. This occurred on October 24, 1945. At the end of December of the same year all the fifty States that had taken part in the Conference (as well as Poland which, without having taken part, was allowed to sign) had ratified the Charter. These States constitute the original members of the Organization, in accordance with Article 3. Article 4 governs the admission procedure for new members. Between original members and admitted members, the United Nations numbers today — after the admission of the successor States of the former Soviet Union and the former Yugoslavia, as well as the admission of some territories which still were under a colonial-type domination — more than 190 members. With very few exceptions, all States of the world are members of the UN: Taiwan (Republic of China), which is still independent from the People's Republic of China, was thrown out the Organization when it was replaced by the latter in the United Nations in 1971 (see § 19); the Turkish Republic of Cyprus, has never been admitted as it has never been recognised by the overwhelming majority of the member States. Switzerland, which for many decades remained out, finally decided to become member, and was admitted to the United Nations in September 2002, after a popular referendum. Other entities which are not States, like the Holy See and, with different standards, many inter-governmental or non-governmental organizations, such as the International Red Cross, have the status of "observer".

C) *Relationships between the League of Nations and the United Nations.*

The League of Nations, which formally survived up until the Second World War, was dissolved in April 1946, when the UN was already fully active. The Assembly of the League met for the last time from 8 to 18 April and, with a unanimous vote, solemnly decreed its own dissolution.

Parallel resolutions of the Assemblies of the two Organizations provided for the transfer of a whole series of functions of a *non-political* nature from the League to the UN. In particular, provision was made for the transfer of the functions carried out by the League Secretariat (typical examples were those functions concerning international agreements, such as custody of instruments of ratification, of adhesion, of denunciation, and so on) and by the various *ad hoc* Committees set up by the League to promote economic and social co-operation among the States. The former were assumed by the UN

Secretariat and the latter by the Economic and Social Council. On the basis of a "common plan", also approved by the two Assemblies, most of the real and personal property owned by the League was acquired by the United Nations.

With regard to the UN, cf. Assembly resolutions of February 12, 1946, part I, A (transfer of Secretariat functions regarding international agreements) and part III ("common plan"), of November 19, 1946 and December 14, 1946 (both covering the transfer of non-political functions of the Secretariat and of various *ad hoc* Committees of the League). As for the League of Nations, the Assembly permitted the transfer of all non-political functions and approved the "common plan" in various resolutions, all of April 18, 1946 (see *A.J.*, 1948, p. 326 ff.; *Int. Org.*, 1947, p. 246 ff.). For other more detailed information on the transfer of functions and property from one Organization to the other, cf. Yearbook of the United Nations 1946-47, p. 110 ff. and p. 261 ff.

The transfer of functions and property did not give rise to any disputes. It would therefore be futile to try to establish whether the transfer was the subject of a real agreement between the two Organizations, or between their Member States, or, yet again, whether there existed unilateral or parallel acts.

Aside from the functions that were expressly "transferred", can it be said that the UN succeeded to the League of Nations? In particular, may one speak of some sort of succession... *mortis causa* (that is, succession governed by customary international law) in the functions of a political nature? This issue came up over the legal situation of Namibia (formerly South West Africa) before its independence in 1990, with regard to the functions that the League exercised over mandated territories (see § 81).

2. *The purposes of the United Nations.*

A detailed analysis of the aims of the United Nations is hardly possible, considering their very general nature. As we shall see when we deal with the functions of the organs, the scope of activity of the United Nations can be better identified in negative rather than in positive terms. It is easier to single out the matters with which the Organization cannot be concerned than those which are within its competence. Of fundamental importance in this regard is the provision of Article 2, para. 7, of the Charter, according to which the United Nations may not intervene in matters "which are essentially within the domestic jurisdiction of any State."

The vagueness of its purposes, which gives the UN the nature of a *political entity*, can be seen from the listing in Article 1 of the Charter. This listing includes: maintenance of international peace and security; development of friendly relations among Nations, based on respect for the principle of equal rights and the self-determination of peoples; the achievement of international co-operation regarding economic, social, cultural and humanitarian issues; promoting respect for human rights and fundamental freedoms without distinction as to race, sex, language or religion. It is obvious how all-inclusive, especially the next to the last of these categories, is.

Even if up to now UN activity has been carried out in all of the above areas, the following can be noted: in the years immediately following the birth of the Organization problems concerning maintenance of peace were considered the most important; between 1950 and 1960 the greatest results were achieved regarding de-colonisation, within the framework of the principle of self-determination of peoples; in the seventies efforts began to be concentrated on co-operation in economic, social, cultural and humanitarian fields, in the hope (which unfortunately today is still only a hope) of eliminating or at least of weakening the serious inequalities existing among the States and therefore of assuring all people equal human dignity and a better future; and, today, after the fall of the Berlin Wall, action is once again being taken with regard to the maintenance of international peace and security, mostly where international peace is threatened or violated by crises arising inside the States themselves.

3. *The organs.*

Article 7 of the Charter establishes as principal organs the General Assembly, the Security Council, the Economic and Social Council, the Trusteeship Council, the International Court of Justice, and the Secretariat. Among them, the Security Council and the General Assembly have a fundamental role. The Council consists of 15 members (11 until 1965 when membership was increased, as the result of an amendment to the Charter, in order to take into account the increase in the over-all membership in the Organization), of whom 5 are permanent members, enjoying the so-called veto power, and 10 are elected for a two-year period by the General Assembly. The Security Council is the organ in the Organization with the greatest powers. It has the exclusive power to decide the measures to be taken against States responsible for aggression or for threats to the peace. The General Assembly, in which all States are represented and have equal weight in the voting, can be concerned with any matter that is within the scope of the Charter, but its powers are very limited and come down, with rare exceptions, to the power to adopt "recommendations", that is, non-binding acts, and to promote co-operation among the States by means of treaties, that is, acts that require the ratification of each State before entering into force. The Secretariat, or, rather, the

Secretary-General who heads it and is appointed by the General Assembly upon the recommendation of the Security Council, is an organ with administrative functions.

Even if they are called principal organs in Article 7, the Economic and Social Council and the Trusteeship Council in effect have a subordinate position with respect to the General Assembly, in so far as they are "under the authority" of the Assembly (Article 60 and Article 87 of the Charter). This means that in carrying out their functions they are compelled to follow the directives of the Assembly. Sometimes their task is limited to the preparation of measures that are then to be formally adopted by the Assembly (see, for example, Article 62, para. 2, Article 85). In any case, they do not have decision-making powers. The Economic and Social Council, whose field of activity is clear from its name, consists of 54 members elected by the Assembly for three years. The Trusteeship Council (trusteeship is an extinct institution, similar to the former system of League of Nations mandates) has a membership which varies, in that the number of its members depends on the number of States administering trust territories (Article 86).

The International Court of Justice, consisting of 15 judges, is defined by Article 92 as the "principal judicial organ" of the United Nations. Its activity is governed both by the Charter and by the annexed Statute. In the settling of disputes between States, the Court presents the traditional characteristics of international tribunals: its jurisdiction rests on agreement between the parties. Perhaps more important than its function in settling disputes is its advisory function. Under Article 96 of the Charter, the General Assembly, the Security Council or other organs so authorised by the Assembly may request the Court to give an advisory opinion on any legal question. These opinions are neither obligatory nor binding: the organ is neither obligated to request them nor required to conform to them.

The structure, functioning and powers of the organs will be analysed in the next chapters. Other organs (subsidiary organs, the Administrative Tribunal, and so on) whose establishment has raised problems in practice or which carry out important functions, will also be taken into consideration.

The Security Council, the General Assembly, the Economic and Social Council, and the Trusteeship Council are organs made up of States. This means that the individuals who, with their vote, concur in making a collective decision are organs of their own State and express the will of their State. The Secretary-General and the International Court of Justice, on the contrary, are organs made up of individuals, meaning that the Secretary and the judges take office as individuals, without expressing the will of any State and without receiving or, rather, with the obligation not to receive, instructions from any State.

4. *The Charter as a treaty.*

BIBLIOGRAPHY: KOPELMANAS, *L'Organisation des Nations Unies*, I, Paris, 1947, p. 165 ff.; KAECKENBEECK, *La Charte de San Francisco dans ses rapports avec le droit international*, in *RC*, 1947, I, p. 113 ff.; DE VISSCHER, *Problèmes d'interpretation judiciaire en droit international public*, Paris, 1963, p. 141; ERLER, *International Legislation*, in *CYIL*, 1964, p. 15 ff.; QUADRI, *Diritto internazionale pubblico*, 5th ed., Naples, 1968, p. 351 ff.; RIDEAU, *Juridictions internationales et contrôle du respect des traités constitutifs des organisations internationales*, Paris, 1969, p. 4 ff.; MACDONALD, *The United Nations Charter: Constitution or Contract?*, in *The Structure and Process of International Law: Essays in Legal Philosophy Doctrine and Theory*, The Hague, 1983, p. 889 ff.; SLOAN, *The UN Charter as a Constitution*, in *Pace Yearbook of International Law*, 1989, p. 61 ff.; DUPUY (P. M.), *The Constitutional Dimension of the Charter of the UN Revisited*, in *MP YUNL*, 1997, p. 1 ff.; FASSBENDER, *UN Security Reform and the Right of Veto: A Constitutional Perspective*, The Hague, 1998, Chapters 1-6 ; MACDONALD, *The Charter of UN in Constitutional Perspective*, in *Austr Y*, 1999 (20), p. 205 ss.

The Charter, of which the Statute of the International Court of Justice is an integral part, is an international treaty. In so far as it gives rise to a set of organs that are designed to carry out basic functions within the international community, such as maintenance of peace, it is usually considered also as a kind of Constitution. For some scholars it should even be considered as the constitution of the international community as a whole. Contributing to this is the fact that some of its provisions foresee the possibility of the Organization taking measures with regard to non-Member States, something considered to be in contradiction with the principle that treaties have no effect on third parties (*pacta tertiis neque nocent neque prosunt)*. When its constitutional nature is accepted, it is usually said that a whole series of unwritten rules, created by means of the practice of the organs and the conduct of the Member States, can be superimposed on the Charter norms. It then becomes a "living" Constitution, as opposed to a merely formal one.

The constitutional aspect of the UN should not be exaggerated. The Charter is and remains a treaty. It is subject to the principles that govern international agreements, and that therefore a State is not bound by it if such State does not express a willingness to adhere to it and to become a member of the Organization. In other words, the UN remains a voluntary community, not a obligatory one, even if today nearly all States are members. As far as the practice is concerned, even if the Charter is considered as an agreement, it is possible to say that unwritten rules have arisen along with, or in derogation of, the provisions laid down in San Francisco. Among the sources of international law, there is customary law. We shall see through the course of this book that customary rules have changed and continue to change the written rules of the Charter. Given the fact that the provisions of the Charter have remained unchanged for fifty years, the customary rules can give a certain flexibility to the action of the organs. However, a great deal of caution is necessary in ascertaining customary law of this kind. It is not enough that a certain principle or a certain rule has been observed over a period of time, even a lengthy period, by the organs, that is, that it has been expressed and upheld by majorities within the organs. It is necessary also to pay attention to the conduct, to the reactions of the individual States, to the capacity of the individual States to effectively oppose majority tendencies. Anyone who undertakes an examination of the practice with this rigorous method will conclude that the number of true customary rules that have been superimposed on the Charter norms is not very high.

The fact that the UN practice has not given rise to many new norms of a customary nature makes the kind of study that we shall undertake in the following chapters more profitable. This will consist in examining the problems of interpretation of the Charter which have arisen since the UN was established. It would not be very useful to undertake such a study, which in each case must involve a judgement as to the legality or illegality of the conduct of the organs and of the States, if new norms to a great extent had come into existence largely through this very conduct, thereby giving them legitimacy.

The provisions of the Charter prevalently govern the functions and the acts of the organs. There are, however, also norms concerned with relations between the Member States. One may mention, first of all, the provisions of Article 2, paras. 3 and 4 (under which the members "shall settle their international disputes by peaceful means" and "shall refrain in their international relations from the threat or use of force"), or of Article 51 which recognises the right of every Member State to act in self-defence against an armed attack and until the Security Council has intervened to maintain international peace and security. Also these norms are closely connected with the functions and the acts of the organs in so far as the possibility of their being applied in practice depends on the actual functioning of the Organization. For example, the prohibition of the use of force does not have much sense unless it is considered within the framework of the Organization normally exercising its powers regarding the maintenance of peace. A treatment of the reciprocal rights and duties of States which is cut off from the treatment of the functions and the acts of the organs would therefore be fruitless, and will not be included here. It is better dealt with in a textbook on public international law.

5. *Interpretation of the Charter.*

BIBLIOGRAPHY: ROSENNE, *United Nations Treaty-Pratice*, in *RC*, 1954, II, p. 295 ff.; ZEMANEK, *Internationale Organisationen als Handlungseinheiten in der Völkerrechts-gemeinschaft*, in *ZöR*, 1956, p. 352; SCHWARZENBERGER, *International Law*, I, London, 1957, p. 517 ff.; BENTIVOGLIO, *La funzione interpretativa nell'ordinamento internazionale*, Milan, 1958, p. 128; DE VISSCHER, *Problèmes d'interpretation judiciaire en droit international public*, Paris, 1963, p. 140 ff.; WENGLER, *Völkerrecht*, Band II, Berlin, 1964, p. 1212; SCHACHTER, *Interpretation of the Charter in the Political Organs of the United Nations, ibid.*, p. 269 ff.; RIDEAU, *Juridictions internationales et contrôle du respect des traites constitutifs des organisations internationales*, Paris, 1969, p. 237 ff.; CAPOTORTI, *Il diritto dei trattati secondo la Convenzione di Vienna*, in *Convenzione di Vienna sul diritto dei trattati (Pubbl. della Soc. Ital. per l'Organizz. Internaz.)*, Padua, 1969, p. 35 ff.; RAMA-MONTALDO, *International Legal Personality and Implied Powers of International Organizations*, in *BYB*, 1970, p. 111 ff.; SKUBISZEWSKI, *Remarks on the Interpretation of the United Nations Charter*, in *Festschrift für Hermann Mosler*, Berlin, Heidelberg, New York, 1983, p. 891 ff.; ID., *Implied Powers of International Organizations*, in *Essays in Honor of S. Rosenne*, Dordrecht, 1989.; GIULIANO, SCOVAZZI and TREVES, *Diritto internazionale*, Parte generale, Milan, 1991, p. 427 ff.

Since it is an international agreement, the Charter must be read according to commonly accepted rules on the interpretation of treaties. While this is uncontested in principle, many attempts have been made to refer to special rules that should be applied both to the Charter and, more generally, to the constitutive agreements of international Organizations. These attempts reflect the commonly held view that the Charter should not be considered only as an agreement but as a Constitution, and they are based on the similarities between the UN organs and the administrative or legislative organs of a State. The International Court of Justice took this direction when it made use of the so-called theory of implied powers in several opinions dealing with problems of interpretation of the Charter. According to the theory of implied powers, which has been developed particularly by the United States Supreme Court in order to extend the powers of the federal government to the detriment of the States, every organ has available not only the powers *expressly* attributed to it by the constitutional provisions but also all the powers necessary for exercising its express powers. In applying the theory of implied powers to the UN organs, the International Court of Justice has considerably extended their reach, even inferring that certain powers of the organs stem directly and exclusively from the objectives of the Organization, objectives which, as we have seen, are extremely vague.

Resort to the theory of implied powers clearly clashes with the once dominant view that international agreements should be interpreted *restrictively* in so far as they would involve in any case limitation of the sovereignty and freedom of the States. Certainly today this view seems completely obsolete and contradicted by the fact that co-operation among the States continues to grow stronger. Indeed, as far as international law is concerned, only general principles usually applicable to all areas of the law should be taken into consideration. Treaty norms should therefore be interpreted broadly or restrictively according to the wording of the text, and its object and purpose. Nevertheless, extreme caution must be used in transferring onto the plane of United Nations and international law doctrines that belong to domestic constitutional law. That there can be an analogy between State organs and UN organs is very questionable as the UN organs lack the effective capacity to impose their decisions on their subjects, which is characteristic of State organs. With regard to the theory of implied powers specifically, it can be applied if it remains within the limits of a broad interpretation, if it serves to guarantee to an organ the full exercise of the powers assigned to it by the Charter. The tendency of the International Court of Justice to use such theory to infer powers from the provisions concerning the general purposes of the Organization does not, on the contrary, seem to be justified and in most cases has proved ineffective.

The advisory opinion of the Court which contained the most precise and also the widest formulation of the theory of implied powers is the well-known one of April 11, 1949 concerning *Reparation for injuries suffered in the service of the United Nations* (ICJ, *Reports*, 1949, p. 174 ff., especially p. 180: "the rights and duties of an entity such as the Organization must depend upon its purposes and functions as specified or implied in its constituent documents..." and p. 182: "... the Organization must be deemed to have those powers which, though not expressly provided in the Charter, are... essential to the performance of its duties". Therefore, implied powers... for implied functions!) Cf. also the opinions of July 13, 1954 on *The Effects of awards of compensation made by the United Nations Administrative Tribunal* (ICJ, *Reports*, 1954, p. 57) and of July 7, 1962 on *The question of certain expenses of the United Nations* (Article 17, paragraph 2, of the Charter) (ICJ, *Reports*, 1962, p. 168). We will go back to each of these decisions when we examine the specific issues they deal with.

The Court has been more cautious when dealing with constituent instruments of the UN specialised agencies which are independent international organizations although linked to the United Nations (see § 73). See the opinion of July 8, 1996 (ICJ, *Reports*, 1996) on the legality of the use by a State of nuclear weapons in an armed conflict, which denies that this question pertains, even implicitly, to the scope of the World Health Organization.

While the common rules of interpretation of treaties apply to the Charter, it is not possible to examine them thoroughly here. Suffice to mention that the tendency prevalent today on the issue is toward abandoning the so-called subjective method, a method borrowed from the realm of contracts in municipal law. This method would require in all cases and as far as possible that the *effective* intentions of the parties be sought, as opposed to their *declared* intentions. As a general rule, on the contrary, international treaties must be given the meaning which is clear in their text, which is evident from the logical connections between the various parts of the text, and which is in harmony with the object and purpose of the act as they result from the text. In a conception of this kind, the preparatory works, in which the effective intentions of the parties should be shown, have a subsidiary function. Recourse may be made to them only when the text presents ambiguities or gaps. In practice the preparatory works serve above all to support and strengthen interpretations that have already been, at least to a certain degree, obtained from the text of the treaty. It is indeed rare, and it is particularly rare with regard to the UN Charter, that the ambiguities of the text do not reflect ambiguities in the preparatory works. This is because behind ambiguous provisions there is nearly always a solution of compromise.

The 1969 Vienna Convention on the Law of Treaties favours the "objective" method of treaty interpretation. Article 31 of the Vienna Convention lays down the general principle: "A Treaty shall be interpreted in good faith in accordance with the ordinary meaning to be given to the terms of the treaty in their context and in the light of its object and purpose"; the only significant exception to the principle is the provision of para. 4, according to which "A special meaning shall be given to a term if it is established that the parties so intended". Art. 32 considers the preparatory work as a supplementary means of interpretation to be used when the examination of the text "leaves the meaning ambiguous or obscure or... leads to a result which is manifestly absurd or unreasonable".

6. *The power to interpret the Charter.*

BIBLIOGRAPHY: KOPELMANAS, *L'Organisation des Nations Unies*, I, Paris, 1947, p. 253 ff.; KELSEN, *The Law of the United Nations*, New York, 1951, p. 738 ff.; SCHWARZ-LIE-BERMANN VON WAHLENDORF, *Mehrheitsentscheid und Stimmenwägung*, Tübingen, 1953, p. 136; SERENI, *Diritto Internazionale*, II, Milan, 1960, p. 984 ff.; SEYERSTED, *Settlement of Internal Disputes of Intergovernmental Organizations by Internal and External Courts*, in *Bruns'Z*, 1964, p. 12 ff.; GROSS, *The United Nations and the Rule of Law*, in *Int. Org.*, 1965, p. 538 ff.; CONFORTI, *La funzione dell'accordo nel sistema delle Nazioni Unite*, Padua, 1968, p. 58 ff.; RIDEAU, *Juridictions internationales et contrôle du respect des traités constitutifs des organisations internationales*, Paris, 1969, p. 237 ff.; ARANGIO-RUIZ, *The Normative Role of the General Assembly of the United Nations and the Declaration of Principles of Friendly Relations* , in *RC*, 1972-III, p. 503 ff. ; BEDJAOUI, *Du contrôle de légalité des actes du Conseil de sécurité*, in *Nouveaux itinéraires en droit. Hommage à François Rigaux*, 1993, p. 69 ff.; ID., *The New World Order and the Security Council. Testing the Legality of its Acts*, Dordrecht, 1994.

One problem that has been much debated concerns the power of the UN organs to interpret the Charter provisions.

In the United Nations there is no organ that has special power to interpret the Charter with binding effects for the other organs and for the member States. Under Article 96 of the Charter the International Court of Justice may give opinions on any "legal question" and therefore also opinions on interpretation of the Charter. However, this activity, on the one hand, may be requested only by the organs and, on the other, does not give rise to binding decisions since neither the organ requesting the opinion nor the States are bound to comply with it. The proposal made at the San Francisco Conference to give the Court a kind of control over the legitimacy of UN acts (a power of control which would have thus implied a kind of monopoly by the Court over the interpretation of the Charter norms) was strongly opposed and then dropped (see U.N.C.I.O., vol. 13, p. 633, p. 645).

On the other hand, the view which would assign the General Assembly a pre-eminent role regarding Charter interpretation with respect to the other organs and the Member States has remained an isolated one. This view finds no basis in the preparatory works of the San Francisco Conference, where it was clearly stated that any conflict between two organs over interpretation of the Charter would have to be settled by an impartial organ, for example, by the International Court of Justice in its advisory function, or by a Committee of jurists especially appointed by the two organs, or even by a joint conference (see U.N.C.I.O., vol. 13, p. 719 f.). Nor does this view find support in the provision of Article 15, para. 2, which requires the organs to submit reports of their activity to the General Assembly, since this provision clearly does not give the Assembly the power to review individual measures taken by the other organs. As for the argument that the Assembly would have the right to a position of pre-eminence in that it incorporates the "legal conscience" of the United Nations, such view is not supported by any objective evidence.

As positions of pre-eminence do not exist, each organ is called upon to interpret the Charter on its own at the time it adopts specific measures. Would such an interpretation be binding for the Member States?

In our view, the answer has to be negative. A positive answer would imply the freedom of the organ to manipulate the Charter, and this would be in conflict with the Charter rules which sanction its "rigidity" (see § 7), or with the rules that lay down special complex procedures for amending the Charter (Articles 108 and 109) and with those requiring that the States co-operate with the Organization but only when it acts "in accordance with the present Charter" (Article 2, para. 5, and Article 25). If the UN organs had the sovereign power to interpret the Charter provisions in a way that was binding on all the Member States, this would be the same as saying that they had the possibility of violating them with impunity, since any decision could be justifiable in the light of a subjective and "special" interpretation of the Charter. On the other hand, the Charter's silence with regard to interpretation (where the attribution of a sovereign power of interpretation by the organs owing to its importance would have required an explicit provision) is an element contributing to proving this negative view. Once again, in confirmation of this, the preparatory works of the San Francisco Charter can be cited, where it was unanimously held that "if any interpretation given by any organ of the Organization... is not generally acceptable, it will be without binding force" (U.N.C.I.O., vol. 13, p. 832).

During the Conference, in Committee IV, which was responsible for the study of legal issues, the question was asked: "How and by what organ or organs should the Charter be interpreted?" While the Committee felt it would be inappropriate to answer this in provisions that were to be part of the Charter, they unanimously approved a statement expressing the view of the Organization's founders. The statement says that there would be no need to codify the principle because "in the course of the operations from day to day of the various organs of the Organization, it is inevitable that each organ will interpret such parts of the Charter as are applicable to its particular functions." It then examines the possibility of a difference of opinion concerning interpretation arising between two States or between two organs, foreseeing that in the former case the dispute would be brought before the International Court of Justice as an organ of quasi arbitration and in the second case there would be recourse to the Court for an advisory opinion, to an *ad hoc* committee of jurists or to a joint Conference. The Commission concluded with the warning that: "it is to be understood, of course, that if an interpretation made by any organ of the Organization or by a committee of jurists is not generally acceptable, it will be without binding force. In such circumstances, or in cases where it is desired to establish an authoritative interpretation as a precedent for the future, it may be necessary to embody the interpretation in an amendment to the Charter. This may always be accomplished by recourse to the procedure provided for amendment". It is clear that the final part of the statement specifically denies the existence of an obligation for the Member States to accept interpretation by the organs. For the history of the Statement, see U.N.C.I.O., vol. 13, p. 631 and p. 633 f.; for the complete text, *ibid*, p. 831 ff.

As a consequence, each Member State may question an interpretation of the Charter made by one of the organs in taking a specific measure. In so doing, the Member State questions whether the measure is in accordance with the Charter and therefore whether it is lawful. What consequences may arise from such questioning and how the differences between the organ and the State may be settled in such cases are issues that have often been raised in practice. They will be examined later in the chapter on UN acts (see § 97).

7. The "rigidity" of the Charter and amendment and review procedures.

BIBLIOGRAPHY: BALLADORE PALLIERI, *Gli emendamenti allo Statuto delle Nazioni Unite*, in *CI*, 1946, p. 193 ff.; PERASSI, *L'ordinamento delle Nazioni Unite*, Padua, 1953, p. 51 ff.; GIRAUD, *La révision de la Charte des Nations Unies*, in *RC*, 1956, II, p. 307 ff.; SCHWELB, *Charter Review and Charter Amendment*, in *ICLQ*, 1958, p. 303 ff.; SCHULZ, *Entwicklungsformen internationaler Gesetzgebung*, Göttingen, 1960, p. 90 ff.; UDINA, *L'Organizzazione delle Nazioni Unite*, Padua, 1963, p. 11 ff.; MORELLI, *Nozioni di diritto internazionale*, 7th ed., Padua, 1967, p. 40; ZACKLIN, *The Amendment of the Constitutive Instruments of the UN and Specialized Agencies*, Leiden, 1968, p. 104 ff.; PANELLA, *Gli emendamenti agli atti costitutivi delle organizzazioni internazionali*, Milano 1986; MUETZELBURG, IN SIMMA (ED.), *Charta der Vereinten Nationen*, München, 1991, p. 1108 ff.

Article 108 provides a specific procedure for the adoption of amendments to the Charter. In order for an *amendment* to enter into force, it must be adopted by a two-thirds majority of the Assembly and then ratified by two-thirds of the members of the United Nations, including all the permanent members of the Security Council (who also have veto power on this matter). The *review* procedure under Article 109 is similar. In the case of review — and this is the only difference between the two procedures — ratification does not occur after an Assembly resolution but after an *ad hoc* Conference (made up of all the Member States) has recommended it. The boundary line between review and amendment is uncertain: recourse should be made to the former to bring about changes that noticcably affect the main characteristics of the Organization.

The two articles (which are also found in other constituent agreements of international organizations) depart from the classic principle of international law that a change in a treaty may occur only with the consent of *all* the contracting States. The procedures which they provide for are to be characterised as procedures which draw their normative force not from general international law but from the UN Charter itself. To point out that the principle of consent has been superseded, Articles 108 and 109 are also cited as examples of provisions creating a kind of "quasi" international legislation. Actually, deviation from the classic principles is lessened by the fact that a State may withdraw from the Organization "if its rights and obligations as such were changed by Charter amendment in which it has not concurred and which it finds itself unable to accept". Withdrawal is not specifically envisaged by the Charter (although it was expressly provided for within the League of Nations: Article 1, para. 3, and Article 26, para. 2 of the Covenant), but at the San Francisco Conference it was said that it was not to be excluded in the case of amendments that a State would not accept (see U.N.C.I.O., vol. 7, p. 267, from which the quotation is also taken). For reasons which will be discussed later (see § 17), the view expressed at San Francisco should be corrected in the sense that the right of withdrawal in the event of amendments (or review) that are not accepted is to be allowed only when such amendments have *noteworthy importance*. Even with these limitations, however, the right of withdrawal in the event of amendments weakens the innovative importance of Articles 108 and 109, in that a Member State will tend to escape from a majority decision precisely when, and only when, an important question is involved.

The provision of special procedures for modifying the Charter involves the impossibility for the United Nations organs to derogate from the Charter when they adopt special measures, and it therefore gives the Charter itself rigidity. This rigidity can be seen not only in Articles 108 and 109 but also in the principle, expressed in Article 25 with regard to the Security Council and in Article 2, para. 5, with regard to all organs, in accordance with which the Member State is obligated to co-operate with the Organization when it adopts measures or takes action "in accordance with the present Charter".

Until now the procedure for revision governed by Article 109 has never been applied. With regard to amendments, the only cases concern issues of secondary importance, specifically, the increase of the number of Security Council members from 11 to 15 (General Assembly res. no. 1991-XVIII of 17 December 1963, entered into force on 30 August 1965) and of the Economic and Social Council, first from 18 to 27 (with the same 1963 resolution), and then to 54 (with res. no. 2846-XXVI of 20 December 1971, entered into force on 24 September 1973).

8. *Present trends to revise the Charter.*

BIBLIOGRAPHY: PERASSI and AGO, *Osservazioni sul problema della revisione dello Statuto delle Nazioni Unite*, in *CI*, 1953, p. 572 ff.; CLARK and SOHN, *World Peace through World Law,* 3rd ed., Cambridge (Mass.), 1966; KÖCK, *Die gegenwartigen Bestrebungen zur Änderung der Satzung der Vereinten Nationen*, in *ZöR*, 1973, p. 25 ff.; BROMS, *The Special Committee on the Charter of the United Nations and the Strengthening of the Role of the Organization*, in *GYIL*, 1977, p. 77 ff.; VIÑAL CASAS, *El Comité especial de la Carta de las Naciones Unidas y del fortalecimiento del papel de la Organizacion*, in *ReD*, 1981, p. 101 ff. and 1983, p. 447 ff.; LEWIN, *La triade contraignante, une nouvelle proposition de ponderaton des votes aux Nations Unies*, in *RGDIP*, 1984, p. 349 ff.; BERTRAND, *Contribution à une réflection sur la réforme des Nations Unies*, Genève, 1985; CHEMILLIER-GENDREAU, *La solution de la crise des Nations Unies: application de la Charte plutôt que revision*, in *RBDI*, 1987, p. 28 ff.; BROMS, *The Present Stage in the Work of the Special Committee on the Charter of the UN and on the Strengthening of the Role of the Organization*, in *Essays in Honor of S. Rosenne*, Dordrecht, 1989, p. 73 ff.; WOLFRUM, *Die Reform der Vereinten Nationen. Möglichkeit und Grenzen*, Berlin, 1989; BARNABY, *Building a More Democratic UN*, London, 1991; ORTEGA CARCELEN, *La reforma de la Carta de Naciones Unidas: algunas propuestas institucionales*, in *ReD*, 1991, p. 389 ff.; MULLER, *The Reform of the UN*, New York, 1992; LEE, VON PAGENHARDT, STANLEY, *To Unite Our Strength. Enhancing the United Nations Peace and Security System*, New York-London, 1992; DJIENA WEMBOU, *Observations sur le processus des réformes en cours aux Nations Unies*, in *RGDIP*, 1993, p. 217 ff.; HEINZE, *Die Vereinten Nationen in Politikfeld internationaler Sicherheit: Wirkungsmöglichkeiten, Grenzen, Reorganisationsprämissen*, Frankfurt am Main, 1993; *International Symposium, Prospects for Reform of the United Nations System*, Rome, 15-16 May, 1992, Padua, 1993; REISMAN, *The Constitutional Crisis in the United Nations*, in *AJ*, 1993, p. 83 ff.; SAKSENA, *Reforming the United Nations*, New Delhi, 1993; CHILDERS, ERSKINE and URQUHART, *Renewing the United Nations System*, Uppsala, 1994; CZEMPIEL, *Die Reform der UNO — Möglichkeiten und Mißverständnisse*, München, 1994; SUCHARIPA-BEHRMANN, *The Enlargement of the UN Security*

Council. The Question of Equitable Representation of and Increase in the Membership of the Security Council, in ZöRV, 1994, p. 1 ff.; FAWCETT and NEWCOMBE (eds.), United Nations Reform: Looking Ahead After Fifty Years, Toronto, 1995; TANZI, Notes on the "Permanent Conference of Revision" of the United Nations Charter at the 50th Anniversary of the Organization, in RDI, 1995, p. 723 ff.; BERTRAND and WARNER (eds.), A New Charter for a Worldwide Organisation ?, The Hague, 1996; WALLENSTEEN, Representing the World: A Security Council for the 21st Century, in Diehl, The Politics of Global Governance, Boulder, 1997; NOYES (ed.), The United Nations at 50: Proposals for Improving its Effectiveness, Washington DC, 1997; FASSBENDER, *UN Security Council Reform and the Right of Veto: A Constitutional Perspective,* The Hague, 1998, Chapters 7-10; FLEURENCE, *La réforme du Conseil de Sécurité: l'état du débat depuis la fin de la guerre froide,* Brussels, 2000; MÜLLER, *Reforming the UN: The Quiet revolution,* The Hague, 2001.

The necessity of revising the Charter has been the object of discussion for a number of years, although a revision has never taken place. Indeed, the following events would have justified changes to the Charter: the number of Member States has tripled in the period from when the Charter was drawn up to the present; the far-reaching and hardly foreseeable phenomenon of decolonisation has occurred; the original ideological conflict between capitalism and socialism, between East and West, has been substituted by the conflict of interest between industrialised and non-industrialised countries, between rich and poor, between North and South. In 1974, the General Assembly created a special Committee made up of a certain number of Member States, with the task of studying the problem (cf. res. no. 3349-XXIX of 17 December 1974). In 1975 this Committee took the name "Special Committee for the United Nations Charter and for strengthening the role of the Organization". Moreover, with regard to the structure of the Security Council, the General Assembly, with resolution no. 48/267 of December3, 1993, decided to establish an "Open-ended working group on the question of equitable representation and increase in the membership of the Security Council and other matters related to Security Council". Lastly, in November 2003 an "High-level panels" was established by the Secretary-General to recommend the changes necessary to ensure an effective action on the part of the United Nations. All this bodies are still working, and up to now no concrete and formal procedure of amendment or revision of the Charter has took place.

There were also many different proposals for changes which came directly from the States. Some of them concerned the Organization's structure, and they range from reinforcing the role of the Assembly (where the Third World States have an overwhelming majority) to enlarging the Security Council in order to guarantee greater representation of the Third World countries, to the abolition or the limitation of the veto (or to extending the veto in order that countries representing different geo-political areas might enjoy it), and so on. Aside from changes in the structure, there has been insistence that several principles declared by the Assembly over the years (see

§ 94) be introduced in the Charter. These concern both principles regarding maintenance of international peace and security, for example, the rules defining aggression (see § 55 *bis*) and principles relating to the field of economic and social co-operation. In this sector declarations and initiatives by the Assembly and by its specially created organs have continued to multiply after de-colonisation, and they are part of the effort to give the world a fairer economic order. We can mention, among others, the Charter of Economic Rights and Duties and the principles of the new international economic order, such as the principle of economic equity, of collective economic security, of the complete and permanent sovereignty of every people over its own natural resources, of the right to a sustainable development, and so on (see § 71). Especially during the seventies, when enthusiasm for the new international economic order was at its peak, and expectation that it could become reality was widespread, a view was held that all these ideas should no longer be entrusted to Assembly documents that were without binding force but should be solemnly made part of the Charter.

In the sector of the maintenance of international peace and security, worthy of mention are the Report presented by the Secretary-General B. Boutros-Ghali to the Security Council in June 1992, a report called "Agenda for Peace" (see *ILM*, 1992, p. 956 ff.), and the Supplement to the "Agenda for Peace", of January 3, 1995 (see Doc. A/50/60 and S/1995/1). More than at a revision of the Charter, these documents aimed at strengthening the role of the Organization within the framework of existing provisions. Worthy of mention is also General Assembly resolution no. 46/36 of December 9, 1991 which sets up in the United Nations a "conventional arms register" where, beginning from January 1, 1992, there is to be registered information, *supplied by the Member States*, concerning the import and export of conventional arms as well as the national stocks at hand. The above cited "Agenda for Peace" (p. 973, para. 71) also refers to this register. If this were a first step towards an efficient system of control by the United Nations over the production and the sale of arms — a system which, involving *direct* inspections, for now is but a utopia — we would be on the right track in pursuing the aim of preventing threats to the peace. Unfortunately still in 1999, in the Report to the fifty-fourth session of the General Assembly, the Secretary-General Kofi Annan was forced to notice that no progress at all had been made within the United Nations on the issue of disarmament (see Doc. A/54/1, par. 122-123).

Programmes aimed at strengthening the role of the Organization are also contained in the Millennium Declaration adopted by the General Assembly on September 8, 2000 (res. 55/2). These are especially devoted to the eradication of poverty, the protection of the environment, the protection of vulnerable people, the strengthening of the role of the General Assembly as "the chief deliberative, policy-maker and representative organ of the UN", and so on. The implementation of the Millennium Declaration is the object of an annual report of the Secretary-General to the General Assembly (the first one is contained in Doc. A/57/270, of July 31, 2002). Cfr. also the Report presented by Secretary-General to the General Assembly with the title "Strengthening of the UN: An Agenda for Further Change" (Doc. A/57/387 of September 9, 2002), which is strictly linked to the Millennium Declaration. The tragic conditions of poor countries and poor people are situations which these, and many other documents, would like to see eliminated or at least mitigated. Such situations, however, still remain to be seriously tackled.

It seems very unlikely that any radical changes in the structure of the United Nations will be made. The attitude of the permanent members of the Security Council is decisive on this. Permanent members have the veto even with regard to ratification of amendments and revision, and they do not seem very inclined to change the existing rules. On the other hand, a single change in the structure of the Security Council, with a widening of the number of members and with the addition of other permanent members, is not in itself sufficient in order to make the United Nations more functional or, most of all, more *credible*. What would change (or, better, would revolutionise) the structure of the Organization in a positive way would be, on the one hand, the *democratisation* of the General Assembly, that is, its transformation from an assembly of governments (see § 30) to an assembly of representatives of peoples and, on the other, the effective control by the Assembly over what the Security Council does. Today we are very far from all this.

Among the trends concerning revision of the UN structures there is one (antithetical to democratising it) favouring a change in the voting system in the Assembly (a system which today is based on the *one State, one vote* principle sanctioned by Article 18, para. 1, of the Charter) through the introduction of the weighted vote, that is, of a vote that is proportionate to the weight, in terms of population, economic resources, contributions to the UN budget, etc., of each country. The weighted vote, whose supporters belong to the Western world, is obviously opposed by less developed countries who hold the majority in the Assembly.

As far as new general principles and aims are concerned, it is unlikely that the Organization would benefit from their addition as general provisions of the Charter. The activities of the Organization is mainly aimed towards obtaining as much co-operation as possible among the States through the instrument of agreement, and the possibility of negotiating equitable consensual solutions to the enormous problems that humanity is facing can be better assured if fewer and less binding objectives are codified. The objectives that the Charter presently indicates (see § 2), precisely because they are all-encompassing and reflect two very general ideals, those of peace and of economic and social co-operation among States, are more than sufficient.

CHAPTER ONE

MEMBERSHIP IN THE ORGANIZATION

Section I

ACQUISITION OF MEMBERSHIP STATUS

9. *Admission.*

BIBLIOGRAPHY: JAENICKE, *Die Aufnahme neuer Mitglieder in die Organisation der Vereinten Nationen*, in *Bruns'Z*, 1950, p. 291 ff.; KELSEN, *The Law of the United Nations*, London, 1951, p. 61 ff.; PERASSI, *L'ordinamento delle Nazioni Unite*, Padua, 1953, p. 15 ff.; GOODRICH-HAMBRO-SIMONS, *Charter of the United Nations — Commentary and Documents*, New York, 1969, p. 85 ff.; GUNTHER, in SIMMA (ed.), *Charta der Vereinten Nationen*, München, 1991, p. 118 ff.

With the exception of the States which signed the Charter at the end of the San Francisco Conference and are considered by Article 3 as original members of the Organization (see § 1 B), a State becomes a member of the United Nations under the admission procedure of Article 4. Paragraph 1 of Article 4 provides that, to become a member of the UN, a State must be peace-loving, accept the Charter provisions and be willing to fulfill its obligations. Admission is decided, under para. 2, by the General Assembly upon the recommendation of the Security Council. A two-thirds majority is required for the Assembly's decision (Article 18, para. 2). Also the Council votes according to a qualified majority, with the possibility of the permanent members exercising the veto (Article 27, para. 3).

10. *Admission requirements.*

BIBLIOGRAPHY: HOMBER, *Admission to the United Nations*, in *BYB*, 1947, p. 90 ff.; SOCINI, *L'appartenenza all'Organizzazione delle Nazioni Unite*, Florence, 1951, p. 22 ff.; FEINBERG, *L'admission de nouveaux membres à la Societé des Nations et à l'Organisation des Nations Unies*, in *RC*, 1952, I, p. 323 ff.; MOSLER, *Die Aufnahme in internationale Organisationen*, in *Bruns'Z*, 1958, p. 285 ff.; DECLEVA, *La qualità di membro delle organizzazioni internazionali*, in *DI*, 1964, p. 198 ff.; WITKIN, *Transkei: An Analysis of the*

Practice of Recognition — Political or Legal, in *HILJ*, 1977, p. 605 ff.; DUGARD, *Recognition and the UN*, Cambridge, 1987.

An analysis of Article 4, para. 1, indicates the following requirements for admission to the UN.: first, membership is open only to States; then, the State must accept the obligations contained in the Charter, be peace-loving and be able and willing to carry out the Charter's obligations.

Acceptance of the Charter's obligations can be considered implicit in the request for admission presented by a State. Art. 134 of the Assembly's rules of procedure and Article 58 of the Security Council's rules of procedure provide that requests are to be submitted to the Secretary-General and that they must contain a declaration made in a "formal instrument" that they accept the obligations contained in the Charter. What is indispensable is that the State's request is made by its organs that have the power to undertake international obligations. This is what the two provisions refer to when they speak of "formal instrument".

Para. 1 of Article 4 provides that the State must be able and willing to fulfill the Charter' obligations "in the judgment of the Organization". The Assembly and the Council thus have full discretionary power in determining whether these two requisites are met. Since being "peace-loving" is only one particular aspect of the willingness to fulfill the Charter's obligations, also the evaluation of this requirement is within the full discretion of the two organs. What about the first (and principal) requirement set by para. 1, that is, the quality of being a State? Is it to be determined by these organs? In other words, does there exist, with regard to Article 4, a notion of a State, more or less corresponding to the notion found in customary international law (the notion of a State as a subject of international law), which the Assembly and the Council must adhere to if they do not want to meet with an unlawful admission?

If Article 4 was to be interpreted in the light of Article 3, which qualifies as States the *original* members of the United Nations, then the notion of a State accepted in Article 4 would depart remarkably from the notion of a State as a subject of international law. In fact, among the original members of the Organization there were entities such as Byelorussia and the Ukraine which at the time could certainly not be considered international subjects (see § 1 B).

However, interpretation of Article 4 must remain independent of Article 3 and the issue of original members. Participation in the San Francisco Conference was very much related to what was happening at the time. In the case of Byelorussia and the Ukraine, in particular, a strong need was felt to prevent the isolation and mistrust of the Soviet Union. Consequently, these events cannot have a decisive influence on the determination of admission requirements. If this is true, then it seems that a State that could be admitted to the UN under Article 4 more or less comes within the definition of the State as a subject of international law. Such State must therefore consist of an *effective and independent system of government of a community within a defined territory*. Such view is supported by a presumption (valid in the absence of elements to the contrary) of the conformity of Article 4 to customary international law, by the basic principle that "the Organization is based on the principle of the sovereign equality of all its members", and, lastly, by the admission practice followed up to now. In fact all of the States that have been admitted so far have had the above-mentioned characteristics — an effective and *independent* system of government of a community within a defined territory.

The requirement of independence as a necessary requisite for an international subject cannot be understood literally. If it were understood as the possibility of acting in complete independence, hardly any State (and perhaps not even the Great Powers) would deserve to be called subjects of international law. This is true not only with regard to phenomena such as satellite States, the presence of foreign military bases on national territory, with relative limitations on sovereignty, but especially with regard to the inter-dependence that increasingly characterizes the entire network of international relations. This being the situation, it seems that the meaning that can be attributed to this requisite is one which stems from a *formal* element: that is, a State is independent when its legal system is original, it draws its power from its own Constitution and is not derived from the legal system or the Constitution of another State. The original character of the Constitution represents a minimum level below which admission of an entity to the UN would become inconsistent with the Charter due to the absence of the requirement of independence. A careful study of the discussions in the Assembly and in the Council regarding certain candidates, which were then admitted, shows that they did not concern this minimum requirement or independence in a legal or formal sense, but independence in a political sense, something quite undefined and not definable. Such discussions were, in fact, of no consequence.

For example, China (at that time represented by the Nationalist Government) and the United States raised objections in the Security Council in 1961 to the admission of Outer Mongolia, held to be a Soviet puppet government (SCOR, 16th year, 971st meet., p. 5 ff. and p. 9). At the same time, the USSR objected to the Republic of Mauritania, whose government had been formed under French influence in a part of the territory claimed by Morocco (*ivi*, p. 39 f.). Although they raised these objections, the United States and China, on the one hand, and the USSR, on the other, *abstained* when the voting took place to avoid the two admission proposals from being blocked by reciprocal vetos; the "deal" was criticised by Morocco before the Security Council (*ivi*, p. 39 f.). For other cases, see SC Rep.. 1946-51, p. 272 f. Cf. also SCOR, 26th year, 1587th meet. (Sept. 30, 1971), n. 86 ff., particularly 106 ff., and GAOR, 26th sess., Pl. meet., 1934th meet. (Sept. 21, 1971), n. 73 ff. (objections of the Yemenite Democratic Republic against the proposal for the admission of Oman, which was then decided by a unanimous vote in the Council and by a very wide majority in the Assembly, with the argument that it was a territory still under British colonial dominion).

In some cases admission was not contested with regard to the requisite of independence but with regard to other requisites or elements of the State as an international subject. For example, in 1981 Guatemala protested against the admission of Belize before both the Security Council and the General Assembly, declaring that Belize was not a State, since it had no territory! Actually, Guatemala was claiming that the territory of Belize, an English colony until independence, belonged to it. The Assembly voted for admission with 144 votes in favour and one contrary, following the unanimous proposal of the Council (cf. SCOR, 36th year, 2302nd meet., Sept. 23, 1981, pp. 1-6 and GAOR, 36th sess., Pl. meet., 13th meet., n. 24, p. 231).

Since Article 4 adopts the traditional notion of a State as an international subject and therefore restricts admission to the UN to those Governments which effectively and independently exercise authority over a *territorial community*. The possible admission of governments in exile (see § 20) or of Organizations or Committees of national liberation (for example, the Palestinian Liberation Organization before 1988 when a Palestinian Authority was installed in the territories occupied by Israel) operating abroad should be considered illegal.

Many of these entities (and among them the Palestinian Authority with the name of "Palestine"), together with inter-governmental and non-governmental organizations, have observer status, a status which gives them the right to participate in the proceedings of the General Assembly, obviously without the right to vote, to receive official documents, to enjoy certain immunities, and so on. As far as Palestine is concerned, it obtained a special observer status within the General Assembly by res. no. 52/250 of July 7,1998. The special status includes, *inter alia*, the right to speak on all agenda items at any plenary meetings of the General Assembly, the right of reply and the right to raise points of order and to co-sponsor draft resolutions and decisions on Palestinian and Middle-East issues. In the recent case of *The Legal Consequences of the Construction of a Wall in the Occupied Palestinian Territories*, the International Court of Justice, which was requested to give an advisory opinion on the legality of the construction of the wall by Israel, has granted a request of Palestine to submit a written statement on the subject, according to Article 66, n.2 of the Statute of the Court ("The Registrar shall…notify any State…or international organization considered by the Court…as likely to be able to furnish information on the question…"). In the view of the Court, submissions of Palestine were to be admitted "taking into account the fact that the General Assembly has granted Palestine a special status of observer and that the latter is co-sponsor of the draft resolution requesting the advisory opinion…" (Order of December 19, 2003).

Lastly, no weight should be given from a legal point of view to the fact that the State to be admitted is not *recognized* by some of the UN Member States. Aside from the question of the nature and value of the recognition of new States, it can be said that Article 4 does not set any conditions on the subject. This can be explained by the UN's aspiration to being a universal organization and to overcoming the positions of its individual members. A different problem is the impossibility, due to the lack of the prescribed majorities in the Assembly and in the Security Council, of admitting a State that is not recognized by the majority of UN members or even by only one of the permanent members of the Council. This is the case, for instance, of the Turkish Republic of Northern Cyprus which was established in 1983, some years after the military intervention of Turkey in the island.

11. *Admission of mini-States*

BIBLIOGRAPHY: FARRAN, *The Position of Diminutive States in International Law*, in *Festschrift für W. Schätzel*, Dusseldorf, 1961 p. 131 ff.; CHAPPEZ, *Les micro-Etats et les Nations Unies*, in *AF*, 1971, p. 541 ff.; SAINT-GIRONS, *L'ONU et les micro-Etats*, in *RGDIP*, 1972, p. 445 ff.; MENDELSON, *Diminutive States in the UN*, in *ICLQ*, 1972, p. 609 ff.; SCHWEBEL, *Ministates and a More Effective UN*, in *AJ*, 1973, p. 108 ff.; HARBERT, *The Behaviour of the Ministates in the UN*, in *Int. Org.*, 1976, p. 109 ff.; ADAM, *Micro-States and the UN*, in *IYIL*, 1976, p. 80 ff.; GUNTER, *What Happened to the UN Ministate Problem?*, in *AJ*, 1977, p. 110 ff.; RAMONAT, *Mikrostaaten in den Vereinten Nationen*, in *Außenpolitik*, 1981, p. 282 ff.

It does not seem that the size (in terms of population and territory) of a State in any way affects the Assembly's or the Council's discretionary power regarding the State's admission. The Organization has had to deal in a number of instances with the question of micro or mini-States. Proposals have been made that measures be studied which would limit their admission to the UN or would assign them a kind of limited participation. In particular, a kind of "associate membership" has been proposed for mini-States which not only have limited population but also few economic resources (the United Arab Emirates would then not be involved!) Such Associate States would enjoy most of the advantages connected with membership status without the obligations. It is obvious that until such innovations are put into effect and specific procedures for implementing them are established, only cautious exercise of the discretionary power of the Assembly and the Council under Article 4 could serve to keep in check the admission of micro-States. Yet, the practice followed up to now has been exactly the opposite. Admission of countries such as the Seychelles, San Marino, Liechtenstein, Tonga and Nauru (the latter numbering more or less 11,000 inhabitants) to the United Nations and granting them full voting rights in the Assembly has certainly not helped to strengthen the role of this organ.

The United States delegate to the Security Council in the Council meeting of Sept. 20, 1965 was the first to suggest the necessity of studying this problem (SCOR, 20th year, 1124 meet., p. 14 f.). In 1969, the Council held a debate on the issue and set up a Committee of experts to investigate it (*ivi.*, 24th year, 1505-1506th meets.). The proceedings of the Committee did not have any important results (after a first provisory report in 1970, published in doc. S/9836, nothing else was done). Several States, however, expressed views on the issue. Some proposed the formula of associate membership for States with "limited population or resources". Others refuted this, mainly with the argument that it would be impossible to introduce limitations after having in recent years already admitted most of the micro-countries (cf. doc. A/AC.182/L.2, n. 135). There have also been various proposals for resolving the problem from private research agencies which have suggested changing the voting procedure in the General Assembly. For example, the proposal of the New York Center for War and Peace Studies is that the majority required for the approval of Assembly decisions should consist not only of the majority of present and voting members but also of the States that represent a certain percentage of the world's population and of the States whose contributions to the UN budget reach a certain percentage (cf. LEWING, *La triade contraignante* etc., in *RGDIP*, 1984, p. 349 ff.).

As we have already noted in discussing Charter revision (see § 8), a real breakthrough in the issue of the General Assembly structure, a breakthrough which would resolve the problem of mini-countries, would be to transform this organ into a world parliament, where all peoples were proportionately represented.

12. *Admission of neutralized States.*

BIBLIOGRAPHY: KOMARNICKI, *The Problems of Neutrality under the UN Charter*, in *T*, 38, 1952, p. 77 ff.; TAUBENFELD, *International Actions and Neutrality*, in *AJ*, 1953, p. 377 ff.; CHAUMONT, *Nations Unies et neutralité*, in *RC*, 1956, I, p. 5 ff.; VERDROSS, *La neutralité dans le cadre de l'ONU particulièrement celle de la République d'Autriche*, in *RGDIP*, 1957, p. 176 ff.; DE NOVA, *Considerazioni sulla neutralità permanente dell'Austria*, in *CS*, vol. VIII, 1956, p. 22 ff.; TESAURO, *Rinuncia alla belligeranza (l'art. 9 della costituzione giapponese)*, in *ADI*, 1966, p. 291 ff.; BINDSCHEDLER, *Das Problem der Beteiligung der Schweiz an Sanktionen der Vereinten Nationen, besonders im Falle Rhodesiens*, in *Bruns'Z*, 1968, p. 1 ff.; ZEMANEK, *Das Problem der Beteiligung des immerwährend neutralen Österreich an Sankitionen der Vereinten Nationen, besonder im falle Rhodesiens, ibid.*, p. 16 ff.; MIELE, *L'estraneità ai conflitti armati secondo il diritto internazionale, II, La disciplina positiva delle attività statuali*, Padua, 1970, p. 496 ff.; HERNDL, *Die Mitgliedschaft Österreichs im Sicherheitsrat der Vereinten Nationen (1973/1974), Neue Aspekte der dauernden Neutralität*, in *Festschrift für Rudolf Bindschedler*, Berne, 1980, p. 527 ff.; HAEGLER, *Schweizer Universalismus, UNO-Partikularismus. Die Bedeutung des Universalitätsprinzips in der Frage des Beitritts der Schweiz zur Organisation der Vereinten Nationen unter bes. Berucks. der Verhandlungen in der Bundesversammlung*, Frankfurt a.M.-New York, 1983; DICHKE, *Völkerrechtliche Probleme eines eventuellen Beitritts der Schweiz zu den Vereinten Nationen*, in *AV*, 1984, Bd. 22, p. 405 ff.; THURER, *UN Enforcement Measures and Neutrality — The Case of Switzerland*, in *AV*, 1992, p. 63 ff.; SCHINDLER, *Kollective Sichereit der Vereinten Nationen und dauernde Neutralitat der Schweiz*, in *Schw. Z.*, 1992, p. 435 ff; INGRAVALLO, *L'ammissione della Svizzera all'ONU e la questione della neutralità permanente*, in *CI*, 2003, p. 265 ff.

It has been debated whether a neutralized State, that is, a State which, on the basis of an international agreement, has undertaken not to wage war or to engage in acts that might lead to war, may be admitted to the UN The debate originated from the fact that some of the obligations imposed by the Charter on United Nations members, specifically the obligations to provide assistance and to participate in UN actions for the maintenance of international peace and security, seem to be incompatible with neutralization. The question of compatibility may be raised, for example, with regard to Article 2, para. 5, which provides that members have a general obligation to assist the UN in all actions, and therefore also in military actions, undertaken against a State. The same can be said with regard to Article 41 which, in connection with Article 39, authorizes the Security Council to require the Member States to adopt the so-called measures not involving the use of force (severance of diplomatic relations, economic sanctions, and so on) with a country responsible for threatening or breaching the peace. Such measures, indeed, may be seen as actions capable of involving in a war the State adopting them. Lastly, the provision of Article 43 should be mentioned, although it has not yet been applied by any member (see § 59). It imposes on the Member States a kind of *de contrahendo* obligation with the Security Council in order to assure their participation in the so-called measures involving the use of force.

The problem of compatibility between status as a UN member and status of a neutralized State arose with the admission of Austria to the United Nations in 1955. The neutralization of Austria is not contemplated by a true international treaty but all the same it can be traced back to an international agreement whose conclusion results from the following elements. On May 26, 1955 the Republic of Austria declared its "perpetual neutrality" in a constitutional provision. Immediately afterwards it informed all the States with which it had diplomatic relations of such provision, inviting them to recognize its neutrality. Fifty-seven States, among them the United States, the USSR, France and United Kingdom, accepted this invitation, some before and some after December 12, 1955, the date when Austria was admitted to the UN The Austrian invitation, on the one hand, and the recognition by the other States, on the other, can be considered as elements of an international convention formalizing the neutralization of Austria.

The status of permanent neutrality has been also adopted by Turkmenistan in 1985.

Lastly, with the admission of Switzerland in 2002 (see § 1 B) another neutralized country is now member of the Organization. The neutrality of Switzerland, already recognized by the Vienna Congress in 1815, was reaffirmed by the Declaration of Paris of 1915. This status of neutrality has been recognized by international contractual instruments; according to some legal scholars it is also the object of an international custom.

The subject of the admission of neutralized States was already discussed at the time of the League of Nations with regard to Switzerland. The League of Nations Covenant provided, at Article 16, that military actions and economic sanctions could be requested of Member States against an aggressor State. In 1920, when Switzerland became a member of the League of Nations, it was once and for all *exempted* from military measures but not from economic measures by a Council resolution (of February 13, 1920). In 1938, another Council resolution (May 14) exempted it from the economic sanctions ordered against Italy for the Ethiopian War. For the text of the two resolutions, whose legality was very doubtful as the Council did not have explicit power to exempt a State from the obligations provided for by the Covenant, cf. *Societé des Nations*, Journal Officiel, 1920, p. 57 and 1938, p. 368 ff. (the second resolution was approved with the abstentions of China and the Soviet Union).

In view of its status, Switzerland decided in 1945 not to seek admission to the UN However, in 1981 the Federal Council sent a message to the National Council (*Message concernant l'adhésion de la Suisse à l'ONU, du 21 décembre 1981*, doc. n. 81.081), proposing the admission. The message specifically dwelt on the issue of the compatibility between neutralization and admission (*Message*, cit., p. 45 ff. and *passim*). A popular referendum, held in 1986, rejected the proposal. After two other messages of the Federal Council, of November 9, 1993 and December 4, 2000, the referendum was again held in 2002 and this time the admission was approved by the majority of the population.

Also in the case of Japan, a problem arose concerning compatibility with the status of a UN member (Japan was admitted in 1956). Article 9 of the Japanese Constitution, which entered into force on May 3, 1947, provides in para. 1 that Japan renounces war as a means of resolving international disputes and adds, at para. 2, that to achieve this purpose "land, sea, and air forces, as well as other war potential will never be maintained. The right of belligerency of the state will not be recognised". It was therefore asked whether para. 2 did not put Japan in the condition of not being able to fulfill the obligation to assist the UN in possible military actions. Actually, over time Article 9 has lost some of its importance, particularly with Japan's ratification of the 1951 peace treaty, which expressly stated that Japan would give the UN every assistance in any action undertaken within the framework of Chapter VII of the Charter.

The problem of compatibility between neutralization and UN membership has two components. One is whether a neutralized State may be admitted to the Organization. The other is whether, once admitted, such a State has the right to invoke its status in order to be exempted from carrying out the Charter obligations regarding maintenance of the peace.

To answer the first question, the requirements which, under Article 4, para. 1, a State must fulfill to be admitted must be taken into account. There is, first of all, the general acceptance "of the obligations contained in the present Charter". Given the clear formula of Article 4, it does not seem that such acceptance may be accompanied by any limits or reservations. Also the acceptance by a neutralized State, therefore, must be unconditional, lest the decision of the Assembly and the Council be illegal. It is indicative that Austria's request, presented in 1952 and never altered, explicitly provided for acceptance "without any reservation" (see *UNT.S.*, 1955, vol. 223, p. 28). It is also indicative that in the long discussions which were held in the Swiss federal organs on the admission of Switzerland before the admittance of this country, and where the main concern was the safeguarding of its neutrality status and the necessity that such neutrality be strongly and solemnly confirmed before becoming a UN member, the view was rejected that this status could be the object of a formal reservation expressed when the application was made. In fact, no such reservation is contained in the request presented by Switzerland in 2002.

There are no other limits to the power of the Assembly and the Council to admit a neutralized State. The ascertainment of the other requisites provided by Article 4, especially that of being "able and willing to carry out" the Charter's obligations come within the full discretion of the two organs (see § 10). Therefore, if the Assembly and the Council believe that a neutralized State is able and willing to carry out the obligations, then the issue is closed.

The preparatory works also indicate the possibility of admitting a neutralized State. During the San Francisco Conference, in Committee 1/2 which was examining the article concerning admission (present Article 4), the French representative proposed that this article should state that neutralization was incompatible with the obligations involved in UN membership (see U.N.C.I.O., vol. 3, p. 383). His proposal was not accepted (ivi., vol. 7, p. 290). Later, Committee 1/1 dealt with neutralization during the study of Article 2, para. 5, which imposes on the Member States the obligation to assist the Organization in any actions it undertakes. The Committee chose not to include any reference to neutralization in Article 2, but expressed the unanimous opinion that a *Member* State could not avail itself of this status in order to free itself from the obligation under Article 2, para. 5, or from any other Charter obligation (*ibid.*, vol. 6, p. 400 f. and 722). It is clear that the San Francisco Conference took for granted the possibility of admitting neutralized States to the UN.

Once a neutralized State has been admitted, may it refuse in specific cases to assist the United Nations when the Organization decides to take action to protect the peace?

It is worth noting at the outset that the answer will be the same whether the neutralization originates in an international agreement or it is the so-called constitutional neutrality. Actually, the problem is not one of "compatibility between treaties" (the UN Charter on the one hand and the neutralization convention on the other). Seen from this perspective, the issue would immediately be closed, in so far as Article 103 of the Charter provides that the obligations under the Charter are to prevail, in the event of a conflict, over obligations under any other international agreement. Here, the issue of compatibility arises, on the contrary, between the Charter, on the one hand, and a factual situation, so to speak, on the other. The whole problem simply consists in asking whether having admitted a State to the UN which has previously declared that it pursues and intends to pursue a policy of neutrality allows the right of the State to continue to pursue such policy even at the cost of failing to meet some of the Charter obligations. From this point of view, it does not matter whether it concerns conventional neutralization or constitutional neutrality.

The Austrian government has occasionally claimed this right in the past. On February 28, 1967, in answering the Secretary-General on the measures to adopt against Southern Rhodesia following Security Council decision no. 232 of December 12, 1966 (a decision that obligated *all* the Member States to interrupt all economic relations with Rhodesia under Articles 39 and 41 of the Charter), the Austrian Republic reserved its position, although at the time only in principle. In particular, it stated that it did not want to "prejudge the question whether Austria, as a permanently neutral State Member of the UN is automatically bound by decisions of the Security Council regarding mandatory sanctions — a question which in the opinion of the Federal Government of Austria can only be decided in each single case on the basis of the specific situation and with due regard to the obligations which result on the one hand from the membership of Austria in the United Nations and on the other hand from its permanent neutrality, of which all States Members of the United Nations have previously been notified" (SCOR, 22nd year, Suppl. 1-2.3.1967, p. 155). This declaration of principle was also expressly referred to in the Austrian answer regarding the subsequent resolution adopted by the Security Council on May 29, 1968, which decreed a complete economic blockade of Southern Rhodesia (cf. SCOR, 23rd year, 7-8.9.1968, p. 176).

The view held by Austria in the Southern Rhodesia case was later abandoned by this State, as can be seen in the official statements made by the Austrian Government during the 1991 Gulf War (see § 60). According to these statements, the right of neutrality cannot be considered "relevant" in the event the Security Council adopts sanctions on the basis of Chapter VII of the Charter (cf. SCHINDLER, *art. cit.*, p. 454). In any case, the view does not seem well-founded. The following elements — Article 103, which confirms the prevalence of Charter obligations over all other obligations; the non-existence in the Charter of a rule providing for "softened" forms of UN membership; the importance of the maintenance of international peace and security in the UN system; the already mentioned clear position taken at the San Francisco Conference, in the sense that a Member State could never invoke its own neutralization — all favour the view that the neutralized State has the same, identical obligations as the other Member States. The fact, then, that, as in the case of Austria, neutralization had been recognized or at least known by the majority of Member States prior to admission does not seem sufficient to alter this conclusion. This fact is counter-balanced by the acceptance without reservations of the Charter obligations that every State must undertake in requesting admission.

As far as Switzerland is concerned, its request of admission made in 2002 states that neutrality status "is compatible with the obligations laid down by the Charter" (Doc. S/2002/801). However, some modifications of the relevant parts of the Swiss Constitution had been already introduced in 2000, in order to permit the participation of the State in peacekeeping operations (even where they are armed). Such participation, as well as the application of measures not involving the use of force (Article 41) have been considered as compatible with neutrality status, being a contribution to the maintenance of the peace and not acts of war.

The compatibility between the status of permanent neutrality and the fulfillment of the Charter obligations has also been recognized by the General Assembly in the case of Turkmenistan (see res. no. 50/80 of December 12, 1995).

That having been said, the requirements of neutralized status can have some influence only as a consequence of the discretion enjoyed by the Security Council regarding actions safeguarding the peace. On the basis of Article 48, the Council may ask that its decisions be carried out by some members and not by others. It therefore may exempt, within the limits allowed by the general interest, the neutralized State. If Article 48 is taken into account, what can be conceded to the position taken by the Austrian government in the Southern Rhodesia case is that the Member States of the Security Council (especially the permanent members) that have recognized the neutralization status have the duty to make an effort in the Council so that, in line with the general interest, the neutralized State is in certain cases exempted from certain measures. On the contrary, this exemption could not be decided on once and for all, because this would be the equivalent of the Council's bringing about a change in the Charter, with the introduction of a "softened" form of UN membership.

13. *The so-called conditional admission and the non-existence of "positive" obligations of the UN organs.*

BIBLIOGRAPHY: KLOOZ, *The Role of the General Assembly by the United Nations in the Admission of Members*, in *AJ*, 1949, p. 246 ff.; JAENICKE, *Die Aufnahme neuer Mitglieder in die Organisation der Vereinten Nationen*, in *Bruns'Z*, 1950, p. 330 ff.; FEINBERG, *L'admission des nouveaux membres à la Société des Nations et à l'Organisation des Nations Unies*, in *RC*, 1952, I, p. 342 ff.; SPERDUTI, *Il principio della buona fede e l'ammissione di nuovi membri delle Nazioni Unite*, in *CI*, 1952, p. 42 ff.; JACOBS and POIRIER, *The Right to Veto United Nations Membership Applications: The United States Veto of the Viet-Nams*, in *HILJ*, 1976, p. 581 ff.; JANEV, *Legal Aspects of the Use of a Provisional Name for Macedonia in the UN System*, in *AJ*, 1999, p. 155 ss.

Can admission be dependent on conditions or requirements different from those provided by paragraph 1 of Article 4?

This problem arose in the early years of the UN with regard to the so-called problem of "package" admission, when for a period of time the USSR paralyzed the admission of a certain number of States with its veto in the Security Council. Although the USSR recognized that these States fulfilled *all* the requirements under Article 4, para. 1, it expressed its intention to vote in their favour only on the condition that certain other States deemed not qualified by the majority of the Council be admitted at the same time. The Soviet attitude, at the time condemned by the Western Powers, and particularly by the United States, was then taken by the latter with regard to the admission of Vietnam (admission blocked in 1975 and 1976 by the United States veto and, in 1975, made conditional on the admission of South Korea).

The admission of the Republic of Macedonia in 1993 can also be considered as a kind of *suj generis* conditional admission. It was subject to the acceptance by the admitted State of "being provisionally referred to for all purposes within the UN as 'the Former Yugoslavia Republic of Macedonia' pending settlement of the difference that has arisen over the name of the State" (see Security Council res. n. 817 of 1993 and General Assembly res. n. 47/225 of 1993).

The issue of "package" admission paralysed UN admissions between 1947 and 1955. It began with the requests for admission by Bulgaria, Finland, Italy, Rumania and Hungary, who had been former enemies of the United Nations members or of some of them but who had ratified peace treaties. When, in the autumn of 1947, these requests were brought before the Council, the Western powers opposed the admission of Rumania, Bulgaria and Hungary. They maintained that these countries did not meet the requirements of Article 4, para. 1, and, in particular, referred to their human rights violations and to the support given by some of them to the Greek civil war. The USSR, on the contrary, held that the five States *all* met the requirements of Article 4 and that therefore *all* had to be admitted. Consequently, the Soviet representative said that its favourable vote for Italy and Finland would be dependent on the admission of the other three States. Faced with the persistent refusal of the Western powers (the majority in the Council), the USSR exercised its veto which then led to the defeat of all the requests (cf: SCOR, 2nd year, 203rd-206th meets.) The issue dragged on in this way until 1955, when the Soviet claim was finally successful, and a "package" of 16 States was admitted to the UN

For the position taken by the United States in the Security Council in 1975 proposing to make the admission of North Vietnam and South Vietnam (at the time not yet unified) conditional on the simultaneous admission of South Korea (and with the possibility of a U.S. vote also in favour of North Korea), see S/PV.1836 (of August 11, 1975) and S/PV.1846 (of Sept. 30, 1975). Several States, mainly of the Third World, spoke out in the Council debate against the American veto, invoking the 1948 opinion of the International Court of Justice (an opinion that will discussed shortly). See, for example, the statements by Tanzania (SCOR, 30th year, 1836th meet.), Algeria (1842nd meet.), India (1844th meet.), Cameroon (1845th meet.), and Mexico (1846th meet.).

The illegality of the practice of conditional admission, confirmed by the 1948 opinion of the Court, was also invoked against China for its veto concerning the admission of Bangladesh in 1972; on this issue, see SCOR, 27th year, 1659th (particularly n. 61 and n. 91) and 1660th (part. n. 11 and n.46) meets.

In 1947, the General Assembly requested an advisory opinion of the International Court of Justice, under Article 96 of the Charter, on the issue of conditional admissions. The question was the following: Can a member of the Security Council or of the Assembly make its consent to the admission of a State to the UN dependent on conditions not expressly provided by Article 4, para. 1, and, in particular, on the condition that other States be admitted together with that State? The advisory opinion of the Court, of May 28, 1948 (in ICJ, *Reports*, 1947-48, p. 57 ff.), was handed down by a majority of nine to six. Close examination of this opinion is useful in so far as it leads to some general conclusions regarding the limits met by the Assembly and the Council concerning both admission and other matters.

Since Article 4 is not concerned with the conduct of the individual Member State in the Security Council or the Assembly, the views expressed by the Court in this opinion, and also by the minority (in the dissenting opinions), refer mainly to these two organs and only indirectly affect individual members. Let us ask, say the judges, whether Article 4, para. 1, places a limit on the conduct of the two organs which would make it illegal to refuse admission for reasons not covered by para. 1; if such limit exists for the organs, it must exist also for the States that make up such organs (cf. ICJ, *Reports*, cit., p. 62 and p. 83).

The Court's opinion is clearly contrary to conditional admission. In the view of the Court, the admission requirements provided for by para. 1 of Article 4 are not only necessary but are also sufficient; to add any other conditions would be illegal. What is their reasoning? The opinion is based mainly on the text of the article. The English text of para. 1, which is not substantially different from the French text, opens with the phrase "Membership in the United Nations is *open* to all other peace-loving States...", and para. 2 adds that "The admission of *any* such State... will be effected...". This clearly indicates, in the Court's view, that it is impossible for the Assembly and the Council, and therefore for the Member States, to be legally entitled to refuse admission to countries which they believe meet the requirements of para. 1 (see *Reports*, cit., p. 62 f.). The spirit of Article 4 is also invoked by the Court (*ivi*, p. 63) but it is not clear in what sense. It would seem to be in the sense that para. 1, in connecting the acquisition of membership status to the capacity to observe the principles and obligations of the Charter, would contain in itself a "legal" regulation of admission, regulation incompatible with an unlimited power of discretion of the organs as to whether or not to admit.

Taking into account the letter and spirit of Article 4, the Court rejects the main argument used by the minority judges to uphold the legality of a refusal of admission that is motivated by considerations extraneous to para. 1. For the judges in the minority, Council and Assembly resolutions concerning admission are acts of a "political nature". They emanate from political organs and in any case involve the examination of political factors. The Council and the Assembly therefore have wide discretionary power on the matter, being free to choose the reasons for their decision. As far as the Security Council is concerned, its discretionary power should also be drawn from the fact that Article 24 entrusts it with "primary responsibility for the maintenance of international peace and security". The Court majority replies that discretionary power regarding admission must not be postulated, but is exactly what is to be demonstrated; that on the basis of an interpretation of the text of Article 4, this discretionary power no doubt exists within very wide limits as far as the ascertainment of the requirements expressly foreseen by para. 1 are concerned, but it certainly ceases to exists once the organ and the States that are members of such organ have come to the conclusion that the candidate possesses them; and that, since the text of Article 4 is clear, neither recourse to Article 24 nor an appeal to the preparatory works is admissible.

For the relevant passages in the opinions of the minority judges, see *Reports*, cit., p. 85 ff.; p. 101 ff.; p. 109 ff.; for the passages of the cited opinion, *ivi*, p. 63 ff.

In our view, a correct solution of the problem may be obtained only by distinguishing between (a) the position of the organs and (b) the position of the individual States that are members of them. In confusing the two positions and in having treated the latter as a reflection of the former, the judges were led to an erroneous approach and ambiguous solutions.

(a) With regard to the position of the organs, no doubt can be raised as to the freedom they enjoy not to admit States even though they meet the requisite conditions of Article 4, para. 1. This is because, in the United Nations system it is inconceivable that there exist *positive obligations*, that is, obligations requiring a certain conduct, on the part of the Assembly and the Council. It is already difficult in municipal law to conceive of such positive obligations with regard to State organs, to say, in other words, that Parliament has the obligation to enact certain laws, or that an administrative body has the obligation to adopt a certain act. However, where remedies exist (dissolution or revocation of the organ, judicial or administrative remedies, and so on) against the inactivity of the organ, such a conception is still possible. On the contrary, it is completely out of place in the case of the Assembly and the Council, given the absolute lack of remedies of this kind. An organ does not exist that can take the place of the Assembly or of the Council in the adoption of an act or that has any power under the Charter to force them to act.

It is true, as the Court says, that the Council and the Assembly are not *legibus soluti*; they are subject to the Charter provisions. But this is true in the sense that their activity, their actions (what they do and not what they do not do), must meet the limits provided in the Charter, and are illegal if they conflict with it. Moreover, the illegality of an act produces important consequences and may be invoked in certain ways and within certain limits by the Member States (see § 97). On the contrary, the possibility that the Assembly and the Council can be compelled to adopt a decision, such as an act of admission, is excluded.

Of course, an act of admission, once it has been adopted, can be considered as illegal if it conflicts with the Charter, and in particular with para 2 of Article 4. It is illegal, for instance, if, as in the above mentioned case of the admission of the Republic of Macedonia in 1993, conditions are laid down by the Security Council and the General Assembly which are not requested by the Charter. The observations of the Court in its advisory opinion of 1948 are exactly applicable to this case.

(b) With regard to the position of the Member States in the Assembly or in the Security Council, it is not Article 4 which answers the question whether there exist any limits to the freedom of the individual member to vote yes or no, or to abstain, in accordance with its "personal" convictions. There is no trace in Article 4 of an evaluation of the behaviour of the individual Member State, and this is why it is necessary once again to avoid the confusion made by the Court between the organ and members of the organ. The voting procedures in the Assembly and in the Council are governed by Articles 18 and 27, which put no limit on the freedom of the vote. All that can perhaps be said, as inferred from Article 2, para. 2, of the Charter, is that the vote is to be exercised in good faith and that a State which persistently violates the principle of good faith may expect to meet with the sanction (up to now never applied) foreseen by Article 6: expulsion. It is evident how far removed this is from Article 4 and how it fits into a more general and completely different framework.

For the view that the rules of procedure in the two organs do not place any limits on the freedom of the vote, see the dissenting opinion of Judge Zoricic, *Reports*, cit., p. 97, who focuses, however, as do the other judges of the majority and of the minority, on the above-cited analysis of Article 4. After having inferred from Article 4 that the Council, and indirectly, the individual member, has discretionary power, judges Basdevant, Winiarski, McNair and Read have recourse to the obligation of good faith in their dissenting collective opinion, in *Reports*, cit., p. 91 f. Judge Alvarez (separate opinion in *Reports*, cit., p. 71) holds the view that the State which acts as did the USSR can be charged with "abuse of rights". The notion of abuse of rights which has often been invoked in UN practice to condemn the abuse of the veto in the Security Council by the Soviet Union, is, however, very much controversial as a notion of public international law.

In 1949, as the practice of conditional admission and the Soviet Union's exercise of the veto continued, the Assembly asked the International Court of Justice a second question. This was whether, in so far as the Security Council was not able to recommend admissions owing to the veto by a permanent member, the Assembly itself... could proceed with admissions on its own initiative. The negative answer of the Court, handed down by a very wide majority, needs no comment and again confirms what we have just said regarding the non-existence, in the UN system, of remedies against the inertia of the organs.

For the second advisory opinion, of March 3, 1950, see ICJ, *Reports*, 1950, p. 4 ff.

14. *Readmission.*

BIBLIOGRAPHY: ROUSSEAU, *Syrie, Problèmes de la reconnaissance du nouvel Etat par les Etats tiers et sa réadmission dans l'ONU*, in *RGDIP*, 1962, p. 413 ff.; DECLEVA, *La qualità di membro delle organizzazioni internazionali*, in *DI*, 1964, p. 187 ff.; LEANZA LAURIA, *La riammissione dell'Indonesia alle Nazioni Unite*, in *DI*, 1967, p. 3 ff.; SCERNI, *La soluzione del caso dell'Indonesia da parte delle Nazioni Unite*, in *CI*, 1967, p. 3 ff.

The procedure under Article 4 is to be followed also in the case of re-admission. Readmission covers both the case of a State which, after having been expelled or having withdrawn from the UN, asks to be readmitted and the case of a State which, after becoming extinct as an international subject (owing to merger or incorporation with another State) and after having, as a consequence, lost its membership status, again acquires its international personality and asks to be readmitted to the Organization. In both cases a new situation exists, which requires carrying out the procedures under Article 4.

The practice varied to some extent in the Indonesian and Syrian cases.

Indonesia left the United Nations in 1965, giving rise to a real case of withdrawal (see § 17) with the consequent loss of membership status. With regard to Syria, this State merged with Egypt in 1958 and at that time lost both its status as an international subject and its seat in the UN When these two States expressed the desire to again become part of the Organization (this occurred with regard to Indonesia in 1966 and to Syria in 1961 when it separated from Egypt), they were readmitted with a simplified procedure. The Security Council did not intervene; nor did the General Assembly take a formal decision. In an Assembly session, the President asked whether there were any objections to restoring the seats of the two States, and after taking note of the unanimous approval, he invited them to again take their seats.

Clearly, the consent of all the Assembly members, and therefore of all the Member States of the UN, made resort to the procedure laid down in

Article 4 appear superfluous. These two cases underline a recurring phenomenon in the United Nations, which consists in the ability of acquiescence of the Member States to remedy even the most obvious illegal acts of the organs (see § 97). Moreover, the simplified procedure followed for Indonesia and for Syria may have practical justification, since they were cases of readmission. Recourse to such procedure in a case of admission would be paradoxical, even if not considered otherwise from a legal point of view.

For the statement of the Assembly President relating to the readmission of Syria and issued in the session of October 13, 1961, see GAOR, 16th sess., Pl. meet., 1035th meet., no. 1 ff. For the one concerning Indonesia issued in the session of September 28, 1966, see GAOR, 21th sess., Pl. meet., 1420th meet., n. 1 ff.

Section II

MODIFICATIONS IN MEMBERSHIP STATUS

15. *Suspension.*

BIBLIOGRAPHY: SOCINI, *L'appartenenza all'Organizzazione delle Nazioni Unite*, Florence, 1951, p. 107 ff.; CIOBANU, *Enforcement Procedure of Article 19 of the UN Charter*, in *RDI*, 1971, p. 423 ff.; ID., *The Scope of Article 19 of the Charter*, ivi, 1972 p. 48 ff.; ID., *Credentials of Delegations and Rapresentation of Member States at the UN*, in *ICLQ*, 1976, p. 351 ff.; ABBOT and others, *The Gen. Ass. 29th Session: the Decredentialization of South Africa*, in *HILJ*, 1975, p. 576 ff.; LAVIEILLE, *La procedure de suspension des droit d'un Etat membre des Nations Unies*, in *RGDIP*, 1977, p. 431 ff.; PATEL, *The Politics of State Expulsion from the United Nations — South Africa, A Case in Point*, in *The Comparative and Int. Law Journal of Southern Africa*, 1980, p. 310 ff.; MAKARCZYK, *Legal Basis for Suspension and Expulsion of a State from an International Organization*, in *IJIL*, 1982, p. 476 ff.; PATEL, *The Legal Aspects of State Expulsion from the United Nations. South Africa a Case in Point*, in *Natal University Law Review*, 1982, p. 197 ff.; HALBERSTAM, *Excluding Israel from the General Assembly by Rejection of its Credentials*, in *AJ*, 1984, p. 179 ff.; ZICCARDI CAPALDO, *Il disconoscimento delle credenziali del Sud Africa come sanzione contro l'apartheid*, in *RDI*, 1985, p. 299 ff.; TABORY, *Universality at the UN: The Attempt to Reject Israel' Credentials*, in *Israel Yearbook of Human Rights*, 1988, p. 189 ff.; SHRAGA, *La qualité de membre non representé: le cas du siège vacant*, in *AF*, 1999, p. 649 ff.

The Charter provides, first of all, for the possibility of total suspension from the exercise of rights related to membership status. Under Article 5, the Member State, against which the Security Council has undertaken preventive or enforcement action, may be suspended from the exercise of all rights and privileges in the Organization by a special decision of the General

Assembly taken upon the recommendation of the Security Council. The Security Council then has the exclusive power to revoke such suspension.

A kind of partial suspension is contemplated by Article 19, on the basis of which a Member State which is in arrears in the payment of its financial contributions due to the Organization (see Article 17) has no vote in the Assembly if the amount of its arrears equals the amount due for the preceding two years. Suspension occurs automatically, and is not dependent on a decision of the organ. Art. 19 adds that the Assembly may prevent this from happening if it ascertains that such delay is beyond the member's control.

> Art. 5 and Article 19 have not given rise, in the practice, to significant problems. Art. 19 should have been applied during the serious crisis which the UN went through between 1961 and 1965, a crisis due to the refusal (for political, not financial, reasons) of a certain number of members to contribute to the expenses incurred by the Organization for peacekeeping actions in the Middle East and in the Congo. In this case (see § 86), in order not to suspend the debtor members from the right to vote, it was preferred... to suspend the Assembly proceedings, and no session was held in 1964.

The Charter does not provide for cases of suspension of rights connected to membership status outside the conditions and procedures under Articles 5 and 19. The decision taken by the General Assembly in 1974 in the South Africa case therefore did not conform with the Charter. This decision, maintained in subsequent years, consisted in refusing the credentials of the delegates of the South African government and in expelling them from the organ's proceedings. Although it was taken in the form of a deliberation over credentials (on the value and limits of these deliberations, see § 21), the Assembly's decision took concrete form in nothing less than the suspension of South Africa from membership rights. This was neither recommended by the Security Council under Article 5 nor justified by arrears in the payment of contributions under Article 19.

The decision taken against South Africa was part of a move to put the country outside the international community and its law. It was supported by the great majority of UN members in the years when the policy of apartheid on the part of the Government of Pretoria was at its most ruthless and was a move aimed at denying the international *legal personality* of any State which practiced apartheid. However, was this move reflected in a precise general rule (of a customary nature) in the international legal system? If the answer is affirmative, not only would suspension of South Africa from Assembly proceedings be justified, but also the loss of its UN seat owing to... the extinction of South Africa as a legal subject would be justified. However, taking into account the relations which many Governments have always maintained with South Africa, it does not seem that this general rule could have taken shape. It has also been held (ZICCARDI CAPALDO) that expulsion of South Africa would not have been illegal in that it would have constituted a kind of collective sanction, a sanction directly imposed by the international community against the crime of apartheid. However, this view leaves us unconvinced, if it is true that the Assembly, as a United Nations organ, is bound by the limitation of powers laid down by the Charter and if it is true that the Security Council has exclusive power regarding sanctions (see § 63).

As early as 1971 the General Assembly had begun to refuse to recognise the credentials of the South African delegates, but it had given this refusal the value of moral condemnation, allowing the delegates to participate in the sessions and to vote (see the statement of the Assembly President, issued in the 28th session, in A/PV.2141 of 5 October 1973). On the contrary, in the 29th session in 1974, after the Security Council had failed to adopt a proposal expelling South Africa from the UN (under Article 6), owing to the vetos of the United States, United Kingdom, and France, the Assembly decided, against the objections of illegality by the Western States and others, to follow up the refusal to recognise credentials with definitive exclusion from the proceedings: cf. A/PV.2281 of November 12, 1974 ; cf. also *UNJY*, 1975, p. 167 f. From that time, the South African Government was no longer present in the Assembly. One cannot say, however, that it was no longer treated as a United Nations member since it continued to participate in the Security Council meetings which concerned it: cf., for example. S/PV.2509 (January 4, 1984), S/PV.2540 (August 16, 1984).

South Africa regained its full membership in 1994, after the ending of its apartheid policy and the calling of free and democratic elections in the country.

Exclusion from General Assembly proceedings was also proposed for several years by the Arab countries with regard to Israel, beginning from 1982 until the end of 1989, but it was always blocked owing to an opposition of the United States and the other Western countries, which was shared by the majority: cf., for the first proposal, A/37/PV.45 of October 28, 1982, and, for the most recent, A/44/PV.32 of October 20, 1989.

At times reservations have been expressed (always during deliberations but without formally requesting exclusion from Assembly proceedings) over one government or another for behaviour contrary to human rights or otherwise to be condemned. Cf., for example, the reservations regarding Chile at the time of the Pinochet regime in the Reports of the General Assembly Credentials Committee during the 1985 (Doc. A/40/747) and 1986 (Doc.A/41/727). Other reservations have been put forward regarding governments which have come to power through force or with the aid of foreign States. However, these reservations concern rather the effects of State succession on membership status, a topic which will be treated later in the Chapter.

The lack of a central government in a country where a war between different factions is going on can lead to a temporary suspension of membership rights. This has been the case of Somalia after 1991 (for the relevant practice, see SHRAGA, *op. cit.*, p. 653 f.; see also § 19 for a similar practice mainly concerning cases of revolutionary change in the Government).

16. *Expulsion.*

BIBLIOGRAPHY: Socini, *L'appartenenza all'Organizzazione delle Nazioni Unite*, Florence, 1951, p. 114 ff.; Sohn, *Expulsion or Forced Withdrawal from an International Organization*, in *HLR*, 1963-64, p. 1397 ff.; Goodrich-Hambro-Simons, *Charter of the United Nations — Commentary and Documents*, New York, 1969, p. 98 ff.; .Kimminich, in .Simma (ed.), *Charter der Vereinten Nationen,* Münche, 1991, p. 142 ff.

Under Article 6, the Assembly, upon the recommendation of the Security Council, may expel from the Organization a Member State which has *persistently* violated the Charter. Also this rule has never been applied. In 1974, a proposal to expel South Africa, a proposal which would have obtained the prescribed majority in the Assembly and was in fact urged by the Assembly, was blocked in the Security Council by the vetos of the United States, United Kingdom and France (cf. S/PV.1796-1808, October 18-30, 1974).

17. *Withdrawal.*

BIBLIOGRAPHY: Kelsen, *Du droit de se retirer de l'Organisation des Nations Unies*, in *RGDIP*, 1948, p. 5 ff.; Gentile, *Il recesso delle Nazioni Unite*, in *CI*, 1951, p. 464 ff.; Singh, *Termination of Membership of International Organizations*, London, 1958, p. 92 ff.; Feinberg, *Unilateral Withdrawal from an International Organization*, in *BYB*, 1963, p. 189 ff.; Dehousse, *Le droit de retrait aux Nations Unies*, in *RBDI*, 1965, p. 30 ff.; Livingstone, *Withdrawal from the United Nations*, in *ICLQ*, 1965, p. 637; Scerni, *Aspetti giuridici del ritiro dalle Nazioni Unite*, in *CI*, 1965, p. 227 ff.; Nizard, *Le retrait de l'Indonésie des Nations Unies*, in *AF*, 1965, p. 498 ff.; Leanza Lauria, *Il recesso dall'Organizzazione delle Nazioni Unite: il caso dell'Indonesia*, in *DI*, 1966, p. 153 ff.; Schwelb, *Withdrawal from the United Nations — The Indonesian intermezzo*, in *AJ*, 1967, p. 661 ff.; Beghé Loreti, *Il recesso dalle organizzazioni internazionali*, Milan, 1967, p. 85 ff., 121 ff., 173 ff.

No Charter provision lays down the possibility for the individual State to unilaterally withdraw from the Organization.

The right of withdrawal was expressly provided for in the Covenant of the League of Nations: Article 1, para. 3 ("Any Member of the League may, after two years' notice of its intention to do so, withdraw from the League, provided that all its international obligations and all its obligations under this Covenant shall have been fulfilled at the time of its withdrawal") and Article 26, para. 2 ("No such amendment shall bind any Member of the League which signifies its dissent therefrom, but in that case it shall cease to be a member of the League"). There were a number of cases of withdrawal from the League (about 20); among the most noteworthy were those of Germany in 1933, of Japan, also in 1933, and of Italy in 1937.

With regard to the practice, the only case of withdrawal that can be cited is that of Indonesia. At the beginning of 1965, this State announced and put into effect its intention to withdraw from the Organization as a protest against the election of Malaysia (a State which came into being, despite Indonesian opposition, from the merger of Malaya with other territories) as a non-permanent member of the Security Council. Notice of withdrawal was given in a letter to the Secretary-General (Doc. A/5857 of January 21, 1965). Although in his letter of reply (Doc. A/5899 of February 26, 1965), the Secretary left open the issue of the legality of Indonesia's conduct, the UN's acquiescence to the withdrawal can be inferred from a series of conclusive acts of the Organization, such as the cancellation of Indonesia from the list of members, the removal of the Indonesian flag and plate from the UN, its exclusion from the budget documents, and so on.

Indonesia came back into the United Nations less than two years later, at the end of 1966.

Because of its peculiar characteristics, and especially because of the rather tenuous and *sui generis* justification brought by Indonesia as grounds for withdrawal, this case testifies for the view that each Member State has a complete and unconditional right to withdraw from the United Nations. Is this view acceptable on the basis of the Charter? The answer is no. The Charter, as an international agreement, must be subject to the principles of international law regarding the unilateral denunciation of treaties. In light of this, and given the lack of an *ad hoc* rule in the Charter, the right of withdrawal from the UN should be allowed only when the conditions of the so-called *rebus sic stantibus* clause are met. As we know, the *rebus sic stantibus* clause concerns the principle that a State may withdraw from an international treaty when there has been a *substantial* change in the circumstances that existed at the time of the adoption of the treaty and that had a *decisive* influence on the conclusion of the treaty.

A partial confirmation of the view that would limit the right of withdrawal from the UN in the event of *substantial* change in circumstances can be found in the preparatory works. In San Francisco, the debate in Committee 2 of Commission 1 between States favourable to withdrawal and those contrary to it was lively. With a majority of 24 States to 19, it was decided not to include a withdrawal clause in the Charter (U.N.C.I.O., vol. 7, p. 261 ff., and, for the vote, p. 266). With a majority of 38 to 2 and with 3 abstentions, the Committee drew up the following report, which was then approved by the Conference in its plenary session:

"The Committee adopts the view that the Charter should not make express provision either to permit or to prohibit withdrawal from the Organization. The Committee deems that the highest duty of the nations which will become members is to continue their co-operation within the Organization for the preservation of international peace and security. If, however, a Member because of exceptional circumstances feels constrained to withdraw, and leave the burden of maintaining international peace and security on the other Members, it is not the purpose of the Organization to compel that Member to continue its co-operation with the Organization... Nor would a member be bound to remain in the Organization if its rights and obligations as such were changed by Charter amendment in which it has not concurred, and which it feels unable to accept, or if an amendment duly accepted by the necessary majority in the Assembly or in a general conference fails to secure the ratification necessary to bring such amendment into effect..." (see U.N.C.I.O., vol. 7, p. 267, for the text of the report and for the Committee vote; *ivi*, vol. 1, p. 619 f., for the approval by the Assembly plenary).

The Committee's report, in the part where it refers to "exceptional circumstances" as a cause justifying withdrawal, is in line with the view based on the *rebus sic stantibus* clause. This is not the case with regard to the part where it allows withdrawal in the event of amendments or revision of the Charter under Articles 108 and 109, in so far as an amendment may concern also issues of negligible importance and therefore involve no *substantial* change in circumstances. Despite the San Francisco report, it would seem that even in the event of changes in the Charter the *rebus sic stantibus* clause must be applied, with the result that the Member State will have the right to withdraw only if the amendment or revision not approved by it touches upon important questions. The San Francisco report cannot pretend to substitute what can be obtained from an objective examination of the Charter.

18. *Effects of State succession on membership status.*

BIBLIOGRAPHY: JENKS, *State Succession in Respect of Law-Treaties*, in *BYB*, 1952, p. 133 ff.; COTRAN, *Some Legal Aspects of the Formation of the United Arab Republic and the United Arab States*, in *ICLQ*, 1959, p. 357 ff.; GONZALES CAMPOS, *Notas sobre la practica de las organizaciones internationales respecto a los effectos de la sucesión de Estados en el estatuto de miembro de la organizacion*, in *ReD*, 1962, p. 465 ff.; *The Effect of Indipendence on Treaties*, A Handbook published under the auspices of the *International Law Association*, London, 1965, p. 222 ff.; ZEMANEK, *State Succession after De-colonisation*, in *RC*, 1965, III, p. 245 ff.; MISRA, *Succession of States: Pakistan's Membership in the United Nations*, in *CYIL*, 1965, p. 281 ff.; GREEN, *The Dissolution of States and Membership of the United Nations*, in HOLLAND and SCHWARZENBERGER, *Law, Justice and Equity; Essays in tribute to G.W. Keeton*, London 1967, p. 152 ff.; O'CONNELL, *State Succession in Municipal Law and International Law, II, International Relations*, Cambridge University Press, 1967, p. 184 ff.; GONÇALVES PEREIRA, *La succession d'Etats en matière de traités*, Paris, 1969, p. 102 ff.; RONZITTI, *La successione internazionale tra Stati*, Milan, 1970, p. 203 ff.; EL-ERIAN, *Representation of States to International Organization (Some Legal Problems)*, in *Festschrift für Rudolf Bindschedler*, Berne, 1980, p. 479 ff.; BLUM, *Russia Takes over the Soviet Union's Seat at the United Nations*, in *EJIL*, 1992, p. 354 ff.; ID., *Membership of the "New" Yugoslavia: Continuity or Break?*, in *AJ*, 1992, p. 830 ff.; HOMANN, *Völkerrechtliche Konsequenzen des Zerfalls der Sowjetunion*, in *Friedens-Warte*, 1993, p. 98 ff.; SCHARF, *Musical Chairs The Dissolution of States and Membership in the United Nations*, in *Cornell International Law Journal*, 1995, p. 29 ff.; WOOD, *Participation of Former Yugoslav States in the UN and in Multilateral Treaties*, in *MPYUNL*, 1997, p. 231 ss.; VITUCCI, *La questione dell'appartenenza della Repubblica federale jugoslava alle Nazioni Unite*, in *RDI*, 2000, p. 992 ff.

Complex problems arise in international law over State succession. It is particularly difficult in some cases to determine whether or not a State is extinct, and, whether, if it is extinct, the rights and obligations under treaties to which it was a party are transmitted to other States by way of succession. These difficulties occur with regard to the United Nations since the extinction of a State as a subject of international law obviously involves the loss of its status as a UN member, and of the related rights and obligations, and since also in UN membership there can be the automatic succession of an old State by a new State. The Charter does not contain provisions on these questions. Therefore they must be solved in the light of principles of customary international law to which, in the absence of evidence to the contrary, one must assume that the Charter refers.

To begin with the most frequently met kind of succession, it can be said that, on the basis of a generally recognized principle, the mere loss or breaking off of part of the territory or of the population residing there does not determine the extinction of a State. The breaking off, by not involving the extinction of the State, has no effect on membership in the UN. The standing as a member of the United Nations, held by the State which suffers the breaking off, remains unchanged. On the other hand, if the territory which has broken off does not come under the sovereignty of another already existing State but forms an independent State (for example, when separation occurs owing to revolutionary and secessionist forces), such territory may become a member of the UN only by seeking admission.

In 1947 when Pakistan was separated from India, India kept the membership status it had acquired in 1945, while Pakistan became a member under the procedure in Article 4. Another example is that of Syria which, after having established the United Arab Republic with Egypt in 1958, decided to become an independent State again in 1961. In this case, the UAR kept its seat, leaving only the problem of the admission of Syria or, rather, its readmission, since the State had been a member before 1958. The "readmission", which should have occurred according to the procedure in Article 4, took place through an abbreviated procedure (see § 14).

All the States which arose following de-colonisation came into being by separation from the so-called "mother country" and were gradually admitted to the UN in accordance with Article 4.

It is not easy to draw a boundary line between a case of separation, followed by the formation of a new State in the part which has split off, and the similar case of dismemberment. While separation does not imply the extinction of the State, the characteristic feature of dismemberment is that one State becomes extinct and two or more new States are formed on its territory. The choice between the one hypothesis and the other depends on the circumstances of each individual case. In particular, the hypothesis of dismemberment must be excluded whenever the government organization of one of the remaining States has retained approximately the same size and features of the government organization of the pre-existing State.

When the dismemberment of a UN Member State occurs, all the new States will be able to join the United Nations only through the admission procedure. The fact that there is only one seat prevents any possibility of succession being contemplated.

A recent striking case of dismemberment, whose effects on membership status were handled in a legally unorthodox way, was that of the

Soviet Union at the end of 1991. The dissolution of this State certainly falls within the hypothesis of dismemberment, as the organization of the former Communist Government crumbled together with the dissolution. In the light of this, all the States that arose from the dismemberment should have become UN members through the admission procedure, with the exception of Byelorussia (now Belous) and Ukraine, which were already members; they actually, for very special reasons, were original members (see § 1 B). Moreover, as has been noted (VILLANI), the admission procedure should have been followed in so far as none of the new States, not even Russia, could have claimed to be the successor of the Soviet Union in the permanent Security Council seat, the seat which had originally been assigned to the USSR in its capacity as a great power. In fact, things developed differently. In an agreement concluded at Alma Ata in December 1991 most of the former Soviet Republics declared themselves favourable to assigning the permanent seat to Russia. The Alma Ata agreement was then acquiesced to by the UN members (some reservations, such as those of Germany and of Japan, were expressed; however, the aim of these two countries was not so much to object to this solution as to plead the case for increasing the number of permanent Security Council members). In short, Russia was considered to be the successor of the Soviet Union, while most of the other Republics were admitted to the UN as new States, the result being that a clear case of dismemberment came to be illegally treated as a case of separation. As often occurs in events of this kind, the illegality was remedied by the acquiescence of the other member States (see § 97).

Another recent case of dismemberment which also deserves mention is that of Yugoslavia. Also in this case the dismemberment hypothesis is preferable to that of the separation from the Yugoslav State of the four former Yugoslav Republics (Croatia, Slovenia, Bosnia Herzegovina and Macedonia) which declared themselves to be independent in 1991. Indeed, it is to be excluded that the fifth former Yugoslav Republic, the Yugoslav Republic (Serbia Montenegro), is the successor of the old Socialist Republic of Yugoslavia, and here also for reasons of the radical changes in the system of government. As for the practice followed by the United Nations, the Organization at first seemed to tend towards continuity, shown by the fact that, until September 1992, the Yugoslav seat in the UN was occupied by the representative of the new Serbia-Montenegro Republic, while the other Republics were gradually admitted under the procedure in Article 4. In September 1992, however, the Security Council recommended (with res. no. 777 of September 19, 1992, which was later on confirmed by res. no. 821 of April 28, 1993) and the General Assembly decided (with res. no. 47/1 of September 22, 1992) that the Yugoslav Republic (Serbia-Montenegro), in so far as it "cannot continue automatically the membership of the former

Socialist Federal Republic of Yugoslavia", would have to apply for admission and, in the meantime, be expelled from Assembly proceedings. The Security Council's and the Assembly's decisions were obviously due to political reasons and some opposition was raised among the Assembly members. For the above-mentioned reasons, the two decisions were, however, correct from a legal point of view. It is indicative, moreover, that the representative of "Yugoslavia" stated in the Assembly, on the very day that this organ decided to expel it, that it would "officially" ask to be admitted to the United Nations. Although subsequent practice has not been without ambiguities (for instance, in some official documents of the United Nations "Yugoslavia" was still treated as a Member State) the Republic of Yugoslavia (Serbia Montenegro) was finally admitted in November 2000 following a regular admission procedure. In 2003 its name was changed to Serbia and Montenegro.

For the discussion carried out in the General Assembly on the Yugoslav case in September 1992, a rather broad discussion but with hardly any legal content, cf. Doc. A/47/PV.2 and Doc. A/47/PV.7. (with the statement by the representative of the Serbia-Montenegro Republic). For the inclusion of Yugoslavia in an official document, see, for instance, the list of defaulting States (Doc. A/CN.2/R.641 of 23 June 1999, p. 14).

As far as less recent practice is concerned, uncertainty between separation and dismemberment arose in the above-cited case of the separation of Pakistan from India, a separation provided for in the Act of the English Parliament which gave final independence to those territories (India Independence Act of 1947). The delegate from Argentina supported the view of dismemberment in the General Assembly, stating that either both States should be considered as successors of the previous Indian State, and therefore original UN members, or that both should apply for admission under Article 4 (cf. GAOR, 2nd sess., 1st Comm., p. 3 f.). The United Nations correctly decided in the sense of the continuity between the new and the pre-existing Indian State and admitted only Pakistan.

The case of Confederation of Mali which split in August 1960 into the two republics of Mali and Senegal can also be cited as an example of dismemberment. The Confederation of Mali was not a UN member, but the Security Council had already decided in June 1960 to recommend its admission to the General Assembly. Once dismemberment had occurred, the Council deemed it necessary to open a new debate over the admission of both States. On this case, see ILC *Yearbook*, 1962, II, p. 105.

Again concerning more recent practice, a non-controversial case of dismemberment was the one between the Czech Republic and the Slovak Republic, both of which were admitted as new States early in 1993 after their split.

Incorporation and unification are some-how opposed to separation and dismemberment respectively. Incorporation occurs when a State, which has been extinguished, becomes part of another State. Unification occurs when two or more States *all* cease to exist and give rise to a new State. Here also it is not always easy to establish the boundary line between the two types. The hypothesis of incorporation is to be preferred to unification whenever there is continuity between the government organization of one of the former

States and the government organization of the State resulting from the unification.

The incorporation of a UN member into another Member State does not give rise to any problems. The incorporating State will maintain its seat while the membership status of the incorporated State will cease to exist.

Thus, after the reunification of Germany, a reunification in which the Democratic Republic became part of the German Federal Republic, Germany continued to take part in all the United Nations organs to which the Federal Republic belonged, while it did not take the place occupied by the Democratic Republic. For example, in the session of January 3, 1991 (Doc. A/45/PV.65) the General Assembly elected Byelorussia as a member of the Information Committee (a subsidiary organ of the Assembly) in the place that "remained vacant" following the disappearance of the Democratic Republic.

In the event of unification between member States, the most traditional solution would seem to be to make the acquisition of membership status of the unified State dependent on the admission procedure under Article 4. This is because it would be by definition a new State and because it would be very difficult to contemplate a hypothesis of succession in membership status, since it would not be clear to which of the former States the succession were to apply.

Although commentators usually speak of unification in referring to what gave rise to the United Arab Republic in 1958, this should rather be considered as a case of incorporation. The continuity between the supreme organs of the United Arab Republic and Egypt, especially the concentration, before and after unification, of broad powers in the person of President Nasser, speaks in favour of the hypothesis of incorporation of Syria into Egypt. As it was a case of incorporation, the solution adopted by the UN, which held that the UAR enjoyed membership status without having to go through the admission procedure under Article 4, seems correct (for the facts concerning this case, cf. ILC *Yearbook*, 1962, II, p. 104).

A phenomenon similar to that of the formation of the UAR took place in 1964 with the merger of Tanganika and Zanzibar, both UN members, into Tanzania. Also in this case, the hypothesis of incorporation of Zanzibar into Tanganika seems preferable, given the continuity between the supreme organs of Tanzania and Tanganika; and also in this case, Tanzania was automatically deemed a member of the Organization (cf. Doc. A/5701). For other cases of incorporation (but of non-Member States in a member State), incorporation which has always left the UN membership of the incorporating country unchanged, see *UNJY*, 1963, p. 161 ff.

19. *Governments created as a result of revolutions or foreign military interventions.*

BIBLIOGRAPHY: QUADRI, *Stato*, in *Nuovo Digesto Italiano*, vol. XII, p. 815 f.; ARANGIO-RUIZ, *Sulla dinamica della base sociale nel diritto internazionale*, Milan, 1954; ID., *La questione cinese*, in *Studi in onore di Tomaso Perassi*, I, Milan, 1957, p. 67 ff.; HIGGINS, *The Development of International Law through the Political Organs of the United Nations*, London, 1963, p. 158 ff.; MCDOUGAL and GOODMAN, *Chinese Participation in the United Nations: The*

Legal Imperatives of a Negotiated Solution, in *AJ*, 1966, p. 671 ff.; BLOOMFIELD, *China, the United States and the UN*, in *Int. Org.*, 1966, p. 653 ff.; CHEN and LASSWELL, *Formosa, China and the UN*, New York, 1967; SPERDUTI, *Sulla questione della rappresentanza cinese alle Nazioni Unite*, in *Studi in onore di Esposito*, Padua, 1973, III, p. 1937 ff.; SHRAGA, *La qualité de membre non representé: le cas du siège vacant*, in *AF*, 1999, p. 649 ff.

What effects do revolutionary changes of government have on state-hood, and, consequently, on UN membership? The problem arises only in the case in which the revolution considerably affects the legal order of the State, so as to modify the previously existing constitutional order. It does not arise when marginal changes concerning powers of the organs occur, even when they are extra-legal. These kinds of changes can certainly be explained in light of the concept of the "living" Constitution, without raising issues concerning the identity of the State.

Cases involving a revolutionary change of government include the possibility of governments being imposed by force and/or with the aid of foreign States.

In UN practice one constant element can be noted: whenever a radical change of regime occurs in a Member State, owing either to domestic revolt or to the intervention of a foreign State imposing a "friendly" government, there is substantial agreement that membership status should not be affected and that a new admission procedure is not necessary. The new Government sends its own representatives to the Organization (or confirms, if it so wishes, those already sent by the former Government) and exercises through them all the rights connected with membership status. The only condition is that it is the Government *effectively* in control of the country. When, for example, following the *coup d'état* in 1948 Czechoslovakia became Communist, it continued to exercise the rights and observe the obligations connected with membership status, with only a change of delegates to the Organization. The same can be said for Cuba, with regard to the establishment of Fidel Castro's regime in 1959, or for Chile after Pinochet took over in 1973. With regard to Governments set up by foreign States, the same solution was found for the Governments formed after the armed interventions by the Soviet Union in Afghanistan and by the United States in Grenada during the eighties, as well as in the case of the Panamanian Government after the capture of Noriega by the United States at the end of 1989. Even if criticism and reservations are sometimes put forward by members during the examination of the credentials of the representatives of the new Governments both in the Security Council and in the General Assembly, the general tendency is toward upholding the continuity between the old and the new Government.

Reservations, although without effect, have been put forward over the years in the General Assembly with regard to the credentials of the representatives of Pinochet's Chile by the Soviet Union and by other States (cf., for example, the USSR statement in 1985, in Doc.A/40/747), with regard to those of the Government of Grenada after the United States' intervention (cf., for example, Doc.A/40/PV.120), with regard to Afghanistan (cf., for example, Doc. A/41/PV.45 and A/43/PV.33), etc.

United Nations practice would seem therefore to confirm the view that the person of the State is not extinguished owing to revolutionary changes of government (*"forma regiminis mutata non mutatur ipsa civitas"*). This view is associated with a certain way of perceiving the State as a subject of international law. It is, first of all, upheld by those who identify the State with its people and who hold that the organization of government, the group of organs exercising power, is present at the international level only as the representative (in the sense of representing the interests) of the human community it governs. However, the same view is also held by those who see the State as a body made up of three elements, population, territory and governmental authority. Changes in the official organs and in the way of exercising such authority would not affect the person of the State, in so far as its continuity would be guaranteed by the permanence of the territory and the population.

Actually, UN practice concerning revolutionary changes in the Member States may be justified also in the light of another conception of the State, on the basis of which the State as an international legal person is identified with the Government in a broad sense, and therefore with the group of organs which exercise, and to the extent that they effectively exercise, power. It is true that whoever adopts a conception of this kind must for coherence recognize that the State becomes extinct when there is a radical change in the political system. Yet it is also true that such recognition is usually accompanied by the acknowledgement that the new Government, or, rather, the new State, succeeds, as a general rule, in the rights and obligations undertaken by the predecessor, provided they are not incompatible with the new political system. Consequently, as far as the UN is concerned, the above-cited practice can be interpreted as a practice of succession of the new State in member status. In fact, this is the preferable interpretation because the view that would have the State correspond to the organization of Government seems most in keeping with the reality of international relations.

Apart from the rather theoretical speculations concerning the exact definition of a State, the issue is still to-day ruled in international law — or at least in United Nations practice regarding the effects of State succession on membership status — by the principle of effectiveness. The fact that a new government is not democratic, or does not respect human rights, or is not peace-loving, etc., has been ever more often put forward as the grounds for the just-mentioned reservations regarding the legality of the credentials of the persons the new governments send as their representatives to the UN However, still today, sooner or later the Government which effectively controls the country occupies the seat in the Organization.

There is not always perfect coincidence between the time when a new government takes over from an old one in the control of a country and the time when the former is installed in the UN seat occupied by the latter. It may happen that the succession within the United Nations occurs sometime before it occurs in the country, and is thus premature. For example, the substitution of the delegates of the Yemenite monarchical Government in the General Assembly by those of the Republican Government in December 1962 was considered by some observers to be premature: in fact, at the time the Republican forces had not entirely defeated the Imam's forces but had only occupied a part, although a considerable part, of the country. By contrast, it may happen that the succession within the United Nations occurs later than that within the country. This was the case of Iraq, which was transformed from a monarchy into a republic in 1958. The representative of the old Government continued to participate for several weeks in Security Council sessions (Iraq at the time was a non-permanent member) in spite of protests by some members of the Council and despite the fact that the new Government had already announced the appointment of another delegate. Another example may be taken from the League of Nations practice. The representatives of the Spanish Republican Government continued to sit in the League Assembly even after the victory of Franco's Government and up until May 1939, when Spain withdrew from the League. Although such anomalies in the timing of a succession are not formally correct, they have little practical relevance because of their very limited duration.

In the recent practice, when different delegations are presented by conflicting governments to represent the same Member State, and the situation within the country is unclear, there is a tendency in the Security Council and the General Assembly to decide that no one is entitled to occupy the seat. The consequence is then that the country in question's membership rights are suspended (see § 15).

On the Yemenite issue, resolved by the Assembly during the examination of credentials, with the seating of the republican delegates and the expulsion of the monarchical delegates from the Assembly hall, see GAOR, 17th sess., Pl. meet., vol. III, 1201st meet., 1202nd meet. On the Iraq case, see SCOR, 13th year, 827th, 834th, and 838th meets., p. 1 ff. On the League of Nations practice in the case of Spain, see *Societé des Nations*, Journal Officiel, 1939, p. 344 for the withdrawal announced by Franco's Government; *ivi*, p. 102 f. for the last appearance in the Council, in February 1939, of the representative of the Republican Government.

For the more recent practice, worthy of mention is the case of Panama in 1989. The Security Council, which had met to discuss the situation in Panama after the fall of Noriega's Government, and in particular the accusations of United States soldiers' illegal entry into the

Nicaraguan Embassy in Panama City, found itself faced with requests of the new Government and also of the old Government to send their representatives to take part in the discussion, as well as with a report of the Secretary-General in which he stated that he "is not in a position to provide an elucidation on the factual situation on the ground" (cf. Doc. S/21047 of December 21, 1989, p. 3). The issue was resolved with both Governments being excluded from the debate (cf. Doc. S/PV.2902 of December 23, 1989) and then was closed with the consolidation of the pro-American Government. In the General Assembly the same occurred when two delegations were appointed in order to represent Cambodia at the fifty-second session, in 1997 (see GAOR, 52nd sess., 38th Pl. meet. and res. no. 54/6 approving the Report of the Credential committee).

Going back to the older practice, a different stand was taken in the case of the Congolese delegation, discussed in the General Assembly between September and November 1960. The Congo, which was admitted to the UN after acquiring independence in June, 1960, was, in the fall of 1960, going through a period of true anarchy. In September, when no Congolese representative had yet taken a seat at the UN, the Chief of State, Kasa-Vubu, and the Prime Minister, Lumumba, removed each other from office, with the subsequent formation of two separate Governments. A third Government, which later joined with the President of the Republic, was formed at the same time by the Chief of the Military Staff, Mobutu. The country was actually governed... by chaos. The General Assembly found itself faced with the opposing claims of Kasa-Vubu and Lumumba to the Congo seat in the UN At the request of several members, the Assembly first decided to postpone any decision. Then, however, with a resolution of November 22, 1960 (approved by a majority of 53 votes to 24, with 19 abstentions), it accredited the representatives of Kasa-Vubu. The decision was justified by the fact that Kasa-Vubu was Head of State and that Article 27 of the Assembly rules of procedure mentions the Head of State as the first among the organs that have the power to accredit representatives in the Assembly. The minority favouring Lumumba insisted, on the contrary, that a decision be postponed until the domestic situation was clarified. Clearly the view supporting postponement had the strongest legal basis. However, the Government headed by Kasa-Vubu later became well-established. For the relevant practice see GAOR, 15th sess., Pl. meet, 896th meet., 912th meet., 917th meet., and 918th-924th meets. See also the report of the Credentials Committee in GAOR, 15th sess., Annexes, item n. 3. A summary of domestic events in the Congo in September 1960 can be found in the annual report of the Secretary-General on the 16th Assembly session, in GAOR, 16th sess., Suppl. n. 1. Cf. also SCOR, 20th year, 1207th meet. and 1227th meet.

Still in the old practice, a very peculiar position was taken by the General Assembly with regard to the Hungarian Government of Kadar between November 1956, when this Government was forcefully established with the support of the Soviet armed forces, and 1962. During this whole period of time the delegates of the Hungarian Government took part in Assembly proceedings, expressing their opinions and exercising their voting right, but... provisionally. In fact, at the 11th Assembly session in 1956-57 Chile challenged the regularity of their credentials. Under Article 29 of the Assembly's rules of procedure, cited by Chile, a representative against whom objections have been raised, may sit in the organ only provisionally, until, first, the Credentials Committee of the Assembly, and, then, the Assembly in plenary have decided the case. However, in every session, between 1956 and 1962, the Assembly decided not to take any decision on the regularity of the Hungarians' credentials, thereby prolonging their provisional participation. For the relevant practice, cf. UN Rep. Suppl. n. 2, vol. II, sub Article 9, n. 9ff., and, for further details, GAOR, 11th sess. Pl. meet., 658th meet.; 12th sess., Pl. meet., 726th meet.; 13th sess., Pl. meet., 792nd meet.; 14th sess., Pl. meet., 852nd meet.; 15th sess., Pl. meet., 995th meet.; 17th sess., Pl. meet., 1202nd meet.

Separate mention is due to the question of Chinese representation, which dragged out for over twenty years, between 1949 and 1971. When the Communist Government of Mao-Tse-Tung was established on mainland China in 1949 and the Nationalist Government of Chiang-Kai-Shek was confined to ruling over only the island of Formosa, the former formally asked to take the latter's seat in the UN, with all the rights and obligations connected with status as a permanent member in the Security Council. The request immediately received the support of the socialist States as well as of a group of Third World States, but met with the very strong opposition of the majority of Member States, led by the United States. Thereafter, the question of Chinese representation was the subject of heated debate and sharp controversy (the moment of greatest tension occurred in 1950 when the Soviet Union abstained in protest from taking part in all the organs in which China was represented) with Mao's Government being completely excluded from United Nations life and with Chiang-Kai-Shek's delegates confirmed in the exercise of all membership rights, including the rights belonging to permanent members of the Security Council. Only in 1971 did the Assembly find the necessary majority (a majority which, beginning in 1961, had been set by the Assembly itself at two-thirds: see § 32) to decide "to restore all its rights to the People's Republic of China and to recognize the representatives of its Government as the only legitimate representatives of China to the United Nations, and to expel forthwith the representatives of Chiang-Kai-Shek from the place which they unlawfully occupy at the United Nations and in all the organizations related to it" (res. n. 2758-XXVI of October 25, 1971).

Unquestionably, the ostracism of the People's Government for so many years and the presence of Nationalist China in the Security Council as a permanent member did not benefit either the prestige or the effectiveness of the Organization. The question of the "two Chinas" should have been resolved in 1950, not in 1971. If this is true, the question remains, however, whether the 1971 decision, in dealing with the issue as a case of turnover of delegates and therefore of a revolutionary change of government within a country, was legal. Serious doubts may arise on this, as the old Nationalist Government did not disappear in 1949 but continued, and still continues today, to govern over a small part (small with respect to the whole of China but not in an absolute sense since it covers 14,000 square kilometers with about 10 million inhabitants), of the Chinese territory. In other words, the Chinese question could have been brought within the principles on separation (see § 18) rather than those on revolutionary changes of Government. Therefore, if one had wanted to resolve it in accordance with law, the old Government should have kept its status as a member (losing, however, the permanent seat in the Security Council, in that it was a Government no longer representing a Great

Power) and the People's Republic should have been admitted to the UN (and been given, as a Great Power, the permanent seat).

More specifically, as far as the Nationalist Government was concerned, the status of permanent member of the Security Council (a capacity given to this Government in 1945 exclusively because it ruled over the Chinese territory as a whole) had already been lost, along with all the related rights, through the effect of the *rebus sic stantibus* principle. The General Assembly, therefore, as some delegations, for example, the Tunisian delegation, had proposed shortly before the decision was taken in 1971 (cf. GAOR, 26th sess., Pl. meet., 1976th meet.), should have only verified the loss of this status, owing to the unexpected and fundamental change of circumstances, without proceeding as it did to the expulsion of Formosa in contempt of the procedure under Article 6 of the Charter. With regard to the People's Republic, its entry into the UN should have occurred through the admission procedure under Article 4. It could have then been given one of the permanent seats in the Security Council even without a formal change in the Charter but in application of the provision in Article 23 which reserves such seats to the Great Powers. It is useless to add that, for purposes of one or the other procedure, no obstacle would have arisen from the presence of Taiwan in the Security Council, a presence which, as we have said, was no longer in accordance with the Charter.

20. *Governments in exile.*

BIBLIOGRAPHY: WALTERS, *A History of the League of Nations*, London, 1967, p. 688 ff.; ARANGIO-RUIZ, *Sulla dinamica della base sociale nel diritto internazionale*, Milan, 1954, p. 156 ff.; RASY, *La question de la représentation Khmer à l'ONU: droit ou politique?*, Paris, 1974; DORFMAN and others, *The United Nations, 28th session, Cambodian Representation*, in *HILJ*, 1974, p. 495 ff.; SCISO, *La questione delle credenziali cambiogiane all'Assemblea generale delle Nazioni Unite*, in *RDI*, 1981, p. 83 ff.; KOENIG, *Die Vertretung Kambodschas bei den Vereinten Nationen*, in *AV*, 1990, p. 266 ff.

The problem of governments in exile must also be resolved on the basis of the principle of effectiveness. This phenomenon may occur following revolutionary changes of government, or in the case of wartime occupation, or of annexation of territories. It may happen (as happened, for example, for the Spanish Republican Government after the civil war in Spain or for the Governments of the territories invaded by the Nazis during the Second World War) that the Government of the country where extra-legal forces have prevailed, and the country has been occupied or annexed to another State, seeks refuge abroad and continues there to be considered and treated as a sovereign entity.

In our opinion, the attempts made in a part of legal literature to give an international legal personality to these entities, which are completely without any effective ruling power over a community, must be rejected. Such attempts do not take into account the fact that international law, although it addresses Governments, still protects the interests of the people who are governed. Such interests are utterly inconceivable without the people to which they are attached.

Consequently, a Government which no longer controls the territory of a member country cannot occupy a seat in the United Nations. If power in the country has been seized by another Government, the latter will have the right to send its own delegates to the UN, in accordance with what was said in the preceding paragraph. If there has been an annexation, the State will cease to exist and so will its status as a UN member. If, lastly, it is a question of belligerent occupation, which is, or should be, characterized by temporariness, the result should be the dormancy of the status as a member during the occupation.

For these reasons, the position taken by the General Assembly between 1979 and 1990 when it was faced with the concurrent claims of the Democratic Kampuchea and of the Government of the People's Republic of Kampuchea to occupy Cambodia's seat in the United Nations, was illegal. With the latter Government established in Cambodia, following the Vietnamese invasion and the flight into Thailand and China of the previous rulers, the Assembly decided in 1979, and it kept to this decision throughout the following years up to 1990, to continue to accredit the representatives of the Democratic Kampuchea, i.e., a coalition Government which included Pol Pot's Khmer Rouge. All this occurred despite the fact that the Democratic Kampuchea no longer had effective control of the country. The decision, taken by the majority and strongly opposed by the minority (countries of the Soviet bloc and various non-aligned countries) was justified mainly for political reasons, which aimed at denouncing the Vietnamese aggression and the nature of puppet government attributed to the Heng Samrin Government, subsequently set up in Phnom Pehn. From a legal point of view, the decision was not, however, acceptable.

For the relevant practice, cf. Report of the Credentials Committee of Sept. 20, 1979 (doc. A/34/500) and the discussions in the Assembly plenary also in 1979, in GAOR, 34th sess., Pl. meet., 3rd and 4th meets. Cf., also, for the following years, A/39/PV.42 and A/37/PV.43 of Oct. 26, 1982; A/38/PV.34 of Oct. 26, 1983; A/39/PV.32 of Oct. 17, 1984; A/42/PV.36 of Oct. 15, 1987; A/43/PV.33 of Oct. 20, 1988; A/44/PV.32 of Oct. 20, 1989. It is indicative that the statements in favour of the Democratic Kampuchea were nearly all based on political grounds, while those favouring the Heng Samrin Government appealed to legal principles, particularly the principle of effectiveness. The argument used by the United States to support the representatives of the Democratic Kampuchea was a curious one (the United States itself said it had a "technical" nature). This was that the representatives of a Government that have been accredited in a previous Assembly session should continue indefinitely to be accredited in subsequent sessions, even if their Government is no longer effective, until a "superior claim" is put forth by another Government, and the "claim" of a puppet Government could not be considered "superior" (cf. GAOR, 34th sess., Pl. meet., 4th meet.).

The problem of the representation of Cambodia had already arisen between 1971 and 1974 and was at that time correctly resolved by the Assembly. These were the years of the struggle between the Government of Prince Sianouk who was forced to seek refuge in Peking and the Khmer Government of Lon Nol who had taken control of the country. In spite of the heated attempts of several Socialist and Third World countries, aimed at expelling the representatives of the Khmer Government, accused of being a puppet Government of the United States, from Assembly proceedings, the Assembly majority decided to the contrary. On the debate, see GAOR, 26th sess., Pl. meet., 2027th meet.; 27th sess., Pl. meet., 2104 meet.; 28th sess., Pl. meet., 2155th meet., 2188th meet.ff., and 2204th meet.; 29th sess., Pl. meet., 2298th-2302nd meets. The position of the majority, which was for approval, was well summarized in a statement by the Japanese delegate who said the Assembly could not arrogate the right to make and to destroy Governments as it pleased (see 28th sess., Pl.meet., 2189th meet.).

The solution given by the Assembly to the question of Cambodian representation in 1979 finds a precedent in the case of Ethiopian representation in the League of Nations. With Ethiopia annexed to Italy in 1936 and its extinction as a State thus having occurred, the League Assembly decided that nevertheless the delegates of Emperor Hailè Selassiè could continue to sit in the organ and have full voting rights. The decision (repeated in subsequent years) was taken expressly for moral and political reasons, to condemn the Italian aggression, but even among its supporters it raised serious doubts of a legal nature (cf. WALTERS, *op. cit.*, p. 690). In fact, Ethiopia, while continuing to maintain a permanent delegate in the League, eventually voluntarily abstained from participating in Assembly proceedings (cf. *Société des Nations*, Journal officiel, 1937, p. 658., *ivi*, 1938, p. 669).

21. *State succession and rules on credentials.*

BIBLIOGRAPHY: FITZMAURICE, *Chinese Representation in the United Nations*, in *Yearbook of World Affairs*, 1952, p. 36 ff.; ARANGIO-RUIZ, *Sulla dinamica della base sociale nel diritto internazionale*, Milan, 1954, p. 145 f.; ID., *La questione cinese*, in *Studi in onore di Tomaso Perassi*, I, Milan, 1957, p. 67 ff. and p. 94 f.; MCDOUGAL and GOODMAN, *Chinese Partecipation in the United Nations: The Legal Imperatives of a Negotiated Solution*, in *AJ*, 1966, p. 671 ff.; CIOBANU, *Credentials of Delegations and Representation of Member States at the UN*, in *ICLQ*, 1976, p. 353 ff.; SCISO, *La questione delle credenziali cambogiane all'Assemblea Generale delle Nazioni Unite*, in *RDI*, 1981, p. 83 ff.; HALBERSTAM, *Excluding Israel from the General Assembly by a Rejection of its Credentials*, in *AJIL*, 1984, p. 179 ff.; ZICCARDI CAPALDO, *Il disconoscimento delle credenziali del Sud Africa come sanzione contro l'apartheid*, in *RDI*, 1985, p. 299 ff.; TABORY, *Universality at the UN: The Attempt to Reject Israel' Credentials*, in *Israel Yearbook of Human Rights*, 1988, p. 189 ff.

Articles 27-29 of the General Assembly's rules of procedure (rules issued on the basis of Article 21 of the Charter) govern the procedure for accrediting the representatives of States in the Assembly. They provide that credentials must be issued by the Head of State or of Government or by the Minister for Foreign Affairs (Article 27); that the Assembly shall, at the beginning of each session, appoint a "Credentials Committee" to examine the credentials and report to the Assembly (Article 28); that a delegate, whose participation in the proceedings of the organ has been challenged by another member, shall be seated temporarily "until the Credentials Committee has reported and the Assembly has given its decision" on his or her position (Article 29). Similar provisions are contained in Articles 13-17 of the Security Council's rules of procedure (which were also issued on the basis of a Charter provision, Article 30). The only differences concern the possibility, granted to the Head of Government or to the Minister for Foreign Affairs, to sit in the organ even without submitting credentials (Article 13) and the attribution to the Secretary-General of the powers that the Assembly rules of procedure give to the Credentials Committee (Article 15).

In all matters concerning credentials, the Assembly and the Council vote by simple majority, since they are procedural matters. The Assembly decides by a majority of those present and voting, under Article 18, para. 3, of the Charter. The Council decides by a majority of nine votes out of fifteen, on the basis of Article 27, para. 2.

Much more succinct are the provisions on credentials in the rules of procedure of the Social and Economic Council (Article 17) which neither indicate the State organ competent to issue credentials nor contemplate the case of "challenging" a representative.

It has been asked in legal literature whether challenges as to delegates' credentials, challenges which the Assembly and the Council may decide upon under Articles 28 and 17 of their respective rules of procedure, can concern the whole Government that the delegate represents. It has been asked, in other words, whether, during the examination of credentials and the relative discussion, they may resolve any doubts as to the right of the Government sending the delegates to occupy a UN seat and to participate in the organ's proceedings. May the Assembly and the Council, during the examination of credentials, ascertain that a State is extinct and therefore refuse to accredit the Government representatives who claim to occupy that seat? May they decide whether, and when, the representatives of a Government formed after a revolution are to be accredited and refuse to accept the credentials issued by the old Government that has sought refuge abroad?

According to one view, the answer should be negative. The cited articles in the rules of procedure would concern only challenges to the qualification of the delegate to represent his or her own Government; they would have been laid down only "for the case of challenges regarding the credentials of a real or false delegate by another real or false delegate *from the same Government*" (ARANGIO-RUIZ). In short, they would refer only to the rather hypothetical case of an individual appearing before the Assembly or the Council or another UN organ and declaring that he or she represents a certain Government, using false documents or presenting credentials from an organ different from the Head of State or the Foreign Minister.

In fact, United Nations practice, as well as the previous League of Nations practice, has been clearly the opposite of this view. All, or nearly all, the problems that have been examined in the preceding sections of this chapter were raised during the examination of credentials and were resolved with decisions regarding the credentials. More than anything, it has been through the decisions on credentials in the League of Nations and in the United Nations that the succession of Governments in the same seat has taken place.

Indeed, the practice seems to be perfectly in accordance with the rules of procedure of the Assembly or of the Security Council. Neither Article 29 of the Assembly rules nor Article 17 of the Council rules, in dealing with challenges to a delegate's credentials and giving the power to the organ to settle such challenges, sets any limit on the subject matter of the challenge.

Article 29 does not even speak of credentials but of objections against the "admission" of delegates. Also the *ratio* of the two articles supports the same view: if challenges concerning the Government as a whole were excluded from the list, one would not know what to include since it would be hard to imagine, and indeed has never occurred in UN practice (as far as we know), that an individual has said that he or she represented a Government without doing so. Nor does the fact that the organs competent to issue credentials are Government organs, such as the Head of State or the Foreign Minister (Article 27, Assembly rules, and Article 13, Council rules) lead to the inference that any investigation aiming to verify the position of these organs, or of the Government to which they belong, is precluded. The indication of the organ competent to issue credentials concerns procedure and says nothing about the examination of credentials with a view to substance. Lastly, it is to be excluded that the matter can be influenced by the rule that the challenged delegate has the right to participate in the organ's proceedings until such organ has come to a decision (Article 29 Assembly rules, Articles 16-17 Council rules). It has been said that if the representatives of two Governments could dispute the seat, both would have the right to speak and to vote in the organs until a decision were made about them, resulting in a breach of the Charter norms that each member has but one vote. The argument is not relevant. Indeed, it is even too obvious, and has always occurred in the practice (see, for example, the Congolese and Yemenite questions: § 19; see also he question of representation of Panama before the Security Council, in SC Rep., Suppl. 1989-1992, Part II, case no. 7) that in cases of this kind the organ must decide immediately and at least before the items on the agenda are set.

Another argument for the view upheld here may be drawn from the fact that the Charter does not provide any special procedure for ascertaining a State's succession. It is therefore only with decisions regarding credentials that the Organization can resolve problems which involve establishing whether a State is extinct as an international subject, whether one Government may succeed to another, and so on.

The only difficulty that may arise is that the Assembly and the Council, within their respective power to decide on credentials, may behave differently when faced with the same case, that is, they may each maintain that a different Government has the right to occupy the same seat in the UN This drawback, which has up to now not been proven to be true in practice, will find a solution only in an agreement between the two organs. It is, moreover, connected with a more basic theme, that of possible divisions between the Assembly and the Council due to the possible differences in the political forces that prevail at the same time in each of the two organs.

In 1950 the General Assembly, precisely in order to avoid disputes between the organs over credentials, recommended that the other organs let the Assembly decide "whenever more than one authority claims to be the Government entitled to represent a Member State in the United Nations" and provided that "this question becomes a subject of controversy in the United Nations" (res. 396-V of Dec. 14, 1950).

Decisions on credentials, as all UN decisions, cannot avoid the principle of legality (see § 97). They are illegal if they are in conflict with the Charter or, if the Charter does not provide otherwise, with international customary law. Because the Charter is not concerned with State succession, it is necessary to refer only to the principles of customary law, that is to say, the principles that have been summarized in the previous sections. Decisions which do not conform to the principle of effectiveness in particular will be illegal.

A decision on credentials, which does not conform (*and only when it does not conform*) to the rules of customary law on State succession may ultimately result in an admission, an expulsion, or a suspension of membership rights effected in contempt of the provisions in Articles 4-6 of the Charter. Therefore, if, through a decision on credentials, the Assembly admits to the United Nations the representatives of a new State (come into being, for example, owing to separation or dismemberment), which on the basis of customary principles does not have the title to succeed a pre-existing Member State, the decision will be illegal, also because it would violate Article 4 which foresees a special procedure for admission. Also, if the Assembly temporarily or definitively expels from its proceedings the representatives of a State that has not undergone any of the changes which under customary law result in extinction of a State (that is, it has not been incorporated, or dismembered, or defeated, etc.), the relative decision will illegally contradict the respective rules on expulsion (Article 6) and on suspension (Article 5).

As we shall see in examining the problem of the illegality of UN acts (see § 97), the lack of a review organ entails that illegal acts can be remedied only by the acquiescence of all the Member States. As we shall also see (*ivi*), acquiescence usually covers acts involving membership in the Organization, and therefore also decisions on credentials. This means that the decisions on credentials succeed in becoming final whether they legally or illegally affect the status as a member. This is the reason for their great importance in the life of the United Nations Organization.

CHAPTER TWO

THE ORGANS

Section I

THE SECURITY COUNCIL

22. *Composition of the Council. Election of non-permanent Members.*

BIBLIOGRAPHY: KELSEN, *Organization and Procedure of the Security Council of the United Nations*, in *HLR*, 1945-46, p. 1087 ff.; BOWETT, *The Security Council*, in WORTLEY, *The United Nations. The First Ten Years*, Manchester, 1957, p. 19 ff.; SCHWELB, *Amendments to Article 23, 27 and 61 of the Charter of the United Nations*, in *AJ*, 1965, p. 834 ff.; GUARINO, *Le recenti modifiche della Carta delle Nazioni Unite*, in *ADI*, 1965, p. 383 ff.; MARSHIK-NEUHOLD, *Die Sicherbeitsrat*, Wien, 1972; REISMAN, *The Case of the Non-permanent Vacancy*, in *AJ*, 1980, p. 907 ff.; BAILEY, *The Procedure of the UN Security Council*, 2nd ed., Oxford, 1988.

The Security Council is composed of permanent members, the so-called five Great Powers, and non-permanent members, elected periodically by the General Assembly. In this regard, Article 23 provides as follows: "The Security Council shall consist of fifteen Members of the United Nations. The Republic of China, France, the Union of Soviet Socialist Republics (today, Russia), the United Kingdom of Great Britain and Northern Ireland, and the United States of America shall be permanent members of the Security Council. The General Assembly shall elect ten other Members of the United Nations to be non-permanent members of the Security Council, due regard being specially paid, in the first instance to the contribution of Members of the United Nations to the maintenance of international peace and security and to the other purposes of the Organization, and also to equitable geographical distribution. The non-permanent members of the Security Council shall be elected for a term of two years... Each member of the Security Council shall have one representative".

Each Member State, permanent or non-permanent, holds in turn the office of President of the Council, on a monthly rotation basis (Article 18, Council rules of procedure).

Until 1965, the year when Article 23 was amended, there were only 11 members of the Council, six of whom were non-permanent members.

During the Cold War period, the formula of "equitable geographical distribution", used by Article 23 with regard to the selection of non-permanent members, gave rise to very sharp clashes, and it was asked whether it referred to physical geography or rather to political geography. The issue arose in reference to a kind of verbal understanding that the Great Powers had made among themselves in 1946 and on the basis of which the six non-permanent seats in the Council were to be distributed as follows: two to Latin America, one to the British Commonwealth, one to the Middle East countries, one to Western Europe and one to Eastern Europe (the understanding is cited in GAOR, 8th sess., Pl. meet., 450th meet., n. 19). In the early years of the United Nations, the East European seat was allocated to a Communist government, for example, to Poland in 1946 and to the Ukraine in 1948. After 1950, the Assembly began to fill the seat with States which, although geographically part of Eastern Europe (or nearly so) had nothing to do with the Communist bloc. In 1952 Greece was elected and, in 1954, Turkey. Strong protests were then made by the Soviet Union which complained both that the 1946 understanding had been breached and that Article 23 had been violated. Apart from the 1946 understanding, whose binding nature is very dubious and which in any case did not bind all the Assembly members but only the five Great Powers, it does not seem that the Article 23 formula can refer to the political situation of the country to be elected. This seems obvious when we consider geographical areas, such as Africa or Asia, which are not characterised by the same kind of political regimes but show the greatest variety.
For a summary of the debates on the allocation of the seat belonging to Eastern Europe, see UN Rep., sub Article 23, nn. 14-22, and, for the most important statements in the General Assembly, GAOR, 4th sess., Pl. meet., 231st meet., n. 10 ff.; 6th sess., Pl. meet., 353rd meet., no. 10 ff.; 8th sess., Pl. meet, 450th meet., n. 22 ff.

The modification of Article 23, which increased the number of Council members to 15, was provided for by the General Assembly with resolution no. 1991-XVIII (lett. A) of December 17, 1963, and entered into force in August 1965 following ratification by two-thirds of the Member States, as prescribed by Article 108.
The 1963 resolution has two parts. In one, the Assembly decides to submit the amendment to ratification by the Member States. In the other it "*further decides* that the ten non-permanent members of the Security Council shall be elected according to the following pattern: (*a*) Five from African and Asian States; (*b*) one from Eastern European States; (*c*) two from Latin American States; (*d*) two from Western European and other States". This second part of the resolution, which is still applied in the allocation of seats, is not, nor is it meant to be, an amendment to the Charter. In fact, it has never been subject to ratification under Article 108. What, then, is its formal value? Certainly it is not binding the Member States. Under the Charter, the Assembly may adopt binding decision only in very specific cases, and this is not one of them. Nor is it possible, in view of the circumstances, to interpret the second part of the resolution as a real international agreement existing between the countries which voted for it. If the States had really intended to

bind themselves, they would have adopted the second part of the resolution as an amendment as well. On the other hand, it would be excessive to say that the decision has no legal value, lowering it, for example, to the level of a "gentlemen's agreement". The best solution is to bring the resolution within the power to make recommendations which very broadly and generally belongs to the General Assembly under Article 10 of the Charter, and to attribute it the typical legal effect of the recommendations of UN organs, that is, the effect of legality (see § 89). A State which follows the criteria indicated by the Assembly could not in any case be accused of violating the provisions of Article 23 on the geographical distribution of seats.

With the geographical distribution adopted in the 1963 resolution, and considering that a permanent member, China, may be numbered among the developing countries, these countries (which are thus guaranteed more than six seats in the Council) enjoy a kind of "collective veto". They are able, if they are in agreement, to prevent the formation of the majority of nine members necessary for the adoption of any decision.

If the Assembly does not succeed in electing one or more non-permanent member of the Council, it is possible that the latter will have to discuss and decide with an incomplete membership. This will have no effect on the validity of a decision. In fact, neither the Charter nor the Council's rules of procedure (issued by the Council itself on the basis of Article 30 of the Charter) prescribe a particular quorum for the sessions. Therefore, the minimum number required to be present corresponds to the number of votes required by Article 27 for the adoption of decisions.

The only case of vacancy of a non-permanent seat occurred in early January 1980 because the Assembly, in the previous December, had not been able to fill one of the two seats assigned to Latin America for which both Columbia and Cuba were contending. The Council nevertheless met during those days but did not have the chance to vote before the seat was occupied by Mexico, elected on January 7 after the withdrawal of the candidacies of the two above-mentioned countries. On the case, cf. REISMAN, *art. cit.* Cf. also the legal opinion issued by the UN Secretariat on December 3, 1979 (in *UNJY*, 1979, p. 164 ff.) which holds that the Council is not legally formed if one or more non-permanent members have not been elected but that, notwithstanding this, it... may nonetheless function so that its primary responsibility regarding maintenance of the peace is not affected.

23. *Voting procedure in the Council:* A) *The nature of the four Powers' Statement at the San Francisco Conference.*

BIBLIOGRAPHY: LEE, *The Genesis of the Veto*, in *Int. Org.*, 1947, p. 33 ff.; JIMENEZ DE ARECHAGA, *Voting and the Handling of Disputes in the Security Council*, NewYork, 1950, p. 42 ff.; BRUGIÈRE, *La règle de l'unanimitè des membres permanents au Conseil de Sécurité, « Droit de veto »*, Paris, 1952, p. 36 ff.; GROSS, *The Double Veto and the*

Four-Powers Statement on Voting in the Security Council, in *HLR*, 1953-54, p. 251 ff.; BROMS, *Voting in the Security Council*, in *Festskrift till L. Hjerner*, Stockholm, 1990, p. 93 ff.; DELON, *La concertation entre les membres permanents du Conseil de Sécurité*, in *AF*, 1993, p. 53 ff.

The voting procedure in the Security Council is outlined in Article 27, which reproduces the Yalta formula (see § 1 A) and confirms the so-called veto power. Under this article, "1. Each member of the Security Council shall have one vote. 2. Decisions of the Security Council on procedural matters shall be made by an affirmative vote of nine members. 3. Decisions of the Security Council on all other matters shall be made by an affirmative vote of nine [seven until 1965] members including the concurring votes of the permanent members; provided that, in decisions under Chapter VI, and under paragraph 3 of Article 52, a party to a dispute shall abstain from voting".

At the San Francisco Conference, several questions were put to the four sponsoring governments (the United States, the USSR, China and the United Kingdom) in order to clarify certain aspects of the Yalta formula which might have created, and which did indeed create, problems of interpretation. Mainly, it was asked how the Council was to vote if it were asked to decide on whether or not a matter was procedural (on the question of the double veto, see § 26). The answer was given in a Statement issued by the sponsoring governments on June 7, 1945 and adhered to by France in its capacity as a future permanent member of the Council.

The nature of the Statement has often been discussed in the Council. The Soviet Union held, in disagreement with the Western Powers, that it is a true international agreement, and, as such, binding on the permanent members. However, if attention is paid to the circumstances in which the Statement was issued and, especially, the position taken at the time by some of the States which signed it, the idea of a formal agreement appears to be unacceptable. The report presented to the President of the United States by the head of the American delegation to the San Francisco Conference has particular significance in this respect. The report indicated the Statement as an explanatory instrument but expressed specific reservations as to the reliability of an anticipatory interpretation made "without any practical experience as to the operation of the Organization or the Security Council". It is clear that such position assumed an intention not to be formally bound.

In our opinion, the Statement should be considered on the same level as the preparatory works. It is true that it was not adopted (but neither was it rejected) by the San Francisco Conference and remained limited to the five Great Powers. Yet it is also true that among these were the States that had drawn up Article 27 at Yalta and then imposed it on the Conference. Consequently, the Statement represented the viewpoint of the "drafters" of the Charter.

The problem of the nature of the Statement should not be over-esti-
mated. Indeed, its content, being the result of compromises, is very ambiguous. As we shall see, it furnishes little help in answering the question the San
Francisco Conference most wanted resolved by the Great Powers, the
question of the double veto. The Statement thus betrays the purpose that it
was meant to fulfill, namely the facilitation of the interpretation of ambiguous
texts, the very function of preparatory works.

For the text of the Statement, see U.N.C.I.O., vol. 11, p. 710 ff. The passage cited
from the report by the Head of the American delegation is reproduced in GROSS, *art. cit.*, p.
255.

24.   B) *The so-called veto power and the significance of abstention by a*
permanent Member.

BIBLIOGRAPHY: WILCOX, *The Rule of Unanimity in the Security Council,* in
Proceedings of the American Society of International Law, 1946, p. 55 ff.; WORTLEY, *The Veto*
and the Security Provisions of the Charter, in *BYB,* 1946, p. 95 ff.; PADELFORD, *The Use of the*
Veto, in *Int. Org.,* 1948, p. 227 ff.; DE PREUX, *Droit de veto dans la Charte des Nations Unies,*
Paris, 1949; LIANG, *Abstension and Absence of a Permanent Member in Relation to the Voting*
Procedure in the Security Council, in *AJ,* 1950, p. 696 ff.; McDOUGAL and GARDNER, *The Veto*
and the Charter: An Interpretation for Survival, in *Yale Law Journal,* 1951, p. 2258 ff.;
BRUGIÈRE, *La règle de l'unanimité des membres permanents au Conseil de Sécurité, « Droit de*
veto », Paris, 1952; DAY, *Le droit de veto dans l'Organisation des Nations Unies,* Paris, 1952;
ENGELHARDT, *Das Vetorecht im Sicherheitsrat der Vereinten Nationen,* in *AV,* 1963, p. 377 ff.;
KAHNG, *Law, Politics, and the Security Council,* The Hague, 1964, p. 124 ff.; JENKS,
Unanimity, the Veto, Weighted Voting, Special and Simple Majorities and Consensus as Models
of Decision in International Organizations, in *Cambridge Essays in International Law; Essays*
in Honour of Lord McNair, London, 1965, p. 48 ff.; STAVROPOULOS, *The Practice of Voluntary*
Abstention by Permanent Members of the Security Council under Article 27, paragraph 3, of
the Charter of the United Nations, in *AJ,* 1967, p. 737 ff.; GROSS, *Voting in the Security*
Council: Abstention in the post-1965 Amendment Phase and its Impact on Article 25 of the
Charter, in *AJ,* 1968, p. 315 ff.; UDECHUKU, *The Problem of the Veto in the Security Council,*
in *International Relations,* 1972, p. 187 ff.; BAILEY, *New Light on Abstentions in the UN*
Security Council, in *International Affairs,* 1974, p. 554 ff.; DAMBAZAU, *UN and the Veto*
Power, in *Nigerian Forum,* 1987, p. 84 ff.

"Veto power" (of the five permanent members of the Council) are the
words commonly used with regard to the provision of Article 27, para. 3,
which provides that decisions on non-procedural matters shall be made by an
affirmative vote of nine members (seven before the Council was enlarged in
1965), which includes all the permanent members. The English text of para. 3
reads as follows: "Decisions of the Security Council... shall be made by an
affirmative vote of nine members including the concurring votes of the
permanent members...". The French text reads: "Les décisions du Conseil...

sont prises par un vote affermatif de neuf de ses membres dans lequel sont comprises les voix de tous les membres permanents...".

  There is no question that, under para. 3 of Article 27, the validity of a non-procedural decision of the Council requires the affirmative votes of all five permanent members. Therefore, even the mere abstention of a permanent member is to be considered a veto (although, in a strict sense, a veto implies the expression of a contrary vote) and is able to paralyze the Council's activity in a particular case. This interpretation is supported, first of all, by the text of para. 3, which expressly requires that the votes of the permanent members "concur" (English text), "are included" (French text) in the "affirmative" vote of the Council majority. The spirit of Article 27 also supports this view, as the Council is responsible under the Charter for the maintenance of international peace and security and that, as the facts have shown, effective action in this area should be supported by the unconditional agreement of the permanent members. Lastly, the San Francisco Statement can be cited in favour of this view: in Article 9 it clearly confirms that Council decisions which do not have a merely procedural nature require the "unanimity of the permanent members plus the concurring votes of at least two [today four] of the non-permanent members".

  Attention must be drawn to the fact that to reach the majority of seven votes [today nine] prescribed by Article 27, para. 3, the Statement considers necessary the votes of the permanent members plus *two votes* [today four] of the non-permanent members. This very clearly means that the Statement requires the affirmative vote of the five Great Powers, and excludes the possibility of the Council deciding with the abstention of even one of them. The view (of STAVROPOULOS) that the Statement is not clear on this is therefore not convincing.

  Notwithstanding the clear words of Article 27, para. 3, the United Nations practice has, since its early years, tended to acknowledge the validity of decisions made with the abstention of one or more permanent members. After some initial uncertainty, this practice became well established through the agreement of all the States. It can be safely said that it gave rise to one of the unwritten rules in the Organization that derogate from the Charter provisions.

  The question of abstention of a permanent member first arose in the Council in 1946 during the examination of the domestic situation in Spain, a situation, according to some Member States, likely to threaten international peace and security. On April 29, 1946, the Council approved, with the abstention of the USSR, a draft resolution proposed by Australia that provided for the creation of a sub-committee to study whether the Franco regime actually constituted a threat to the peace. The Soviet representative, after stating he did not approve the draft resolution in that it was dilatory, declared he would abstain so as not to make its adoption impossible; however, he invited the Council (and the United States adhered to this) not to consider his conduct as "a precedent capable of influencing in any way the question of the abstention of permanent members of the Security Council" (cf. SCOR, 1st year, 39th meet., part. p. 243). Thereafter, the abstentions of the permanent members began to be more frequent, *without any longer raising any exceptions or reservations whatsoever.* Important decisions, for example, concerning the admission of new States, the setting up of international peacekeeping forces, and so on, have often been taken with the abstention of permanent members. As we have said, it is now a well-established practice which has given rise to a customary norm (on the possibility that the Charter may be derogated from by customary rules, see § 4).

The customary rule that permits the validity of decisions taken with the abstention of one or more permanent members was in no way influenced by the changes in the number of members of the Council introduced in the Charter in 1965. It has been held that since there are now 15 (instead of 11) members of the Council and that 9 votes (instead of 7) are sufficient for the adoption of a resolution, the customary rule should no longer be in effect. Otherwise, the Council could issue a decision even when *all* the permanent members abstained. To the contrary, such an eventuality is not able by itself alone to nullify a rule shaped over a period of time. In introducing changes to the Charter in 1965, the Member States did not show any intention spe-cifically concerning abstention, thereby letting it be understood that they intended to leave things as they were. Indeed, the practice after 1965 has been consistent with the previous practice.

In the sense that the practice has given rise to a customary rule on abstention, and that such rule has remained unchanged since 1965, the International Court of Justice has also expressed a view. This was in its opinion of June 21, 1971 on the Namibia (South West Africa) question. Cf. ICJ, *Reports*, 1971, p. 22. On the Namibia question, see § 81.

A form of abstention exists in *non-participation* in the vote (in the vote, not in the discussion). Also on this point the practice has become well-established, especially in the years immediately following the entry of Com-munist China in the Council. By not participating in a vote, a State (if it is a permanent member), while not intending to prevent the adoption of a reso-lution, wants to more strongly emphasize its dissent (but not with different legal effects) with respect to a case of abstention. Non-participation in a vote implicitly carries with it the intention to contest the measure and to be disas-sociated from its effects (on this point, see § 97).

For several years after its entry in 1971, Communist China did not participate in voting on resolutions concerning the establishment and the functioning of peacekeeping forces or observation forces. Cf., for example, for the resolutions on peacekeeping operations in the Middle East, SCOR, 28th year, 1973, 1760th meet., 33rd year, 1978, 275th meet. Various Arab countries and Third World countries joined China in non-participation with regard to the Middle East resolutions. Also other permanent members (for example, France, in the case of res. no. 376 of October 17, 1975, on the admission of the Comoros Islands) have resorted to the practice of non-participation in the vote.

By mitigating the rigidity of Article 27, para. 3, the customary rule on abstention has allowed the Security Council to adopt resolutions which otherwise would not have been adopted. Yet it is clear that in the end this rule weakens the capability of the Council to act effectively to protect the peace, since this capability depends to a large degree on the consent of the permanent members.

25. C) *Absence of a permanent Member.*

BIBLIOGRAPHY: KUNZ, *Legality of the Security Council Resolutions of June 25 and June 27, 1950*, in *AJ*, 1951, p. 137 ff.; GROSS, *Voting in the Security Council: Abstention from Voting and Absence from Meeting*, in *Yale Law Journal*, 1951, p. 209 ff.; GENTILE, *Astensione ed assenza volontaria di un membro del Consiglio di Sicurezza*, in *RDI*, 1954, p. 347 ff.; KAHNG, *Law, Politics, and the Security Council*, The Hague, 1964, p. 132 ff.; LABOUZ, *L'Organisation des Nations Unies et la Corée. Recherches sur la fiction en droit international public*, Paris, 1980.

Again with regard to Article 27, para. 3, the question arises as to whether the Security Council can legally decide on non-procedural matters, if one or more of the permanent members is absent during the sessions when they are being discussed.

On this issue practical examples are not abundant. Two cases can be cited, both involving the USSR. In 1946, Iran brought a complaint before the Council, claiming Soviet interference in its internal affairs (Russian troops were stationed in Azerbaijan!), but soon after announced it was withdrawing its complaint as the two countries had come to an agreement. Contrary to the Soviet view (shared by France and supported also in a memorandum from the Secretariat), which was that the agreement had eliminated any dispute or situation that might endanger the peace and had thus made any UN intervention unwarranted, the Council decided, in its 36th session of April 25, 1946, to keep the question on the agenda. The USSR then said that it would not take part in the sessions in which the Iranian question was being discussed, thereby challenging beforehand the validity of eventual decisions of the organ. The Council, in any case, did not adopt a resolution.

The second case, which occurred in 1950, is more interesting. The USSR abandoned the Council for more than six months to protest against the failure to substitute Communist China for Nationalist China in the Council (see § 19). Before withdrawing, the Soviet delegate declared that he would refuse to recognize all resolutions passed in his absence. And, on his return, he confirmed this intention. This time the Council, despite the Soviet Union's withdrawal, took two decisions, no. 83 of June 27, 1950 and no. 84 of July 7, 1950, which were at the basis of the Korean War (see § 60).

In both cases, the majority of the Council members expressed the view that the absence of a permanent member should be the same as abstention from the vote and that therefore the organ could proceed to take decisions on any matter.

On the Iranian question, cf. SCOR, 1st year, 33rd, 36th, 40th and 43rd meet. (the above cited Secretariat's memorandum is reproduced in SCOR, 1st year, 33rd meet., p. 143 ff.). For the Russian statements of 1950, see SCOR, 5th year, 461st meet., p. 9 f. and 480th meet., p. 2 ff. Cf. also the telegram from the USSR deputy foreign minister to the Secretary-General, of June 29, 1950 (doc. S/1517, published in SCOR, 5th year, Suppl. for June, July and August 1950, p. 29 f.).

Considering that the practice is limited, that one of the permanent members, the Soviet Union, had throughout its existence insisted on the illegality of decisions taken in its absence, and that caution must be used in ascertaining customary rules that have developed within the framework of the Charter (see § 4), it is impossible to say that an unwritten rule has been shaped with regard to absence similar to the one which confirms the validity of a resolution when a permanent member abstains. All that can perhaps be said, in the light of the provision of Article 27, para. 3, and together with the customary rule on abstention, is that the consequences of the absence from voting depend on the meaning that the State that is absent gives it. If the State is absent in order to paralyze the activity of the Council (as the Soviet Union was in the above-mentioned cases), its position is equivalent to a negative vote and triggers the provision of Article 27, para. 3. On the contrary, if it intends only to dissociate itself from the vote without preventing adoption; if, in other words, it attributes to absence a meaning which does not differ, even if it is more striking, from non-participation in the vote, it remains within the framework of the customary rule on abstention.

26. D) *The problem of the double veto.*

BIBLIOGRAPHY: LIANG, *Notes on Legal Questions Concerning the United Nations; The so-called « Double Veto »,* in *AJ,* 1949, p. 134 ff.; RUDZINSKI, *The so-called Double Veto,* in *AJ,* 1951, p. 443 ff.; GROSS, *The Double Veto and the Four-Power Statement on Voting in the Security Council,* in *HLR,* 1953-54, p. 262 ff.; ID., *The Question of Laos and the Double Veto in the Security Council,* in *AJ,* 1960, p. 118 ff.; KAHNG, *Law, Politics, and the Security Council,* The Hague, 1964, p. 112 ff.

The veto power provided in Article 27, para. 3, can be exercised when a decision is not merely procedural but concerns a "substantive" issue. With regard to decisions of a procedural nature, Article 27, para. 2, provides that they shall be made by the affirmative vote of any nine members of the Council.

The problem of the double veto is usually stated in the following terms. Since Article 27 makes a distinction, for voting purposes, between procedural decisions and substantive decisions, how will the Council vote when it must decide whether or not a matter which is brought before it concerns procedure? Will it vote on the preliminary question according to the provision of para. 2 of Article 27, which excludes the right of veto, or according to the provision of para. 3, which allows it?

The problem had already arisen at the time of the League of Nations with regard to Assembly and Council acts, which, under Article 5 of the Covenant, could be either procedural or non-procedural. According to Article 5, procedural matters were subject to the rule of simple majority, and non-procedural matters to the rule of unanimity. This vote applied also to preliminary questions (for reference, see GROSS, *art. cit.*, p. 252 ff.).

The Charter does not provide elements for resolving the problem of the double veto. The text does not help, as both the above mentioned solutions can lead to consequences that may be challenged on the basis of Article 27. Those who want to say that the preliminary question must be decided by simple majority, will run the risk of attributing a procedural character to resolutions which objectively do not have it and thus of circumventing the veto power. Those, vice versa, who want to treat the preliminary question in the same way as a matter of substance, will contravene the rule of para. 2, by extending the veto to resolutions that are clearly procedural. Neither can it be said that any light is shed by the preparatory works, in particular, by the Four Powers Statement at the San Francisco Conference (see § 23). It is indicative that the Statement has from time to time been invoked in the Council to support one or the other view. In fact, its text, specifically regarding the problem of the double veto, is elastic and ambiguous because it was the result of compromise. The Four Powers affirm, on the one hand, the principle that the preliminary question must be resolved with the greater majority, and therefore with the possibility of exercising the veto, but they confirm, on the other, that the Charter itself distinguishes between procedure (Articles 28-32) and substance (Chapters VI and VII), that the distinction made by the Charter is so precise as to make improbable the necessity that the Council make a preliminary decision, and that in any case such a decision could be reached when the organ was faced with matters of "great importance". In the light of this, it would be difficult to attribute the Statement a purpose other than that of recognizing and, at the same time, of neutralizing the right of veto.

Most of the Statement (part I, nos. 1-5) aims at confirming that a procedural matter, for which the veto is excluded, comes within the provisions... concerning procedure (Articles

28-32 of the Charter). Then, with regard to the problem of voting on the preliminary question, the Statement concludes (part II):

"1. In the opinion of the delegations of the Sponsoring Governments, the Draft Charter itself contains an indication of the application of the voting procedures to the various functions of the Council.

2. In this case, it will be unlikely that there will arise in the future any *matters of great importance* on which a decision will have to be made as to whether a procedural vote would apply. Should, however, such a matter arise, the decision regarding the preliminary question as to whether or not such a matter is procedural must be taken by a vote of seven [today nine] members of the Security Council, including the concurring votes of the permanent members" (our italics).

If a solution to the so-called problem of the double veto is not offered by the Charter, neither can it be seen from practice, which is very inconsistent.

In the early years of the United Nations, the Council decidedly seemed to take the position that the preliminary question was subject to the veto. It did so, first of all, in 1946, during the examination of the domestic situation in Spain, a situation which some members believed was likely to threaten international security. On that occasion, when a dispute arose over whether or not a resolution confirming the Assembly's right to be concerned with the Franco regime was procedural, the majority decided that the preliminary question was to be voted on under Article 27, para. 3, and the resolution was then blocked by the veto of one of the permanent members. The same result was reached, and following the same procedure, in 1947 with regard to a resolution requesting that the Assembly consider the question of Greek border incidents and, in 1948, regarding a draft resolution for the appointment of a sub-committee to collect documents and testimonies on the *coup d'état* (and consequent coming to power of the Communist regime) in Czechoslovakia.

For the practice concerning the double veto in the case of the Spanish question, see SCOR, 1st year, 49th meet., p. 400 ff., partic. p. 413 ff. In this case the draft resolution stated "... The Security Council decides that, without prejudice to the rights of the General Assembly under the Charter, the Council shall keep the situation in Spain under continuous observation and shall maintain it upon the list of matters of which it is seized". The resolution was clearly procedural, since its operative part required that the Spanish question was to be kept on the agenda. Nonetheless, the Soviet Union captiously held that at least one part of it, the part concerning the "rights of the General Assembly" went beyond procedure. The USSR thus said that, since there was disagreement as to the nature of the resolution, the veto principle should apply. In the end, its view prevailed, despite the reservations of same countries such as the Netherlands (*ivi*, p. 422 ff.) and Australia, (*ibid.*, p. 424 ff.) These reservations were mainly based on the fact that the Statement, cited by the USSR, had no legal relevance for the non-permanent members of the Council.

On the case concerning Greek border incidents (the UN was concerned for a long time in the post-war era with the support given by Communist countries to the Greek guerrillas), cf. SCOR, 2nd year, 202nd meet., p. 2397 ff. In this case the draft resolution, presented by the United States, and blocked by the Soviet Union, established that "... the

Security Council... requests the General Assembly to consider the dispute between Greece on the one hand and Albania, Yugoslavia and Bulgaria on the other, and to make any recommendations with regard to that dispute which it deems appropriate under the circumstances" (*ibid.*, p. 2369). The draft clearly involved an application of Article 12 of the Charter, under which the General Assembly shall not make any recommendation with regard to disputes or situations with which the Security Council is concerned "unless the Security Council so requests". The Western powers held that such a request was purely of a procedural nature. On the contrary, the Russian view was that, when Article 27, para. 2, speaks of decisions on procedural matters, it is referring to the "internal" procedure of the Council and not to relations between organs as well. In any case, the Soviet Union was successful in requesting that the vote on the preliminary question as to the nature of the resolution be taken according to para. 3 of Article 27, and then exercised its veto.

For the practice relating to the Communist *coup d'état* in Czechoslovakia, see SCOR, 3rd year, 288th, 300th, and 303rd meets. On this occasion, since it was obvious that the Soviet Union intended to block any intervention of the Council, Chile presented a draft resolution that was limited to the setting up of a sub-committee of three members instructed "to receive or to hear... (any) evidence, statements and testimonies and to report to the Security Council at the earliest possible time". The discussion, which immediately flamed up, over whether or not the resolution was procedural was carried out both in the light of the Charter and on the basis of the Four Powers' Statement. The Western view was that it concerned a subsidiary organ under Article 29 of the Charter and therefore was a subject that came within the part of the Charter dedicated to procedure and considered by the Statement (part I, no. 2) as pertaining to procedural matters. By contrast, the USSR held that it involved a true request by the Council under Article 34 (on investigation), that is, an article in Chapter VI of the Charter and expressly used as an example in the Statement (part 1, nos. 4 and 5) of a provision concerning matters of substance. An impartial examination shows that the Western view was not correct and, in particular, that Article 29 was not appropriately cited. The setting up of a subsidiary organ is in fact admissible only when it may be assigned functions that the principal organ is able to carry out. It is clear, in other words, that, if the Council cannot proceed with an investigation under Article 34 owing to the veto of a permanent member, neither can it transfer such a function to a subsidiary organ. Also in the Czechoslovak case, the USSR won, by having the view prevail that the preliminary question as to the nature of the resolution was subject to the veto.

It thus seemed that the practice tended to be in favour of the right of veto, even if, especially in the Czechoslovak case, many governments protested against the abuse of this right and tenaciously defended the procedural nature of the resolutions being discussed. As early as 1950, however, the Council began to change its view when it decided not to take into account the veto of Nationalist China with regard to the Formosa question. This case concerned a resolution inviting Mao's government to explain its own point of view before the Council (convened on Soviet initiative to discuss the American presence in Formosa) and the Chinese-Nationalist delegate held that, owing to the dispute over Chinese representation in the UN (see § 19), the invitation went beyond the area of procedure. When the preliminary question was put to the vote, the President stated, amid the protests and reservations of Chiang-Kai-Shek's delegate, that the majority had voted against the latter's view and that this was sufficient to admit Mao's representative to the discussion. Actually, it cannot be said that this case was very important in the context of the practice concerning the double veto, since, as clearly emerges from a reading of the Council records, Nationalist China's ability by itself alone to block a resolution appeared... pretentious even to the United States. Much more interesting is a subsequent case which occurred in 1959, during the examination of the question of the infiltration of Communist guerrillas in Laos. Here the Council was called upon to decide whether the appointment of a subcommittee to examine the situation was a procedural matter. It was called upon to give an opinion on a problem identical to the one it had already discussed and resolved in 1948 with regard to the Czechoslovak crisis. Yet this time the majority, favourable to the procedural nature, decided not to take into account the contrary opinion and veto of the Soviet Union. The sub-committee was thus appointed, in spite of the Russian statement concerning the absolute invalidity of the resolution.

On the Formosa question, see SCOR, 5th year, 504th-507th meets. (for the most important statements of the Chinese representative, see 505th meet., p. 18 f., 506th meet., p. 3 and 5 ff., 507th meet., p. 2 ff. and 8). On the Laos case, see SCOR, 14th year, 847th meet. (for the USSR declaration that the resolution, approved despite its veto, was "illegal" and "cannot be regarded as having any legal force", see 848th meet., p. 23).

The problem of the double veto was touched upon also in December 1971, during the examination by the Council of questions relating to the war between India and Pakistan.

On that occasion, the USSR proposed several times that the Council hear a representative of the new State of Bangladesh that was coming into existence but then withdrew its proposal in the light of the opposition of several members, particularly of the representative of the People's Republic of China (cf. SCOR, 26th year, 1607th meet., Dec. 5, 1971, n. 25 ff. and 1613th meet., Dec. 13, 1971, n. 77 ff., partic. n. 122). In the meeting of December 13, 1971, before the USSR withdrew the proposal, the President was ready to put it to a vote and had noted that he would have considered the question one of procedure and not of substance (in line, therefore, with the solution given to the problem of the double veto in 1950, with regard to the Formosa question).

What is, then, the correct solution to the problem of the double veto? In fact, a solution does not exist because the problem is not correctly posited. Moreover, the uncertainty of practice strengthens our view. It is useless to ask whether the majority is competent to decide the question of whether a decision is procedural or substantive since neither the Council, nor any other UN organ, has the absolute and sovereign power to interpret the Charter and to impose its interpretation on the individual members (see § 6) The Council, therefore, will never be able, within its own discretion, to decide which resolutions the Charter assigns to one or the other category. All that one can say is that if a State believes that the organ has adopted a substantive resolution with the legal majority for a procedural resolution, it will accuse it of having violated the Charter and will put forward its reservations with regard to the legality of the act (as China and the USSR did respectively in the cases of Formosa and Laos). Reservations of this kind do not concern only the double veto but rather are recurring aspects of United Nations practice. They arise from the fact that the Charter does not give the UN organs the powers to sovereignty interpret the Charter and such organs lack the capacity to assert their authority over the individual State. What consequences derive from challenges of the legality of UN acts is a problem that will be examined later (see § 97).

The only case that has practical importance with regard to the so-called double veto is that of a resolution adopted with the legal majority for a procedural matter and questioned by a permanent member who has opposed its veto (see the questions of Formosa and Laos) and possibly also by other dissenting members. On the contrary, if the Security Council decides to vote with the greater majority on a resolution which some members believe is procedural (see the Spanish, Greek and Czechoslovak questions), the exercise of the veto will block its adoption, thus making any reservation about the legality of the majority's conduct useless. As we have had occasion to note elsewhere (see § 13), there is no point in speaking of illegality in the case of the inertia of a UN organ.

27. E) *Abstention from voting by a Member party to a dispute.*

BIBLIOGRAPHY: LIANG, *The Settlement of Disputes in the Security Council: The Yalta Voting Formula*, in *BYB*, 1974, p. 354 ff.; JIMENEZ DE ARECHAGA, *Voting and the Handling of Disputes in the Security Council*, New York, 1950, p. 25 ff.; KELSEN, *The Law of the United Nations*, London, 1951, p. 258 ff.; TAVERNIER, *L'abstention des Etats à un différend (art. 27, par. 3, in fine, de la Charte)*, in *AF*, 1976, p. 283 ff.; TANZI, *Diritto di veto ed esecuzione della sentenza della Corte internazionale di giustizia tra Nicaragua e Stati Uniti*, in *RDI*, 1987, p. 293 ff.

After having established that non-procedural decisions of the Security Council are to be taken by an affirmative vote of nine members and having at-tributed the right of veto to the permanent members, Article 27, para. 3, adds that a member State of the Council which is "party to a dispute" shall abstain from voting in the decisions under Chapter VI and under para. 3 of Article 52. This latter article is concerned with a rather specific case, namely, the relations between the Security Council and international organizations of a regional character (see § 67). Chapter VI is much more important since it authorizes the Council to investigate (Article 34) and to contribute to the solution of disputes, particularly disputes likely to endanger international peace and security, by recommending that the parties seek peaceful means of settlement such as negotiation, mediation, arbitration, etc. (Articles 33 and 36), or by dealing itself with the merits of a dispute in order to indicate a solution (Article 37).

The principle *nemo judex in re sua* is therefore confirmed by the Charter. It is regrettable, however, that this principle, specifically restricted to the subjects covered in Chapter VI, has limited scope. Some very important resolutions are excluded from its sphere of application, such as those concerning action (and sanctions) in the event of threats to the peace and of acts of aggression (Chapter VII) and those which affect membership status, especially the resolution in which the Council recommends that the General Assembly expel a Member State from the United Nations, a resolution without which the Assembly cannot act (Article 6). Another important matter which does not come under the *nemo judex* principle is the one covered in Article 94, para. 2, under which the Council may make recommendations or decide upon measures to take against a State which, having been party to a dispute brought before the International Court of Justice, refuses to comply with its decision. Since the right of veto applies for these decisions, the non-existence of an obligation to abstain on the part of the member whose case is before the Council means that it is *impossible* for the organ to take action against a permanent member.

An example is offered by the United States' refusal to comply with the International Court of Justice's decision of June 27, 1986 in the case between the United States and Nicaragua concerning *Military and Paramilitary Activities in and Against Nicaragua* (in ICJ, *Reports*, 1986, p. 14). The decision was unfavourable to the United States, and was contested by the last country, which held that the case was not within the Court's competence. Nicaragua had recourse to the Security Council under Article 94, para. 2, of the Charter and the organ drew up a draft resolution, which, although it received 11 favourable votes and three abstentions, among them, those of France and the United Kingdom (abstentions of permanent members do not prohibit the adoption of a resolution: see § 24), was blocked by the United States veto. Cf. Doc. S/PV.2715 of October 10, 1986 and S/PV.2718 of October 10, 1986. The draft (published in Doc. S/18428) was limited to urgently requesting "full and immediate compliance" with the Court's decision.

With regard to the application of the *nemo judex in re sua* principle, the Charter has certainly regressed with respect to the League of Nations Covenant. The Covenant, after having laid down at Article 5 the criterion of unanimity for decisions made by the collegial organs of the League, provided in various rules that a Member State of the Council was to abstain if it were directly interested in an issue. The obligation to abstain was foreseen not only by Article 15, paras. 6 and 7, of the Covenant, with regard to subjects *roughly* corresponding to those in Chapter VI of the Charter, but also by Article 16, para. 4, regarding expulsion. From an examination of paras. 1 and 2 of Article 16 (which concerned subjects corresponding to Chapter VII of the Charter but organizing differently the measures to be taken for protection of the peace), it is possible to see that with regard to the recommendation contemplated by para. 2, the vote of a directly interested Member State of the Council was also not to be counted for purposes of unanimity.

According to the Permanent Court of International Justice (opinion no. 12 of November 21, 1925), in PCIJ, *Series B*, no. 12, p. 32) the obligation of a Member State of the League Council to abstain was to be considered to extend to all cases in which an international treaty asked the Council to settle a dispute, since it was "a well-known rule according to which no one can be a judge of his own case".

Interpretation of the last part of Article 27, para. 3, presents considerable difficulties. What is meant by a dispute? And when can it be said that a Member State of the Security Council is party to it? The difficulties arise, first of all, from the fact that the definition of an international dispute is not clear and that the various current definitions can lead to misunderstandings if used for the purposes of Article 27, para. 3. Let us take the well-known definition given in 1924 by the Permanent Court of International Justice in the *Mavrommatis* case (Judgement of August 30, 1924, in PCIJ, *Series A*, no. 2, p. 11) and upheld by the International Court of Justice (cf. ICJ, *Reports*, 1962, p. 328), according to which a dispute would be "a disagreement on a point of law or fact, a conflict of legal views or interests between two persons". If one were to adopt a concept of this kind here, all the members of the Security Council would nearly always have to abstain from decisions taken on the basis of Chapter VI of the Charter. On the other hand, even assuming, as it seems correct, that a restricted notion is the right one and saying that in a dispute a conflict of interests arises between States when it is accompanied by each one's claim to have its own interest prevail, difficulties and uncertainties still exist. Considering the very great political importance that the questions brought before the Council usually have, it is not hard to find in them specific interests of a certain number of members, particularly of certain permanent members, and also clear evidence of their intention to have them prevail.

Other difficulties stem from the fact that some of the most important provisions of Chapter VI of the Charter speak both of a "dispute" and of a "situation" likely, if continued, to endanger the peace. This is the case in Article 34 on the Council's power to investigate, and also in Article 36 ("The Security Council may, at any stage of a dispute... or of a situation... recommend appropriate procedures or methods of adjustment"). Most observers have no doubt, given the very clear text of the last part of Article 27, para. 3, that the obligation to abstain concerns only disputes and not situations as well. This leads to the necessity to distinguish between them.

A case which very well illustrates the above mentioned uncertainties was the one which occurred in 1951 regarding the restrictions imposed by Egypt on the passage of ships through the Suez Canal. In that year, Israel brought a complaint before the Council, denouncing the Egyptian measure aimed at blocking the Suez Canal to ships directed toward Israeli ports and carrying arms, oil and other material that could be used in war operations. The Israeli government held that this measure was contrary to international law, to the UN Charter and to the general armistice agreement concluded in 1949 between the two countries. It is worth noting that before Israel appealed to the Council, several States whose ships had been affected by the Egyptian blockade had hastened to vibrantly protest against Egypt. They included, among others, the United States, United Kingdom, and France, permanent members of the Council, as well as the Netherlands and Turkey, which in 1951 were non-permanent members. When the question was brought before the Council and the discussion phase was over, a draft resolution was proposed which urged Egypt to lift the restrictive measures on Suez traffic. It was at that point that the Egyptian representative, invited to participate in the Council meetings under Article 32 of the Charter, raised the problem of the applicability of the last part of Article 27, para. 3, maintaining that the five countries mentioned above had an obligation to abstain from the vote in that they were parties in the case. A heated discussion was carried out on the point, but in the end the Council decided that the obligation did not exist, and the draft, voted on by all, reached the prescribed majority. If the Egyptian view had been accepted, the Security Council would have been paralysed, since at the time it was composed of 11 members and Article 27 then required a majority of at least 7 members.

The arguments used by Egypt were mainly of a substantive nature, while those put forward by the five countries, and expressed by the British representative had a decidedly formal character. Egypt said: 1) that the interests of the United States, Great Britain, France, Holland and Turkey were directly involved and that the protests of these countries, combined with the Egyptian resistance, constituted the typical grounds for an international dispute; 2) that Article 27, para. 3, last part, confirming the *nemo judex in re sua* principle, was applicable whenever a Member State of the Council was directly interested, and apart from whether or not there was, technically speaking, a real dispute. In turn, the British delegate held: 1) that *only* Israel had had recourse to the Council against Egypt and that therefore *only* Israel was party to the dispute with Egypt; 2) that the Council could not reject this formal criterion and resort to a rigid application of the *nemo judex in re sua* principle without paralysing the Council (because of the likelihood that any question relating to maintenance of the peace could involve a number of States).

The problem of interpretation of Article 27, para. 3, last part, had also been confronted from a general point of view, a few years before the Suez discussions, in the General Assembly in the Interim Committee set up by the Assembly for matters pertaining to international peace and security. The interpretation given by the Interim Committee, in a 1948 report, was very near in spirit to the one given by the British delegate in the Suez case, in that it was based on purely formal criteria, making the existence of a dispute for the purposes of Article 27, para. 3, depend on the way in which a matter was brought before the Council. The report of the Interim Committee was adopted contrary to the opinion of the United States which at that time supported the view... later upheld by Egypt. The problem was one of substance, the U.S. said, and must be resolved, whether or not it is technically a dispute, simply by taking into account the "principle of justice that one cannot be at the same time both judge and party".

For the discussions in the Council in the case of the Suez Canal blockade, see SCOR, 6th year, 553rd, 555th meet. (partic. 553rd meet., p. 23 ff., 555th meet., p. 1 ff and p. 14 ff). The 1948 report of the Interim Committee is in GAOR, 3rd sess., Suppl. no. 9, p. 7 f. For the proposal of the United States in the Interim Committee, see A/AC.18/SC.3/4.

The interpretation of Article 27, para. 3, last part, was also discussed by the Council in February 1946, during the examination of the Syrian and Lebanese question (Syria and Lebanon had brought charges before the Security Council that French and English troops had failed to withdraw from their territories). On that occasion, even before the discussion on the merits had taken place or a draft resolution had been presented, the question was put in the following terms: How must the Council vote to establish whether or not a dispute exists and therefore whether France and United Kingdom must abstain? While some maintained that the question was procedural, requiring a vote by simple majority, others held that it was a question of substance to be decided by the qualified majority (with the right of veto). In short, the problem was addressed as a problem of the double veto (see § 26). On the fallacy of this approach, we remember the criticisms already made in the previous paragraph. It is evident that the problem does not consist in asking how the Council must vote, but rather what is the objective interpretation of Article 27, para. 3, last part. In the Syrian-Lebanese case, debate was finally cut off by the attitude of France and United Kingdom, which stated they would abstain although they believed that, in this particular case, a dispute did not exist (the draft resolution invited the parties to negotiate the troop withdrawal). Cf. SCOR, 1st year, 19th and 23rd meet.

In our view, it should be excluded that the obligation to abstain contemplated by Article 27, para. 3, is to be decided on the basis of formal criteria and that, in particular, it is incumbent only upon the States which bring a complaint before the Council and those against which the complaint is made. This is certainly not the spirit of the provision, since it is without question that the aim of the *nemo judex in re sua* principle is to avoid the judgment of an interested party. It is sufficient, moreover, to consider the absurd consequences that would be reached by accepting such formalistic view. A group of governments could get around the obligation to abstain by entrusting only one among them to bring the issue before the Council.

Considering that the criterion must be a substantive one, we believe that a satisfactory answer can be reached only if the concept of dispute in a technical sense (a concept that has been elaborated by international case law and therefore on different occasions and for different purposes) is abandoned, and the meaning of the obligation to abstain is determined in accordance with the rational of the provision in Article 27, para. 3.

A balanced solution, taking into account that the provision should not be given a broad interpretation, thereby compromising the normal functioning of the Council, could be the following. The States obligated to abstain are those which in a given *draft resolution* are shown to be concerned parties, either because they may benefit from it or because they may be harmed by it, and provided that their favourable or unfavourable position has a *sui generis* nature, i.e., provided that their position is different from any other Member State of the United Nations and of the international community. In other words, it is useless to seek to resolve the problem of abstention in abstract terms, by looking at the issue brought before the Council and asking whether such issue is or is not a dispute. On the contrary, attention must be paid, to the specific measure of the organ in order to determine which subjects are effectively and *individually* involved. There is not any safer way to satisfy the rule of Article 27, para. 3, last part, without unduly extending its content.

Again with reference to the case of the Suez Canal blockade, there is no doubt that the United States, Great Britain, France, the Netherlands and Turkey did not have an obligation to abstain. Indeed, the invitation that Egypt allow navigation through the Canal, an invitation contained in the draft resolution then made by the Council itself, did not acknowledge that these five States had any rights that were greater than or different from those of any other member of the international community.

It is important to stress the necessity that, for purposes of the provision in Article 27, para. 3, last part, the concept of international dispute in the technical sense be abandoned, that is to say, in the sense that it is a conflict between two States in which one claims something and the other resists. The *nemo judex in re sua* principle finds application in domestic law also in situations that are not characterized by a dispute between two or more persons, for example, in the criminal law field. It does not seem incorrect to express this principle by saying that whoever judges cannot be "party to the dispute". In a certain sense, every person who is the object of a judgment of an organ always has a relationship with the community to which the organs belongs, which can be defined as a "dispute". The same can be said of the position of the individual State with respect to the Security Council, on the condition that the word "dispute" is not given the technical meaning that it usually has in international law.

Lastly, no literal argument can be inferred against our view from the last part of Article 27, para. 3. It is also useless to establish whether a question brought before the Council is, instead of a dispute, one of the "situations" mentioned in Chapter VI of the Charter. In any case, one must look in the sense specified above, at the addressees of the draft resolution. On the other hand, the distinction between dispute and situation is fleeting and for various reasons, as we shall see, completely useless (see § 52).

The contrary view held by the International Court of Justice in its opinion of June 21, 1971 on Namibia (see § 81) can be therefore criticised. The Court held that the clause which appears at the end of para. 3 of Article 27 of the Charter "... also requires for its application the prior determination by the Security Council that a dispute exists and that certain members of the Council are involved as parties to such a dispute" (cf. ICJ, *Reports*, 1971, p. 23). Actually, in this particular case, the objection raised by South Africa, maintaining that the Court did not have competence, was inconsistent for another reason. South Africa held that the resolution in which the Council had requested an opinion of the Court on the Namibia question was illegal because some members of the Council should have abstained in so far as they were "parties to the dispute". However, regardless of any other consideration, the last part of Article 27, para. 3, refers only to decisions "under Chapter VI and under paragraph 3 of Article 52", without mentioning the requests for advisory opinions of the Court under Article 96.

In shifting attention to the specific draft resolution of the Council, the advantage of largely eliminating uncertainties over whether to classify an issue as belonging under Chapter VI or Chapter VII of the Charter is also assured. The obligation to abstain covers only the matters in Chapter VI, and since a precise boundary line between the two chapters does not exist (see § 49), only an examination of the specific draft resolution can answer the question, even only approximately, whether the Council is acting according to Chapter VI or Chapter VII.

Confirmation may be found in the debate over the applicability of the last part of Article 27, para. 3, which preceded the adopted of res. no. 502 of April 3, 1982 on the Falklands/Malvinas question. A draft resolution had been introduced which, after having established that Argentina had broken the peace, asked for the immediate cessation of hostilities, the withdrawal of Argentinian troops from the Falkland/Malvinas islands, and the start of negotiations between Argentina and Great Britain. Then, Panama, indicating this last request, raised the issue of whether Great Britain should abstain as party to the dispute. The majority of the Council correctly favoured the English view that the resolution clearly came under Chapter VII, and permitted Great Britain to vote. The entire discussion concerned, as it should have, only the *draft* resolution. Cf. Doc. S/PV.22350 of April 3, 1982, p. 81 ff.

There are cases in which the Council, confronted with draft resolutions which clearly remained within the framework of Chapter VI but directly involved permanent members, allowed these members to vote and to exercise the right of veto. Cases of this kind must be strongly criticized. One of them occurred in 1983 when the draft resolution concerning the shooting down of a South Korean jetliner by the Soviet Union was not approved because of the Soviet veto (and despite the favourable vote of nine Council members) (cf. Doc. S/PV.2476 of September 12, 1983). The draft resolution (published in Doc. S/15966/rev.1), without making any reference to Chapter VII and without describing the downing of the aircraft as a threat to the peace (it was in fact a police action, although a very brutal one), simply provided for an investigation. It is disturbing that during the discussion no Member State of the Council even mentioned the USSR's obligation to abstain.

The same can be said of res. no. 457 of December 4, 1979 which asked the Iranian government to put an end to the illegal detention of staff members of the United States Embassy in Teheran, requesting also that both governments take the necessary measures to peacefully settle any unresolved issues. The United States, an interested State to which the resolution was addressed, took part in the adoption of the resolution which remained within the framework of Chapter VI. In this case, however, its participation had no influence from a legal viewpoint since the resolution was unanimously approved. Nevertheless, a unanimous condemnation by the other members of the Council, which represented the various components of the international community, would have had more force had the United States abstained.

A similar example is the participation of the United States, Great Britain and France in res. no. 731, approved by the Security Council on January 21, 1992. This resolution requested Libya to hand over to these three countries the Libyan citizens suspected of having organized the attacks against the PAN AM and UTA aircraft which had exploded in flight over Scotland (Lockerbie) and Chad. This resolution (unlike a subsequent resolution, no. 748 of March 31, 1992, in which the Council enacted enforcement measures against Libya) also came within Chapter VI. In spite of this, and in spite of the reservations put forward by the Libyan representative before the Council (cf. Doc. S/PV.3033, p. 24 f.), the United States, Great Britain and France were admitted to the vote. In this case also, the resolution was unanimously approved.

28. F) *Approval by "consensus"*.

BIBLIOGRAPHY: DE LACHARRIÈRE, *Consensus et Nations Unies*, in *AF*, 1968, p. 9 ff.; D'AMATO, *On Consensus*, in *CYIL*, 1970, p. 104 ff.; CHAI, *Consultation and Consensus in the Security Council*, New York, 1971; BASTID, *Observations sur la pratique du consensus*, in *Festschrift für Wilhelm Wengler*, Berlin, 1973, I, p. 11 ff.; CASSAN, *Le consensus dans la pratique des Nations Unies*, in *AF*, 1974, p. 456 ff.; CASSESE, *Consensus and Some of its Pitfalls*, in *RDI*, 1975, p. 754 ff.; SPERDUTI, *Consensus in International Law*, in *IYIL*, 1976, p. 33 ff.; BESTELIU, *The Significance of Negotiations for the Adoption through Consensus of Decisions within the United Nations System and Other International Conferences*, in *Revue Roumaine de sciences sociales*, 1983, 2, p. 139 ff.; ID., *Some Remarks Concerning Reservations to the Decisions of International Organizations, with Special Reference to the Decisions Adopted by Consensus within the UN*, in *Revue roumaine d'études internationales*, 1987, p. 443 ff.

As we have seen, Security Council decisions are valid if they are taken by a favourable vote of at least nine members and, in the case of non-procedural decisions, without the negative vote of the permanent members. Whenever at least nine votes are in favour of a certain text, the general will of the Council must be considered expressed. From a legal point of view, it does not matter how such will is shown: as in all collegial bodies, it may be in the form of a vote by roll-call, by hand-raising, by acclamation, by failure to object to the President's statement aiming to ascertain, on the basis of the outcome of a debate, whether a certain decision has been adopted, and so on. In this variety of forms, and therefore with little relevance from a legal point of view, practice of approval by (or the expression of) consensus has to be included.

The use of the term consensus has spread throughout the United Nations and other international organizations. Although it has also become part of official acts, its use retains some ambiguities. Generally, the term is used to mean a decision which reflects the agreement of all the members of an organ and which is made without a formal vote, usually with a statement (uncontested and in fact, agreed upon, *and often agreed upon outside official meetings*) of the president of the organ. However, these two elements — unanimous agreement and the lack of a formal vote — are not always combined. It may occur, for example, that the text does not reflect unanimity but is accompanied by the specific statement of one of the members that he "dissociates himself" from the consensus. It may also occur that the consensus is even... put to a vote and obtains negative votes! All this confirms that, aside from terminology which is often linked only to what is in current fashion, the only thing that counts is the possibility of ascertaining the general will of the organ members according to the minimum majority required by the Charter. Nor is it possible to fashion, as has been done in legal literature (BASTID) precisely with reference to the Security Council, an *ad hoc* customary norm which would give legality to consensus. Indeed, the Charter does not establish rigid procedures for the calculation of votes nor may it be considered automatically fulfilled if a decision has been agreed upon by all members or by a very wide majority of members. Altogether different is the problem (on this, see CONFORTI, *Le rôle de l'accord dans le système des Nations Unies*, in *RC*, 1974, II, p. 271 ff.) of whether a resolution (either adopted by a formal vote or by consensus), whose *content* is contrary to the Charter, may have the force, on the basis of customary international law, of an agreement among States.

As examples of decisions by consensus adopted by the Security Council through a presidential statement, see, among many others: SCOR, 26th year, 1576th meet. (August 26, 1971), no. 4; 28th year, 1684th meet. (January 15, 1973), no. 10; 1704th meet. (March 21, 1973), no. 192 and 1730th meet. (July 22, 1973), no. 335 (admission of the two Germanies); S/PV.2005 of November 11, 1977; S/PV.3053 of February 19, 1992 (condemnation of the attacks on the Venezuelan Embassy in Tripoli); S/PV.3072 of May 12, 1992 (the sending of a mission of the Secretary-General in Nagorno-Karabac).
        For an example of "dissociation" from consensus (specifically of China with regard to the border incidents between Iran and Iraq), see SCOR, 29th year, 1764th meet. and S/11229 in Suppl. Jan.-Feb.-March 1974. Examples of when consensus has been put to a vote and approved with contrary votes are not found in Security Council practice, but they appear in General Assembly practice (see, for example, GAOR, 26th sess., Pl. meet., 1957th meet, October 7, 1971, nos. 208-218).
        Sometimes, not only has consensus been reached in informal meetings but it has not even been declared by the President during an official meeting, but only announced in an *ad hoc* document. Cf., for example, SCOR, 27th year, Suppl. Apr.-May-June 1972, p. 32 f. (S/10611) and p. 128 (S/10705) which report, respectively, consensus on increasing the number of UN observers in the Israeli-Lebanese sector and consensus on the condemnation of air piracy. This practice, which has been sporadic and thus has not set any standard, was quite rightly criticised by the Italian delegate to the Security Council. In a letter to the President, he pointed out that it weakened the importance of Council decisions: cf. Suppl. cit., p. 133, S/10711 (published also in IYIL 1975, p. 311 f.).

The practice of consensus, as we can easily imagine, has contributed to rendering the content of relevant resolutions vague and ambiguous. It also often happens that the States which take part in consensus say, on the one hand, that they approve the decision as a whole and therefore do not want to block, by abstention or by a negative vote, unanimous adoption but, on the other hand, they have specific reservations regarding certain parts of the decision. This last point, which is the only really important one in the practice of consensus, will be discussed later, in the context of challenges to the legality of UN resolutions (see § 97).

29.   *Participation in Security Council meetings of States which are not members of the organ.*

BIBLIOGRAPHY: KELSEN, *Organization and Procedure of the Security Council of the United Nations*, in *HLR*, 1945-46, p. 1090 ff.; SALOMON, *L'ONU et la paix; Le Conseil de Sécurité et le réglement pacifique des différends*, Paris, 1948, p. 157 ff.; JIMENEZ DE ARECHAGA, *Voting and the Handling of Disputes in the Security Council*, New York, 1950, p. 56 ff.; GROSS, *Voting in the Security Council and the PLO*, in *AJ*, 1976, p. 470 ff.; LORD, *Taiwan's Right to Be Heard before the Security Council*, in HENCKAERTS, *The International Status of Taiwan in the New World Order*, London, 1996, p. 133 ff.

Articles 31 and 32 of the Charter and Article 39 of the Council rules of procedure are relevant for this issue. According to Article 31, a Member State of the United Nations which is not a member of the Council may participate in the proceedings of the organ, without vote, any time the Council "considers that the interests of that Member are specially affected". This provision, which leaves the invitation to the complete discretion of the Security Council, does not raise any legal problems. The same can be said, and for the same reason, of Article 39 of the rules of procedure, on the basis of which the Council may invite any person (physical) whom it considers competent to supply information or to give assistance in matters within its competence.

The rule contained in Article 32 is different. It provides that any member of the United Nations which is not a member of the Council and any State which is not a member of the United Nations *shall* participate in the discussions, without vote, whenever "it is party to a dispute under consideration by the Security Council". In this case, the Security Council therefore may not refuse to hear the non-Member State. It has only, the article continues, to lay down the conditions for the participation in the discussion. Article 32 is important not only because it limits the discretionary power of the Council but also because, unlike Article 31, it is also concerned with non-Member States of the United Nations It is only through Article 32 that they may take an active part in meetings. It is true that the representatives of a non-Member State can also be invited on a purely personal basis pursuant to Article 39 of the rules of procedure, but Article 39 has a very limited importance in that it does not allow any real participation in the discussion.

The principle set out in Article 32 and valid for any activity of the Council, whether it comes within the scope of Chapter VI, of Chapter VII or of any other parts of the Charter, is basically the principle that if a State brings a charge or is charged (any problem the Council is concerned with either directly or indirectly pertains to international security), it must be heard. Also with regard to Article 32 (as, as we have seen in the previous paragraph, for the last part of Article 37, para. 3), it would be inappropriate to adopt a formal approach to the term "dispute" and to say that Article 32 does not apply when the Council is seized of a "situation" or a question which is not technically an international dispute. It would be very odd, for example, if a State against which the Council intended to initiate a procedure for expulsion from the United Nations, under Article 6 of the Charter, or against which the Secretary-General had brought the attention of the Council, under Article 99, did not have the right to express its views within the organ. Just as in the case of the last part of Article 27, para. 3, it was a matter of specifically defining the *nemo judex in re sua* principle, here one must apply the principle that both the accused and the accuser must be heard.

Also in practice an invitation under Article 32 has been sometimes made independently of the existence and ascertainment of a real dispute. For example, in 1946, during the examination of the Greek question (Greece was at the time torn apart by fighting between Communist guerrillas and the legitimate government), Albania and Bulgaria, which had been accused of supporting the guerrillas, were allowed to take part in the discussions, even though the Council had undertaken the question as a situation, not as a dispute. The President held, and the Council agreed, that the invitation was to be extended to the two States (which, at the time, were not UN members) in consideration of "spirit" of Article 32 (cf. SCOR, 1st year, 84th meet., partic. p. 607 ff.). By contrast, the decision taken by the Council in its meeting of June 26, 1950, and confirmed in its meeting of September 1, 1950, during the Korean conflict, to invite South Korea and not North Korea as well to the meetings must be considered arbitrary. This exclusion was justified not so much by the absence of a dispute, as by the fact the North Korea was the aggressor State. The Soviet Union fervently argued against this reasoning, holding correctly that the intention of Article 32 is that the accused State may defend itself (cf. SCOR, 5th year, 494th meet., p. 10 ff., partic. p. 17). Also worthy of criticism was the failure to invite South Africa (also those accused of crimes must be heard!) when the Security Council requested an opinion of the International Court of Justice — handed down on June 21, 1971 — on the Namibia question (see § 81). In this case the Court adopted a view in support of the attitude of the Council, hinging upon the circumstance that the Namibia question had been listed on the Council agenda as a situation, not a dispute (cf. ICJ, *Reports*, 1971, p. 22 f.). However, in subsequent meetings on the Namibia question, despite some efforts to the contrary, South Africa was invited to attend (cf., for example, SCOR, 26th year, 1584th meet., September 27, 1971, n. 1 ff.).

It has been asked in practice what Article 32 means by a State when its speaks of non-Member States of the United Nations. The problem has been raised mainly with regard to revolutionary governments or to governments formed in parts of territories formerly controlled by Member States of the United Nations, for example, the Indonesian government in 1947 or that of Bangladesh in 1970. To avoid extending an invitation under Article 32, appeal has often been made to the precariousness or to the lack of general recognition of the government in question. It is true that the practice is on the whole extremely variable, that political reasons have nearly always prevailed, and that at various times different standards have been adopted depending on the majority. In our opinion a legally correct solution can be inferred only from

the notion of State contained in the Charter with regard to admission (see §
10). Invitation under Article 32 would not therefore depend on recognition
and would be extended when (and only when) the government effectively and
independently exercises power over a territorial community. In all other cases,
only the limited "hearing" under Article 39 of the Council's rules of
procedure could take place.

> In the case of Indonesia's war of independence from the Netherlands, in August
> 1947, the majority of the Council invited the Indonesian government, which already controlled
> a large part of Indonesian territory, to participate in the meetings. This invitation, in the opinion
> of some members of the majority, was obligatory on the basis of Article 32. According to other
> members of the same majority, it was based only on "reasons of fairness and justice". In the
> view of the minority, it was a clear violation of Article 32 since Indonesia was not a sovereign
> State and had not been recognised by any other State. The first of these opinions seems to be
> correct. On this question, see SCOR, 2nd year, 181st meet., p. 1918 ff. and 184th meet., p. 1954
> f. A more or less similar question was discussed (and an identical solution was adopted) in
> 1948 with regard to the invitation extended to the provisional Israeli government to participate
> in the discussion on the Middle East crisis: see SCOR, 3rd year, 330th meet., p. 2 ff. On the
> contrary, in 1968, during the examination of the Czechoslovak question (the Soviet Union had
> occupied Czechoslovakia), the Council decided not to invite the German Democratic Republic,
> maintaining, as the majority of States affirmed during the discussion (cf. SCOR, 23rd year,
> 1445th meet.), that it... was not a State! Bangladesh was also denied an invitation, despite
> Soviet support, during the discussion of the Indo-Pakistani conflict (December 1970), a conflict
> which arose over the establishment of this State (cf. SCOR, 26th year, 1606-1613th meets.).

A rather *sui generis* form of invitation was devised by the majority in
the Council during the meeting of December 4, 1975 with regard to the case
of the Palestinian Liberation Organization. The PLO was invited to participate
in the proceedings "not on the basis of Article 37 [which essentially
corresponds to Article 31 of the Charter and, as Article 31, is limited to the
Member States of the UN] or rule 39 of the provisional rules of procedure of
the Security Council", but with "the same rights of participation as are
conferred when a Member State is invited to participate under rule 37" (*sic!*).
The Western powers unsuccessfully opposed this invitation, holding that the
form under which the invitation was extended had no foundation in any
provision of the Charter or of the rules of procedure and that the only way to
invite the PLO was through Article 39 of the rules of procedure, with all the
limitations connected to it. After that, the United States formally continued for
many years to challenge the invitation under Article 31 and to insist that the
applicable article was Article 39. The challenge was certainly well founded,
since the PLO was not a State but a national Committee operating abroad.

> For the December 4, 1975 meeting, see S/PV.1859. For subsequent ones, see, among
> many, S/PV.1993 (March 25, 1977), S/PV.2280 (June 12, 1981), S/PV.2540 (May 21, 1984),
> and, lastly, S/PV.3026 (January 6, 1992). The United States always voted against these
> decisions. France and United Kingdom (and other Western States, non-permanent members of

the Council) abstained after 1976. It has been complained in legal literature (GROSS, *op. cit.*, p. 477 ff.) that the United States did not resort to the practice of the double veto (on this, see § 26) in the 1975 meeting, thereby letting the resolution pass as a purely procedural matter and therefore valid despite the negative vote of permanent members.

Also in the General Assembly, the PLO was for many years invited to participate in the capacity of an observer in the sessions and the work of the General Assembly, as well as in the proceedings of all the international conferences held under the auspices of the Assembly (cf. res. 3237-XXIX of November 22, 1974).

On the contrary, in other cases similar to that of the PLO, for example, in the case of representatives of Polisario, the Security Council held only the hearing provided for by Article 39 of the rules of procedure (cf. S/PV.2151 of June 20, 1979).

Another "special" form of invitation was used between 1992 and 2000 with respect to the Federal Republic of Yugoslavia (Serbia and Montenegro) after the decision taken by the General Assembly, upon recommendation of the Security Council, not to allow this State to "... continue automatically the membership of the former Socialist Federal Republic of Yugoslavia" (see § 18). The representative of Serbia and Montenegro was correctly invited to participate in the Council's discussions on the former Yugoslavia crisis as an individual person, without a reference to rule 37 or rule 39 of the provisional rules of the procedure, but he was admitted to seat... behind the nameplate "Yugoslavia" (see for example: 3135th meet., November 13, 1992; 3201st meet., April 19,1993; 3336th meet., February 14, 1994; 3428th meet., September 23, 1994 ; 3478th meet., January 12, 1995). Legally speaking this was nonsense.

Section II

THE GENERAL ASSEMBLY

30. *Composition of the Assembly. Subsidiary organs.*

BIBLIOGRAPHY: RAY, *Commentaire du Pacte de la Société des Nations*, Paris, 1930, p. 137 ff.; SCHÜCKING-WEHBERG, *Die Satzung des Völkerbundes*, I, 3rd ed., Berlin, 1931, p. 420 ff.; BALL, *Bloc Voting in the General Assembly*, in *Int. Org.*, 1951, p. 3 ff.; BOWETT, *The Law of International Institutions*, London, 1963, p. 37 ff.; BAILEY, *The General Assembly of the United Nations, A Study of Procedure and Practice*, New York, 1964, p. 21 ff.; GOODWIN, *The General Assembly of the United Nations*, in LUARD, *The Evolution of International Organizations*, New York, 1966, p. 42 ff.; WERNERS, *The Presiding Officers in the UN*, Haarlem, 1967; XYDIS, *The General Assembly*, in BARROS (ed.), *The United Nations, Past, Present and Future*, New York, London, 1972, p. 64 ff.; FINLEY, *The Structure of the UN General Assembly (its Committees, Commissions and Other Organims 1946-77)*, 2 vols., Dobbs Ferry, N.Y., 1990; POULANTZAS, *The Interim Committe or "Little Assembly": A Subsidiary Organ of the General Assembly of the United Nations Organization*, in *Revue de droit international, de sciences diplomatiqus et politiques*, 1993, p. 251 ff. .

All the Member States of the Organization are represented in the Assembly. Every member has the right to have five representatives (Article 9, para. 2) but has only one vote (Article 18, para. 1).

The difference between the number of delegates and the number of votes had already been envisaged by the League of Nations Covenant with regard to the League Assembly. Article 3, para. 4, of the Covenant gave every State three representatives and one vote. The main purpose of the provision, according to the drafters, was to allow the participation in Assembly discussions of several people, representing the same State but expressing different, and perhaps even contrasting, views and interests. The right to vote, it was said, cannot be divided and would be exercised by the organs (the executive power) responsible for the foreign policy of each country. It would be wise, however, that each government ensure that more than one "voice" was heard in the discussion phase, accrediting, for example, a representative of the opposition in Parliament, of a trade association, and so on. As President Wilson solemnly declared during the peace conference (session of February 14, 1919), in this way one would have been able to partially get around the fact that the League Assembly was an assembly of State delegates and not a world Parliament.

It does not seem that, either at the time of the League of Nations or today at the United Nations, the intention of the drafters of the Covenant has been followed in practice. Already in the League Assembly, there were not many "discordant voices" (only a few governments, among them, Belgium and Hungary, accredited members of opposition parties). They have actually disappeared in the UN Assembly. Although the delegations of many States are not made up exclusively of organs of the executive branch, it is impossible to find any trace of non-conformist political views in the statements of delegates in the General Assembly.

The plurality of delegates has also practical purposes since the Assembly proceedings take place, as do the proceedings of any collegial organ which has broad composition and broad competence, both in plenary session and in various committees and subcommittees. Indeed, considering that the Assembly committees and subcommittees are so numerous, even five delegates assigned to each State by Article 9, para. 2, of the Charter would not be sufficient for these purposes. Articles 25, 26, 100 and 101 of the Assembly rules of procedure are of help. These articles provide that five substitute delegates and an unspecified number of counselors, experts, etc., may be part of the delegation. The head of the delegation may invest the former with the same powers as the representatives. The latter may participate in committees without, however, being eligible for the offices of president, vice president or rapporteur in such committees.

The delegation is accredited (by the Head of State or Government or by the Minister for Foreign Affairs: Article 27, rules of procedure) at the opening of every Assembly session. Under the provisions of Article 20 of the Charter, the sessions are regular annual sessions and special sessions. Every year, usually the Tuesday of the third week in September (Article 1, rules of procedure), the regular session opens. Special sessions are convoked by the Secretary-General at the request of the Security Council or of a majority of the members of the United Nations.

The organization of Assembly activities, which has its basis in the rules of procedure, can be outlined as follows. At every session a President and various vice presidents are elected. The activities are mostly carried out in the Main Committees, where every member is represented and which prepare the resolutions to be submitted to the Assembly plenary. The Main Committees are: the First Committee (disarmament and international security); the Second Committee (economic and financial); the Third Committee (social, humanitarian and cultural); the Fourth Committee (special political and de-colonisation); the Fifth Committee (financial and budgetary); the Sixth Committee (legal). Two committees are concerned with important procedural matters. The General Committee, consisting of the President of the Assembly, the vice-presidents and the Chairmen of the Main Committees, is competent for the drawing up of the agenda to be submitted to the Assembly. The Credentials Committee, consisting of nine members, examines the credentials of the delegates and reports to the Assembly.

Making use of the competence given to it by Article 22 of the Charter, the Assembly has over the years gradually established a whole series of subsidiary organs of a permanent nature for pursuing special purposes. Some of them have been established principally to undertake studies. Others represent the forum in which the States negotiate agreements and seek to promote international cooperation in specific fields. Others, again, oversee operational tasks, in particular, the management of funds received through the voluntary contributions of Member States. The organs created within the framework of economic cooperation and development are very important.

The following are examples of the most important organs (their structure will be examined later, in the framework of the UN functions in the economic and social field): the United Nations Conference of Trade and Development (UNCTAD), whose task is to promote international trade for the principal purpose of accelerating the development of economically disadvantaged countries; the United Nations Institute for Training and Research (UNITAR), for the training of officials in developing countries on general subjects concerning international co-operation; the United Nations Development Program (UNDP), whose governing council, consisting of 37 countries, oversees, in co-operation with various specialised United Nations agencies (see § 73), an extensive system of multilateral technical assistance to low-income countries; the United Nations Children's Fund (UNICEF), which furnishes aid to governments requesting it for the health, nutrition, social protection, education, and professional training of children and adolescents; the United Nations Environment Program (UNEP), which is concerned with the environment.

Among the permanent organs set up by the Assembly which do not concern the field of economic co-operation, the international law Commission deserves special mention. This commission consists of a certain number of experts (who sit as individuals, not as government representatives) and its purpose is to contribute to the codification and progressive development of international law.

Other important subsidiary organs, whose tasks mainly involve research and study, are the following: the Disarmament Commission, the Special Committee for Peacekeeping Operations, the Committee on the Peaceful Use of Extra-Atmospheric Space, the Special Committee for the United Nations Charter and the strengthening of the role of the Organization, the Special Committee on principles of international law covering friendly relations and co-operation among the States, the Commission on the permanent sovereignty over natural resources.

See also § 72.

The organs created by the Assembly in the field of economic coopera-tion and development (which in turn have given birth to other organs and to a complex bureaucratic apparatus), together with the organs created by the Economic and Social Council, have very often acted without specific coor-dination and in the end have resulted in a waste of energy and funds not unlike an over-bureaucratized State administration. On this point, see also § 38.

31. *Voting procedure in the Assembly.* A) *The "present and voting" majority.*

BIBLIOGRAPHY: HOVEY, *Voting Procedure in the General Assembly*, in *Int. Org.*, 1950, p. 420 ff.; COSENTINO, *Astensione*, in *Rassegna Parlamentare*, 1959, p. 89 ff.; BAILEY, *The General Assembly of the United Nations, Study of Procedure and Practice*, New York, 1964, p. 132 ff.; GROSS, *On the Degradation of the Constitutional Environment of the UN*, in

AJ, 1983, p. 582 f; MINDAOUDOU, *La notion de majorité comme preuve de démocratie à l'Assemblée générale des Nations Unies*, in *African Journal of International and Comparative Law*, 1996, p. 447 ff..

Article 18 provides that decisions of the Assembly be made by a majority (simple or qualified) of the members present and voting. This provision gives rise to the question, which is often raised also for collegial bodies in municipal law, of whether abstentions should be taken into account in calculating the majority. Is abstention equivalent to a vote? If so, the majority is to be calculated by summing the votes in favour, the votes against and the abstentions, with the consequence that the number of votes necessary for the adoption of a decision will increase. If not, it will be necessary to count only the negative and favourable votes, and therefore arrive at approval more easily. Article 86 of the Assembly rules of procedure resolves the problem in this second sense, establishing that "... the phrase 'members present and voting' means members casting an affirmative or negative vote". However, the question remains whether the provision in the rules of procedure and the practice, which has always conformed to it, are compatible with Article 18 of the Charter.

Article 86 of the rules of procedure was adopted at the second Assembly session in 1947. At the first regular session, in 1946, and at the first special session, at the beginning of 1947, the problem was raised, in the absence of rules on the point, twice. Both times, after a discussion in which views were put forward in favour of one or the other solution, the view consistent with the present Article 86 prevailed. Cf. GAOR, 1st sess., 2nd part, 1st Comm., 13th meet., p. 43 ff., 1st Comm., 57th meet., p. 346 f.

Domestic law literature has discussed at length the possibility of considering abstention as demonstration of a vote and including it in the calculation of the majority. As always, arguments favouring one view or the other may be, and have been, used. It has been said, by those who want to count abstention, that by abstaining, a member of the body takes a middle course which is neither more nor less significant than a yes or no vote, and that the abstaining member expresses his will and this will is to yield to the opinion of the majority, whether it is favourable or unfavourable to the draft resolution. Excluding those who abstain from the list of voters would mean unjustifiably putting them at the level of absentees. The contrary view points out the literal meaning of the word abstention. It adds that the voter who abstains in a certain sense gives up his right to vote, to effectively take part in the voting procedure. Mainly, however, this view holds that counting abstention for purposes of the majority gives it the same value as a negative vote. There are also views between these two extremes, such as the one that abstention should not be counted only when it is formally announced before the vote. The extent to which this issue is debatable can be shown by those cases in which, even in the presence of an identical provision on the required majority for the approval of a decision, two collegial bodies behave in opposite ways. This is what happens, for instance, in Italy where Article 64, para. 3, of the Constitution provides that both houses of Parliament decide "by the majority of the members present" and where abstentions are counted in the Senate while they are not counted in the Chamber of Deputies.

It is difficult to establish which solution Article 18 of the Charter actually favours. A deciding element in favour of the view that excludes abstentions in counting the majority, the view underlying Article 86 of the Assembly rules of procedure, is one of the arguments already mentioned: the fact that abstention would not otherwise be different from a negative vote. Yet this argument, instead of interpreting the provision, indicates only the consequence, however serious, of one of its possible interpretations. One should rather consider the aspect of the greater or lesser facility in arriving at the adoption of Assembly resolutions. If abstentions do not count, the number of votes necessary for approval is reduced and the Assembly may more easily decide. Considering that this organ, unlike the Security Council, does not as a rule have real decision-making powers, the less rigid interpretation, which would facilitate its functioning, is perhaps more in conformity with the spirit of the Charter. Under this aspect it is therefore not difficult to acknowledge that Article 86 of the rules of procedure correctly interprets Article 18.

One scholar (GROSS) has held the opinion that Article 86 and the underlying interpretation more favourable to the adoption of a resolution could have been justified when there were few members of the United Nations, while today it would no longer be justified, given the great increase in the number of Assembly members. It is not easy, however, to understand what difference this makes. As for the view (held by the same author) that, if Article 86 of the rules of procedure were eliminated, Article 18 would necessarily have to be interpreted in the sense that abstentions are to be counted in determining the majority, it is difficult to establish on what historical, textual or logical arguments such view is based.

32. B) *Simple majority and qualified majority.*

BIBLIOGRAPHY: KOO, *Voting Procedures in International Political Organizations*, New York, 1947, p. 231 ff.; HOVEY, *Voting Procedure in the General Assembly*, in *Int. Org.*, 1950, p. 412 ff.; VALLAT, *Voting in the General Assembly of the United Nations*, in *BYB*, 1954, p. 237 ff.; KERLEY, *Voting on Important Questions in the United Nations General Assembly*, in *AJ*, 1959, p. 324 ff.; SALERNO, *La procedura di voto della Assemblea Generale delle Nazioni Unite sulle c.d. questioni importanti*, in *ADI*, 1966, p. 312 ff.; WILCOX, *Representation and Voting in the United Nations General Assembly*, in FALK-MENDLOVITZ, *The Strategy of World Order, III, The United Nations*, New York, 1966, p. 272 ff.; WOLFRUM, in SIMMA (ED.), Die Charta der Vereinten Nationen, München, 1991, p. 275 ff.

There have been discussions both in legal literature and in practice about the system adopted in Article 18, paras. 2 and 3, for distinguishing Assembly decisions that are to be made by a simple majority of present and voting members from those requiring a qualified two-thirds majority.

After establishing that decisions on "important questions" are to be made by a two-thirds majority, para. 2 of Article 18 lists a number of questions of this kind (including, among others, recommendations with respect to maintenance of the peace and decisions concerning member status in the UN, the Trusteeship Council, budgetary questions, etc.). Para. 3 provides that the Assembly shall decide by simple majority on "other questions" and that by simple majority it may indicate new "categories of questions to be decided by a two-thirds majority", in addition to those listed in para. 2.

Making use of the power given it by Article 18, para. 3, the Assembly has gradually introduced other categories requiring the two-thirds majority, by including them in its rules of procedure or in an annex to these rules. For example, Article 19 of the rules of procedure provides that the request to include an item on the agenda of an Assembly special session may be approved only by a two-thirds majority if it is made after a certain date. Article 81 provides that when a proposal (usually a draft resolution) has been adopted or rejected, it may not be reconsidered during the same Assembly session unless a two-thirds majority of the members present and voting decide otherwise. Annex III, F (no longer of use after Namibia's acquisition of independence) provided that decisions on reports and petitions concerning the South-West African Territory (today Namibia) under South African administration were to be made with the qualified majority. More recently, a proposal was presented, again within the meaning of Article 18, para. 3, that the qualified majority is required also for resolutions which repeal a previous resolution, but it was rejected by the Assembly.

> For the discussion on this proposal, carried out during the Assembly session of January 16, 1992, see A/46/PV.74. Actually, even if it was formulated in general terms, the proposal concerned a specific case being examined by the Assembly. Its aim was to make more difficult the adoption of a draft resolution which, owing mainly to the insistence of the United States, revoked res.no. 3379-XXX of November 10, 1975. Under this latter resolution zionism was to be considered as a form of racism. The draft was then approved by a wide majority (111 votes in favour, 25 against and 13 abstentions) and became res. 46/86.

The most important problem concerning the vote procedure is whether the list of questions contained in Article 18, para. 2 is exhaustive or is only a list of examples. If the list is exhaustive, the Assembly may decide by a two-thirds majority only on the questions listed, except, obviously, for the possibility of creating an additional category on the basis of para. 3, i. e. for the possibility of deciding that in future all resolutions of a certain kind and with a certain purpose, will be voted on by the two-thirds majority. If, on the contrary, it is held that para. 2 contains only a list of examples, the Assembly may decide *in individual cases* (and therefore without resorting to para. 3) whether a question is important and whether it should be voted on with the qualified majority.

The practice has followed this second interpretation. In a number of cases (the last one occurred in 1998, when the Assembly voted on the question of equitable representation and increase in the membership of the Security Council, and related matters) the Assembly has decided that a certain resolution, not included in the list, was to be considered important and to be voted on by the two-thirds majority. Moreover, in making this decision it has a number of times stated that it did not want to be bound for the future by para. 3. This has led the organ to behave differently, and without any substantial justification, in identical cases. For example, in the first session, in 1946, it was decided that the two-thirds rule was to apply to the request for an advisory opinion of the International Court of Justice, because the request was connected to another draft resolution requiring this majority. During the fourth session, in 1949, the simple majority was proposed and accepted although the same connection existed. In another example, simple majority and greater majority were adopted at different times for resolutions concerning non-self-governing territories (Article 73 of the Charter).

The Assembly's tendency to endorse the view that the list in para. 2 is not exhaustive has often led to perplexity and opposition within the organ itself. Therefore, while it is to be excluded that the practice has given rise to an *ad hoc* customary rule, it will be useful to investigate what is the acceptable interpretation from an objective point of view.

For the question of the representation in the Security Council see res no. 53/30 of November 23, 1998, adopted by the General Assembly after two days and a half of heated debate on the reform of the Security Council (GAOR, 53rd sess., 63-66th meets.). The resolution, after a reference to Chapter XVIII of the Charter (which already states that a two-third majority is needed for the approval of amendments to the Charter) says that the Assembly "determine not to adopt any resolution or decision on the question of equitable representation on and increase in the membership of the Security Council and related matters without the affirmative vote of at least two third of the members of the General Assembly". Of course, from the legal point of view we are discussing here, the determination contained in the resolution is important as far as the "equitable representation and related matters" are concerned, since the increase in membership, needing an amendments to the Charter, is already covered by chapter XVIII, Article 108.

For the practice concerning the case of the request for opinions of the International Court of Justice, see GAOR, 1st sess., 2nd part, Pl.meet., p. 1048 ff. and 4th sess., Pl. meet., 270th meet., n. 126 ff. The details of the cases concerning non self-governing territories were the following. Up until the eighth Assembly session, in 1953, draft resolutions concerning information about non-self-governing territories were voted on by the two-thirds majority. On the contrary, in the eighth session, the Assembly decided for the simple majority, as proposed by Mexico (cf. GAOR, 8th sess., Pl. meet., 459th meet., no. 6 ff. and partic. no. 35 f.). In the 11th, 12th, and 13th sessions, the Assembly again adopted the two-thirds rule, amidst the protests of Mexico and of other States (cf. GAOR, 11th sess., Pl. meet., 657th meet., no. 1 ff., Pl. meet., 722nd meet., no. 14 ff.; 12th sess., Pl. meet., no. 1 ff.). Subsequently, the voting was once again by simple majority: cf., for example, resolutions 35/27 of November 11, 1980, 36/50 of November 24, 1981 and 37/30 of November 23, 1982 on the question of East Timor, adopted respectively by 58 votes to 35, 54 votes to 32, and 50 to 36.

    For other cases in which it was discussed and decided each time whether a question was to be voted by the two-thirds majority, cf., again as an example, GAOR, 16th sess., Pl. meet., 1043rd meet., nos. 6-25 (the Assembly decided to vote by two-thirds majority on a draft resolution presented by Czechoslovakia on the effects of atomic radiation. The draft was considered as not approved since it received only a simple majority); GAOR, 20th sess., Pl. meet., 1385th-1390th, 1400th, 1405th, 1407th and 1408th meet. (here it was decided to apply the simple majority rule to a draft resolution, which then became res. no. 2105-XX of December 20, 1975, on the observance of the Declaration concerning the independence of colonial peoples). For other information on the practice, see SALERNO, *art. cit.*, p. 312 ff.; see also, further on this paragraph, regarding the question of Chinese representation.

Textual arguments have been used to reach conclusions on this subject. For example, in favour of the view that has had the widest following in practice, i.e. in favour of the opinion that the list of questions in para. 2 is a pure catalogue of examples, the English text of the article has been cited. In introducing the list with the phrase "The questions [the important questions to be decided by the two-thirds majority] shall include:..." the text would let it be understood that the Assembly is free to consider other questions as important. On the contrary, others have made reference to the French text, which introduces the list with the phrase "Sont considerées comme questions importantes:...", a phrase which would seem to support the exhaustive nature. In fact no textual argument can lead to a certain conclusion. The same must be said for those who, once again in favour of the opinion that the list contains only examples, put emphasis on the fact that para. 2 says: "Decisions... on important questions shall be made by a two-thirds majority... These questions shall include...". If the qualified majority were to apply only to the questions listed, they say, para. 2 would speak directly of the questions to be decided by the two-thirds majority, as there would be no practical necessity for qualifying them as important. If, then, para. 2 adopts this terminology, this implies that the Assembly is free to declare the importance of other questions and decide them by the two-thirds rule. To the contrary, it can be said that such a serious problem cannot be resolved by discussions over whether or not a phrase is superfluous.

    In our opinion, despite the prevailing tendency in practice (followed also by the United Nations Secretary-General Perez de Cuéllar: cf.: *Memorandum* of November 4, 1985 in *UNJY*, 1985, p. 130 f.) and notwithstanding the respective strengths of the textual arguments, the view to be preferred is the one holding that the list in para. 2 is exhaustive. This is for a reason of systematic interpretation, that is, a connection which must exist between para. 2 and para. 3 of Article 18. If the list were not exhaustive, and the Assembly could decide on a case-by-case basis whether a question was to be voted by a two-thirds majority, would there still exist the need to have the procedure under para. 3 which entails adding, in the future, other categories of questions to be decided by two-thirds majority? If para. 3 has a purpose, it can only be that of avoiding the Assembly's decision on a case-by-case basis. The view supporting the exhaustive nature of the list is also confirmed in the preparatory works. They reveal that the procedure under para. 3 was considered the *only* acceptable procedure for extending the two-thirds majority to questions not included in the list in para. 2.

During the San Francisco Conference, it was debated whether certain questions should be included in the list in para. 2 as important questions. In some cases (for example, regarding the election of the Secretary-General) it was decided not to do so also because the Assembly would have always been able, on the basis of para. 3, to later add the question to the list. In these discussions, mention was never made of the possibility of the Assembly voting by the two-thirds majority on questions not listed in para. 2 or not added under para. 3. (Cf. UNC.I.O., vol. 8, p. 364 ff., partic. p. 389 f. and p. 510 ff.).

The procedure provided by para. 3 needs to be given a closer look. On the basis of this procedure, as we have said, the Assembly may decide that in the future all questions belonging to the same category shall be decided by two-thirds majority. May the Assembly, after having introduced a certain category, eliminate it later? The question is a very delicate one and is the pivot around which the whole interpretation of Article 18, para. 2 and 3, revolves. In our view, it would be difficult to hold that once a category had been added to the list of questions to be decided by two-thirds majority, it could not be eliminated. If this were so, Article 18, para. 3, would acknowledge that the Assembly had the power to modify the Charter by simple majority, in derogation of the provisions of Articles 108 and 109 on amendments and review; moreover, resort to Articles 108 and 109 would be necessary whenever the necessity was felt to restore the simple majority system for the additional category. Although this view has been held, such a rigid system cannot be attributed, in the absence of an express prevision to para. 3.

One could object that admitting the revocability of a category under para. 3 would come into conflict with our opinion in favour of the exhaustive nature of the list in para. 2. It could be said: If the Assembly has the power to introduce and eliminate categories, does this not mean that it is then free to act on a case-by-case basis? Does it not mean that it is ultimately free, even if only through the creation or elimination of a category, to decide each time whether or not to vote by the two-thirds rule? And is this not the conclusion reached by those who deny the exhaustive nature of the list? Such an objection has to be rejected for the following reason. In speaking of categories, para. 3 *authorizes the Assembly to make only general and abstract decisions*. According to the purpose of para. 3, a category cannot be *introduced* for contingent reasons and with regard to individual cases, nor can it be *eliminated* for contingent reasons and with regard to individual cases. It may be introduced and eliminated only with a well-pondered and generally motivated measure. For example, the measures with which the Assembly has introduced several additional categories in its own rules of procedure — measures which have been mentioned above and which all-in-all represent the only serious examples of application of para. 3 — respond exactly to these requirements. On the contrary, the rule of the case-by-case basis, even if disguised under the *form* provided by para. 3, does not constitute an application but rather a violation of this paragraph. And such violation involves violation of the rights of the minority. "We should not change the rules in the middle of the game", the United States delegate correctly observed in the 39th General Assembly session in 1984 (A/39/PV.98, sess. of December 12, 1984, p. 1792) in strenuously but unsuccessfully opposing a decision made by the organ that all resolutions, and their relative amendments, on the question of apartheid would require from then on a two-thirds majority vote. In fact, the decision had clearly been proposed and was adopted for the sole purpose of preventing a United States amendment, which had just been introduced, from being voted on by a simple majority.

Another example of resort to para. 3 to disguise a decision on a specific case was the one, above reported, of the proposal regarding resolutions repealing previous resolutions, a proposal put forward for the sole purpose of making the repeal of the declaration on zionism more difficult. In this case, however the proposal was not successful.

The situation is, then, identical to that of rules of procedure of collective bodies, for example the rule of procedure of the General Assembly or of the Security Council (see § 96), of Parliamentary rules of procedure, and so on. There is no doubt that, just as they are issued by the majority, rules of procedure can be modified by the same majority. However, it is necessary that the modification be general and abstract and that it be made only after an examination of the reasons that objectively make it necessary. On the contrary, the view cannot be held that the majority, which has the power to modify a rule of procedure, may also not apply it in individual cases. The individual failure to apply would constitute a violation of the rules of procedure and mean violation of the rights of the minority.

In conclusion, the Assembly practice, which tends to establish case by case whether a certain question not included in the list in para. 2 must nevertheless be voted by a two-thirds majority, is illegal. Under the Charter, the

Assembly may adopt the two-thirds rule for a question not included in the list only through the procedure described in para. 3, deciding in a general and abstract way that all the questions of a certain kind shall in the future be decided by the two-thirds majority. Such decision could then later be revoked but always in a general and abstract way.

Once again to show its illegality, separate mention should be given to the attitude taken by the Assembly regarding the voting procedure on the question of Chinese representation, before the question was resolved in favour of Communist China (see § 19). Until the 15th session (1960), the problem had never arisen as to what majority should be required to vote on the Communist proposal aiming to substitute Mao's delegates for those of Chiang-Kai-Shek in the United Nations. On the other hand, until that time the States favouring Formosa had constituted the great majority in the Assembly. At the 16th session, in 1961, a draft resolution was presented for the first time (by the United States together with other countries) and approved. The draft decided "in conformity with Article 18 of the Charter" that "any proposal to change the representation of China is an important question". At the 20th session, in 1965, the Assembly confirmed the 1961 resolution, expressly deciding that "this resolution is still valid". Similar confirmation occurred in subsequent sessions up until November 20, 1970. On that date, the proposal to substitute the delegates of Communist China for those of Nationalist China received for the first time a simple majority of the votes cast (51 in favour, 49 against, and 25 abstentions) but was not adopted owing to the decision that had made the Chinese question an important question to be decided by the two-thirds majority (cf. GAOR, 25th session, Pl. meet., 1913th meet.).

It is not clear whether with the 1961 resolution the Assembly intended to introduce a category under para. 3 of Article 18, or if, in conformity with the practice that had always been followed and starting from the assumption that the list in para. 2 is a mere catalogue of examples, it had intended to take a decision limited to the session underway. Nor was this uncertainty cleared up in the subsequent practice. The fact that the Assembly felt the need several times in a row to confirm the two-thirds rule testifies for the latter solution, since the procedure in para. 3 has unlimited efficacy in time. Considering, however, that the resolutions after 1961 seemingly had the character of restatements ("the 1961 resolution is still valid"), resort to para. 3 is conceivable. In any case, whether the first or the second interpretation is the right one, Article 18 was not respected. If the Assembly intended to act on the basis of para. 2, its action would be in contempt of the exhaustive nature of the list of important questions. As for para. 3, this authorises the introduction of "additional categories of questions" to be decided by the two-thirds rule. It is clear that the Chinese question could not be considered a category but an individual specific case (exactly as Albania held several times: cf., for one of its last statements, GAOR, 25th sess., Pl. meet., 1913th meet., no. 24), and that the treatment given by the Assembly to the Chinese question shows exactly that para. 3 has no other function than that of guaranteeing the general and abstract nature of Assembly decisions on the voting procedure.

The resolutions which considered the Chinese question important are the following: Res. December 12, 1961 (1668-XVI); November 17, 1965 (2025-XX); November 29, 1966 (2159-XXI); November 28, 1967 (2271-XXII); November 19, 1968 (2389-XXIII); November 11, 1969 (2500-XXIV) and November 20, 1970 (2642-XXV). For the debate in the XVI session in 1961, see GAOR, Pl. meet., 1080th meet.

An altogether different problem (on this, see § 19) is whether the Chinese question, in involving the Charter provisions on admission and expulsion, could be decided by an Assembly resolution, no matter whether it was passed by a simple majority or by a two-thirds majority.

One final point needs to be discussed. Up to now the rules which the Assembly should follow when it is faced with a question *not included in* the enumeration in para. 2 have been examined. It may occur, however, as it has occurred, that the Assembly is faced with question over which there is *some doubt* as to whether it belongs to one of the listed categories: a question that some members believe belongs to the list and others believe does not. The problem has arisen, for example, of whether a draft resolution stating that a certain State "should" be admitted to the UN, or another one recommending that the Security Council re-examine its policy on admission, belonged to the category "admission of new members to the United Nations" (a category which clearly concerns specific admission of a given State, and therefore the resolutions governed by Article 4 of the Charter). It has been also asked whether in the category "suspension of the rights and privileges of membership" there could be included the case of an invitation, made by the Assembly to the Member States, to renounce the right to present opinions to the International Court of Justice in the exercise of its advisory function; whether there belonged to the category "recommendations with respect to the maintenance of international peace and security" decisions relating to the inalienable rights of the Palestinian people or those on the aggressive and peace-threatening policy of Israel; whether there belonged to the category of "budgetary questions" the decision to qualify certain expenses as ordinary expenses under Article 17, if such qualification was made in the abstract, before the expenses were incurred and actually noted in the budget; whether, again concerning "budgetary questions", there were to be included the mere setting of criteria for allocation of the financial burden among the Member States or regarding travel allowances for Secretariat officials, and so on. In these and in similar cases, the Assembly has always held that it could decide (by simple majority) whether a question was included in the enumeration in para. 2. In our opinion this is a classic problem of interpretation of the Charter and the considerations we made about the power of the UN organs to interpret the Charter (see § 6) should be applied: the interpretation given by the General Assembly to para. 2 in a concrete case is not binding for the Member States and may be challenged by any of them.

For the practice cited, cf. GAOR, 6th sess. (1951-52), Pl. meet., 370th meet., no. 77ff (question of the admission of new members); 10th sess. (1955), Pl. meet., 541st meet., no. 126 ff. (renunciation of the right to present opinions to the Court); 25th sess. (1970), Pl. meet., 1921st meet., no. 74 ff. (question of the inalienable rights of the Palestinian people; *ivi*, no. 25, protests of the Israeli delegate that the Assembly had decided to vote by simple majority); 21st sess. (1966), Pl. meet., 1492nd meet., no. 17 ff. (qualification of the expenses of the Capital Development Fund as ordinary expenses); 27th sess., A/PV.2108 of December 13, 1972 (principles on the sharing of expenses); 28th sess., A/PV.2206 of December 26, 1973 (travel allowances for officials); 39th sess., A/PV.101 of December 14, 1984 (aggressive policy of Israel). In this last case, the United States, in maintaining that para. 10 of a draft resolution against Israel (which then became res. 39/146A) should come under the category of resolutions regarding maintenance of peace, was first opposed to the question of the applicability of the two-thirds rule under Article 18, para. 2, being put to the vote. Resolutions on the maintenance of the peace, the US delegate said, are, under para. 2, to be adopted by a two-thirds majority and the Assembly *cannot* decide otherwise without violating the Charter:. This view was correct. Immediately afterwards, however, the United States accepted "in a spirit of accommodation" that the Assembly decide on the preliminary question, and the organ decided by simple majority (69 in favour, 28 against, with 23 abstentions) that the two-thirds rule should not apply to the cited para. 10. Para. 10 was then adopted with 69 votes in favour, 39 against, and 26 abstentions, in clear violation of para. 2 of Article 18.

33. C) *Approval by "consensus"*.

BIBLIOGRAPHY: see § 28.

The practice of consensus has already been dealt with in treating the voting procedure in the Security Council, and there is no need to resume the discussion. Worthy of mention here is the fact that in the General Assembly more often than in the Security Council States, while participating in the adoption of a measure by consensus, expressly reserve their position regarding some parts of it. Even if this can be explained by the large number of States sitting in the Assembly and therefore by the impossibility of reaching really unanimous decisions, it certainly does not lead us to consider the practice of consensus as entirely commendable. It is indicative that some important or even historical Assembly resolutions adopted by consensus, such as resolutions no. 3201 S-VI of May 9, 1974 and 3202 S-VI of May 16, 1974 on the new international economic order, stand out for the number and the quality of the reservations expressed against them (see § 97).

Section III

THE SECRETARIAT

34. *Appointment of the Secretary-General.*

BIBLIOGRAPHY: SCHWEBEL, *The Secretary-General of the United Nations*, Harvard University Press, 1952, p. 30 ff.; BAILEY, *The United Nations Secretariat*, in LUARD, *The Evolution of International Organizations*, New York, 1966, p. 97 ff.; GORDENKER, *The UN Secretary-General and the Maintenance of Peace*, New York, 1967, p. 34 ff.; SMOUTS, *Le Secretaire général des Nations Unies*, Paris, 1971, p. 17 ff.; SESSA, *Il Segretariato delle Nazioni Unite*, in *CI*, 1972, p. 328 ff.; PARKER, *Electing theUN Secretary-General after the Cold War*, in *Hastings Law Journal*, 1992, p. 161 ff.

The office of Secretary-General ("the chief administrative officer of the Organization", under Article 97) is held by an individual who is not the organ of any State and must not seek or receive instructions from any government (Article 100). The Secretary-General is appointed, under Article 97, by the General Assembly upon the recommendation of the Security Council. Since it is a non-procedural matter, the Council's decision may be vetoed by one of the permanent members.

The text and the rational of Article 97 indicate that there must be perfect agreement between the Assembly and the Council on the appointment of the Secretary-General. This agreement must cover all details of the appointment. Since Article 97 does not set the length of the term of office, it must in some way be agreed upon by the Assembly and the Council. When (and only when) no final date is set, the closest solution to the rational of Article 97 is that the Secretary will hold office until his mandate is revoked by the Assembly on the recommendation of the Council.

In 1950, when the term of office of the then Secretary-General Trygve Lie, a term which had been previously agreed upon to last five years, expired, the Assembly decided to extend it for a further three years. Since this occurred without the recommendation of the Security Council (although only after ascertaining that the Council was unable to reach a decision owing to reciprocal vetos of the permanent members), the extension was challenged by some countries as illegal. In the light of Article 97 there were good grounds for this challenge.

Trygve Lie had been appointed in 1946 on the recommendation of the Security Council (on January 29, 1946) after the Assembly had established (res. no. 12-I of January 24, 1946) that the first Secretary was to have a term of office of five years and that the appointment would be renewed for another five years, with the understanding that there would be the possibility of setting different terms in the future. Since the Council's decision took place after the Assembly's, it must be held that an agreement between the two bodies had been made for a five-year appointment. It follows that, in 1950, the Assembly could not have decided without a new recommendation by the Council. On the contrary, the majority in the organ expressed the view that since Article 97 had not set any term, the Assembly could make use, for purposes of the extension, of the original proposal. The Communist bloc lined up against the majority opinion. The Soviet Union stated that it would not recognise Trygie Lie "as the lawful holder" of the office of Secretary-General. For the discussion, see GAOR, 5th sess., Pl. meet., 296th meet., no. 13 ff.; 297th and 298th meet. (*ivi*, no. 1 ff., partic. nos. 43, 46 and 49 the Soviet statement).

In 1953, when the extended term was over, the Security Council recommended the appointment of Hammarskjold without indicating when his term would expire, but the Assembly set (res. no. 709-VII) a five-year appointment, referring to the original resolution of January 29, 1946, which had provided for this term also for the second Secretary-General. In 1957, it was the Council, again recommending Hammarskjold, which set the five-year term. With Secrctary U Thant, appointed in 1961 after the death of Hammarskjold, the practice of a three-year term was introduced, again on the Council's initiative. However, with Secretary Waldheim, appointed in 1971, and reconfirmed in 1976, the five-year tern returned. Also Secretary Perez de Cuéllar, appointed at the end of 1981, Secretary B. Boutros-Ghali, appointed in 1992, and the present Secretary Kofi Annan, whose term began on January 1, 1997 and was renewed for a further term to last from January 2002 until December 31, 2006.

35. *The Secretariat staff and the legal nature of the employment relationships.*

BIBLIOGRAPHY: LISSITYN, *Case-note on the ICJ's Advisory Opinion on the « Effect of Awards » Case*, in *AJ*, 1954, p. 655 ff.; COHEN, *The United Nations Secretariat — Some Constitutional and Administrative Developments*, in *AJ*, 1955, p. 295 ff.; BASTID, *Le statut juridique des fonctionnaires de l'ONU*, in *The United Nations: Ten Years' Legal Progress*, The Hague, 1956, p. 145 ff.; ID., *Les tribunaux administratifs internationaux et leur jurisprudence*, in *RC*, 1957, II, p. 347 ff.; FRIEDMANN and FATOUROS, *The United Nations Administrative Tribunal*, in *Int. Org.*, 1957, p. 13 ff.; SEYERSTED, *Settlement of Internal Disputes of Intergovernmental Organizations by Internal and External Courts*, in *Bruns'Z*, 1964, p. 1 ff.; DURANTE, *L'ordinamento interno delle Nazioni Unite*, Milan, 1964, p. 194 ff. and p. 363 ff.; KOH, *The United Nations Administrative Tribunal*, Louisiana State University Press, 1966; BAADE, *The Acquired Rights of International Public Servants*, in *American Journal of Comparative Law*, 1966-67, p. 251 ff.; QUADRI, *Diritto internazionale pubblico*, 5th ed., Naples, 1968, p. 85 ff. and p. 559 f.; MERON, *Staff of the UN Secretariat: Problems and Directions*, in *AJ*, 1976, p. 659 ff.; TAVERNIER, *Les accors de recrutement des fonctionnaires des Nations Unies par voie de concours*, in *AF*, 1980, p. 503 ff.; MERON, *In re Rosescu and the Independence of the International Civil service*, in *AJ*, 1981, p. 910 ff.; ID., *Charter Powers of the UN' Secretary-General with Regard to the Secretariat and the Role of General Assembly Resolutions*, in *Bruns'Z*, Bd. 42, 1982, p. 731 ff.; BARNES, *Tenure and Independence in the United Nations International Civil Service*, in *N.Y. Univ. Journal of Law and Politics*, 1982, 4, p. 767 ff.; ZYSS, *Le regime commun des Nations Unies*, in *RGDIP*, 1987, p. 341 ff.; BETTATI, *Recrutement et carrière des fonctionnaires internationaux*, in *RC*, 1987, IV, p. 171 ff.; BULKELEY, *Depoliticing UN Recruitment: Establishing a Genuinely International Civil Service*, in *New York Univ. Journal of International Law and Politics*, 1990, p. 749 ff.; VV. AA., *International Administration: Law and Management Practices in International Organizations*, New York, 1990; MERON, *« Exclusive Preserves » and the New Soviet Policy toward the UN Secretariat*, in *AJ*, 1991, p. 322 ff.; PELLET and RUZIE, *Les fonctionnaires internationaux*, Paris, 1993; AMERASINGHE, *The Law of the Intenational Civil Service, as Applied by International Administrative Tribunals*, 2 vols., New York, 1994; MILLER, *Le droit applicable oar le Tribunal administratif des Nations Unies*, in *Le contentieux de la fonction publique internationale*, Paris 1996, p. 219 ff.; ACKERMAN, *The Internal Judicial System of the United Nations*, in *Justice*, 1997, p. 33 ff.

Under the Secretary-General there is a very large bureaucratic system for carrying out the executive functions of the United Nations.

According to Article 101 of the Charter, the status of staff members, and in particular their appointment and the rights and obligations connected to their employment relationship with the Organization, are regulated by rules laid down by the Assembly. With regard to their appointment, Article 101, para. 1, provides that the staff "shall be appointed by the Secretary-General under regulations established by the General Assembly". It is obvious therefore that the normative power of the Assembly must be of a general and abstract nature without infringing upon individual appointments made by the Secretary-General. In the practice, however, especially from the seventies on and especially in the area of economic cooperation, a tendency has taken root in the Assembly to condition the appointment of higher-level officials both by requiring previous consultation with the Member States and by subjecting the appointment to subsequent confirmation by the Assembly itself. Since this practice has not given rise to any significant reaction and since the Secretary-General has gone along with it, a customary rule has perhaps become superimposed on Article 101, para. 1. There are, however, some scholars (MERON) who still insist that such practice is illegal.

The principle of *independence* from their Member States extends from the Secretary-general to the Secretariat staff. "In the performance of their duties", says Article 100 of the Charter, "the Secretary-General and the staff shall not seek or receive instructions from any government or from any other authority external to the Organization... Each member of the United Nations undertakes to respect the exclusively international character of the responsibilities of the Secretary-General and the staff and not to seek to influence them in the discharge of their responsibilities." The principle is clearly aimed at safeguarding such responsibilities and their performance. It is difficult to say that it applies in the recruitment phase, that is, to the active role that the national governments may play either in the form of designation or under the guise of expressing agreement. Interventions of this kind — which are usual in the practice and are kept in check by the requisites of efficiency, competence and integrity which, under Article 101, must be given paramount consideration in hiring — do not seem illegal in that they take place in the phase preceding the performance of the function. On the other hand, if the Secretary-General yields to such interventions and consequently refuses to establish a given employment relationship, no legal effect is produced.

The *renewal* of an employment contract is another matter. It has been asked in practice whether the fact that a national government had "vetoed" the extension of a fixed-time contract can constitute a just cause for the failure to renew it when the renewal has been requested by the UN office of the staff member. The United Nations Administrative Tribunal (an organ which will be dealt with in a moment) has correctly tended toward the view that, when it is not a matter of State employees seconded to the Organization but of ordinary employees, the non-renewal is illegal and gives rise to the employee's right to compensation. This is because, according to the Tribunal, Article 100 of the Charter would prevent the Secretary-General from "... legally invoking a decision of a government to justify his own action with regard to the employment of a staff member" (decision in the *Levcik* v. *Secretary-General* case, on which see MERON, in *AJ*, 1981, p. 918).

State interference in the assignment of positions in the Secretariat has also occurred through the "exclusive preserve" practice, that is, succession in vacant positions by citizens of the same country to which the previous staff member belonged. This practice, however, was finally prohibited by res. no. 43/224 of the General Assembly in 1989.

The employment relationship between staff members and the Organization, resulting from Assembly resolutions and regulations issued by the Secretary-General as delegated by the Assembly, is characterized by the existence of a judicial organ, the Administrative Tribunal. The Tribunal was set up by the Assembly with res. no. 351-IV of November 24, 1949 (modified by subsequent resolutions no. 782-VIII of December 9, 1953, no. 957-X of November 8, 1955, no. 50/54 of December 11, 1995, and no. 52/56 of December 15, 1997) which approved its statute. It consists of seven independent persons elected by the Assembly and it is competent to decide disputes arising from non-observance of the rules on the employment relationship. Its judgments cannot be appealed against, except when new and decisive facts are discovered, or clerical or arithmetical mistakes are made including errors arising from any accidental slip or omission. When this is the case, the Secretary-General or the employee may apply for a revision within one year, in the first case, or for correction, at any time (Article 12 of the Statute). An application for revision, which could be received in the past by the International Court of Justice, has been abolished in 1995 (General Assembly res. no. 50/54 of December 11, 1995).

The establishment of the Administrative Tribunal (which was not something new, since a similar organ had existed in the League of Nations), was intended to meet obvious considerations of justice. Indeed, employment disputes in international organizations, similar to disputes concerning employment relations with foreign sovereign entities, are still today considered in various States as not within the competence of domestic tribunals. If a staff member, dismissed by an international organization or by a foreign embassy, has recourse to the courts of the State where the organization's headquarters or the embassy is located, his case will usually be dismissed owing to the principle of international law on the immunity of foreign States from civil jurisdiction, a principle which extends to unions of States and which, as far as the United Nations are concerned, is confirmed by Article 105, para. 1, of the Charter. This immunity must then be counter-balanced by the possibility for the worker to have judicial protection elsewhere. In the event of an employment relation with a foreign State, the legal system of such State will provide such protection. In the same way, in the case of an international organization, judicial protection of employees must depend on the remedies that the organization itself makes available. The United Nations Administrative Tribunal falls within this framework.

Judicial remedies regarding employment are provided by many international organizations (the United Nations, specialised Agencies, European Communities, etc.).

Resolutions and regulations concerning the UN Secretariat staff make up a whole system of rules. It has been subject to debate (and the debate concerns all international organizations) whether these are true legal rules. Those who favour their legal nature ask whether with such norms the Organization has created a separate and original legal system or a system which draws its validity from the Charter and therefore directly from international law. To understand these debates, which are largely theoretical, a useful tool is the opinion handed down by the International Court of Justice in 1954 in the *Effects of Awards of Compensation Made by the United Nations Administrative Tribunal* case (see ICJ, *Reports*, 1954, p. 47 ff.).

In 1952, the Secretary-General dismissed without notice several staff members of U.S. nationality, accusing them of "disloyalty toward the host country" for having refused to testify before the McCarthy Committee of the United States Senate which at the time was investigating "subversive" activities. However, the Administrative Tribunal declared these dismissals unlawful and ordered either the re-employment of the dismissed staff or the awarding of substantial compensation. The case came before the General Assembly in its eighth session (in the autumn of 1953) during the approval, under Article 17 of the Charter, of the UN budget item concerning the payment of this compensation. When strong criticism arose in the Assembly over the decision of the Tribunal (which was accused by some members of having issued judgements that were clearly unjust with regard to the Organization), and there was strong support for the idea that the funds should not be allocated, the General Assembly decided to seek an advisory opinion of the International Court of Justice under Article 96 of the Charter. The request was worded as follows: "Having regard to the Statute of the United Nations Administrative Tribunal and to any other relevant instruments and to the relevant records, has the Assembly the right on any grounds to refuse to give effect to an award of compensation made by that Tribunal in favour of a staff member of the United Nations whose contract of service has been terminated without his assent?".

An identical case had been presented in the League of Nations, but it was at the time when the League was breaking up. Since it was about to dissolve, the League Assembly decided (res. of April 18, 1946) not to follow up several judgements of the League's Administrative Tribunal which had awarded compensation to staff members of the Organization.

The Court gave a negative answer to the Assembly's question. The advisory opinion can be divided, from a logical viewpoint, in two parts. In the first part, the Court raised the problem of interpretation of the constitutive instruments of the Tribunal, especially of the Statute, and asked whether or not the Assembly, in adopting them, intended to reserve for itself the power to review the Tribunal's decisions. In the Court's view, no doubts could arise about this. Taking into account Article 1 ("A Tribunal is established by the present Statute..."), Article 2, para. 3 ("In the event of a dispute as to whether the Tribunal has competence, that matter shall be settled by the decision of the Tribunal"), and Article 10 ("decisions of the Tribunal shall be final and without appeal") of the Statute, the Court concluded that the Assembly intended to create a true judicial body and not a mere subordinate institution with only advisory or subsidiary functions. Consequently, the Tribunal's judgments were *res iudicata* between the parties, that is, between the individual staff member, on the one hand, and the Organization, represented by the Secretary-General, on the other. Therefore, the decisions awarding compensation were binding, by virtue of the Statute of the Tribunal, on the United Nations and on the Assembly itself.

In the second part, the Court raised a problem of Charter interpretation, and asked whether the Assembly had the power to create a Tribunal of such a nature. Here also its view was very clear. This power was implicitly granted (on the so-called implicit powers, see § 5) by Article 101 of the Charter, which gives the Assembly the power to issue regulations regarding employment relationships of the staff members, requiring, among other things, that "conditions of service" be such as to "secure the highest standards of efficiency, competence and integrity" of the staff. Also implicit was the power to create a Tribunal for the purposes of "justice" pursued by the United Nations, considering that the staff members, owing to the Organization's immunity from the jurisdiction of State courts, would have no one to turn to for judicial protection.

The Court also examined, in detail, the reasons adopted by several States to support the Assembly's power to revoke Tribunal decisions. These reasons can be found in the opinions of the dissenting judges, annexed to the judgment. The principal ones were based on Article 22 and Article 17 of the Charter. It was held, first of all, that the Tribunal, as an organ created by the Assembly, was nothing other than one of the subsidiary organs referred to in Article 22, and that this subsidiary nature implied complete subjection to the principal organ. Regarding Article 17, it was said that in so far as this article gave the Assembly the power to examine and approve the budget, it gave the organ the freedom not to approve an expense; and such freedom would certainly be in conflict with the obligation to pay compensation awarded by the Tribunal. The Court rejected both views. With regard to the former, it pointed out the extraneousness of Article 22 to the case under discussion, since it was an article providing for the establishment of organs for exercising the Assembly's own functions, and the function of the Administrative Tribunal was certainly not among them. With regard to Article 17, the Court's opinion was that, in meeting expenditures that arise from previous Assembly decisions (in this case, the decision establishing the Tribunal), the Assembly had no alternative regarding the budget than to honor the engagements it had undertaken.

> No doubt the argument based on Article 17 was poorly chosen, in that it could be proposed with regard to... staff salaries (on problems of interpretation of Article 17, see § 86 ff.). By contrast, the Court's view that the setting up of the Tribunal was only a way to regulate the employment relationship was a sound one.
> There were other arguments raised against the view taken by the Court, and also rejected by it. Some observers held that the review power of the Assembly should be allowed at least in the case of a judgement that was clearly invalid (for example, for excess of power, for manifest injustice, and so on), analogously to what may happen with regard to decisions taken by international arbitrators in interstate disputes which a party does not comply with when it maintains that they are vitiated by a defect of this kind. However, the analogy can certainly be refuted owing to the different nature of the situation existing between a UN staff member dispute and a dispute between States; what is at stake here is the institutional nature of the Administrative Tribunal.

The conclusions reached by the Court are basically correct even if, in our view, they were incomplete. It is not enough to say that the Statute of the Administrative Tribunal denies a review power by the Assembly and that the establishment of the Tribunal occurred legally under the Charter. There is a more general problem which is the key to the entire matter, although no trace of it appears in the opinion of the Court. This is the question whether the Assembly, in regulating the employment relationship in the United Nations, must do so, on the one hand, according to the principle of generality and abstractness and, on the other, to the principle of the non-retroactivity of its decisions. One could, in fact, hold that the very power exercised to establish the Tribunal could be exercised not only, obviously, to abolish it but also to modify the regulations in the sense of not recognizing some decisions already handed down. The only way to refute this thesis is to show that, under the Charter, the Assembly may proceed in the matter only with general, abstract and non-retroactive rules. In domestic legal systems, these three characteristics of the law are ever less frequently considered essential. It is especially the third characteristic that can be sacrificed when the common good or higher principles of social justice so require. What, then, in the case of the rules governing the Administrative Tribunal? It is prudent to interpret the Charter in the sense of generality, abstractness, and non-retroactivity. On the one hand, the power attributed to the Assembly by Article 101, para. 1, with regard to the employment relationship is clearly a power of general law-making. On the other hand, the respect for the "principles of justice" that Article 1, para. 1, imposes on the Organization seem to testify in the sense that the Assembly cannot destroy, with regard to the past, what it itself has created and this is especially true when no higher social need can be found as in the specific case in favour of retroactivity.

The Court only incidentally touched upon the subject of non-retroactivity, when, in confirming that the Assembly had the power to establish a real Tribunal for settling disputes between the United Nations and its staff, it conceded that that Assembly itself may abolish the Tribunal, repealing its Statute, or "... amend the Statute and provide for review of the *future* decisions of the Tribunal...". Cf. ICJ, *Reports*, 1954, p. 61 (our italics).

The opinion that the General Assembly could repeal the decisions of the Administrative Tribunal has never been brought up again, even in relation to decisions whose reasoning raised perplexities.

Cf., for example, the statements of Great Britain and the United States in the Fifth Committee in the 41st Assembly session (Doc. A/C.5/41/SR.39 of December 3, 1986) regarding an Administrative Tribunal decision (no. 370) which had awarded large amounts but which, in spite of this, in the view of the two States, had to be upheld in that it was the result of a legal procedure respecting the rule of law.

In view of the thesis correctly held by the International Court of Justice on the irrevocability of Administrative Tribunal decisions, and in view of the fact that the Assembly's power to establish such a Tribunal and, more in general, to regulate the status of UN staff finds its basis as well as its limits in the Charter, that is, in a set of legal norms, the full legal character of the regulation of the employment relationship in the Organization cannot be questioned. Whoever holds that the rules on the status of staff members are not true legal norms appeals to the argument that their observance by the Organization rests *in the final analysis* (and therefore also when there is a decision of the Administrative Tribunal) on the general will of the Organization itself. Against such general will, the individual could have no effective remedy. He could flaunt his judgment, obtained after a regular proceeding before the Administrative Tribunal, but he would have no way to force the United Nations to carry it out. This argument, however, casts too wide a net, since also in municipal law the possibility of enforcing judgments against the Public Administration is still today very far from being guaranteed in all countries.

As we noted, it is questioned whether the norms which regulate the status of staff members belong to an autonomous and original legal order (to an order which, like the legal order of a State, finds in itself the reason of its own force) or whether they draw their validity, through the Charter, from international law. This second solution seems to be the preferable one, in that it better underlines the uncontestable fact: that the rules regarding staff can never be in conflict with the Charter provisions. In fact, it was exactly in the light of the Charter that a good part of the question dealt with by the International Court of Justice, on the effects of Administrative Tribunal awards, was formulated and resolved. It is true that the supporters of the "original nature" of the United Nation's internal legal order usually consider the rules on staff members as subordinate to the Charter, maintaining that the Charter provisions are ambivalent and that they have, on the one hand, the nature of international norms and, on the other, that they can be construed as constitutional norms of an original legal system. The dispute over the "original nature" acquires then a purely theoretical value and thus can best be left to the philosophers.

36. *Privileges and immunities of UN Officials.*

BIBLIOGRAPHY: KUNZ, *Privileges and Immunities of International Organizations*, in *AJ*, 1947, p. 852 ff.; PREUSS, *Immunity of Officers and Employees of the United Nations for Official Acts: The Ranallo Case*, in *AJ*, 1947, p. 555 ff.; KING, *International Administrative Jurisdiction*, Brussel, 1952; BEDJAOUI, *Fonction publique internationale et influences nationales*, London, 1958, p. 173 ff.; JENKS, *International Immunities*, London, 1961, p. 111 ff.; BLOCH, *La fonction publique internationale et européenne*, Paris, 1963; LANGROD, *La fonction publique internationale*, Leiden, 1963; FOCARELLI, *L'ammissione al transito ed al soggiorno negli Stati Uniti della missione dell'OLP presso le Nazioni Unite*, in *CI*, 1989, p. 25 ff.; DAVID, *L'avis de la Cour Internationale de Justice du 15 déc. 1989 sur l' applicabilité de la section 22 del' art. VI de la Convention sur les privileges et immunités des Nation Unies (affaire Mazilu)*, in *AF*, 1989, p. 298 ff.; PONS RAFOIS, *Applicabilidad de la seccion 22 del articulo VI de la Convencion sobre los privilegios e immunidades de las Naciones Unidas (Opinion consultiva del Tribunal Internacional de Justicia de 15.12.1989)*, in *ReD*, 1991, p. 39 ff.; BOTHA, *Are United Nations Special Rapporteurs Entitled to Privileges and Immunities?*, in *South African Yearbook of International Law*, 1989/90, p. 191 ff.; OXMAN, *Difference Relating to Immunity from Legal Process of a Special Rapporteur of the Commission on Human Rights*, in AJ, 1999, p. 913 ff.

Customary law provides that diplomatic agents enjoy a series of privileges and immunities *vis-à-vis* domestic law (personal inviolability, exemption from civil and criminal jurisdiction, tax exemptions, and so on). By contrast, there do not exist customary rules which require States to grant the same treatment to the officers and employees of international organizations. Thus it is only by means of an agreement that a State may undertake such obligations. There are treaty provisions regarding the immunity of staff members of every organization. They can be contained in the convention which sets up the organization, in the agreements concluded by the organization with member or non-Member States, particularly with the State in which it has its headquarters, or, lastly, in agreements concluded between the Member States.

As far as Secretariat staff and, more generally, United Nations officials are concerned, the Charter is limited to confirming in Article 105, para. 2, a framework principle concerning immunity ("... officials of the Organization shall... enjoy such privileges and immunities as are necessary for the independent exercise of their functions..."), leaving to the General Assembly the task of proposing to the Member States the conclusion of agreements for a detailed regulation of the subject (Article 105, para. 3). Among the agreements presently in force, special mention should be given to the General Convention on the Privileges and Immunities of the United Nations, of February 3, 1946, to which a large number of States are party, and the Convention between the United Nations and Switzerland (a State where a number of offices of the Organization have their seats) of July 1, 1946.

These and numerous other conventions (which provide immunity for UN officials in individual countries: see, as examples, Article VIII of the United Nations-Thailand Convention of May 26, 1954 on the Economic Committee for Asia and the Far East; Article VI of the United Nations-Ethiopia Convention of June 18, 1958 on the Economic Committee for Africa; the United Nations-Egypt Convention of September 12, 1950 regarding the United Nations Office for Palestinian refugees; the United Nations-Jordan Convention of August 20, 1951; the United Nations-Egypt exchange of notes, of February 18, 1957, regarding the status of the United Nations Emergency Forces in Egypt) are collected in UNLS, *Legislative Texts and Treaty Provisions Concerning the Legal Status, Privileges and Immunities of International Organizations*, 1959, p. 183 ff. For more recent conventions, see the first part of UNJY where they appear under the heading "*Legal Status of the UN and Related Intergovernmental Organizations*".

Article VI, sect. 22, of the General Convention on the Privileges and Immunities of the United Nations provides that also experts who perform "missions" on behalf of the United Nations shall enjoy various immunities during the period of their missions, such as exemption from measures limiting their personal freedom, immunity regarding acts done by them in the exercise of their function, the inviolability of correspondence, the right to receive documents, and so on. Under the advisory opinion of the International Court of Justice of December 15, 1989, in the case of the *Applicability of Article VI, Section 22, of the Convention on the Privileges and Immunities of the United Nations* (in ICJ, *Reports*, 1989, p. 177 ff.), by "mission" there must be meant, within the meaning of sect. 22, not only the sending of experts in one or more countries but any task assigned to persons, such as the preparation of reports, the carrying out of research or investigations and the like. The opinion, issued upon the request of the Economic and Social Council, originated in the *Mazilu* case. Mr. Mazilu was a Romanian citizen who, in his individual capacity, was seated in the Subcommittee for the prevention of discrimination and the protection of minorities (a subsidiary organ of the Human Rights Commission, in turn a subsidiary organ of the Economic and Social Council). For political reasons, the Romanian government in power at the time prevented Mazilu from leaving Romania in order to reach the United Nations headquarters, from receiving documents from the United Nations, and from preparing a report assigned to him by the Subcommittee.

On Article VII, sect. 22, see also the Advisory opinion of the International Court of Justice of April 29. 1999, in the case of *Difference relating to Immunity from Legal Process of A Special Rapporteur of the Commission on Human Rights*. In this case the expert on mission on behalf of the United Nations, M. Cumaraswamy, was prosecuted in his country, Malaysia, for an interview given to a magazine, which was considered defamatory vis -a -vis Malaysian courts. The opinion is important not only because the Court confirms its previous judgment in the Mazilu case but also for the assertion that it is up to the Secretary-General to assess whether a UN agent has a right to immunity. In the Court's opinion, the national courts must given the greatest weight to the assessment of the Secretary-General, an assessment which creates a presumption in favour of immunity which can be rebutted only in exceptional circumstances.

Generally, treaty provisions on the immunity of UN officials are of two types. They either describe in detail the kind of immunity and its scope or they (and this is usually the case of rules concerning higher ranking officials) refer to the norms of customary international law regarding diplomatic immunity. As an example of the first type, there is section 18 of Article V of the cited general Convention, on the basis of which UN officials shall "... (*a*) Be immune from legal process in respect of words spoken or written and all acts performed by them in their official capacity; (*b*) Be exempt from taxation on the salaries and emoluments paid to them by the United Nations; (*c*) Be immune from national service obligations; (*d*) Be immune, together with their spouses and relatives dependent on them, from immigration restrictions and alien registration;..." and so on. As a rule of the second type, there is section 19 of the same Article V of the general Convention, which provides that, in addition to the immunities and privileges specified in section 18, the Secretary-General and all Assistant Secretaries General, together with their spouses and minor children, shall enjoy the "privileges and immunities, exemptions and facilities accorded to diplomatic envoys, in accordance with international law". The rules contained respectively in sections 15 and 16 of Article V of the Convention of July 1, 1946 between the United Nations and Switzerland are identical.

Special mention should be made with regard to the United States (the UN host country). The U.S adhered to the general Convention only in 1970. Prior to that time, the only norm binding this country on the international plane with regard to the immunities and privileges of UN officials was Article 105, para. 2, of the Charter. In fact, the headquarters agreement concluded between the United States and the Organization on June 26, 1947, did not contain specific rules on immunities. Nor can it be held, as some scholars maintained prior to 1970, that the agreement had incorporated the general Convention (sect. 26 of the agreement, under which "the provisions of the present agreement shall be complementary to the provisions of the General Convention...", far from proceeding to such incorporation, can be explained by the fact that the United States had stated in 1947 that it wished to accede *promptly* to the general Convention). Actually, the subject was regulated by domestic laws, both federal laws and New York State laws, including the *International Organizations Immunities Act* of 1945 and subsequent amendments.

The immunities and privileges of officials are granted in the interest of the Organization which, through the Secretary-General, may always waive them in specific cases. Section 20 of Article V of the general Convention (and similar provisions are contained in the other above-cited conventions) provides as follows: "The Secretary-General shall have the right and the duty to waive the immunity of any official in any case where, in his opinion, the immunity would impede the course of justice and can be waived without prejudice to the interests of the United Nations. In the case of the Secretary-General, the Security Council shall have the right to waive immunity".

If a UN Member State is not a party to any of the conventions on immunity, it is nevertheless bound by the principles of Article 105, para. 2. Its organs, and in particular, its courts, shall be in such case called upon the not easy task of interpretation and shall have to decide what immunities are actually necessary for the independent performance of the function. On the other hand, it does not seem that a very general formula, as is the one used by Article 105, para. 2, automatically involves the extension of all the usual diplomatic immunities to United Nations officials.

In the same sense, cf. the United States decision of November 11, 1946 by the City Court of New Rochelle in the *Westchester* v. *Ranallo* case in *Annual Digest of Public International Law Cases*, 1946, p. 168 ff. The American court rejected the argument of a UN employee (the Secretary-General's driver) that Article 105 would guarantee all officials and employees of the Organization the enjoyment of immunities and privileges belonging to diplomatic agents.

Since no immunity is granted by customary law, a non-Member State of the United Nations which is not bound by special treaty provisions has no obligation to concede immunities or privileges to Secretariat officials.

37. *The protection of UN Officials.*

BIBLIOGRAPHY: LIANG, *Notes on Legal Questions Concerning the United Nations — Reparations for Injuries Suffered in the Service of the United Nations*, in *AJ*, 1949, p. 460 ff.; WRIGHT, *Responsibility for Injuries to United Nations Officials*, *ibid.*, p. 95 ff.; ID., *The Juridical Personality of the United Nations*, *ibid.*, p. 509 ff.; EAGLETON, *International Organization and the Law of Responsability*, in *RC*, 1950, I, p. 323 ff.; SCHWELB, *The*

International Character of the Secretariat of the United Nations, in *BYB*, 1953, p. 80 ff.;
HARDY, *Claims by International Organizations in Respect of Injuries to their Agents*, in *BYB*,
1961, p. 516 ff.; WEISSBERG, *The International Status of the United Nations*, New York, 1961,
p. 170 ff.; RITTER, *La protection diplomatique à l'égard d'une organisation internationale*, in
AF, 1962, p. 427 ff.; SEYERSTED, *Objective International Personality of Intergovernmental
Organizations*, in *Nordisk Tidsskrift for International Ret*, 1964, p. 9 ff.; ID., *Jurisdiction over
Organs and Officials of States, the Holy See and Intergovernmental Organizations*, in *ICLQ*,
1965, p. 494 ff.; QUADRI, *Diritto internazionale pubblico*, 5th ed., Naples, 1968, p. 564 ff., 611
ff., 649 ff., 756 ff.; BLOOM, *Protecting Peacekeepers: The Convention on the Safety of United
Nations and Associated Personnel*, in *AJ*, 1995, p. 621 ff.; BOURLOYANNIS-VRAILAS, *The
Convention on the Safety of United Nations and Associated Personnel*, in *ICLQ*, 1995, p. 560
ff; RUZIÉ, *La sécurité du personnel des Nations Unies recruté sur le plan local*, in *Journal du
droit international*, 1999, p. 435 ff.; URIOS MOLINER, *La Conventión sobre seguridad del
personal de las Nacionas Unidas y el personal associado*, in *ADcI*, 1999 (XV), p. 547 ff.

If a UN official suffers injury against his person or his property while
he is on a mission in the territory of a State, what are the consequences with
regard to the relationship between this State and the Organization? The
question arose in the past and has arisen again in recent times with the tragic
attack on the headquarter of the UN Mission in Baghdad, which took place on
August 19, 2003. Such matters are regulated by the Convention on the Safety
of UN and Associated Personnel, signed in New York on December 9, 1994,
entered into force on January 15, 1999 and ratified up until now by 72 States.
The Convention states that State Parties "shall take all appropriate measures
to ensure the safety and security of UN and associated personnel…" (Article
7). The Convention does not envisage a duty on the State to indemnify either
the victim, or her/his relatives, or the United Nations, when an offense to a
UN official or associated person has occurred. It is rather necessary to explore
general international law in order to understand this matter.

Classic international law, and specifically the branch of international
law that concerns the treatment of aliens, provides for diplomatic protection.
The State whose citizen has suffered injury abroad, either to his person or to
his property, has the right to act at international level (with protests, requests
for arbitration, threat of reprisals or retaliation, and so on) against the State in
whose territory the wrong occurred and for the purpose of obtaining
compensation for damage. Does the United Nations have a similar right with
regard to its officials? And on what conditions and within what limits? The
question was the subject of an International Court of Justice opinion (in the
case of reparation for injurics suffered in the service of the United Nations, in
ICJ, *Reports*, 1949, p. 174 ff.), handed down in 1949 at the request of the
General Assembly and occasioned by the killing of several UN officials who
were in the Middle East to negotiate and oversee the truce between Arabs and
Jews.

The killing in Jerusalem on September 17, 1948 of Count Folke Bernadotte, sent by the UN as a mediator between Arabs and Jews, and of Colonel André P. Serot, a UN observer, gave rise to strong emotion at the time. The two crimes were committed by Jewish extremists and the Israeli government was immediately openly accused by the UN Secretary of not having taken suitable measures to prevent them.

To approach the subject of the protection of officials correctly and to evaluate the Court's opinion fully, let us begin with the subject of the treatment of aliens.

A general principle of international law imposes on the States the so-called duty to protect aliens. Under this principle, the State must make available suitable measures *to prevent and to punish* wrongful acts against the person or the property of an alien committed on its territory. The standard of suitability should be commensurate to what is usually made available for all individuals in a civilized State, that is, in a State "which normally sees to the need for order and security in the society under its control" (QUADRI). The duty of the territorial State to protect aliens *formally* exists with the State of which the alien is a national, even if, from the viewpoint of *substance*, its purpose is the protection of individual interests and property.

The general duty to protect also covers the case of the alien who is an organ or official of his own State and who is abroad on an official mission. With regard to measures aimed at *preventing* injury to aliens who are organs, especially injury to their person, the care taken by the territorial State must be greater than that taken for private aliens. If, for private persons, the State may limit itself to normal police supervision, for aliens who are organs it must adopt measures which are all the more intense the higher their rank and the more dangerous their mission. Indeed, the general principle of the protection of aliens requires the State to protect them with *suitable* measures. The suitability cannot but depend on the rank of the individual to be protected and the activity he is performing.

Moreover, although already assured by the general principle of the protection of all aliens, the protection of an alien who is an organ or an official is also contemplated and made obligatory by an *ad hoc* principle of international law. The specificity of such a norm is shown by the fact that it, unlike the more general principle, does not protect individual interests and property but an interest that is solely of the State: by safeguarding the person of the official or of the organ, the function of the State is safeguarded. The specificity of such norm becomes evident in the infrequent case of aliens who are citizens of one State and organs of another. The obligation of protection in such case exists, in international practice, both regarding the national State and regarding the State of which the alien is an organ. In the former case, it is to protect the citizen and, in the latter, to protect the State function.

As far as the pathological aspects of the subject are concerned, a State which fails to protect any foreign citizen on its territory is internationally obligated to pay compensation for damage. Such compensation, as we have already mentioned, may be the subject of international procedures by the State of which the injured individual is a citizen, the so-called diplomatic protection. Although it is the State which acts at international level, although compensation is due to it and only to it, and although it may also, for political reasons, decide not to take any action (and all this owing to the non-existence of individual rights at the international level), the fact is important that the general principle on the protection of aliens basically protects individual interests. It is well-known, in fact, that compensation concerns personal and property damage suffered by the victim and awarded on the assumption (an assumption usually verified) that it is intended, through the national State, for the victim himself or for persons entitled through him.

Also when the victim is a foreign organ or official on a mission, diplomatic protection is to be exercised by the national State on the basis of the above cited principle and in order to obtain compensation for damage for the victim or for his heirs. However, in such case the State may also complain that the rule for the protection of the State function has been violated and therefore claim that it be compensated for the damage caused to such function, that is to say, the damage that it has suffered through the loss or the injury of its organ or official. In fact this second claim may usually appear to be covered by diplomatic protection. However, it becomes a separate claim in the event, although quite rare, of an alien who is the organ or official of a State different from the State of which he is a national.

In the above framework the problem of the protection of UN officials must be inserted. This problem consists in asking whether the States in whose territory the officials are performing their function have obligations towards the United Nations that are identical or similar to those described above; whether towards the United Nations there exists a duty of protection of the function, and whether, next to this, there is also a duty of protection of the official as an individual; whether, as a result, the UN may act at the international level against the State that has failed to protect its official in order to compensate for the damage caused to the function and also (alongside the national State of the official) the damage caused to the victim himself or to persons entitled through him.

A rather different framing of the problem is found in the above-mentioned 1949 opinion of the International Court of Justice. This was because of the way the question put to the Court by the General Assembly was formulated.

The Assembly (resolution of December 3, 1948) had formulated its question as follows: "In the event of an agent of the United Nations in the performance of his duty suffering *injury in circumstances involving the responsibility of a State*, has the United Nations as an Organization the capacity to bring an international claim against the responsible government with a view to obtaining the reparation due in respect of the damage caused a) to the United Nations; b) to the victim or to persons entitled through him? In the event of an affirmative reply on point b), how is action by the United Nations to be reconciled with such rights as may be possessed by the State of which the victim is a national?" (ICJ, *Reports*, 1949, p. 175, our italics).

The Court declared at the outset that it took it for granted that the States, whether members or non-members of the United Nations, have an obligation to protect UN officials. The existence of an obligation to protect, it stated, is to be admitted since it implicitly results from the Assembly's question, and specifically from the part of the question which speaks of "circumstances involving the responsibility of a State". Therefore, to stay within the limits of the question (staying within such limits is a constant practice of the Court in its advisory function), it is necessary only to see what occurs after the failure of the obligation to protect and, in particular, whether the United Nations has the competence to bring an international claim (with protests, requests for submission to arbitral organs, to Committees of enquiry, and so on) for the reparation of damage caused either to itself or to the victim (*Reports*, cit., p. 177).

With all due respect, the Court in this way falls into a basic fallacy, whose consequences can be seen throughout the opinion. The fallacy consists in wanting to resolve the doubts pertaining to the procedural phase of the protection of United Nations officials, especially the doubt whether the Organization may act only for reparation of damage caused to the function or also for damage caused to the victim, without first clarifying what is the substantive regulation of the matter and particularly what is the content of the norms requiring the territorial State to protect the official on a mission. On the contrary, as we have seen with regard to the treatment of aliens, the possibility and the limits of an international legal action for reparation depend exactly on the way in which the matter is regulated at a substantive level.

Unquestionably, there exists a duty to protect UN officials (and the same can be said for other international organizations) in order to *protect the function*. Such duty derives from general international law and specifically from the application by analogy to the United Nations (as to other international organizations) of the principle that the State which accepts on its territory a foreign organ or official on a mission has an obligation, towards the State that the official represents, to protect him. The rationale of the principle, which consists in protecting the State function, easily covers the hypothesis of the function exercised for a collectivity of States.

Since it is a matter of the application of a rule of general international law, the obligation to protect falls on both Member States and non-Member States, obviously on the assumption that they have agreed that a UN mission be present on their territory. With regard to Member States, confirmation of the existence of the obligation may be implicitly found in several Charter provisions. There is, first of all, Article 2, para. 5, according to which "members shall give the United Nations every assistance in any action it takes in accordance with the present Charter...". There is also Article 105, para. 2, in the part in which it provides that officials of the Organization shall enjoy such privileges and immunities as are "necessary for the independent exercise of their functions in connection with the Organization". Since this last provision actually prescribes a privileged treatment of the official in protection of his function, it must be held that it implicitly prescribes the more limited obligation to protect.

Consequently, the United Nations may bring an international claim against a State which fails to protect an official adequately and request reparation for damage caused to his function, that is, damage that the Organization itself has suffered through the loss or injury of its agent.

Also the Court's opinion holds that the United Nations as subject of international law (a status that the Court forcefully recognised at a time when legal literature used to raise strong reservations about the personality of international organizations as distinct from the personality of Member States) may claim reparation for damage caused to the function against both Member States (*Reports*, cit., p. 180 f.) and non-Member States (*ivi*, p. 184 f.). However, the Court does not ask what the legal basis of the claim for reparation is. *What are the international rules whose violation may be invoked by the United Nations?* It does not ask this because, as we said above, it takes it for granted that an obligation to protect exists. It is clear, it says in substance, that if the State violates an obligation which it hypothetically has toward the Organization, it must compensate the damage caused to it!

Having said that, it is to be excluded that the States have, toward the United Nations, an obligation *to protect the official as an individual.* Consequently, it is to be excluded that the United Nations may bring an international claim against a State which has not adequately protected an official, after he has been admitted to its territory, for reparation of damage caused to the official himself.

This negative conclusion has to be reached first (and therefore at least with regard to non-Member States) from the viewpoint of general international law. It is not possible, in fact, to extend the very general principle which is applied with regard to the treatment of aliens and which imposes on the territorial State a duty to protect the individual. Such a duty is imposed vis-a-vis the State with which there exists the closest link, that is, the nationality link, which by its very nature justifies the capacity of the national State to act for the protection of individual interests. It would be absurd, in view of this, to set up an analogy between the relationship of citizenship and the relationship of mere service that links the official to the United Nations.

Still on the plane of customary international law, it is not possible to hold that a customary rule, of similar content to the rule on the treatment of foreign citizens, has grown up specifically with regard to the United Nations, or to international organizations in general. There do not exist sufficient elements in practice to support such a view. On the other hand, the growing up of a rule of this kind would have to have been accompanied (and there is also no trace of this in practice) by the taking away from the rules on the treatment of aliens the protection of all individuals who are UN officials or officials of any international organization. Indeed, it would be absurd if international law imposed the same obligation towards both the national State and the Organization, with the final result of allowing both of them to defend the interests of the individual and to claim reparation of damage caused to him or to persons entitled through him (*ne bis in idem*).

Neither, lastly, is there in the Charter a duty to protect similar to the one imposed by the rule on the protection of aliens. If the already cited provisions of Article 2, para. 5, with regard to assistance to the United Nations, and Article 105, para. 2, on the privileges and immunities of officials, testify in favour of a duty to protect the function, it would be completely arbitrary, in the absence of any textual or historical argument on the matter, to utilize them also for purposes of the protection of the official as an individual. The same can be said of Article 100 which confirms the independence of officials "from any government or any other authority external to the Organization", obligating the Member States to respect it. No stratagem can make this provision say that a UN agent is removed from the "authority" of the State of which he is a citizen as far as the defense of his individual interests is concerned. All that can perhaps be concluded is that the national State has a duty to consult with the United Nations if it intends to undertake legal action in diplomatic protection and such action might compromise the independence of the official. However, it is obvious how theoretical such an hypothesis is.

On the contrary, in its opinion of 1949 the Court firmly decided that the United Nations may act in the protection of the individual, asking reparation for damage caused to the victim or to persons entitled through him, that is, *from both Member States and non-Member States* (ICJ, *Reports*, cit., p. 181 ff. for Member States, p. 184 ff. for non-Member States). It is on this point (which has been criticised in legal literature) more than anywhere else that a certain superficiality of the opinion appears. With regard to the Member States, the Court refers to Article 2, para. 5, and Article 100 of the Charter but not in order to extract a rule imposing on the Member States the obligation to protect the official as an individual. The duty to protect, unfortunately not better specified, is still assumed as a hypothesis. From Article 2, para. 5, and Article 100, the Court infers only the United Nation's power to act in the protection of an official as an *implied power* (see § 5) necessary for the effective functioning of the Organization. With regard to non-Member States, the Court limits itself even to stating that United Nations action in defence of an individual is to be allowed... once the responsibility of the territorial State has been admitted, even by way of hypothesis.

According to the Court (*Reports*, cit., p. 185 f.), the UN action for individual damages would be in competition with that of the national State. The United Nations and the national State would however have to find a solution with "goodwill and good sense", taking into account that the State which failed in its obligation to protect would not be compelled to pay twice over!

The opinion of the Court has not been followed by a significant practice and is for this reason that, as we have said, a customary rule on the protection of the UN officials as individuals has not grown up.

Section IV

THE ECONOMIC AND SOCIAL COUNCIL
AND THE TRUSTEESHIP COUNCIL

38. *Composition and functions of the Economic and Social Council.*

BIBLIOGRAPHY: FINER, *The United Nations Economic and Social Council*, Boston, 1946; LEWIS, *The Economic and Social Council*, in WORTLEY, *The United Nations. The First Ten Years*, Manchester 1957, p. 34 ff.; TOWNLEY, *The Economic Organs of the United Nations*, in LUARD, *The Evolution of International Organizations*, New York, 1966, p. 246 ff.; SHARP, *The United Nations Economic and Social Council*, New York, 1969; SCHWELB, *The 1971 Amendment to Art. 61 of the UN Charter and the Arrangements Accompanying it*, in *ICLQ*, 1972, p. 497 ff.; VIRALLY, *L'Organisation mondiale*, Paris, 1972, p. 87 ff.; SCHWELB, *Entry into Force of the Second Amendment to Article 61 of the UN Charter*, in *AJ*, 1974, p. 300 ff.; RUCZ, *Le Conseil Economique et Social de l'O.N.U. et la coopération pour le développement*, Paris, 1983; OUNAIES, *La réforme du Conseil Economique et Sociale des Nations Unies*, in *Etudes internationales, 1998*, p. 55 ff.

The Council, which is a subsidiary organ of the General Assembly, in that it has the task of promoting international cooperation in the social and economic field "under the authority of the General Assembly" (Article 60), consists of 54 members of the United Nations who are elected for a three-year period (Article 61). They meet in regular session twice a year and in special session when the majority of its members so requires or in a series of other cases provided for in its rules of procedure (cf. Articles 1-4, rules of procedure).

The number of members of the Council was brought from 18 to 27 in 1965 (with the same resolution that increased the members of the Security Council from 11 to 15) and was then increased to 54 in 1971. The Assembly resolution which introduced the increase through an amendment to Article 61 (res. no. 2847-XXVI of December 20, 1971) entered into force on September 24, 1973 following ratification by two-thirds of the Member States as provided for by Article 108 of the Charter.

Besides the part relative to the amendment, the 1971 resolution contains a part in which the Assembly "decides... that... the members of the Economic and Social Council shall be elected according to the following pattern: *a*) Fourteen members from African States; *b*) Eleven members from Asian States; *c*) Ten members from Latin American States; *d*) Thirteen members from Western European and other States; e) Six members from the Socialist States [today, former Socialist States] of Eastern Europe". On the significance of the "decision", which has not been ratified by the States, the remarks concerning the similar "decision" which in 1965 accompanied the increase in the number of Security Council members (see § 22) are applicable.

Each member of the Council has one vote. Resolutions are adopted by a majority of the members present and voting (Article 67).

Article 60 of the Council's rules of procedure interprets the expression "members present and voting" as including only members who vote in favour of or against a resolution. This interpretation, identical to the one given by Article 88 of the General Assembly's rules of procedure seems correct for the same reasons applicable in the case of the Assembly (see § 31).

The rules of procedure (Article 41) provide also that, for decisions to be valid, the majority of members of the Council must be present. There may be some doubts as whether this provision is in conformity with the Charter, which is silent on the matter.

On the basis of Article 69, the "Economic and Social Council shall invite [*convie* in the French text] any member of the United Nations to participate, without vote, in its deliberations on any matter of particular concern to that Member". Unlike Article 31, which is concerned with invitations made by the Security Council (see § 29), Article 69 is formulated in such a way as to leave no margin for the organ's discretional power in deciding whether a subject is "of particular interest" for that State.

There are numerous subsidiary organs that have been set up by the Council over the years in accordance with Article 68 of the Charter ("The Economic and Social Council shall set up commissions in economic and social fields and for the promotion of human rights, and such other commissions as may be required for the performance of its functions"). The most important of these organs are the *functional Commissions* (for statistics, population, social development, human rights, the conditions of women, drugs, crime prevention and criminal justice, science and technical assistance for development, sustainable development, etc.) and the *regional economic Commissions* (for Europe, Asia and the Far East, Latin America, and Africa), all consisting of representatives of governments. However, to these two types of commissions there have been added a myriad of intergovernmental Committees and Committees of experts, such as the Economic Committee, the Committees for coordination, for housing, for building and planning, for the application of science and technology for development, and for development planning, and so on.

Under various aspects, the subsidiary organs of the General Assembly (see § 30) involved in the economic and social field are also linked up with the Council. Many of them (for example, UNICEF, UNCTAD, UNDP) must follow its directives. In turn, the Assembly, as the organ to whose "authority" the Council is subject, has the necessary power to give directives to the subsidiary organs of the Council as well as to the Council itself. In conclusion, *all* the UN organs operating in the economic and social field, all organs today competent in the field of development, may be considered arranged in a hierarchy with the General Assembly at the top and immediately below it the Economic and Social Council.

The impressive number of bodies concerned with development, their creation at different times, the similarity or the close affinity between their tasks and areas of competence have entailed that, despite the directing function assured by the Assembly and the Council, the whole machinery concerned with development has functioned in a very chaotic way, with little coordination and a great waste of energy. Beginning from the end of the 1970s the General Assembly has sought with a series of resolutions — deserving of special mention are res. 32/197 of December 20, 1977 and, more recently, res. 45/264 of May 13, 1991, res. 46/219 of December 20, 1991 and res. 46/235 of April 13, 1992 — to put some order in the system, mainly to eliminate waste, overlapping among organs and fragmentary interventions.

39. *The Trusteeship Council.*

BIBLIOGRAPHY: MERON, *The Question of the Composition of the Trusteeship Council*, in *BYB*, 1960, p. 250 ff.; GOODSPEED, *The Nature and Function of International Organization*, New York, 1967, p. 532 ff.; GOODRICH-HAMBRO-SIMONS, *Charter of the United Nations — Commentary and Documents*, New York, 1969, p. 519 ff.; BLUM, *The Composition of the Trusteeship Council*, in *AJ*, 1969, p. 747 ff.; RADIVOJEVIC, *United Nations Reform and the Position of the Trusteeship Council,* in *Review of International Affairs*, 1988, p. 27 ff.

This is an organ whose importance is now diminished, with the disappearance of the institution of trusteeship (an institution similar to the former mandate system of the League of Nations and consisting of a colonial type of government of territories under the control of the United Nations) as a result of de-colonization.

The Council operates under the direction of the Assembly (Article 87), except when it performs its functions with regard to territories considered totally or partially as strategic areas. In this case, it is subordinate to the Security Council (Article 83).

Under the Charter, its composition should vary. In fact, Article 86 states: "The Trusteeship Council shall consist of the following Members of the United Nations: *a*) those Members administering trust territories; *b*) such of those Members mentioned by name in Article 23 [the permanent members of the Security Council] as are not administering trust territories; and *c*) as many other Members elected for three-year terms by the General Assembly as may be necessary to ensure that the total number of members of the Trusteeship Council is equally divided between those Members of the United

Nations which administer trust territories and those which do not". However, in 1994, with the independence of Palau, the last remaining trust territory (belonging to the group of Marianne, Caroline and Marshall islands, all entrusted to the United States after the Second World War as strategic areas), the Trusteeship Council has ceased to be in operation.

Due to the disappearance of the institution of trusteeship, the Council has no work to perform for the time being. For some proposals which aim at giving it new functions see § 80.

Section V

THE INTERNATIONAL COURT OF JUSTICE

40. *Organization of the Court.*

BIBLIOGRAPHY: DUBISSON, *La Cour Internationale de Justice*, Paris, 1964, p. 11 ff.; ROSENNE, *The World Court*, 3rd ed., Leiden, 1973, p. 43 ff.; McWHINNEY, *The World Court and the Contemporary International Law-Making Process*, Alphen aan den Rijn, 1979; WALDOCK, *The International Court of Justice as Seen from Bar and Bench*, in *BYB*, 1983, p. 1 ff.; ROSENNE, *Procedure in the International Court: A Commentary on the 1978 Rules of the International Court of Justice*, The Hague, 1983; GUYOMAR, *Commentaire du règlement de la Cour Internationale de Justice*, 2nd ed., Paris, 1983; ROSENNE, *The Law and Practice of the International Court of Justice*, 2nd ed., Dordrecht, 1985, p. 165 ff.; McWHINNEY, *The International Court of Justice and the Western Tradition of International Law*, Dordrecht, 1987; STARACE, *Corte Internazionale di Giustizia*, in *Enciclopedia giuridica Treccani*, vol. IX, 1988; BENVENUTI, *Corte internazionale di giustizia*, in *Digesto (dir. pubbl.)*, vol. IV, 1989; ROSENNE, *The World Court. What it is and how it works*, 4th ed., Dordrecht, 1989; ORAISON, *L'evolution de la composition de la Cour Internationale de Justice siègeant en séance plenière de 1945 à nos jours*, in *Revue de dr. int., de sc. dipl. et pol.*, 1999, p. 61 ff.

The International Court of Justice is considered by Article 92 of the Charter as the "principal judicial organ of the United Nations", since it was basically intended to settle legal disputes between States. It organization is governed by a Statute annexed to the Charter which is an integral part of the Charter, as provided in Article 92.

The fifteen members of the Court are elected in a personal capacity (they do not represent their own State, nor may they "exercise any political or administrative function or engage in any other occupation of a professional nature": Article 16 of the Statute) and are chosen "among persons of high moral character, who possess the qualifications required in their respective countries for appointment to the highest judicial offices, or are jurisconsults of recognized competence in international law" (Article 2, Statute). Their term lasts nine years (five of the first judges served a term of nine years, five of six years and the other five of three years, in order to allow for partial renewal of the Court in the future), but they may be re-elected at the end of their term (Article 13, Statute). In the performance of their functions the judges enjoy diplomatic privileges and immunities (Article 19, Statute).

The privileges and immunities of the judges were specified in an agreement between the Court and the Dutch government (the seat of the Court is at the Hague) on June 26, 1946, and the agreement was approved by the General Assembly with res. no. 90-1 of December 11, 1946.

The Assembly resolution, besides approving the agreement, contains a recommendation addressed to all members of the United Nations. In it, it is requested that, if a judge is residing in a country different from the one in which he usually resides, in order to be "at any time" at the Court's disposal, he be given diplomatic immunities by the State of residence. It is also requested that diplomatic immunities be given by transit States, in case the judge has to travel for official reasons, and that all States recognise the passes issued by the Court to judges and to clerks and other employees of the Court.

The immunities recommended by the Assembly, especially those requested from the State of residence, do not seem completely justifiable in the light of Article 19 of the Statute which limits diplomatic immunities to the period when functions are being performed by the Court. Worthy of noting is also that the recommendation speaks of "judges" rather than "members of the Court" (the expression used in Article 19). As results from Assembly proceedings (cf. GAOR, 1st sess., 2nd part, 6th Comm., 22nd meet., p. 104 ff.) this was meant to refer not only to the 15 regular judges but also to the so-called *ad hoc* judges who, on the basis of Article 31 of the Statute, a State party to a case before the Court may appoint if none of the regular judges have the nationality of such State and there is a judge of the nationality of the other party. Under this aspect also, the Assembly recommendation seems more liberal than Article 19.

41. *Election of judges.*

BIBLIOGRAPHY: EAGLETON, *Choice of Judges for the International Court of Justice*, in *AJ*, 1953, p. 462 ff.; RUDZINSKI, *Election Procedure in the United Nations*, in *AJ*, 1959, p. 95 ff.; DUBISSON, *La Cour Internationale de Justice*, Paris, 1964, p. 31 ff.; BAILEY, *The General Assembly of the United Nations, A Study of Procedure and Practice*, New York, 1964, p. 184 ff.; ROSENNE, *Election of Members of the International Court of Justice: Late Nominations and Withdrawls of Candidacies*, in *AJ*, 1976, p. 546 ff.; ID., *The Election of Five Members of the International Court of Justice, ivi*, 1982, p. 364 ff.; MCWHINNEY, *Law, Politics and « Regionalism » in the Nomination and Election of World Court Judges*, in *Syracuse Journal of International Law*, 1986, p. 1 ff.; ORAISON, *L'evolution de la composition de la Cour Internationale de Justice etc.*, in *Revue du droit international de sciences diplomatiques et politiques*, 1999, p. 61 ff.

The election system is regulated by Articles 4-12 of the Statute of the Court. It is divided into the following phases.

First, the Secretary-General draws up a list of candidates, who have been nominated by the so-called national groups in the Permanent Court of Arbitration or, with regard to States which are not members of the 1907 Hague Convention which gave rise to this Court, from groups formed in a similar way (Articles 4-7). The national groups include experts in the field of international law appointed by their respective governments. In entrusting to them, rather than directly to the governments, the nomination of candidates for the office of judge of the International Court of Justice, the aim was to emphasise the irrelevance of political factors that *should* prevail on the subject.

The list of candidates is then submitted to the General Assembly and to the Security Council which proceed "independently of one another" to elect the judges (this is under Article 8; although they do not have a joint session, the Assembly and the Council usually meet at the same time). The candidates who obtain the absolute majority of votes in both organs are considered elected, with Article 10, para, 2, specifying that in the Security Council the right of veto by the permanent members may not be exercised. "If, after the first meeting held for the purpose of the election, one or more seats remain to be filled, a second and, if necessary, a third meeting shall take place" (Article 11).

If the Assembly and the Security Council do not succeed, after three meetings, in covering all or part of the vacant seats, the task of electing the judges passes to a committee of six members, of whom three are appointed by the Assembly and three by the Council (Article 12, paras. 1 and 2). If the committee is not successful either, the judges who are already on the Court shall proceed by co-option, drawing upon the list of candidates drawn up by the Secretary-General (Article 12, para. 3).

Various problems have been raised in practice with regard to the interpretation of the above rules. There was debate, for example, over the meaning of the term "meeting" adopted in Articles 11 and 12. During the first session, in February 1946, the General Assembly adopted the view that "meeting" meant "a vote" and that therefore after three unsuccessful votes, the appointment of the committee in Article 12 would become necessary. This interpretation seemed too restrictive to some delegates in the Assembly, particularly the delegate from El Salvador. He proposed, unsuccessfully, that meeting should mean the entire day, with the possibility, therefore, of more than one vote on the same day (for the debate, see GAOR, 1st sess., 1st part, Pl. meet., 24th meet., p. 344 f.). The problem was then resolved by Article 151 of the Assembly rules of procedure and Article 61 of the Security Council rules of procedure, which have the same wording, and according to which "any meeting of the Assembly (or of the Council) held... for the purpose of the election of members of the Court shall continue until as many candidates as are required for all the seats to be filled have obtained in one or more ballots an absolute majority of votes". The two articles thus codify an expedient which is often resorted to in the practice of collegial bodies. This consists in considering a session extended until it reaches the purpose for which it is being held. In this way, however, the possibility envisaged by Article 12 (the appointment of a committee after three unsuccessful meetings) narrows to the sole eventuality, which has never occurred, that, for three times, the lists of those elected respectively by the Assembly and the Council do not coincide.

It has been also asked whether Article 10, para. 1, in providing that the Assembly and the Council vote by "absolute majority" means half plus one of those voting or half plus one of the members of the body. Although the text of the provision ("absolute majority *of votes*"), tends toward the former solution, it is rather ambiguous. By contrast, the second interpretation is clearly supported by the preparatory works, during which it was said that the adjective "absolute" was adopted (as it is adopted in American practice) to mean a majority of the members of the body: see U.N.C.I.O., vol. 17, p. 330. The practice has conformed to this solution: cf. UN Rep., vol. I, *sub* Article 18, no. 23. Lastly, as Article 10 speaks of absolute majority, the votes necessary in the Security Council are 8 out of 15 and not 9 out of 15 as prescribed in general by Article 27 of the Charter for Council decisions.

CHAPTER THREE

THE FUNCTIONS

Section I

GENERAL LIMITS TO UNITED NATIONS FUNCTIONS

42. *Limits* ratione personae *and* ratione materiae.

Article 1 of the Charter, in listing the purposes of the United Nations and in thereby indicating the areas in which the Organization may act, adopts a very flexible and general formulation (see § 2). On the basis of Article 1, there is practically no subject, whether pertaining to the political sphere or to the economy or to social and cultural relations, and so forth, that cannot come within the competence of the United Nations.

Owing to the indeterminacy of the UN's purposes, the Charter provisions, from which it is possible to deduce some general limits to the Organization's activity, have special significance. They contribute, although from a negative point of view, towards better clarification of the sphere of its competence. The first limit is a limit *ratione personae*. This can be found in the provisions which establish when the United Nations may be concerned with relations involving non-Member States. Since the United Nations has reached universality, this limit has no practical relevance. Then, there is the limit *rationae materiae*, the so-called limit of domestic jurisdiction, to which the Charter dedicates Article 2, para. 7: "Nothing contained in the present Charter shall authorise the United Nations to intervene in matters which are essentially within the domestic jurisdiction of any State...". The provision of Article 2, para. 7, is a true key provision in the Charter system and, as such, has given rise to very animated discussion and disagreement within the United Nations. Although, as we shall see, the limit of domestic jurisdiction has undergone some important customary restrictions, it still plays a role in the UN system.

43. *The United Nations and non-Member States.*

BIBLIOGRAPHY: WEINBERG, *Völkerbund und Nichmitgliedsstaaten*, Münster, 1932; KELSEN, *Sanctions in International Law Under the Charter of the UN*, in *Iowa Law Review*, 1946, p. 499 ff.; ID., *Membership in the UN*, in *Columbia Law Review*, 1946, p. 410 f.; VERDROSS, *Nazioni Unite e terzi Stati*, in *CI*, 1947, p. 439 ff.; KUNZ, *Revolutionary Creation of Norms in International Law*, in *AJ*, 1947, p. 123 ff.; KELSEN, *The Law of the United Nations*, London, 1950, p. 106 ff.; FALK, *The Authority of the United Nations over Non-Members*, Princeton, 1965; BINDSCHEDLER, *Das Problem der Beteiligung der Schweiz an Sanktionen der Vereinten Nationen, besonders im Falle Rhodesiens*, in *Bruns'Z*, 1968, p. 5 ff.; SCHNECK, *Das Problem der Beteilgung der Bundesrepublik Deutschland an Sanktionen der Vereinten Nationen, besonders im Falle Rhodesiens*, in *Bruns'Z*, 1969, p. 269 ff.; FALK, *The Authority of the United Nations to Control Non Members*, in *The Status of Law in International Society*, Princeton, 1970, p. 5 ff.; THURER, *UN Enforcement Measures and Neutrality — The Case of Switzerland*, in *AV*, 1992, p. 69 ff.; SCHINDLER, *Kollektive Sichereit der Vereinten Nationen und dauerne Neutralität der Schweiz*, in *Schw. Z.*, 1992, p. 458 ff.

The problem of the relations between the United Nations and non-Member States, which was strongly felt particularly in the early years of the post-war period, has lost its importance as the Organization has become universal. Since Switzerland joined the United Nations in 2002, the only two States which are outside the Organization are Taiwan and the Turkish Republic of Cyprus (see § 1 B). Nevertheless, the problem still deserves some observations. This is because it may occur that a newly formed State goes through a period of time while waiting to be admitted and in the meantime there is the problem of its relations with the United Nations. Such event occurred, for instance, in the case of the Republic of Yugoslavia (Serbia-Montenegro) which was admitted to the United Nations (see § 18) in November 2000, but ceased to have formal links with the former Yugoslavia in September 1992. Article 2 of the Charter lists, from para. 1 to para. 5, the principles on which the Organization is based, requiring, in particular, that the Member States: fulfill in good faith the Charter obligations (para. 2); peacefully settle their disputes (Article 3); abstain from the threat or use of force (Article 4); assist the Organization in the actions it takes and refrain from assisting States against which the Organization is taking preventive or enforcement action (para. 5). After this, para. 6 of Article 2 provides: "The Organization shall ensure that states that are not members of the United Nations act in accordance with these Principles so far as may be necessary for the maintenance of international peace and security".

What are the kinds of pressure that the United Nations may use with regard to a third State in order to reach the aim set in Article 2, para. 6? As the provision is silent on the matter, the answer must be found in the specific rules of the Charter on the powers of the organs, especially of the General Assembly and of the Security Council, concerning maintenance of the peace.

Article 2, para. 6, must be linked, first of all, to the use of those kinds of pressure that have no mandatory effect. Both the General Assembly and the Council have the power to make recommendations to the States, that is, resolutions that do not bind the States (see § 89)). Worthy of mention from this point of view are the provisions of Article 11, para. 2 ("The General Assembly may discuss any questions relating to the maintenance of international peace and security... and... may make recommendations with regard to any such questions to the State or States concerned") and the various provisions of Chapter VI, particularly Article 33, para. 2, Article 36, and Article 37, para. 2, which give the Security Council the power to recommend settlement of disputes likely to endanger the peace. All the provisions cited, in indicating the addressees of the recommendations with expressions such as "States concerned" or "parties to a dispute" and thereby avoiding, unlike a number of other provisions, reference to only the Member States, clearly intend to apply also to third States. Consequently, Article 2, para. 6, does not add anything more than what can be already inferred directly from these provisions.

Article 2, para. 6, must then be connected to Chapter VII of the Charter, specifically with regard to Articles 39, 41, and 42 which authorise the Security Council, for purposes of maintenance of the peace, to take enforcement measures against States. Under the procedures governed by these articles, the Council shall "determine the existence of any threat to the peace, breach of the peace, or act of aggression" (Article 39). Then, it may order the so-called measures not involving the use of armed force, such as interruption of economic relations by the UN Member States with the country responsible for the threat or aggression (Article 41), or undertake military action, if it believes that the measures not involving the use of armed force are or have proved to be inadequate (Article 42). Also the provisions of Articles 39, 41 and 42 are formulated in such a way as to be interpreted in the sense that any country, member or non-member, may be the object of enforcement measures. Article 2, para. 6, therefore, does not add anything to these provisions either.

In authorising the United Nations to take action with regard to countries outside the Organization, it does not seem that Article 2, para. 6, or, rather, the various provisions of the Charter which have been cited here, involve a serious departure from customary international law, particularly from the rule that treaties cannot create obligations for third States. A departure of this kind cannot be seen in the power of the Assembly and the Security Council to address recommendations to third parties, since they are acts that, by definition, are not binding on the addressees. No issue arises, then, if the Council addresses recommendations to a non-Member State. Nor is the conclusion different with regard to enforcement measures that the Council may adopt against a State on the basis of Chapter VII of the Charter.

Actually, since such measures, even those not involving the use of armed force, are envisaged in the event of a threat to, or a breach of, the peace, they postulate the existence of an armed conflict, both international or internal, or of a situation very close to it. When adopted with regard to non-Member States, they appear as measures taken against another State by a group of States, or by all the States within the international community and which have entrusted to the Security Council, as stated in Article 24, para. 1, of the Charter, "primary responsibility for maintenance of international peace and security". Situations of this kind have always existed and have always given rise to actions and reactions which, amounting to one of the pathological aspects in the life of the relations between States, escape a precise evaluation under international law and, even more, under the principle of the non-effect of treaties, with regard to third parties. From this point of view, it must rather be said that the above provisions of Chapter VII, far from creating obligations for non-Member States, are provisions... in their favour. This is because, unlike what occurs in traditional war situations, *the Security Council is bound to the observance of Charter, especially as far as procedures are concerned.*

It is indicative in this respect that hardly ever in practice have non-Member States (or their supporters in the United Nations) raised the objection of non-membership whenever the Council or the Assembly have made them the object of measures such as those governed by Chapter VII. They have nearly always preferred to resort to other objections, such as the non-observance of procedural rules by the two organs, the violation of the domestic jurisdiction principle under Article 2, para. 7, the Assembly's lack of competence on the basis of Chapter VII, and so on. To give a recent example, also in the case of the Republic of Yugoslavia (Serbia-Montenegro), which between 1992 and 2000 was not a UN member, (see § 18) and against which the Security Council has had recourse to Article 41 of the Charter (see § 58), it does not seem that the objection of non-membership in the Organization was ever raised.

For less recent practice, we may recall that, when between April and June 1946, the Security Council, at the request of Poland (a request expressly based on Article 2, para. 6), was discussing whether or not to resort to the measures in Chapter VII against Franco's government in Spain, at the time a non-member, the objections which were raised by some States and which eventually prevented the Council from taking action, were all based on Article 2, para. 7. They were based on the fact that the Fascist nature of the government was a purely domestic situation and as such unlikely to threaten international peace and security (cf. SCOR, 1st year, 34th meet. and 44th-49th meets.). Also in the discussions that took place over the UN actions against North Korea and Communist China, in 1950-51, there is no trace, not even in the statements by the representatives of the People's Republic who were sometimes allowed to participate in the proceedings, of objections based on the non-membership of the two States in the Organization. In this case, the Security Council adopted two resolutions, respectively, no. 83 of June 27, 1950 and no. 84 of July 7, 1950, which accused North Korea of aggression and recommended that the Member States intervene with military means in the defence of South Korea. The Soviet Union sternly challenged the two resolutions, mainly for the reason that the Security Council had decided in its absence. It challenged also the participation of the representative of Nationalist China, which, in its opinion, constituted a violation of Article 27, para. 3, of the Charter (see § 25). As for the Assembly, it recommended an embargo on all war material directed toward China and North Korea (res. no. 500-V of May 18, 1951), which gave rise to objections, by the Communist Bloc States, which were based only on the lack of competence of this organ to take measures under Article 41 (cf. GAOR, 5th sess., Pl. meet., 330th meet., n. 37 ff., 64 ff., 85 ff., and 101 ff.). Also res. no. 221 of April 9, 1966 and no. 232 of December 16, 1966, adopted by the Security Council, can be cited. The two resolutions were adopted under Chapter VII, against Southern Rhodesia and objected to in the same year by South Africa and Portugal, although solely regarding alleged violations of procedural rules (see doc. S/7271 and S/7392).

In conclusion, Article 2, para. 6, appears to be a simple provision on the powers of the Organization. It confirms in general terms the powers that the Assembly and the Security Council have available towards non-Member States regarding maintenance of the peace. These powers are already envisaged by specific Charter provisions and are not in any way particularly revolutionary from the viewpoint of customary international law.

It has been asked whether the non-Member State which refuses to co-operate with the Security Council in actions taken against a State responsible for threatening the peace or for aggression contravenes the prohibition against threatening or using force or in any case is responsible for complicity with the aggressor. As it has been pointed out (cf. THURER, *art. cit.*, p. 75) these views do not seem convincing and are not confirmed by practice.

The practice we are referring to, which revolved around Switzerland before 2002, testifies that this State has nearly always co-operated with the Council with regard to measures not involving the use of armed force. Sometimes, however, it has not fully co-operated. For example, it did not do so in the case of the economic sanctions against Southern Rhodesia, decreed by res. no. 232 of December 16, 1966. In a note of February 13, 1967, addressed to the Secretary-General, the Swiss government stated that it "cannot submit to the mandatory sanctions of the United Nations" and offered only to control imports from Rhodesia so that its territory would not be a place of transit for goods directed to other countries (see SCOR, 22nd Suppl. for Jan., Feb., March, 1967, p. 117). In any case, it seems that Swiss participation in sanctions was usually the result of free choice rather than the fulfilment of a true legal obligation: cf., for example, the *note verbal* of November 8, 1990 to the Secretary-General (in Doc. S/AC.25/1990/33) which stated that Switzerland would "independently" apply the air embargo measures against Iraq, provided for by res. no. 670 of 1990.

Various other Charter provisions concern non-Member States. Under Article 32, such States must be invited to Security Council discussions concerning disputes to which they are a party (see § 29). They may bring before the Council or the Assembly any dispute to which they are a party as long as they accept the obligations of peaceful settlement provided by the Charter. They may, lastly, under Article 50, consult the Security Council in seeking to resolve possible economic difficulties caused to them by a measure taken by the Council in protection of the peace. The problem of whether real rights for non-Member States derive from these provisions is purely theoretical. The objection that is usually raised with regard to the possibility that an agreement creates rights for third parties is that the parties to the agreement may refuse to the third parties, even in individual cases, benefits which accrue to such rights. This objection is not, however, conclusive here, since the third party faces not individual States but organs obligated to respect the Charter.

Worthy of mention are also the provisions of Articles 102 and 103. The former provides that agreements entered into by the Member States, and therefore also agreements entered into with non-Member States, cannot be invoked before UN organs if they are not registered with the Secretariat. Article 1, no. 3, of the *Regulations on the Implementation of Article 102 of the Charter*, adopted by General Assembly res. no. 97-I of December 14, 1946 (and amended by resolutions 364 B-IV of December 1, 1949, 482-V of December 12, 1950 and 33-141 A of December 19, 1978) establishes that "registration may be made by any of the contracting parties", meaning by this, as was specifically said in the Assembly when such regulations were drawn up, that also non-Member States may register a treaty (cf. *UN Rep.*, *sub* Article 102, no. 43 f.). The provision of Article 103 confirms the prevalence of the obligations "of the members of the United Nations under the present Charter" over their obligations "under any other international agreement". Such provision is clearly aimed at the Member States, but it too may involve third States in the sense that the latter certainly could not invoke before the UN organs agreements entered into with member countries that were in conflict with the Charter provisions.

As far as we know, the fact that the provisions of Articles 32, 35, para. 2, 50, 102 and 103 concern non-Member States has never given rise to questions in practice.

44. *The domestic jurisdiction clause (Article 2, para. 7).*

BIBLIOGRAPHY: ULLMANN, *Ausschliessliche Zuständigkeit der Staaten nach Völkerrecht*, Bonn-Köln-Berlin, 1933; PREUSS, *Art. 2 para. 7 of the Charter of the UN and Matters of Domestic Jurisdiction*, in *RC*, 1949, vol. 74, p. 547 ff.; RAJAN, *United Nations and Domestic Jurisdiction*, 2nd ed., London, 1961; BINDSCHEDLER, *La délimitation des compétences des Nations Unies*, in *RC*, 1963-I, p. 391 ff.; ROSS, *La notion de « compétence nationale » dans la pratique des Nations Unies*, in *Mélanges offerts à Henry Rolin*, Paris, 1964, p. 284 ff.; VERDROSS, *La « competence nationale » dans le cadre de l'Organisation des Nations Unies et l'indépendance des Etats*, in *RGDIP*, 1965, p. 314 ff.; ID., *Les affaires qui relèvent essentiellement de la compétence nationale d'un Etat d'après la Charte des Nations Unies*, in *« Akrothinia » Vallindas*, Salonicco, 1966, p. 45 ff.; ID., *The Plea of Domestic Jurisdiction Before an International Tribunal and a Political Organ of the United Nations*, in *Bruns'Z*, 1968, p. 33 ff.; SPERDUTI, *Il dominio riservato*, Milan, 1970; ID., *Competenza nazionale e competenza internazionale nel sistema delle Nazioni Unite*, in *CI*, 1970, p. 494 ff.; OUCHAKOV, *La compétence interne des Etats et la non-intervention dans le droit contemporain*, in *RC*, 1974, I, p. 1 ff.; CONFORTI, *La nozione di Domestic Jurisdiction nelle riserve all'accettazione della competenza della Corte Internazionale di Giustizia*, in *CS*, 1975 (XIV), p. 215 ff.; CANÇADO TRINDADE, *The Domestic Jurisdiction of States in the Practice of the UN and Regional Organizations*, in *ICLQ*, 1976, p. 715 ff.; WATSON, *Autointerpretation, Competence and the Continuing Validity of Article 2 (7) of the UN Charter*, in *AJ*, 1977, p. 60 ff.; JONES, *The United Nations and the Domestic Jurisdiction of States*, Cardiff, 1979; SANG-

SEEK, *Domestic Jurisdiction in the UN*, in *Korean Journal of International Law*, 1986, p. 96 ff.; DELANEY, *Article 2(7) of the UN Charter: Hindrance to the Self-Determination of Western Sahara and Eritrea?*, in *Emory International Law Review*, 1990, p. 413 ff.; ARANGIO-RUIZ, *Le domaine réservé (Cours général de droit international public)*, in *RC*, 1990, VI, p. 1 ff.

"Nothing contained in the present Charter", states *Article* 2, para. 7, "shall authorise the United Nations to intervene in matters which are essentially within the domestic jurisdiction of any State or shall require the members to submit such matters to settlement under the present Charter; but this principle shall not prejudice the application of enforcement measures under Chapter VII".

The limit of domestic jurisdiction (in French, *domain reservé*) is the only general *ratione materiae* limit on the activity of the Organization. It has been much discussed in practice, and much has been written about it in legal doctrine. Various positions have been taken on its precise sphere of application. They range from the more conservative views — defended to the nth degree by the Socialist States — which tend to widen such sphere, to the more progressive ones more favourable to international co-operation in different areas of the domestic life of States. The latter hold that such limit has nearly been eliminated in practice, since there is almost no matter that lies outside the Organization's authority.

Article 2, para. 7, has as a precedent Article 15, para. 8, of the Covenant of the League of Nations. The Covenant provision, however, did not limit the authority of the whole League but only that of the Council, with regard to the peaceful settlement of disputes. It reads as follows: "If the dispute between the parties is claimed by one of them, and is found by the Council, to arise out of a matter which by international law is solely within the domestic jurisdiction of that Party, the Council shall so report, and shall make no recommendation as to its settlement". The Dumbarton Oaks proposals (see 1 A) were directly inspired by this rule. The provision in the proposals was nearly identical to the one in the Covenant, placing a limitation only on the Security Council with regard to the peaceful settlement of international disputes.

Chapter VIII, Sec. A., of the Dumbarton Oaks proposals (corresponding to what is now Chapter VI of the Charter), after having described in paragraphs 1 to 6 the functions of the Security Council with regard to the pacific settlement of disputes, provided as follows in paragraph 7: "The provisions of paragraphs 1 to 6 of Section A should not apply to situations or disputes arising out of matters which by international law are solely within the domestic jurisdiction of the state concerned". The most important difference in this text with respect to that of Article 15, para. 8, of the Covenant laid in eliminating the Council's authority to decide whether or not a matter was within domestic jurisdiction.

It was at the San Francisco Conference, on the initiative of the sponsoring States that the present wording of Article 2, para. 7, was agreed upon. This provision differs from the former provision in the Covenant not only because it has been elevated to a general principle limiting the activity of the whole Organization (with the sole exception of the enforcement measures under Chapter VII of the Charter) but also because of the very different way in which it indicates the limit of domestic jurisdiction ("matters which are *essentially* within the domestic jurisdiction" of a State, rather than a "matter which *by international law* is *solely* within the domestic jurisdiction" of a State), and, lastly, because it does not say who is to decide whether or not a matter is within domestic jurisdiction.

The principal problems of interpretation that Article 2, para. 7, has raised can be listed as follows: A) What is meant by domestic jurisdiction? B) What meaning does the word "intervene", used in para. 7, have, and, therefore, what activities of the Organization are subject to the domestic jurisdiction clause? C) What importance does the exception in the last part of para. 7 have, in which the domestic jurisdiction clause cannot be invoked regarding the application of "enforcement measures" under Chapter VII? D) Who is to decide whether or not a matter is within domestic jurisdiction?

45. A) *The notion of domestic jurisdiction.*

BIBLIOGRAPHY: see § 44.

Three issues need to be analysed in this paragraph. First of all it is important to recall the notion of domestic jurisdiction in force at the time of the League of Nations with regard to Article 15, para. 8, of the Covenant (the so-called legal notion of domestic jurisdiction). One must then ask if and in what sense Article 2, para. 7, accepted a different notion, and, lastly, one must seek to establish whether the practice has given rise on this matter to unwritten rules which have become superimposed on the Charter.

I. *The legal notion.*

In allowing international law to decide which matters are within the exclusive competence of the State, Article 15, para. 8, of the Covenant of the League of Nations adopted what can be called the legal notion of domestic jurisdiction. This notion had its fullest, most precise and most acceptable formulation in a well-known decision of the Permanent Court of International Justice in 1923. Domestic jurisdiction, said the Court, includes matters in which the State *is free from international obligations* of any kind; only in these matters, in fact, is it the exclusive *"maitre de ses décisions"*. The description given by the Court was then purely *negative*.

> The Court opinion (PCIJ, *Series B*, no. 4, p. 7 ff.) was handed down on February 7, 1923, at the request of the Council of the League of Nations. A dispute between France and Great Britain concerning certain decrees issued by France in Tunisia and Morocco had been brought before the Council. These decrees had conferred, in certain circumstances, French nationality on aliens, among them, British subjects born in these territories. The French view was that the Council was not competent in the disputes, as a matter of citizenship was within the domestic jurisdiction of the State under Article 15, para. 8, of the Covenant. Great Britain held the opposite view, maintaining that the two decrees violated international obligations which France had undertaken towards it. After having given the above cited definition of domestic jurisdiction (p. 23 f.), the Court held that the question of citizenship belonged, in principle, to domestic jurisdiction in that it was a matter not regulated by international law, but stated that in the case before it France's objection had to be rejected since it was a question of deciding whether or not the French measures violated agreements made with Great Britain (p. 24 ff.)
>
> The legal notion of domestic jurisdiction was confirmed by the Permanent Court in its judgement of August 30, 1924 in the *Mavrommatis* case (PCIJ, *Series A*, no.2).

From the definition given by the Court, what is clear, first of all, is the *relative* nature of domestic jurisdiction, which depends on the range of international obligations undertaken by a particular State. More specifically, since international obligations arise either from general customary law or from treaty law and since the former are equal for all States, the sphere of domestic jurisdiction of each country varies in function of the number of treaties which it has entered into. The question whether or not a matter is within the domestic competence of a given State depends on whether this matter is regulated by customary international law and, moreover, whether, although unrelated to customary law, it is the subject of obligations freely agreed upon by such State. Of course, if such a treaty obligation exists, then the matter will cease to belong to the domestic jurisdiction of the State solely with regard to the relationships within the contracting Parties.

The legal notion of domestic jurisdiction has then a *historical* nature, since the number of obligations weighing on States may vary in time as a result of the (continual) evolution of both international customs and treaties.

Can there be a *positive* notion of domestic jurisdiction? In other words, what are, at least *roughly*, matters in which international law does not impose obligations on the States?

With regard to customary law, the traditional view has always been that the State does not suffer limitations with regard to the treatment of its own *citizens*, or regarding its own *organization of government*, or, lastly, in activities concerning the use of its own *territory*. This formula, which calls to mind the classic "elements" of a State, can still be used today, but only with great caution. Although it still corresponds – indeed with some important exceptions (see § 44 III) - to reality with respect to the organization of governmental powers and to the utilisation of the territory, a different view must be taken with regard to relations between the State and its own subjects. This is so because of the far-reaching developments that the protection of human rights has also undergone from the viewpoint of customary international law. Consequently, the formula must be verified case by case.

As for treaty law, it would be absurd to go into depth regarding the matters it does not regulate, as this would involve... a listing of the conventions entered into by each country. Generally speaking, one can say that the States, which once were certainly reluctant to undertake obligations in the matters left to domestic competence by customary international law (so that the two spheres of domestic jurisdiction, under customary law and under treaty law, in the end almost coincided), have now modified this position. The most significant aspect of the development of treaty law today is the tendency for treaty norms to invade all sectors of a State's domestic life. Apart from agreements regarding the protection of human rights, worthy of mention are the many kinds of treaties which have assured co-operation in the economic, social and cultural fields, in particular, those treaties which provide for economic integration among the contracting parties, by substituting domestic law in the regulation of customs tariffs, foreign trade relations and so on.

II. *The notion under Article 2, para. 7.*

While Article 15, para. 8, of the Covenant speaks of a "matter which by international law is solely within the domestic jurisdiction of the State", Article 2, para. 7, of the Charter takes away from the UN's sphere of action "matters which are essentially within the domestic jurisdiction". What is the importance of the change and, in particular, of eliminating the reference to international law? Must it be held, as many do, that the legal notion has been substituted by another one of a different nature? And if so, which?

It does not seem that the framers of the Charter intended to make radical or revolutionary changes in the notion of domestic jurisdiction that had been affirmed at the time of the League of Nations. The preparatory works do not offer any traces of such changes. Indeed, the most important element offered by the San Francisco Conference proceedings is, as legal scholars well know, the speech made by the American delegate John Foster Dulles on behalf of the sponsoring powers regarding the text of Article 2, para. 7, to explain the reasons why it was formulated differently from Article 15, para. 8, of the Covenant. It is considered authoritative, not only because of the prestige of the speaker but also because it expressed the viewpoint of the powers that had drawn up Article 2, para. 7. From this speech, and also from the statements of the delegates of other countries, it is possible to conclude that the elimination of the reference to international law and the substitution of the adverb "essentially" ("matters which are essentially within the domestic jurisdiction") for the adverb "solely" in Article 15, para. 8, was not meant to disavow the old legal notion of domestic jurisdiction but only to widen its scope. In what sense? The drafters of Article 2, para. 7, were mainly concerned about the possibility that international conventions relating to matters traditionally within domestic jurisdiction (relations between State and citizen, economic policy, etc.) would continue to increase. These were matters which the Charter itself (for example, the provisions concerning respect for human rights in Articles 55 and 56) made the object of international co-operation. Besides the matters in which a country was free from *any whatsoever* international obligation (as under Article 15, para. 8, of the Covenant), they also wanted to remove from the UN's sphere of action those matters in which a country was bound by agreements only by way of exception since such matters would *normally* come within the sphere of freedom of the States. In short, the drafters wanted everything that *in principle* (that is, despite the existence of individual agreements) was not regulated by international rules to be subject to the limit of domestic jurisdiction. The formula "matters *essentially* [and no longer solely] within the domestic jurisdiction" was deemed the most suitable for expressing this intention.

Dulles' speech can be found in the *Verbatim Minutes* of Committee 1 of Commission 2 of the Conference, unpublished (on microfilm at the UN Library in Geneva). Actually, the summary appearing in U.N.C.I.O., vol. 6, p. 507 f., omits the most interesting passages (passages that can also be found in RAJAN, *op. cit.*, pp. 42-44). The speech as a whole tends to present the limit of domestic jurisdiction under Article 2, para. 7, as *broadened* with respect to the limit in Article 15, para. 8, of the Covenant. Such broadening was made necessary by the remarkable extension of the UN's sphere of action and was aimed at preventing a State from being brought before the Organization for the sole fact of having concluded an agreement on a matter usually not regulated by international law. Particularly enlightening on this is the passage in which Dulles explains why the reference to international law has been abolished. What, he wonders, should this reference mean? "Does it mean that whenever you have a treaty which deals with any subject that treaty is international law, and therefore the fact that a subject is dealt with by a treaty means that it is no longer domestic?... Does it mean that because this Charter is a treaty which makes international law, every subject which it deals with is no longer a matter of domestic jurisdiction? If so... the whole purpose of that limitation is done away with, because it would mean that all these matters we talk about [economic and social relations], this whole social life of every State which is dealt with... by this Charter would, under the interpretation of the international law phrase, be no longer a matter of domestic jurisdiction, and therefore, the whole effect of the limitation swept away". In line with this passage, then, there is the part of the speech which supports the substitution of the adverb "essentially" for the adverb "solely" used in Article 15, para. 8, of the Covenant. The use of the adverb "solely", Dulles says, "would destroy the whole legal effect of the limit of domestic jurisdiction; indeed, what today in the world is solely domestic?"

Also a statement by the Australian delegate must be cited (Australia took a very active part in the approval of Article 2, para. 7, and was responsible for the final formulation of the last part of the article relating to cases not within the limit of domestic jurisdiction; see § 46). This statement was contrary to a Belgian proposal intending to reinsert in the text of Article 2, para. 7, both the reference to international law and the adverb "solely" in place of "essentially". Regarding the reference to international law, the Australian delegate stated that he believed "*that there was no other possible criterion that could be used*" and that, therefore, he did not see the necessity of mentioning it in the article. With regard to the adverb "exclusively", the Australian delegate "agreed with Mr. Dulles that matters *solely* within domestic jurisdiction were constantly contracting". He gave the example of an agreement on full employment, an agreement that up to a few years before would have been unthinkable because it concerned a matter that was "essentially" domestic even if, precisely because of the existence of the agreement, it was no longer "solely" domestic. The appropriateness of changing the adverb was to make the limit not totally worthless (see U.N.C.I.O., vol. 6, p. 511 f.).

Returning to Dulles's speech, the American delegate's main concern, which led to the necessity of emphasising the broadening of the limit of domestic jurisdiction, was to avoid that the Charter provisions on economic and social co-operation, on respect of the limit of national sovereignty, and so on, would lead the United Nations to interfere in the internal affairs of the Member States (the relationships between these provisions and Article 2, para. 7, and therefore the part of the speech specifically concerned with them will be discussed later on). There was also considerable concern, in relation to American domestic policy, that the US Senate would not ratify the Charter, as it had not in the past ratified the League of Nations Covenant, if the limit of domestic jurisdiction was not strongly defended.

Not only the historical background and the preparatory works of Article 2, para. 7, but also the text of the provision speak in favour of the legal notion of domestic jurisdiction, in the sense (made clear by the adverb "essentially") of bringing within domestic jurisdiction those matters that are *in principle* free from international obligations. Indeed, it would be impossible to give a convincing meaning to the notion of domestic jurisdiction in Article 2, para. 7, if it were not anchored to international law. Frankly, no merit can be seen in the attempts that have been made to build up a notion of a moral character, on the basis of which, in order to invoke the domestic jurisdiction clause, in a given matter, the State would have to prove not so much that it were free from legal obligations as that it was not bound by "principles of international social ethics" (SPERDUTI). On the same line, a political notion of domestic jurisdiction, appealing to the element of interest rather than to that of law, has been held. Outside of domestic jurisdiction, and therefore subject to UN action, would be conduct which, although it does not violate the rights of others, and although it remains within the State's own community in some respect is apt to be essentially injurious to the interests of other States (ROSS) and thus have important consequences at the international level. In our view, all these efforts practically empty Article 2, para. 7, of any meaning, and, ultimately, reach the result (in open contrast with the basic importance given to the provision by the framers of the Charter) that it is as if the article did not exist. The idea that the United Nations is to be concerned with questions and only with questions that can have international repercussions is something that has already been made very clear in those Charter provisions which lay down the powers of the organs as well as by the very nature of the United Nations as an entity which was created to promote and bring about international co-operation. Article 2, para. 7, would have no meaning even if we were to agree with the view (ARANGIO-RUIZ) that domestic jurisdiction would not constitute a *ratione materiae* limit but would only bind the United Nations (and the same could have been said of the League of Nations Council on the basis of Article 15, para. 8, of the Covenant) not to interfere with the governmental functions exercised by the States within their own territories and "directly" regulate relations between individuals. Even if Article 2, para. 7, did not exist, it is difficult to see how the United Nations could directly exercise governmental functions (especially taking into account that UN acts are taken in the form of recommendations) over individuals who are subjects of their respective States. It is true that some Charter provisions provide that the United Nations may undertake the administration of territories: Article 81 expressly provides so (or, rather, provided, since it concerns a matter that is now obsolete) with regard to the trusteeship territories (see § 80). Some other cases of administration of territories under the control of the Security Council have also occurred in practice (see § 60 *bis*). However, all this is not related to domestic jurisdiction as a general limit to the Organization's activity.

Most of the views which depart from the legal notion of domestic jurisdiction tend, in the last analysis, to disparage this notion to the advantage of the UN's powers, and thus move in a direction that is exactly the opposite of what the drafters of the Charter wished. Indeed, these views, more than offering an objective interpretation of Article 2, para. 7, want to propose an interpretation that would justify the UN practice as it has been developing since the early years of the Organization's existence. As we shall see shortly, this practice shows the tendency of the organs to reject, in various sectors, exceptions based on domestic jurisdiction. Yet it does not seem that the best way to proceed in the light of such practice is to have Article 2, para. 7, say things that it does not say and that are its negation. The best way is to ask, as we will do, whether the practice has modified, or, even, annulled Article 2, para. 7, and given rise to norms of a customary nature.

It is also necessary to dispel a misunderstanding that is at the basis of all the attempts to deny the legal notion of domestic jurisdiction. This misunderstanding consists in the belief that acceptance of this notion entails that the United Nations cannot discuss the political aspects of an issue or reach political solutions regarding it. It is said that if organs such as the General Assembly or the Security Council or the Economic and Social Council were to refrain from intervening in questions not governed by international law, they would in the end only be concerned with legal disputes and become nothing more than a court of justice, thus betraying their functions which are eminently political. Actually, all that Article 2, para. 7, asks is that the United Nations not be concerned with a situation involving a particular State (we shall soon see that a different conclusion may be required for decisions of general applicability) except when there is damage, threat or the possibility of damage to the *rights* of others. On the contrary, there is nothing that prevents the Organization from being concerned with the non-legal aspects of such situation or recommending political solutions even if they are not legally orthodox.

Arguments against those who accept the political notion of domestic jurisdiction and uphold the UN's competence in anything that has significant international repercussions can be found in the preparatory works for Article 10 of the Charter concerning the functions of the General Assembly. This article was initially formulated as follows: "The General Assembly has the right to discuss any matter coming within the sphere of international relations...". But this formulation was substituted by the present one ("The General Assembly may discuss any questions or any matters within the scope of the present Charter...") as a result of the Soviet delegate's insistence that the former wording could have brought the Assembly to interfere in matters of domestic jurisdiction. Cf. UNC.I.O., vol. 5, p. 522 ff. and p. 535 ff.

There is, then, a question of great importance for purposes of interpretation of Article 2, para. 7, to clarify. Various provisions of the Charter, beginning with those that establish the purposes of the United Nations, concern matters usually not regulated — or, better, that were not regulated at the time the Charter was drawn up and entered into force — by international law and thus by tradition were included in the domestic jurisdiction. One can say, in fact, that *all* these matters are taken into consideration by the Charter as the possible subject matter for deliberation by the UN organs. It is sufficient to mention that the Charter enables the United Nations: to pursue the "principle of self-determination of peoples" (Article 1, para. 2), an objective that may lead, especially if self-determination is given a literal meaning, to interference in the most intimate issues in the life of a State, such as matters concerning the form of government; to promote and encourage respect for human rights and fundamental freedoms for all (Article 1, para. 3, Article 55 (*c*), Article 56); to promote, in addition to a high standard of living and full employment, "conditions of economic and social progress and development" (Article 55 (*a*) and Article 56), that is, everything that comes within the objectives of a modern State community. How was this compatible, with the domestic jurisdiction clause? Need we then hold, as some observers do, that the Charter "internationalised" these matters once and for all, practically nullifying Article 2, para. 7? In fact, as we shall see, it is exactly on the basis of the above-cited provisions that the UN organs have given rise to a practice which tends to negate Article 2, para. 7.

In our view it is possible to reconcile the rules on the UN's competence in "domestic" matters with Article 2, para. 7, without sacrificing either. Such reconciliation can be attained by holding that in those matters, or, rather, in all matters of domestic jurisdiction, the Organization may adopt only resolutions of general applicability (drafts for multilateral conventions, recommendations addressed to *all* the States, and so on), while it is precluded from adopting resolutions concerning *individual* States. This is objectively the only convincing solution if we consider the opening phrase of Article 2, para. 7 (*"Nothing contained in the present Charter* shall authorise the United Nations to intervene..."), if we consider that Article 2, para. 7, expressly prohibits interfering in the domestic jurisdiction "of any State" ("d'un Etat", in the French text), and if we consider, lastly, that the text of the often-cited provisions makes it clearly understood that they refer to initiatives of a general nature. This same solution is supported by the San Francisco Conference proceedings and by the above-mentioned speech by the American delegate Dulles.

During the drawing up of Article 55 in Committee 3 of Commission II, the United States initially asked that a different wording be examined which made it clear that in economic and social matters there would be no interference in the domestic affairs of individual States. The Committee decided not to change the formulation, holding that the change was useless (according to the Australian delegate) because of the presence in the Charter of Article 2, para. 7. However, it was unanimously decided, again as proposed by the United States, to include the following statement in its final report: "The members of Committee 3 of Commission II are in full agreement that nothing contained in Chapter IX [including the present Article 55] can be construed as giving authority to the Organization to intervene in the domestic affairs of the Member States". Cf. U.N.C.I.O., vol. 10, p. 57 ff. and p. 83.

With regard to Dulles's speech which we have already mentioned above, it was exactly concerning the provisions on economic and social co-operation that the American delegate uttered the most often quoted words of his speech, "Is it going to be", he said, "an organization which deals essentially with the governments of the Member States, and through international relations? Or is it going to be an organization which is going to penetrate directly into the domestic life and the social economy of each one of the member-states?... None of us had the idea that the Economic and Social Council... was going to have the right to decide itself what pattern of social order is wanted and go behind the governments to intervene directly to impose that pattern on each one of the 50 member-states". It must be excluded that Dulles meant to say that Article 2, para. 7, prevents the United Nations from taking decisions that are binding for the citizens of the Member States, since no provision in the Charter provides for, nor did the draft discussed in San Francisco contain, binding powers of this kind. The passage of the speech was to be interpreted exactly in the sense that economic and social questions of a domestic nature were to be dealt with on a general and abstract level, and resolved only through international co-operation, that is, through agreement.

Some of the general and abstract resolutions adopted by the Organization, for example, the General Assembly's Declarations of Principle (see § 94), in a certain sense perform a *de lege ferenda* function in that they promote the undertaking of new legal obligations by the States. This function is sometimes cited as a proof against the legal notion of domestic jurisdiction since such obligations do not exist when the resolutions are adopted. The proof is not convincing if it is held, as it is held here, that resolutions of general character, i. e. resolutions addressed without distinction to *all* the States do not come within the provision of Article 2, para. 7.

III. *Developments in the practice.*

The very abundant UN practice (especially of the General Assembly) on the question of domestic jurisdiction indicates that the Organization has always, or nearly always, rejected the exceptions based on Article 2, para. 7. It has always, or nearly always, said that it could discuss and decide despite protests by the individual State or individual States addressed by the resolution. The areas in which this has occurred more than most are those of the liberation of peoples under a colonial regime, the protection of human rights and the struggle against governments imposed by force or against governments considered oppressive. In each of these areas the activity of the Organization has ultimately unfolded in a direction that was contrary to Article 2, para. 7. So, with regard to human rights, one of the areas where UN interventions have been increasing and intensifying since the seventies (see § 74 ff.), not only the General Assembly has adopted, from the beginning of its existence, a large number of resolutions of a general and abstract nature (which should have not gone beyond the meaning of Article 55 (*c*) and Article 60) but has also shown a tendency to see that human rights are respected within *individual countries*. Also, there has been interference in domestic jurisdiction of single States by the discussions undertaken or the resolutions adopted by the Assembly or the Security Council to condemn Fascist governments such as the Franco regime in Spain, or governments established by force (the *coup d'état* in Czechoslovakia in 1948, the setting up of the Kadar government in Hungary in 1956, and so on), or the puppet governments imposed by foreign Powers (the filo-Vietnamese government in Cambodia beginning in 1979, the Afghanistan government set up by Soviet troops in 1980, and so on). As for the colonial question, it is well known that the United Nations played a dominant role in the process of de-colonisation; that the General Assembly took all responsibility in the matter, including deciding if and when the various peoples subject to foreign rule were to gain independence, thereby realising the most far-reaching type of intervention in the internal affairs of the colonial powers; and that this competence was certainly not provided for by Article 73 of the Charter, which is concerned with non-self-governing territories in a very general way and without any specific commitment for the Organization (see § 78).

How is this practice to be evaluated?

Our opinion has always been, in the same way as in evaluating the practice concerning other parts of the UN system, that one needs to proceed with the necessary caution and rigidity of method in trying to ascertain the existence of unwritten rules which may have modified or abrogated Charter provisions. In this regard (see § 4), it is not enough that a certain rule has been observed over a period, even a long period, of time by the organs, that it has been confirmed and defended by the majorities that have over time been formed in such organs. It is also necessary to look at the conduct and the reactions of individual States, at their capacity to counteract effectively the tendencies of the majorities. It is precisely by following this rigorous method, we maintained, in the previous editions of this book, that the original meaning and the basic concept of Article 2, para. 7, still remained alive and vital, except for the formation of individual specific unwritten rules derogating from it, particularly of norms relating to the areas of human rights and de-colonisation. Also for human rights, we held that their violations, despite the general ratification of the two important United Nations covenants on human rights in 1966 and other international agreements promoted by the United Nations (see §§ 76-77), came within the matters "essentially" belonging to domestic jurisdiction, and that the only, however important, exceptions were the so-called gross violations, that is, severe and brutal violations, such as apartheid, genocide, torture and so on. We held so because there was a compact group of States (the Socialist States of Eastern Europe) whose existence and behaviour could not be ignored. Even though they had ratified the above-cited covenants and conventions on human rights, these States still continued, with persistence and efficacy, to invoke Article 2, para. 7, with the exception that we have indicated.

The Socialist States had staunchly defended the view that the existence of treaty obligations could not affect domestic jurisdiction in a matter, such as human rights, which "essentially" belonged to this domain. This occurred as early as 1948 and 1950 when Bulgaria, Romania and Hungary had been accused in several General Assembly resolutions (res. nos. 272-III, 249-IV and 385-V) of violating the provisions of the peace treaties they had signed which obligated them to respect human rights (for the statement by the Communist delegates invoking Article 2, para. 7, cf. GAOR, 3rd sess., Gen. Comm., 59th meet.p. 22 and p. 26 ff.; 5th sess., Pl. meet., 284th meet., no. 166 ff.). To cite a more recent example, the same view was defended before the Commission on Human Rights (see § 38), on the Polish question (a question never dealt with by the General Assembly). When the government of General Jaruzelsky was accused in 1982 of committing gross human rights violations in Poland, such as the arbitrary arrest of thousands of persons, the suppression of the freedom of expression and of association, etc., thus violating the United Nations covenants ratified by Poland (cf. res. no. 1982-26 of the Commission), the Polish and Soviet delegates, besides protesting the charge of gross violations, held that the intervention was illegal in so far as it was contrary to both Article

2, para. 7, and Article 40 of the Covenant on Civil and Political Rights (Article 40 provides, as the only form of international supervision over the implementation of the provisions in the Covenant, the sending by the States parties of periodical reports to a special organ, the Human Rights Committee (see § 77). Such reports are limited to the human rights situation in the State's own territory. According to a restrictive interpretation of Article 40 which was strongly upheld by Socialist States, they could not be the subject of specific criticism of individual countries. For the positions of Poland and the Soviet Union, cf. *Int. Comm. on Human Rights*, 38th sess., 57th meet. (Doc. E CN.4/1982/SR.57 of March 18, 1982, no. 33 ff.).

With the fall of the Socialist regimes of Eastern Europe, today the situation has changed. The domestic jurisdiction clause has finally vanished as far as human rights are concerned. However, what is important to note is that the protection of human rights, as it is understood in today's international community, goes well beyond the respect for one right or another and affects all relations in which the human person and his dignity is in some way involved. In the name of human rights, any distinction between international wars or wars between States and internal wars or civil wars has been abolished for the purpose of any type of UN action. In short, any situation within a given State which is injurious to human dignity — from mistreatment of minorities and gross violations of human rights, like genocide, ethnic cleansing, massive deportations and so on, to the adoption of economic and social policies detrimental to the population, to suffering imposed on the civilian population by civil wars — is now the object of UN action, whether or not it constitutes the violation of a specific international obligation. This is very clear to anyone who looks through the collections of resolutions by the General Assembly, the Security Council, and the Economic and Social Council and their subsidiary organs, as well as the records of the sessions where such resolutions are adopted.

Unquestionably, everything concerning human rights, including the treatment of minorities, goes beyond the limit of domestic jurisdiction. For a recent Security Council resolution concerned with minorities, cf. res. no. 688 of April 5, 1991 which condemned repression of Iraqi civilian populations, particularly in the areas inhabited by Kurds, considering such repression a threat to the peace. This resolution, which can be characterised as a resolution under Article 39 of the Charter (see § 56), involves an interference in Iraqi domestic affairs, interference considered lawful for the reason we have stated. It is then odd that the resolution contains a reference, in its preamble, exactly to Article 2, para. 7 !

Another matter which is no longer covered by the domestic jurisdiction clause is the constitutional regime of countries where a civil war has taken place and some form of national conciliation is ongoing with the help of the United Nations. Both the Security Council and the General Assembly normally intervenes in these procedures, promoting, and monitoring the execution of agreements among the different factions on the future constitutional regime of the country (see §§ 56 and 63).

Aside from the matters we have indicated, if a rigorous method is adopted, if attention is paid not only to the tendencies of the majority but also to the attitude of the individual States, or, rather, of individual groups of States, the domestic jurisdiction clause may still be and still is invoked for those sectors which international law *in principle* leaves to the discretion of the individual State. In accordance with the already-mentioned formula utilised to identify a positive notion of domestic jurisdiction (see § 45 I), what remains "essentially" within domestic jurisdiction are the relations concerning the organization of government (the form of State and of Government, the organization of public offices and the like) and the utilisation of the territory.

Of course, the whole matter of domestic jurisdiction does not have precise contours and it is influenced by the fact that international law is continuously evolving and expanding. Taking into consideration what has occurred up to now in United Nations practice, it is difficult to say whether a sector has ceased to belong to domestic jurisdiction because international law has expanded or because UN practice has given rise to departures from Article 2, para. 7. The truth is that most often the evolution of international law is exactly due to pressure from the United Nations and to the insistence with which it pursues certain values.

46. B) *The meaning of "intervene".*

BIBLIOGRAPHY: see § 44. *Adde*: LAUTERPACHT, *International Law and Human Rights*, London, 1950, p. 166; GILMOUR, *The Meaning of "Intervene" within Article 2 (7) of the UN Charter — An Historical Prospective*, in *ICLQ*, 1967, p. 330 ff.

Article 2, para. 7, prohibits the Organization from "intervening" in matters that are within the domestic jurisdiction of a State.

Legal scholars are nearly all in agreement in rejecting the view (LAUTERPACHT) which would give the term "intervention" the same meaning that it has under classic international law, that is, dictatorial interference carried out with the threat or use of force. If this view were correct, Article 2, para. 7, would once again lose any meaning. The UN organs, generally speaking, lack means of enforcement with regard to the States, and usually only issue recommendations, acts that do not claim to make the conduct requested obligatory. On the other hand, the only examples of dictatorial interference of the United Nations are the enforcement measures under Chapter VII of the Charter, exactly those measures that the last part of Article 2, para. 7, allows to be taken even if matters of domestic jurisdiction are involved!

An argument in favour of the above criticised view may be found in the preparatory works, specifically in the part of the speech by the American delegate Dulles at the San

Francisco Conference (quoted at § 45 II *in fine*) where, in commenting on Article 2, para. 7, he holds that the Organization must not "go behind the governments to intervene directly to impose a social order [a certain pattern of social order] in each one of the 50 member-states". We have seen, however (*ivi*), that this phrase is to be understood in a different sense.

Once an interpretation based on the traditional meaning of the term intervention is excluded, Article 2, para. 7, must be intended as prohibiting the organs from exercising, in matters of domestic jurisdiction, the normal powers given them by the Charter.

Of the two stages in which the examination of a question is usually divided, the discussion stage and the decision stage, the latter unquestionably falls under the prohibition. The organ must abstain from taking any resolution, whether it is a recommendation addressed to the State or to the States concerned, whether it is an act of an organising nature, such as the establishment of a committee of inquiry, or whether, lastly, it is a decision of an operational nature, as, for example, a General Assembly decision to undertake a study of the economic or social situation within a given country. However, the discussion stage must also be considered covered by the prohibition. This stage, owing to the lack of real decision-making powers of the organs, to the political importance that the questions examined usually have, and to the fact that the United Nations constitutes a centre where world public opinion is reflected, has an importance that is equal to if not greater than the decision-making stage. Of course the organ may undertake a discussion in order to establish whether or not a matter comes within domestic jurisdiction, but the discussion must be kept within the limits necessary for this purpose. The natural, even if not the only, time for such discussion is before a matter is placed on the agenda. Placing a question of domestic jurisdiction on the agenda does not therefore constitute an intervention under Article 2, para. 7, as long as such placement occurs in order to discuss and assess whether the question has purely a domestic nature or not.

The problem of whether the mere examination or the mere discussion of a matter is prohibited by Article 2, para. 7, has been debated in practice usually at the time of the drawing up of the agenda. The States which object on the basis of this Article usually say that a question of domestic jurisdiction should not even be listed on the agenda. The States contrary to the exception usually answer that placement never constitutes an intervention under Article 2, para. 7, as the discussion stage is always lawful. Both views are to be corrected in the sense we have stated. For the relevant practice, cf. UN Rep., *sub* Article 2, para. 7, no. 346 ff., partic. no. 351, Suppl. no. 1, no. 121 ff., partic. no. 123 and Suppl. no. 2, no. 139 ff.

It has been asked in legal literature and in practice whether only resolutions addressed to certain countries amount to intervention under Article 2, para. 7, or whether general and abstract resolutions (recommendations addressed to all the States, drafts for multilateral agreements, and so on) also do. In our view (see § 45 II), Article 2, para. 7, prohibits only the former and leaves the Organization free to adopt the latter in any matter, even in the most domestic matter. This, however, does not concern the meaning of the term "intervene" but, as we have seen, concerns the relationships between Article 2, para. 7, and various other Charter rules.

47. C) *The significance of the exception in the last part of Article 2, para. 7.*

BIBLIOGRAPHY: see § 44.

The last part of Article 2, para. 7, provides that the domestic jurisdiction clause cannot be invoked when the Security Council decides to use the enforcement measures ("mesures de coércition" in the French text) under Chapter VII. As is very clear in the preparatory works and as can be deduced from the purpose of the provision, which is to ensure at all events that the Security Council intervenes when faced with a threat to the peace, with a breach of the peace, or with an act of aggression, Article 2, para. 7, last part, means to refer not only to the measures of a military nature under Article 42 but also to the measures not involving the use of armed force governed by Article 41.

At the San Francisco Conference, the great powers had proposed to take all of Chapter VII (corresponding to Chapter VIII, Sect. B, of the Dumbarton Oaks proposals) away from the domestic jurisdiction clause. However, the Conference decided to accept, with their consent, an Australian amendment restricting the exception to the "enforcement" measures. The Australian memorandum which accompanied the presentation of the amendment expressly indicated as "enforcement measures" the measures provided by Articles 3 and 4 of Chapter VIII of the Dumbarton Oaks proposals, which correspond to the present Articles 41 and 42 of the Charter (see U.N.C.I.O., vol. 6, p. 439 f., nos. 15-17 of the memorandum). This fact dispels any doubt about the applicability of Article 2, para. 7, last part, also to Council interventions on the basis of Article 41, although the use of the term "enforcement measures" (and, in the French text, the term "mesures de coercition") may more immediately bring to mind the measures involving the use of force under Article 42. It is, moreover, indicative that the report of Committee 1 of Commission 1, where the Australian amendment was approved, speaks, in commenting on the amendment, of "enforcement action (preventive and coercitive)" and, in the French text, of "mesures *preventives* et coércitives", with very clear reference, then, also to measures not involving the use of armed force (*ibid.,* p. 488 and 492).

The main purpose of the Australian amendment was to avoid that the domestic jurisdiction clause could be dropped with regard to recommendations that the Security Council may issue under Article 39, the opening article in Chapter VII. These recommendations have nothing to do with enforcement measures; they consist in indicating to the States involved in a case of threat to the peace, breach of the peace or an act of aggression how to settle the dispute or remove the situation which has given rise to the case. They therefore are quite similar to the recommendations covered in Chapter VI regarding the pacific settlement functions of the Council (see § 56). Since it is the same kind of recommendation, it would not be right, Australia held, that the domestic jurisdiction clause was not applicable for the former while it was applicable for the latter. This was all the more so since the unfairness would be turned against small and middle-sized States which, unlike the great powers who possess the right of veto, would not have available other means able to prevent the interference of the Council in their domestic affairs (cf. U.N.C.I.O., vol. 6, p. 437 ff., nos. 7-13 of the cited Australian memorandum).

All cases of Security Council intervention that are covered by Articles 41 and 42 fall outside the principle of non interference with the domestic jurisdiction. On the basis of Article 41, the Council may either decide (the decision has a binding character) what measures not involving the use of armed force must be adopted by the Member States against a given State or may limit itself to *recommending* the adoption of such measures (see § 58). Even for recommended measures, therefore, domestic jurisdiction cannot be invoked.

Although not provided for in Article 2, para. 7, last part, one should also exclude from the domestic jurisdiction clause all those Security Council resolutions which constitute or may constitute the necessary conditions for, or are fundamental for the purposes of, an effective intervention on the basis of Articles 41 and 42. Therefore the following must be considered as falling outside the limit of domestic jurisdiction; namely those resolutions in which the Council decides to carry out an investigation, that is, to acquire factual elements on a given situation, provided that the investigation is aimed at ascertaining whether the conditions exist for the possible application of Articles 41 and 42. The fact that the power of investigation is set out under Article 34, that is, by an article in Chapter VI and not in Chapter VII of the Charter, is not a decisive element, for reasons we will explain later (see § 51)

Council resolution no. 4 of April 29, 1946 was therefore fully lawful. This resolution appointed a sub-committee of five members entrusted with the task of gathering documents and testimonies on Franco's Fascist regime in Spain and consequently with determining "whether the situation in Spain has led to international friction and does endanger international peace and security, and if it so finds, then to determine what practical measures the United Nations may take". In its report, the sub-committee reached the conclusion that a real threat to the peace did not exist and that, therefore, none of the series of measures set out in Articles 41 and 42 and in Chapter VII in general could be taken (see SCOR, 1st year, 1st series, Spec. Suppl., p. 1 ff.). Since the matter was one of domestic jurisdiction, the report should have stopped at this point. On the contrary, it stated that the Spanish situation came within the framework of Chapter VI (regarding the dispute-settlement functions of the Council) and expressed the view that the Council was empowered under Article 36 to recommend appropriate procedures or methods of adjustment (*ibid.*, p. 10). As was noted in the Council during the examination of the report (cf. SCOR, 1st year, 46th meet., p. 345 ff.), a recommendation of this kind would have surely been contrary to Article 2, para. 7. In fact, the sub-committee's proposal was also politically useless and purely and simply revealed the Council's impotence. If the Council had seriously wanted to deal with fascism in Spain, the only viable weapon would have been the legitimate one offered by Articles 41 and 42. In the end, the Council did not take any decision and referred the case to the General Assembly, thereby burying it.

Equally lawful was res. no. 203 (para. 2) of May 14, 1965 which ordered an investigation into the internal situation in the Dominican Republic.

For other references to the practice concerning investigations, see § 51.

Other decisions which are clearly functional to the interventions under Articles 41 and 42 and likewise also outside the limit of domestic jurisdiction are the invitations which, under Article 40, the Security Council may address to parties involved in a situation that is a threat to the peace or a breach of the peace or an act of aggression in order to call upon them to adopt "provisional" measures to prevent a worsening of the crisis. A typical measure of this kind, in case of war, is the "cease-fire" (see § 57). This measure may be therefore requested also with regard to a civil war.

On the occasion of Indonesia's war of independence, the Council adopted, on August 1, 1947, a resolution which asked the parties involved to cease hostilities immediately and to seek a solution through arbitration or other peaceful means. It was correctly noted, in the Council and in consideration of a protest by the Dutch delegate, that at least the part of the decision concerning the cease-fire, in so far as it came within the framework of Article 40, left open the question of the lack of jurisdiction of the organ under Article 2, para. 7 (cf. SCOR, 2nd year, 193rd meet., p. 2175).

The cease-fire in civil wars is now commonly recommended or decided by the Security Council without protests from the parties concerned.

To cite a different example, it must be held that the defence used by the Israeli government against Council resolution no. 250 of April 27, 1968 was groundless. This resolution requested Israel to postpone a military parade in Jerusalem so as not to increase tension of the area (a resolution within the framework of Article 40). The Israeli government held that the matter concerned its own domestic jurisdiction (cf. *UNMC*, 1968, May, p. 24).

Recommendations referred to in Article 39, the opening article in Chapter VII, do not come within the exception set out in Article 2, para. 7, last part, and thus are covered by the domestic jurisdiction clause. Their purpose is to indicate to the interested States how to resolve disputes or eliminate the situation at the origin of the threat to the peace, breach of the peace or the act of aggression (see § 56). Evidence of this is given, first of all, by the preparatory works, since, as we have seen above, the reference in Article 2, para. 7, last part, to "enforcement measures" (rather than to the entire Chapter VII) was wanted in order not to subject recommendations under Article 39 to the limit of domestic jurisdiction. Further evidence comes from a contextual approach, and precisely from the circumstance that the recommendations under Article 39 not only are not closely functional to the measures of Articles 41 and 42, but they are entirely identical to those provided by Chapter VI, particularly by Articles 36 and 37, that is, by the chapter (on the peaceful settlement of disputes) for which the domestic jurisdiction clause was especially conceived (see § 56).

Some members of the Security Council who, during Indonesia's war of independence, when they were faced with the above cited res. no. 27 of August 1, 1947 inviting the parties to a cease-fire and recommending that they seek a solution through arbitration, correctly maintained that the Council had competence regarding the invitation (under Article 40) but not regarding the recommendation.

48. D) *Competence to interpret Article 2, para. 7.*

Who has competence to decide whether or not a question falls within domestic jurisdiction? Does such a decision belong to the organ before which the exception of domestic jurisdiction is raised, and is it binding for the government which raises the objection and for dissenting governments? The problem of the power to interpret the Charter has been dealt with in general terms (see § 5) and there is no reason to depart from those considerations here. It is sufficient to add that the problem of the competence to interpret the Charter was discussed at San Francisco, and has been examined in legal doctrine, mainly with regard to Article 2, para. 7.

Section II

MAINTENANCE OF THE PEACE: FUNCTIONS OF THE SECURITY COUNCIL

49. *Chapters VI and VII of the Charter.*

BIBLIOGRAPHY: HERNDL, *Reflections on the Role, Function and Procedures of the Security Council of the UN*, in *RC*, 1987-VI, p. 322 ff.; PETROVIC, CONDORELLI, *L'ONU et la crise yougoslave*, in *AF*, 1992, p. 32 ff.; DUPUY (P.M.), *Sécurité collective et organisation de la paix*, in *RGDIP*, 1993, p. 617 ff.; DURCH (ed.), *The Evolution of UN Peacekeaping: Case Studies and Comparative Analysis*, New York, N.Y., 1993; HAHLBOHM, *Peacekeeping im Wandel: die friedenssichernden Einsätze der Vereinten Nationen nach dem Ende des Ost-West-Konflikts*, Frankfurt am Main, 1993; WHITE, *Keeping the Peace: The United Nations and the Maintenance of International Peace and Security*, Manchester, 1993; BROWN, *The role of the United Nations in Peacekeeping and Truce-Monitoring: What Are the Applicable Norms*, in *RBDI*, 1994, p. 559 ff.; FERENCZ, *New Legal Foundations for Global Survival: Security Through the Security Council*, Dobbs Ferry-New York, 1994; DINSTEIN, *The Legal Lessons of the Gulf War*, in *ZöRV*, 1995, p. 1 ff.; ORTEGA CARCELÉN, MARTÍN, *Hacia un Gobierno Mundial. Las nuevas funciones del Consejo de Seguridad de Naciones Unidas*, Salamanca, 1995; RATNER, *The New UN Peacekeeping*, New York, 1995.

Chapters VI (Articles 33 ff.) and VII (Articles 39 ff.) lay down the functions of the Security Council, the organ assigned by the Charter "the primary responsibility for the maintenance of international peace and security" (Article 24). Since the end of the Cold War and the fall of the regimes in Eastern Europe, this organ has once again become active (as it was in the very early years of the life of the United Nations). Chapter VI is dedicated to the peaceful settlement of disputes. Aside from some provisions (Articles 34 and 35) which govern general aspects of Council activities, and therefore within the systematic order of the Charter must be linked not only to the other provisions of Chapter VI but also to the provisions in Chapter VII (see §§ 50-51), Chapter VI regulates the Council's exercise of a merely conciliatory function. Chapter VII concerns "action" for the maintenance of the peace; it assumes that the peace has been breached or threatened and enables the Council to adopt a series of measures to restore peace, which may or may not involve the use of armed force.

The different features of Security Council actions on the basis of either Chapter VI or Chapter VII may be summarised as follows.

First, the peaceful settlement function under Chapter VI deals with matters that only potentially could disturb the peace and is performed with regard to a dispute or situation "the continuance of which is likely to endanger the maintenance of international peace and security" (cf. Articles 33, 36, and 37). By contrast, Chapter VII concerns crises that are underway, specifically the existence "of a "threat to the peace", a "breach of the peace", or an "act of aggression" (cf. Article 39).

Secondly, the protagonists of the relationships governed by Chapter VI are, more than the Council itself, the parties to the dispute, or the States involved in a situation potentially prejudicial to the peace. Given its role of peacemaker, the Council has only the function of urging the States involved so that the endangering disputes or situations may be settled. However, such settlement remains a matter that is completely dependent on the will, and therefore on the agreement, of the States directly concerned. It is not by chance that Article 33, the opening article of Chapter VI, places in the foreground the obligation on the parties to the dispute to resolve it by peaceful means. Vice versa, in the cases envisaged by Chapter VII, the main role belongs to the Council. Most of its actions, far from requiring the co-operation of the States (or the groups fighting within a country) who are the authors of the crisis, are directed against them. What is important is rather the obligation of the other States to co-operate to make effective the measures decided upon for the maintenance of the peace (the breaking of diplomatic relations, economic blockades, use of force, and so on).

The different degree of gravity of the situation to be dealt with and the different role played by the Council is reflected in the instruments the Council has available on the basis of either chapter. The typical act through which the pacific settlement function under Chapter VI is performed is the recommendation (cf. Articles 36 and 37) which is without binding force. By contrast, Chapter VII, while providing for the possibility of recommendations, is characterised by the Council's power both to issue decisions (cf. Article 41), that is, acts binding the States they address, and to adopt resolutions of an operational nature (Article 42), that is, resolutions with which the Council does not address the States but decides itself to undertake certain actions (on operational decisions, see § 92). Moreover, the conciliation function cannot, owing to its nature, be carried over into resolutions which acquire a sanctioning nature with regard to one or more States. Whereas the imposing of sanctions against States which breach or threaten the peace is the typical measure governed by Chapter VII.

Lastly, the whole conciliatory function of the Council is subject to the exception of domestic jurisdiction set out in Article 2, para. 7, an exception that the framers of the Charter had originally put exactly at the end of the provisions of Chapter VI (see § 47). Vice versa, according to the same Article 2, para 7, the exception is not admissible when the Council takes enforcement measures on the basis of Chapter VII. In fact, in recent times, the Council has mainly acted with regards to domestic affairs and mainly for humanitarian reasons (see § 55). Obviously, the exception of domestic jurisdiction is not admissible even as far as the Chapter VI is concerned, when the Council intervenes in situations for which, as we saw, the limit of domestic jurisdiction has been superseded in practice.

Ascertaining whether a Council intervention comes under Chapter VI or Chapter VII also has practical consequences from the point of view of Article 27, para 3. According to this paragraph, it is only when confronted with a draft resolution that is within the framework of Chapter VI that a Member State of the Council, which is directly and individually affected by the resolution, is obliged to abstain from participating in the vote (see § 27).

These differences can serve as a starting point. As will be made clear from an analysis of the rules on the peaceful settlement function under Chapter VI and from the rules of Chapter VII, a very sharp dividing line between the two groups of provisions cannot be drawn. There are cases where Council interventions under Chapter VI may be mixed with interventions governed by Chapter VII (for example, Chapter VII also contains, in Article 39, conciliatory action: see § 56). In cases of this kind, the exact classification of a Council resolution in one chapter or the other can only be the result of careful interpretation aimed at establishing which of the distinguishing features outlined above are mainly present.

Often in the past Council resolutions did not indicate the articles in the Charter, or even the chapters, on the basis of which they have been adopted. In recent times this cases have considerably diminished, although not disappeared, since the Council often declares that it is acting under .Chapter VII. It still may happen, for instance, that the grounds for the decisions are connected to one chapter, while the operative part is within the framework of another. It may happen, for example, that the Council decides upon measures not involving the use of armed force of the kind governed by Article 41, but in the preamble to the resolution it avoids stating the existence of a threat to the peace or a breach of the peace and qualifies the situation in which it is intervening with terms that bring it within the situations covered by Chapter VI. It would be out of place, given the highly political nature of the Council functions, to treat the contradiction between the grounds and the operative part in the light of formal criteria... borrowed from administrative law, and conclude, or only raise doubt, that it is the cause of the illegality of the resolution! The only problem foreseeable is that of the exact classification of the act under Chapter VI or Chapter VII. In classifying an act, the operative part is more important, since it is the part of the act that will have practical effects. One could in fact adopt, as a valid criterion for any resolution, the rule that the act is characterised by its operative part and that examination of the grounds may help only if the operative part leaves open doubt as to whether it belongs under Chapter VI or Chapter VII.

It is also of utmost importance to note that in recent times the Council has adopted a series of resolutions, (such as the authorisation of the use of force by States, institution of criminal tribunals, administrations of territories, etc.) which can hardly fit into one or other Article. A legal examination of such cases will ascertain whether sufficient practice has been established in order to justify the conclusion that customary rules have arisen within the UN system. The issue will be treated in the framework of Chapter VII.

50. *The power to seize the Council.*

BIBLIOGRAPHY: KELSEN, *The Law of the United Nations*, London, 1950, p. 372 ff.; JIMENEZ DE ARECHAGA, *Voting and the Handling of Disputes in the Security Council*, New York, 1950, p. 47 ff.; CAVARÉ, *Les sanctions dans la cadre de l'ONU*, in *RC*, 1952, I, p. 263 ff.

Article 35 (a general provision that can refer to any function of the Security Council) grants all States the power to seize the Council. Under para. 1, the Member States may come before the Council, bringing to its attention any dispute or any situation which might lead to international friction. Under para. 2, non-Member States may also seize the Council although with certain limitations, and specifically they can only bring to its attention a dispute to which such State is a party and provided that it states its intention to settle the dispute peacefully.

Although it is included among the provisions on the Security Council functions, Article 35 is also concerned with the power to bring a matter before the Assembly. This is further evidence that it has the nature of a quite general rule.

Worth mentioning also is Article 37, which does not merely provide an option but creates a true obligation to seize the Council. This obligation is incumbent on the parties to a dispute who have failed to settle the dispute between themselves through peaceful means. Since, however, it is an obligation pertaining only to the conciliation function of the Council, it would be better to discuss it with regard to such function (see § 52.). The same can be said about Article 38, which provides for the possibility that all parties to a dispute agree to bring it before the Council, in which case certain limits, which should be inherent to the conciliation function of the organ, do not apply.

Matters may also be brought before the Council by the General Assembly and by the Secretary-General.

The Assembly "may call the attention of the Security Council to situations which are likely to endanger international peace and security" (Article 11, para. 3). The Secretary-General may bring to its attention, under Article 99, "any matter which in his opinion may threaten [in the French text: "mettre en danger"] the maintenance of international peace and security". The two provisions, taking into account the reference to situations that may endanger, as well as threaten the peace, are rules of general applicability: the

Assembly and the Secretary may turn to the Council both when they believe that a matter requires action under Chapter VII and to request the conciliation function under Chapter VI.

At the request of the Secretary-General the Council has several times undertaken the examination of very important cases, for example, the Congolese crisis in 1960 (see § 59), the Cypriot crisis in 1947 (see Doc. S/11339), and the crisis resulting from the capture and detention of hostages in the United States Embassy in Tehran in 1979 (see Doc. S/13646).

The power of the General Assembly to seize the Council is also provided for by Article 11, para. 2 (first part). According to this provision, the Assembly, after having discussed a question regarding maintenance of the peace, may make recommendations to the Council concerning such questions. The other rule in Article 11, para. 2 (last part), which requires that the Assembly refer to the Council any question "on which action is necessary", more than being concerned with procedure, confirms the Assembly's lack of competence to perform functions of the kind envisaged in Chapter VII (see § 63).

When the States, the Assembly or the Secretary-General act on the basis of the above-cited provisions, the Security Council *must meet*. This can be understood from the letter and spirit of the norms themselves. Article 3 of the Council's rules of procedure strictly conforms to these norms. It requires the President to call a meeting of the organ whenever it is requested under Articles 35, 11 and 99.

Obviously, this concerns only the convocation of the organ. Once it has met, the Council must ascertain whether the conditions necessary for the exercise of its functions exist. If the conditions do not exist, it will not include the matter referred to on its agenda. It may be said that the Council President is authorised to carry out a *prima facie* investigation to exclude cases that are of manifest inadmissibility, for example, cases that have already been rejected by the Council and presented again within a very short time without any change of circumstances. This is all the more true since it is customary in the Council for the President to consult all the members before calling a meeting.

Article 2 of the rules of procedure considers separately the case where a meeting of the Council is requested by a Member State of the organ, and also requires that the President call the meeting. This provision is independent from Article 3 which, referring to all the UN Member States, already includes the requests of members of the Council. In the first place, Article 2 is relevant mainly when the Council is already considering a question, included on the agenda, and it is only a matter of moving forward or postponing meetings that have already been decided upon or of urging the President in the event that the Council has entrusted him with convening at his discretion for subsequent meetings. Moreover, according to the interpretation given to Article 2 in practice, the request of a Council member takes away from the President the above mentioned power of *prima facie* investigation: he is in any case obligated to convoke the Council.

For the practice concerning convocation, cf. SC Rep. (and subsequent supplements) *sub* Chapter I, part. I. An exemplary case regarding Articles 2 and 3 of the rules of procedure can be found in SCOR, 20th year (1965), 1220th meet, p. 3 ff. In this meeting, the President stated that he had convoked the Council to examine the situation in the Dominican Republic (a situation that had for some time already been placed on the Council agenda by the Socialist States who maintained that it was a situation likely, owing to the presence of United States troops in the territory, to endanger the peace), despite the fact that the preliminary consultations he had held with the majority of the Council members were *prima facie* in the sense that the meeting was useless. At the insistence of a member of the organ (the USSR), he felt he was obligated to convene the meeting. Cf. also: SCOR, 21st year (1966), 1276-77th meet. (protests of the United States, Great Britain and other countries over the President's delay in calling a Council meeting on the Rhodesian question); Doc. S/14683 of September 10, 1981 and A/15699 of September 18, 1981 (containing, respectively, the formal request for convening a meeting of the Council, on the basis of Article 35 of the Charter and of Article 3 of the rules of procedure, by Guatemala for examining their dispute with the United Kingdom regarding the territory of Belize, and the formal protest by Guatemala that a Council meeting had not been called); Doc. S/PV.2977 (Part I) of February 13, 1991 (protest by Cuba for the failure to call a Council meeting concerning the Gulf War — the Council had not met for 28 days since the outbreak of hostilities — despite the request by several members).

We should emphasise that convocation of the Council is one thing and the Council's performance of its functions is another. The latter includes the ascertainment of the conditions (for example, real danger to the peace) necessary to be able to undertake action, and such ascertainment may have positive or negative results.

The confusion between these two moments gave rise to a strange debate in the very early years of the United Nations, during the examination of the Iranian question. It was asked whether, since Iran had seized the Council under Article 35, para. 1, to protest against the stationing of Russian troops on its territory, but then had stated that it had reached an agreement with the Soviet Union, the Council could, in spite of this, keep the question on the agenda, as the majority wanted. The problem of the legality of the majority decision was approached, both within the organ and in a memorandum of the Secretariat, in the sense that it would have to be established whether the Council... could act *ex officio* or would have had to defer to the decision of the State which had requested the meeting! The fallacy of such an approach is clear, and it is clear that it is useless to pose a problem of *ex officio* action if it is true, as it is true, that the Council may always be activated by a single State and therefore, even more so, by the majority of its members. The only question that in this particular case should have been asked was whether, an agreement between the parties having been reached, international peace and security were still in danger. It concerned the *objective* conditions for carrying out the functions of the Council.

For references to the documents, see § 25. Cf. also SC Rep. *sub* Chap. II, part. IV, case no. 56.

51. *Investigation.*

BIBLIOGRAPHY: JIMENEZ DE ARECHAGA, *Le traitement des différends internationaux par le Conseil de Sécurité*, in *RC*, 1954, I, p. 41 ff.; KERLEY, *The Powers of Investigation of the UN Security Council*, in *AJ*, 1961, p. 892 ff.; GOODRICH-SIMONS, *The UN and the Maintenance of International Peace and Security*, Washington, 1962, p. 173 ff.; MARCUS-HELMONS, *Les Nations Unies et les commission d'enquête*, in *Annales de droit et de sciences politiques*, 1962, p. 123 ff.; GOODRICH-HAMBRO-SIMONS, *Charter of the UN — Commentary and Documents*, New York, 1969, p. 265 ff.; BERG, *The 1991 Declaration on Fact-finding by the United Nations*, in *EJIL*, 1993, p. 107 ff.

"The Security Council", Article 34 states, "may investigate ["peut enquêter" in the French text] any dispute or any situation which might lead to international friction or give rise to a dispute, in order to determine whether the continuance of the dispute or situation is likely to endanger the maintenance of international peace and security".

Considering the location of Article 34 in Chapter VI and the language adopted ("in order to *determine* whether the... dispute or situation is likely *to endanger* the maintenance... of peace..."), we should conclude that the Council may make use of an investigation only to decide whether or not to exercise the conciliation function under Chapter VI itself. On the contrary, the provision is to be interpreted in a broader sense, as attributing a general and all-encompassing power of investigation. Taking into account the rational of the provision, which is to enable the Council to acquire all the necessary factual elements regarding an international situation in order to determine its potentiality of danger, the investigation may constitute the premise for the exercise of any one of the powers of the Council regarding maintenance of the peace, and therefore also the powers envisaged in Chapter VII. On the other hand, it would be absurd if the Charter were to attribute the power to investigate in relation to the conciliation function and not in relation to the functions under Chapter VII as well. There do not exist, in fact, in Chapter VII provisions in which a power of this kind can be found. Even Article 39, when it says that "The Security Council *shall determine* ["constate" in the French text] the existence of any threat to the peace, breach of the peace, or act of aggression and shall make recommendations or decide what measures shall be taken in accordance with Articles 41 and 42..." does not seem to cover decisions that are limited to making investigations.

The fact that Article 34 gives the Council a general and all-encompassing power means that the organ is free either to decide purely and simply in favour of an investigation or to link the investigation to a certain function, deciding, for example that investigations are to serve only to ascertain whether conditions exist for exercising the conciliation function, or for an action to restore the peace, and so on. It is clear that the second hypothesis should occur when the Council has already taken a certain direction and the investigation should furnish only additional elements.

Although there are some examples of "restricted" investigations in practice, the resolutions that can be referred to Article 34 are mostly of a general nature. This shows the clear intention of the Council not to link the power of investigation to one or another of its functions.

As examples of general resolutions, cf.: res. no. 15 of December 19, 1946, which appointed a Commission to investigate Greek frontier incidents during the civil war in that country ("Whereas", the resolution reads, "... there have been presented to the Security Council oral and written statements... relating to disturbed conditions in northern Greece... which conditions... should be investigated *before* the Council attempts to reach *any conclusions*... the Security Council resolves that... the Security Council under Article 34 of the Charter establish a Commission of Investigation to ascertain the facts relating to the alleged border violations... between Greece on the one hand and Albania, Bulgaria and Yugoslavia on the other"; res. no. 4 of April 29, 1946 which appointed a subcommittee of five members of the Council to gather statements and documents to establish whether the existence of the Fascist regime in Spain could "lead to international friction" (a situation which is typically a subject of the conciliation function) and "endanger international peace and security" (a situation typically referring to Chapter VII); res. no. 132 of September 7, 1959 which was limited simply to deciding (with regard to guerrilla infiltration in Laos) "to appoint a subcommittee consisting of Argentina, Italy, Japan and Tunisia", and instructing this subcommittee "to examine the statements made before the Security Council concerning Laos, to receive further statements and documents, and to conduct such inquires as it may determine necessary and to report to the Security Council as soon as possible"; res. no. 189 (para. 5) of June 4, 1964 on border incidents between Vietnam and Cambodia; res. no. 203 (para. 2) of May 14, 1965 on the domestic situation in the Dominican Republic, in which the Secretary-General was invited "to send, as an urgent measure, a representative to the Dominican Republic for the purpose of reporting to the Security Council on the present situation"; res. no. 295 of August 3, 1971, appointing a mission of three members of the Council to be sent to Guinea to ascertain the situation caused by Portuguese raids; res. no. 348 (para. 5) of May 28, 1974 on border incidents between Iran and Iraq; res. no. 377 of October 22, 1975 and no. 379 of November 2, 1975, in which the Secretary-General was invited to consult with all parties concerned on the question of Western Sahara and to report to the Council in order to enable it to take appropriate measures; res. no. 404 of July 2, 1977 appointing a mission of three members of the Council to investigate acts of violence committed in Cotonou, in Benin, by mercenaries brought by an aircraft which had landed without authorisation and was from an unknown point of departure; deliberation of April 4, 1983 (resulting from a statement issued on the same date by the President of the Council and reported in Doc. S/15680) which entrusted the Secretary-General with the task of carrying out investigations on cases of mass intoxication in several Arab territories occupied by Israel.

As an example of an investigation linked to specific objectives, cf. res. no. 61 of November 4, 1948 appointing a committee of five members of the Council entrusted with the task of assisting the UN mediator in Palestine and, in the event of breaches of the truce between Arabs and Israelis, to "report to the Council on further measures it would be appropriate to take under Chapter VII of the Charter".

The fact that, on the basis of Article 34, an investigation may be decided on without reference to a specific function of the Council has practical consequences concerning the exception of domestic jurisdiction and the voting procedure in the organ. With regard to domestic jurisdiction, the exception can be raised in the case of the conciliation function but not in that of the enforcement measures set out in Chapter VII (cf., Article 2, para. 7, last part). It is evident, then, that resolutions that in a general manner give rise to an investigation, which in turn can lead to the adoption of such measures, do not meet the limit of domestic jurisdiction. For similar reasons, general resolutions on an investigation *always* come under the rule of the last part of Article 27, para. 3, according to which "in decisions under Chapter VI... a party [a member of the Council] to a dispute shall abstain from voting". This is specifically due to the possibility that the Council may restrict itself, following the investigations, to the exercise of the conciliation function under Chapter VI.

It may happen that the investigation is expressly linked by the Council to the conciliation function or to the measures under Chapter VII. When this is the case, the relative resolution will follow, as far as domestic jurisdiction and the cited provision of Article 27, para. 3, last part, are concerned, the regime of the function to which it is linked.

The Council may carry out an investigation either directly or, as usually occurs, by creating an *ad hoc* subsidiary organ under Article 29 (for example, a Commission of inquiry composed of several members of the Council, of the diplomatic staff of members States, of UN officials, and so on), or by entrusting the Secretary-General who will act in accordance with Article 98.

Also when it is accompanied by the creation of a subsidiary organ under Article 29, the resolution regarding an investigation has a substantive and not a procedural nature for purposes of the majorities prescribed by Article 27, para. 3. On this point, which gave rise to the question of the double veto, see § 26.

The power of investigation may also be exercised with regard to situations and disputes in which the Council has already intervened in exercising its functions in maintenance of the peace, but where it intends to follow further developments with a view to further interventions. From this point of view, the establishment of subsidiary organs (truce commissions, observation corps) to oversee respect for truces and armistices in international and internal wars or to monitor, to avoid or to investigate into violations of human rights is covered by Article 34. For all these measures, which pertain either to Chapter VII or to the matter of human rights in a broad sense, the limit of domestic jurisdiction does not exist (see § 45 III). Article 34 also furnishes the framework for the creation of subsidiary organs such as Commissions of good offices, of mediation, and so on, to which the Council may assign, besides their conciliation functions (in accordance with Article 36 or Article 39) functions of investigation as well. Examples of truce commissions, observers, commissions of good offices and of mediation with functions of investigation are abundant in practice.

The establishment of groups of military observers is to be kept separate from the establishment of UN armed forces, including peacekeeping forces, on the basis of Chapter VII (see § 59 *in fine*). This is even more true as far as non-military groups of observers are established by the Council.

Cf., for example, for less recent practice, res. no. 39 of January 20, 1948 (appointment of a Commission of three Member States of the United Nations with tasks of investigating and mediating the Indo-Pakistani question); res. no. 48 of April 23, 1948 (truce commission for Palestine, composed of career consuls of the Member States of the Council); res. no. 50 of May 29, 1948 (military observers in Palestine), res. no. 67, para. 4 (b) of January 28, 1948 (military observers in Indonesia); res. no. 80 of March 14, 1950 (appointment of a UN representative for India and Pakistan); res. no. 100 of October 27, 1953 (supervision of the suspension of works carried out by Israel in the de-militarised zone in Palestine); res. no. 171 of April 9, 1962 (supervision of the truce in Palestine); res. no. 179 of June 11, 1963 (military observers in the de-militarised zones along the border between Yemen and Saudi Arabia: see also the Report of the Secretary-General on the situation in Yemen, the basis for the Council resolution, in SCOR, 18th year, Suppl. for April, May and June 1963, p. 33 f.); res. no. 209 of September 4, 1965 and no. 210 of September 6, 1965 (supervision of the truce between India and Pakistan by military observers); res. no. 234 of July 9, 1967 (supervision of the truce in the Suez Canal zone).

For the more recent practice, particularly for the practice concerning the creation of military or non-military groups of observers, cf., for example, res. no. 619 of August 9, 1988 (setting up of UNIMOG, a group of military observers for supervising the cease-fire between Iran and Iraq; res. no. 644 of November 7, 1989 (setting up of ONUCA, a group of observers in Central America); res. no. 653 of April 20, 1990 and res. no. 656 of June 8, 1990 (monitoring the cease-fire in Nicaragua by the ONUCA); res. no. 687, part B, para. 5, of April 3, 1991 and res. no. 689 of April 9, 1991 (setting up of UNIKOM, a groups of observers for the respect of the demilitarised zone between Iraq and Kuwait after the Gulf War); res. no. 690 of April 29, 1991 (creating MINURSO, the UN Mission for a Referendum in Western Sahara); res. no. 693 of May 20, 1991 (creating ONUSAL, the UN Observer Mission in El Salvador); decision of January 29, 1993, resulting from a statement by the President, relating to the sending of a mission in Georgia to provide, among other things, for monitoring the cease-fire between the parties in conflict (cf. Doc. S/PV.3169); res. no. 846 of June 22, 1993 (setting up of UNOMUR, the UN Observer Mission in Uganda-Rwanda); res. no. 846 of June 22, 1997 (creation of MONUA, the UN Observer Mission in Angola); res. no. 1161 of April 9, 1998, requesting the Secretary-General to reactivate the International Commission of Inquiry set up in conformity with previous resolutions in order to collect information and reports relating to the sale and supply of arms to the former Rwandan government forces.

The question of whether the act which gives rise to an investigation is a decision (which as such binds the States to co-operate with the investigating organs), or a mere recommendation (and therefore an act without binding force) has been discussed in practice and in legal doctrine. It has been held, in favour of the first view, that the investigation may, *owing to its very nature*, only be decided upon and not recommended, and, as a consequence, Article 25 of the Charter has been invoked. According to this article, "The Members of the United Nations agree to accept and carry out the decisions of the Security Council in accordance with the present Charter". The supporters of the non-binding nature have insisted on the fact that the provision concerning investigations appears in Chapter VI and that, on the basis of Chapter VI, as was often repeated during the preparatory works, the Council has at its disposal only the tool of recommendation and therefore does not have binding powers.

Such a discussion arose, in the early years of the United Nations, over the question of Greek frontier incidents. After the already mentioned Commission of investigation had been appointed to shed light on the accusations that Albania, Yugoslavia and Bulgaria were fostering the civil war in Greece, these three countries refused to co-operate with the Commission and refused to allow Commission members to enter their territories. The legality of this refusal (particularly the refusal by Yugoslavia which, at the time, among the three, was the only UN member) was examined with regard to whether the resolution ordering the investigation had the nature of a decision or of a recommendation (cf. SCOR, 2nd year, 162nd meet., p. 1418-1427; 166th meet., p. 1522 ff.; 167h meet., p. 1541 f.; cf. also SC Rep. 1946-51, chap. X, part II, case no. 13).

In our view, the problem of the position of Member States with regard to an investigation is completely unrelated to the alternative of a recommendation or a decision and also to the distinction between Chapter VI and Chapter VII. The resolution providing for an investigation is not a *normative* act, neither in the sense of a mandatory prescription (decision) nor in the sense of an expression of an only desired outcome (recommendation). It is an *operational* resolution, with which the Council does not lay down rules on conduct but simply acts (on operational resolutions, see § 92). The answer to the question of whether, and up to what point, the Member States are obligated to co-operate must thus be sought elsewhere. With regard to the existence of the obligation, it is sufficient to go back to Article 2, para. 5, under which "all Members shall give to the United Nations every assistance in any action it takes in accordance with the present Charter". It is clear, on the other hand, that an obligation to co-operate is inherent to any constitutive agreement of an international organization. However, this is not the heart of the problem, at least that regarding investigation. The heart of the problem consists in asking, up to what point co-operation must be lent, and, specifically, whether it must be lent up to the maximum concession that can be asked of a sovereign State, that is, to open its territory (or a territory controlled by it) to the Council or to its subsidiary investigating organs. We believe that the answer must be negative, since when the Charter has required such a concession in relation to certain actions by the United Nations, it has said so expressly (see, as an example, Article 43 and the rights of passage it governs). We believe, however, that in light of the general duty to co-operate, a State which closes its frontiers to an investigation must at least furnish an adequate reason for doing so.

In the light of the Charter, therefore, the refusal of Albania, Bulgaria and Yugoslavia in the above-cited case cannot be condemned. The same is to be said, again in the light of the Charter, of Israel's refusal in 1968 to allow entry in the occupied Arab territories to a representative of the Secretary-General, who had been entrusted, by res. no. 259 of September 27, 1968, with the task of investigating the living conditions and the security of inhabitants (on this case, see *UNMC*, 1968, Oct., p. 3).

Quite a different question is whether the refusal of a State to open its territory to, and to fully co-operate with, the investigating organs can be considered by the Council as a threat or a violation of international peace according to Article 39 and engendering enforcement measures within the framework of Chapter VII.

Various resolutions recently adopted against Iraq, which demand the opening of the territory to, and full co-operation with, UN inspectors in order to investigate its programme of development of weapons of mass destruction, can be cited in this respect. The last and most important one is res. 8.11.2002 n. 1441 which warned Iraq that it would face "serious consequences" if co-operation with the inspectors was refused or incomplete.

52. *The peaceful settlement function under Chapter VI.* A) *Factual Conditions.*

BIBLIOGRAPHY: EAGLETON, *The Jurisdiction of the Security Council over Disputes*, in *AJ*, 1946, p. 513 ff.; SALOMON, *L'ONU et la paix. Le Conseil de Sécurité et le règlement pacifique des différends. (Le chapitre VI de la Charte des Nations Unies)*, Paris, 1948; KELSEN, *The Settlement of Disputes by the Security Council*, in *International Law Quarterly*, 1948, p. 173 ff.; WEHBERG, *Der Sicherheitsrat und das friedliche Streitverfahren*, in *Die Friedens-Warte*, 1948, p. 311 ff.; BRUGIÈRE, *Le développement des procédures de réglementation pacifique des conflits et la compétence du Conseil de Sécurité, ibid.*, 1949, p. 257 ff.; DELBEZ, *L'évolution des idées en matière de réglement pacifique des conflits*, in *RGDIP*, 1951, p. 5 ff.; ZENKER, *Le Conseil de Sécurité et le réglement pacifique des différends*, Paris, 1952; VERDROSS, *Idées directrices de l'Organisation des Nations Unies*, in *RC*, 1953, II, p. 32 ff.; JIMENEZ DE ARECHAGA, *Le traitement des différends internationaux par le Conseil de Sécurité*, in *RC*, 1954, I, p. 60 ff.; UBERTAZZI, *Contributo alla teoria della conciliazione delle controversie internazionali davanti al Consiglio di Sicurezza*, Milan, 1958; GOODRICH and SIMONS, *The UN and Maintenance of International Peace and Security*, Washington, 1962, part. III; ARANGIO-RUIZ, *Controversie internazionali*, in *Enciclopedia del diritto*, vol. X, 1962, p. 419 ff.; SERENI, *Le crisi internazionali*, in *RDI*, 1962, p. 553 ff.; CHABRA, *The UN Security Council; its Composition, its Voting Procedure and its Function in the Peaceful Settlement of Disputes during its first Fifteen Years*, Cincinnati, 1963; BOWETT, *The UN Peaceful Settlement of Disputes*, in *David Davies Memorial Institute Study Group on the Peaceful Settlement* etc., *(Report)*, London, 1966, p. 161 ff.; VILLANI, *Controversie internazionali*, in *Novissimo Digesto Italiano (Appendice)*, 1980, p. 711 ff.; FYODOROV, *The UN Security Council and the Pacific Settlement of International Disputes*, in *International Affairs* (Moscow), 1982, 4, p. 19 ff.; SOHN, *The Security Council's Role in the Settlement of International Disputes*, in *AJ*, 1984, p.

402 ff.; MURPHY, *The Conciliatory Responsibilities of the United Nations Security Council*, in *GYIL*, 1992, p. 190 ff.

According to Articles 33, 36 and 37, the peaceful settlement function applies to "disputes or situations the continuation of which is likely to endanger the maintenance of international peace and security".

It is difficult to say where exactly the difference lies between dispute and situation. The preparatory works do not shed any light on the matter. As far as the definition of "situation" is concerned, the starting point is the fact that even a situation must be such as to endanger the peace. Consequently, a situation must have *as a minimum* the following characteristic: on the one hand, the claim of one or more States that others act in a certain way (either at the international level or, for cases where the limit of domestic jurisdiction does not exist, at the domestic level), and, on the other, the refusal to act in this way. The questions that have been brought before the Council up until now have all had this characteristic. However, demand and refusal (or resistance) are the classic elements of an international dispute, and one could therefore be tempted to say that, for purposes of the peaceful settlement function, a distinction between dispute and situation does not exist. In favour of this conclusion, one could note: firstly, that the States, in seizing the Council, usually speak of a situation even when they are clearly bringing their own very special disputes; secondly, that the Council has hardly ever been concerned with the difference; thirdly, that even the legal doctrine which has sought to examine the topic is abundant with theoretical observations but miserly with practical examples; and, lastly, that the classic notion of international dispute is so broad as to be able to take in any matter brought before the Council (see, on this point, § 27). Perhaps all that can be concluded, in simply adopting a quantitative criteria, is that in a dispute a claim to the effect that others act in a certain way comes from one or from few States, whereas in a situation (especially in the case of a domestic situation in a country) there are more or many States or even the entire international Community involved. The necessity that in any case there are opposing parties is found in the spirit of Chapter VI and, more simply, in the very fact that the function of the Council is limited to settling disputes.

It would be mistaken to identify *situations* with the attitude taken by a State in the sphere of domestic jurisdiction. In the first place, a dispute between two given States may also touch upon matters of domestic jurisdiction, for example, the treatment of a minority in the light of the treaties in force between the two States. Secondly, when a domestic situation, for example, a situation arising from the failure to respect human rights, is not brought to the attention of the Council by a State or by a group of States but by the General Assembly or by the Secretary-General, there can still be identified a group, perhaps a very large group, of States, or even a group composed of all the States, who are pressing to have the situation settled.

When we speak of domestic situations, we speak of situations for which the limit of domestic jurisdiction does not exist, or does not exist any more (see § 45 III). Of course, other domestic situations cannot be dealt with by the Council under the provisions of Chapter without infringing Article 2, para. 7, of the Charter.

Besides being fleeting, the difference between dispute and situation is also of no practical use. It is true that some articles of the Charter seem to assume such differences, in that their provisions are limited to disputes. This is the case of Article 27, para. 3, last part, according to which "in decisions under Chapter VI,... [a member of the Council] a party to a dispute [under consideration by the Security Council] shall abstain from voting". Similarly, Article 32 which gives the right to participate in Council sessions to any State which "is party to a dispute under consideration by the Security Council...", and to Article 37 which, in addressing the most important competence of the Council under the peaceful settlement function, the power to enter in the merits of a question (see § 54), refers solely to disputes. However, as far as the first two articles are concerned, we have already noted in ascertaining their exact rational, that their sphere of application is ultimately completely independent from the notion of dispute (see § 27 and § 29). As for Article 37, we shall see in a moment that practice has considerably widened its scope, so as to make it useless to strive for a precise determination of the factual circumstances set out by it.

The difference between disputes and situations, for the purposes of Article 37, has occasionally been discussed in the Council, although without any practical result being reached, with the aim of establishing whether or not... the organ had to keep to the qualification of dispute or situation given to a certain case by the State bringing the issue. Cf. the cases of nationalisation of the Suez Canal and of the Indo-Pakistani dispute (which India insisted on calling a situation) at the earl stage of their dispute for the possession of the territories of Jammu and Kashmir: cf. SC Rep, Suppl. 1956-1958, sub. Chap. X, part. IV, case nos. 7 and 9.

The peaceful settlement function is limited to disputes and situations "the continuance of which is like to endanger the maintenance of international peace and security". With this redundant language, Articles 33 ff. requires that matters brought before the Council have certain gravity. The gravity may depend either on the matter being disputed, or on the means and intensity with which the States directly concerned claim to have their respective interests or points of view prevail. In any case, as can be seen in an even superficial reading of Article 33, para. 2 ("The Security Council shall...") and Article 37, para. 2 ("If the Security Council deems..."), the Council enjoys broad discretionary power in deciding whether a question actually may endanger the peace and therefore deserves to be dealt with. The only limit to the discretion of the organ is the fact that... some kind of difference, whatever it may be, exists between the States. If there are no differences between States, the peace cannot be endangered.

Under this aspect, the behaviour of the Council in examining the already mentioned Iranian question was to be considered unlawful (see § 50). In this case, the majority decided to keep the question on the agenda although Iran and the USSR had together announced that they had resolved it by agreement, and that new elements had not appeared.

Given the discretion enjoyed by the organ in deciding whether or not a question may endanger the peace, Article 38 in the end borders on irrelevance. Under this article, the Council "may, if all the parties to a dispute so request, make recommendations... with a view to a pacific settlement of the dispute". This means that the peaceful settlement function may also have as its subject disputes that do not endanger the peace, when, and only when, all the parties (and therefore not only one of them or even a third State or the Secretary-General or the Assembly, as in the other cases: see § 50) agree in bringing the matter before the Council. It is a useless norm since the provisions regarding the peaceful settlement of endangering disputes defer to the Council the judgement as to their dangerous nature. It would be a different matter if it were held that in the case of Article 38 the Council *was obligated* to be concerned with a question or at least to place it on the agenda. However, such a view would be contrary to the letter of Article 38 ("The Council may..."). Moreover, it would be unfounded from a general point of view, since it is inconceivable that UN organs could enter positive obligations to engage in a given course of conduct (see § 13).

There is no trace of Article 38 in practice.

53. B) *Indications to the States of "procedures or methods" for settling differences that may endanger the peace.*

BIBLIOGRAPHY: see § 52.

Article 33, para. 1, which opens Chapter VI, obliges the parties to a dispute to seek a solution by peaceful means (cf. Article 2, para. 3). It indicates, by way of example, negotiation, enquiry, mediation, conciliation, arbitration, judicial settlement, and resort to regional agencies or arrangements.

Article 33, para. 2, and Article 36 give the Council the power to urge the parties to a dispute and, more generally, the States whose differences are likely to endanger the peace, to have recourse to procedures of this kind. The difference between Article 33, para. 2, and Article 36 is that the former refers to a *general* request by the Council while the latter provides that the organ indicate which *specific* means ("procedure or method") among the ones in Article 33, para. 1, or among others of a similar nature, is appropriate for a given question. In both cases, as in the whole peaceful settlement function, the Council may issue only recommendations. Those do not bind the States to follow the recommended course of conduct.

The subjects regulated by Article 33, para. 2, and Article 36 are also dealt with in Chapter VII at Article 39. According to Article 39, the Council, faced with a threat to the peace, a breach of the peace, or an act of aggression not only may adopt enforcement measures but may also make recommendations to the States concerned, of the kind provided for in Chapter VI (see § 56). Actually, it may be difficult to establish whether a certain Council resolution comes within the framework of Article 33, para. 2, or Article 36, in that it refers to a mere dispute or situation likely to endanger the peace, or can be traced back to Article 39. It is mainly difficult to distinguish between a situation "likely to endanger the peace" and a situation that is a "threat to the peace". What criterion should be adopted in practice? In accordance with what we have said previously regarding the delimitation between Chapter VI and Chapter VII (see § 49), Article 39 covers those resolutions which indicate not only procedures or methods for settling a dispute or a situation, but also adopt one of the measures for protecting the peace set out in Chapter VII, or expressly state they are confronted with conduct of States that can be considered a threat to the peace, a breach of the peace or an act of aggression, or, again, intervene in a situation characterised by the use of military force and therefore objectively definable as a breach of the peace.

Of the two articles, Article 36 is the more important. It authorises the Council to intervene "at any stage" of a dispute or situation endangering the peace and it authorises interventions of various kinds. The most simple intervention is the indication of the procedure or method to follow to reach a settlement. It operates as an invitation to the interested States, depending on the case, to negotiate, seek a solution by mediation, submit the dispute to arbitration, and so on. In addressing the States, the Council must take into account the procedures that have already been adopted by the parties (Article 36, para. 2) and the necessity that when the disputes have a legal nature, recourse should be had to the International Court of Justice (Article 36, para. 3).

Cf., for example, the following resolutions: res. no. 2 of January 30, 1946, regarding the already mentioned Iranian question in which, once it had been ascertained that the USSR and Iran had begun negotiations, the parties were invited to continue and to inform the Council on their progress; res. no. 22 of April 9, 1947, which invited Great Britain and Albania to submit to the International Court of Justice their dispute regarding the Corfu Channel (Great Britain held Albania responsible for damage suffered by several of its ships which were passing through the waters of the Channel in October 1946, waters which had been mined by Albania; in turn, Albania claimed the violation of its sovereignty since British authorities had, in the following days, begun an operation of mine-removal; the decision was handed down by the Court on April 9, 1949, in ICJ, *Reports*, 1949, p. 4 ff.); res. no. 93 of May 18, 1951, including an invitation to Israel and to Syria to bring questions regarding the implementation of the armistice agreement of July 20, 1949 before a mixed armistice Commission, created after the 1948 war between Arabs and Israelis and consisting of representatives of the two parties; res. no. 144 of August 19, 1960, adopted in relation to the tension created between Cuba and the

United States following the coming to power of the Castro regime and recommending that the members of the Organization of American States act as a mediator between the two countries; res. no. 385 of August 25, 1976, which invited Greece and Turkey to negotiate an agreement for settling the dispute over the delimitation of their respective portions of the continental shelf, keeping in mind the competence of the International Court of Justice in legal matters; res. no. 530 of March 19, 1983, which, having expressed concern about the danger of a military clash between Nicaragua and Honduras, recommended that they resolve their disputes through the mediation of the Contadora group (Columbia, Mexico, Panama and Venezuela); res. no. 616 of July 20, 1988, which acknowledged the establishment of an ICAO Commission of investigation regarding the shooting down of an Iranian civilian aircraft by the United States naval forces in the Straits of Hormuz in 1988; res. no. 658 of June 27, 1990, no. 690 of April 19, 1991, and no. 809 of March 2, 1993, inviting Morocco and the Polisario Front to co-operate with the Secretary-General to resolve the question of Western Sahara; res. no. 1073 of September 28, 1996, calling, *inter alia*, for the immediate resumption of negotiations within the Middle East peace process (see para. 3 of the resolution).

A second kind of intervention that can come within the framework of Article 36 is when the Council does not only invite the States to have recourse to a certain procedure or method, but itself provides for such procedure or method. This is the reason for the Council's creation of subsidiary organs, which are composed in different way (by members of the organ, by Secretariat officials, by UN Member States) and which may assist the parties in settling disputes or situations. Examples of Commissions of good offices, of mediation, of conciliation, and so forth, are numerous in practice. However also in these cases, as in general in the exercise of the peaceful settlement function (see § 49), the protagonists remain the States concerned, with the Council's task that of stimulating agreement among them. The role and the powers of the Commissions created by the Council do not differ in any way from those of similar organs set up outside of the United Nations and used by the States in accordance with Article 33, para. 1.

Cf., for example, the various resolutions adopted regarding the Indo-Pakistani and Middle East questions, in periods of truce: res. no. 39 of January 20, 1948 (creation of a Commission of three members of the United Nations with the tasks of investigating and exercising "mediatory influence to smooth away difficulties" between India and Pakistan); res. no. 47 of April 21, 1948 (Commission of five UN members with functions of good offices between the parties); res. no. 107 of March 30, 1955 (invitation to Egypt and Israel to co-operate with the Chief of Staff of the UN Commission encharged with supervising the truce in the Middle East, and to discuss the situation existing along the armistice line between the two countries); res. no. 242 of November 22, 1967, adopted several months after the Israeli Six-Day War and including a request addressed to the Secretary-General to send his own special representative to the Middle East (this was the beginning of the Jarring Mission which was to last several years) to favour the pacific settlement of the question. Cf. also, and again as examples, res. no. 367, para. 6, of March 12, 1975, inviting the Secretary-General to exercise his good offices in order to reach a solution to the Cyprus question; res. no. 457, para. 4, of December 4, 1979, containing the same invitation with regard to the taking and the detention of American Embassy staff in Tehran; res. no. 765 of July 16, 1992 and no. 772 of August 17, 1992 (sending of a representative of the Secretary-General and of observers in South Africa);

res. no. 1398 of March 25, 2002, no. 1430 of August 14, 2002 and no. 1466 of March 14, 2003 (boundary dispute between Ethiopia and Eritrea).

See also the examples listed at § 51, concerning the groups of observers with functions both of mediation or conciliation and investigation.

Aside from the above mentioned cases, any recommendation, whose purpose is to facilitate agreement among the States directly concerned, can come within the scope of Article 36. The only thing that the Council cannot or, rather, should not do on the basis of Article 36 is *to enter into the merits* of questions, that is, to recommend how to resolve a given difference, to say who is wrong and who is right, or to express condemnation for certain conduct of a State and to request, as a consequence, that it cease. The power to recommend solutions on the merits (the so-called terms of settlement, as opposed to procedures and methods under Article 36) is provided by the following Article 37 and must, or, rather, should be exercised in the presence of special and more rigid conditions. We use the conditional tense because these pre-requisites have been abandoned in practice and therefore can be considered eliminated by custom (see § 54). Today the Council is completely free, when faced with a dispute or situation which threatens to endanger the peace, both to indicate procedures and methods of settlement and to recommend solutions on the merits, during any stage of the dispute or situation.

The procedures and methods of settlement under Article 36 are those, and only those, aimed at facilitating agreement among the States. It is absurd, considering the spirit of Chapter VI, to consider measures applying sanctions or involving the use of force, even as an exception and for very limited purposes, as procedures of "settlement", and to bring them within the framework of Article 36. No merit has the view, held in legal doctrine as well as in the Security Council itself, that certain resolutions, such as recommendations addressed to the Member States to adopt economic measures against given States, or resolutions to set up UN armed forces, should come within the framework of Chapter VI and in particular of Article 36. This view holds that such resolutions would not come completely within the cases governed by Article 41, regarding economic sanctions, and Article 42, on measures involving the use of force. It is often said that the Council acts in these cases in between Chapters VI and VII. As we shall see, this view has been upheld in the Council for political reasons but is legally untenable (see §§ 58 and 59).

54. C) *The indication of "terms of settlement"*.

BIBLIOGRAPHY: see § 52.

Recommending "terms of settlement", that is, suggesting to the States how to settle, *in the merits*, a given dispute, certainly comes within the framework of the peaceful settlement function. The powers of the Council on the subject are provided by Article 37.

As in the case of Article 33, para. 2, and Article 36, there is a problem of co-ordination of Article 37 with Article 39, which also authorises the Council to recommend solutions on the merits. The criterion for distinguishing the recommendations that come within Article 37, on the one hand, and Article 39 on the other, is the same criterion which should be used in order to distinguish between Article 39 and Article 33, para. 2 and Article 36. On this point, see § 56.

Article 37 contains, first of all, at para. 1, a provision of a procedural nature. This provision substitutes for the generic term *may* (which refers to the *right* of every State, on the basis of Article 35, to bring a matter before the Council: see § 50), a precise *obligation* of the parties to a dispute likely to endanger the peace to refer it to the Council. This obligation arises only when the States are not able to settle the dispute by the means indicated by Article 33, para. 1 (and in spite of possible recommendations made by the Council on the basis of Article 33, para. 2, and Article 36). In other words, it arises only when the possibility of an agreement between the parties proves to be unrealistic.

In disputes brought before the Council in this way, the Council may intervene, under para. 2 of Article 37, by recommending terms of settlement (in the French text, "termes de règlement"), and thus make proposals on the merits, deciding who is wrong and who is right, indicating the reciprocal concessions that the parties must make in the interests of peace, expressing condemnation of a given State conduct, such as, for instance, the gross and systematic violation of human rights, and then requesting that it ends.

Article 37, para. 2, also says that the Council may, instead of entering in the merits, decide to take action... under Article 36. The indication of this second possibility is redundant, since it is already stated, in very broad terms, by Article 36 itself.

In the Dumbarton Oaks proposals, no mention was made of the Council's power to recommend terms of settlement (cf. para. 4 of Chapter VIII, sec. B, corresponding to the present Article 37). However, the Sponsoring Powers themselves proposed it at the San Francisco Conference (see U.N.C.I.O., vol. 12, p. 181).

Article 37 subjects the power to enter in to the merits of questions to the following conditions: the existence of a dispute; recourse to the Council by the parties to the dispute (or at least by one of them); the proven impossibility of reaching agreement between the parties through the means available under Article 33, para. 1.

Literally, para. 1 of Article 37 seems to require that *all* the parties to the dispute have recourse to the Council. However, during the proceedings of the San Francisco Conference, the possibility of a unilateral recourse was explicitly and unanimously allowed: see U.N.C.I.O., vol. 12, p. 47.

The phrase "should the parties to a dispute... fail to settle it by the means indicated" in Article 33 does not mean that all these means (negotiation, mediation, conciliation, arbitration, etc.) must be attempted before the Council intervenes! It is enough that, given the circumstances, an agreement between the parties is not foreseeable.

> Cf., in this sense, the intervention of the Egyptian delegate during the examination by the Council, in 1947, of the dispute between Egypt and Great Britain regarding the presence of British troops in Egyptian territory. In protesting against a draft resolution (then not adopted) which stated (clearly for purposes of delay) that "the means of settlement provided by Article 33 of the Charter have not been exhausted", the Egyptian representative pointed out the impossibility that the Charter could require prior resort to these means *cumulatively* considered (see SCOR, 2nd year, 193rd meet., p. 2165 f.).

It is useless to dwell on the conditions required by Article 37 for the Council to recommend terms of settlement. As all commentators usually point out, the Council practice, except for very rare cases, has clearly tended, since the early years of the United Nations, to give the organ a great amount of freedom on this matter. The Council has entered into the merits of questions, without encountering significant opposition of a procedural nature by the States involved, whenever it has wished to do so. It has done so in questions submitted to it as "situations" rather than as "disputes", with regard to cases that were not brought before it by one of the parties to the action, and, finally, without being concerned with investigating if resort to the means under Article 33 was effectively impossible, but even intervening in the initial stage of a dispute. Consequently, it is possible to say that, owing to a custom, the power to indicate terms of settlement under Article 37 exists within the same broad limits with which Article 33, para. 2, and Article 36 grant the power to recommend and to indicate procedures or methods of settlement. Such custom has given the peaceful settlement function, a function which by nature does not adapt very well to procedural limits, a remarkable degree of effectiveness. Indeed, the provisions of Chapter VI on the peaceful settlement function are uselessly and inexplicably long-winded. Would it not have been sufficient to lay down in general terms the Council's power to recommend how States should act in the case of situations likely to endanger the peace? That is exactly what the customary rule which has developed from the practice does!

Examples of resolutions indicating terms of settlement (sometimes together with procedures or methods of settlement) can be found, first, in the practice on the Middle East question, in periods of truce. Cf. res. no. 42 of March 5, 1948 (regarding implementation of the partition plan for Palestine prepared by the General Assembly with res. no. 181-III of November 29, 1947); res. no. 89 of November 17, 1950 (on the regulation of passage of Beduins through the demilitarised zone); res. no. 95 of September 1, 1951 (recommendation to Egypt that the restriction on traffic through the Suez Canal be eliminated); res. no. 242 of November 1967 (indicating some general points for the solution of the Middle East question, such as the withdrawal of Israel from the Arab territories occupied during the Six-Day War in the summer of 1967, the reciprocal obligation to respect territorial integrity, the freedom to navigate in international waterways in the region, etc.); and, more recently, no. 607 of January 5, 1988, no. 608 of November 14, 1988, no. 636 of July 7, 1989, no. 672 of October 12, 1990, no. 681 of December 20, 1990, no. 694 of May 24, 1991, and no. 699 of June 17, 1991 (obligation of Israel to respect, in the Arab territories, the rules on belligerent occupation and to end the deportation of Palestinian civilians). Various times, then, terms of settlement, and, in particular, the necessity of plebiscites under the aegis of the United Nations, have been proposed to India and Pakistan in order to settle their territorial disputes (cf., for example, res. no. 47 of April 21, 1948, no. 80 of March 14, 1950, no. 91 of March 30, 1951, no. 122 of January 24, 1957). With regard to other questions, cf. for example, res. no. 3 of April 4, 1946 (withdrawal of Russian troops from Iranian territory); res. no. 138 of June 23, 1960 (invitation to Israel to "make appropriate reparation in accordance with the Charter of the United Nations and the rules of international law" to Argentina for the abduction of the Nazi criminal Eichmann by Israeli agents in Argentine territory); res. no. 226 of October 14, 1966 and res. no. 241 of November 15, 1967 (request that Portugal take appropriate measures so that its territory would not become a base of operations for mercenaries on their way to the Congo); res. no. 264 of March 20, 1969 (invitation to South Africa to withdraw from the territory of Namibia); res. no. 278 of May 11, 1970, incorporating a report of the Secretary-General, favourable to granting full independence to the Bahrain Islands, and the consequent rejection of the claims of Great Britain and Iran to exercising form of "protection" over such islands; res. no. 348 of May 28, 1974 (invitation to Iran and Iraq to... carry out the agreement concluded by the two States to resolve their border disputes); no. 457, para. 1, of December 4, 1979 (request to the Iranian government to immediately free staff of the American Embassy in Tehran); no. 573 of October 4, 1985 (request for compensation for damage caused by Israel in an attack on Tunisian territory); no. 637 of July 27, 1989 (approval of the agreement of Guatemala City of August 7, 1987 for peace, democratisation, reconciliation, development and justice in Central America); no. 649 of March 12, 1990 and no. 774 of August 26, 1992 (settlement of the Cypriot problem through a bi-municipal and bi-zonal federation between the Greek and Turkish communities); no. 731 of January 23, 1992, asking the Libyan government to agree to the request of the governments of the United States, Great Britain and France for co-operation in ascertaining responsibility for the terrorist attacks on the PAN AM 103 and UTA 772 flights, and, in particular, to deliver to these governments two Libyan citizens considered responsible for the attacks; no. 825 of May 11, 1993 (invitation to the People's Republic of Korea to respect the Treaty on the Non-proliferation of Nuclear Weapons); no. 1044 of January 31, 1996 (calling upon the government of Sudan to extradite to Ethiopia three suspects wanted in connection with the assassination attempt on the life of the President of Egypt occurred in Addis-Abeba); no. 1117 of June 27, 1997 (again on the settlement of the Cypriot problem trough a single bi-municipal State).

Many of the above listed resolutions did not fulfil the procedural requirements set forth in Article 37.

55. Action with respect to maintenance of the peace under Chapter VII. General remarks.

BIBLIOGRAPHY: KELSEN, *Collective Security and Collective Self-Defense under the Charter of the United Nations*, in *AJ*, 1948, p. 783 ff.; CAVARÉ, *Les sanctions dans le cadre de l'ONU*, in *RC*, 1952, I, p. 191 ff., part. p. 255 ff.; STONE, *Aggression and World Order (A Critique of UN Theorie of Aggression)*, London, 1958; McDOUGAL and REISMAN, *Rhodesia and the United Nations: The Lawfulness of International Concern*, in *AJ*, 1968, p. 1 ff.; VEROSTA, *Der Begriff « International Sicherheit » in der Satzung der Vereinten Nationen*, in *Internationale Festschrift für Alfred Verdross*, München, 1971, p. 533 ff.; LAMBERTI ZANARDI, *La legittima difesa nel diritto internazionale*, Milan, 1972, Chap. IV ff.; SCHWEBEL, *Aggression, Intervention and Self-Defence in Modern International Law*, in *RC*, 1972, II, p. 411 ff.; COMBACAU, *Le pouvoir de sanction de l'ONU. Etude théorique de la coercition non militaire*, Paris, 1974; ZOUREK, *Enfin une définition de l'agression*, in *AF*, 1974, p. 9 ff..; BRUHA, *Die Definition der Aggression*, Berlin, 1980; SCHAEFER, *Die Funktionsfähigkeit des Sicherheitsmechanismus der Vereinten Nationen*, Berlin, 1981; SCISO, *L'aggressione indiretta nella definizione dell'Assemblea Generale delle Nazioni Unite*, in *RDI*, 1983, p. 253 ff.; COMBACAU, *The Exception of Self-Defence in UN Practice*, in CASSESE (ed.), *The Current Legal Regulation of the Use of Force*, Dordrecht, 1986, p. 22 ff.; GREIG, *Self-Defence and the Security Council: What does Article 51 Require?*, in *ICLQ*, 1991, p. 366 ff.; ELLIOTT, *The New World Order and the Right of Self-Defence in the UN Charter*, in *Hastings International and Comparative Law Review*, 1991, p. 55 ff.; BERES, *After the Scud Attacks: Israel, « Palestine », and Anticipatory Self-Defense*, in *Emory International Law Review*, 1992, p. 71 ff.; SUCHARITKUL, *The Process of Peace-Making Following Operation «Desert Storm»*, in *ZöRV*, 1992, p. 1 ff.; GAJA, *Reflexions sur le rôle du Conseil de Securité dans le nouvel ordre mondial*, in *RGDIP*, 1993, p. 297 ff.; *Le dévelopment du rôle du Conseil de Sécurité (Colloque de l'Académie de droit international de La Haye, 1992, préparé par R-J. Dupuy)*, Dordrecht, 1993; KAIKOBAD, *Self-Defence, Enforcement Action and the Gulf Wars, 1980-88 and 1990-91*, in *BYIL*, 1992, p. 299 ff.; CARON, *The Legitimacy of the Collective Authority of the Security Council*, in *AJ*, 1993, p. 552 ff.; FRAUDENSCHUB, *Article 39 of the UN Charte Revisited: Threats to the Peace and the Recent Practice of the UN Security Council*, in *ZöRV*, 1993, p. 1 ff.; HUTCHINSON, *Restoring Hope: UN Security Council Resolutions for Somalia and an Expanded Doctrine of Humanitarian Intervention*, in *HILJ*, 1993, p. 624 ff.; LILLICH, *Humanitarian Intervention Through the United Nations: Towards the Development of Criteria*, in *Bruns'Z*, 1993, p. 557 ff.; STEIN, *Das Attentat von Lockerbie vodem Sicherheitsrat der Vereinten Nationen und dem Internationalen Gerichtshof*, in *AV*, 1993, p. 206 ff.; BAILEY, *The UN Security Council and Human Rights*, 1994; DINSTEIN, *War, Aggression and Self-Defence*, Cambridge, 1994; PICONE (ed.), *Interventi delle Nazioni Unite e diritto internazionale*, Padua, 1995; ÖSTERDAHL, *Threat to the Peace: The Interpretation by the Security Council of Article 39 of the UN Charter*, Uppsala, 1998; Bermejo Garcia, *Questiones actuales referents al uso de lafuerza en el derecho internacional*, in *ADe*, 1999, p. 3 ; CONDORELLI, *Les attentas du 11 septembre: où va le droit international ?*, in *RGDIP*, 2001, p.85 ff .

Chapter VII covers the most important powers of the Security Council, which should serve the purpose of the maintenance of world order. It constitutes the basis for the adoption of enforcement measures regarding States responsible for breaching the peace and even for the establishment of armed forces in the service of the United Nations. The collective security system, as the powers given by Chapter VII to the Council are called, functioned poorly and rarely up until the fall of the Berlin Wall, owing to the Cold War and the reciprocal veto's of the Soviet Union and the permanent Western members. Starting with the Gulf War, however, this system has had a second life and has once again become important. At the present time the Council actions taken on the basis of Chapter VII are the most relevant and important UN activities, in accordance, moreover, with what had been the idea of the framers of the Charter. Although the period of veto is not definitively over, particularly as far as large and important crises are concerned, the number of resolutions providing for very limited interventions of the Security Council under Chapter VII is, however, still impressive.

One of the main features of the current action of the Security Council on the basis of Chapter VII is the intervention in a State's domestic affairs. This could be where a civil war is going on or a massive violation of fundamental human rights has occurred or where a post-conflict situation arises which needs the assistance to the local authorities.

Another important feature is the increasing number of measures which are taken by the Council without any justification in the light of the provisions of the Charter. Often, in taking such measures, the Council expressly states that it is acting in the framework of Chapter VII since a threat or a breach of the peace has occurred. In examining this practice from a legal point of view, it is necessary to ascertain whether the practice can be somehow fitted into one of the provisions of the chapter, even broadly interpreted, and, if not, whether it has brought about a customary rule or it must simply be considered as illegal even if politically understandable. In the following pages we will firstly examine the provisions of Chapter VII and the related practice and then consider the practice which has no basis in such provisions.

55 bis. The determination of a threat to the peace, a breach of the peace, or an act of aggression.

BIBLIOGRAPHY: See § 55. *Adde*: DELBRÜCIK,, *The Fight Against Global Terrorism : Self-Defense or Collective Security as .international Policy Action ?*, in *GYIL*, 2001, p. 9 ff; ZAMBELLI, *La constatation des situation de l'article 39 del Chartedes Nations Unies, ecc.*, Bâle, 2002;CHAn, *La notion de pouvoir discrétionnaire appliqué aux organizations internationals*, in *RGDIP*, 2003, p. 535 ff.

Under Article 39, the first article in Chapter VII, the exercise of the powers set out under the article presumes the existence of a threat to the peace, a breach of the peace or an act of aggression.

In determining whether or not, in a specific case, there exists a threat to the peace, a breach of the peace, or an act of aggression, the Security

Council enjoys broad discretionary power ("The Council", Article 39 simply states, "shall determine the existence...", etc.). This discretionary power may be exercised especially with regard to the hypothesis of "threat to the peace". This is actually a very vague and elastic hypothesis which, unlike aggression or breach of the peace, is not necessarily characterised by military operations or operations involving the use of armed violence. It therefore covers the widest range of behaviour by a State. As a threat to, or a breach of, the peace, domestic situations become important, both with regard to conduct of the State itself (for example, the Council may hold, as it did in the case of South Africa and of Southern Rhodesia, that a generalized policy of racial discrimination constitutes a threat to the peace: see § 58) and with regard to a civil war situation in which a State, that is, a legitimate government, is no longer identifiable, but there are only factions fighting among themselves (as was the case of the intervention in the Congo in 1960 and is the case of the intervention in Somalia in 1992: see 59). Indeed, as we have already seen, one of the salient features of the present stage of interventions by the Council on the basis of Chapter VII is the humanitarian nature of the intervention and the lack of a distinction between international war and civil war. Of course, for this whole subject, the exception of domestic jurisdiction is not admissible. First of all, this exception is expressly excluded by Article 2, para. 7, last part, with regard to decisions concerning enforcement measures. Secondly, also for the other decisions that come within Chapter VII, decisions which, as we shall see, consist mainly of recommendations governed by Article 39 (see § 56), the limit of domestic jurisdiction has been eliminated in the practice with regard to situations in which human rights are at stake (on this point, see § 45 III).

The Council enjoys, then, a very wide discretionary power. At the San Francisco Conference, various proposals were made that the Charter be more detailed with regard to the conditions for the applicability of Chapter VII and, in particular, that it define aggression or at least list a certain number of typical cases which would justify an intervention by the Council. There was also clear concern that wide discretion of the organ could be detrimental to small or middle-sized States, possibly targeted by the Council, whereas the major powers, shielded by their right of veto, would have nothing to fear even in the event of their being in the position of the accused. However, it was easy to object that the opening of such issues would have brought the Conference to a standstill, especially if one took into account the precedent of the heated and fruitless debates that had characterised the attempts at defining aggression in the League of Nations in the period between the two world wars (on these debates, see STONE, *op. cit.*, p. 27 ff.) So, in the end, the present wording of Article 39 was preferred, with the stated purpose of allowing the Council to decide how to act on a case by case basis (cf. U.N.C.I.O., vol. 12, p. 505).

The discretionary power of the Council, as laid down by Article 39, has remained integral even after the adoption by the General Assembly, with res. no. 3314-XXIX of December 14, 1974, of a Declaration of principles (on the characteristics of this kind of act, see § 94) on the definition of aggression. The Declaration, issued after several years of work by a special Committee, lists a series of cases of aggression. They range from military invasion or occupation, even if temporary, to bombardment by land, sea or air forces, to the blockade of ports or coasts, to the sending of bands of mercenaries or to a State allowing its territory to be used for attacks against another State's territory (so-called indirect armed aggression), and so on. This is a list that does not affect Article 39 and the powers of the Security Council. Indeed, the Declaration recognises that the Council may, taking into account the circumstances of each specific case, conclude that the commission of one of the acts listed does not justify its intervention (Article 2); that the Council may consider other acts not listed as aggression (Article 4); and that, more in general, the definition of aggression contained in the resolution shall not prejudice the functions of UN organs as they are provided for by the Charter. This being the situation, it is useless to raise the problem (which in any case would have to have a negative answer) of whether the Assembly has the power to bind the Council on this matter.

A committee of 15 Member States for the study of aggression had been appointed by the General Assembly already in 1950 with res. no. 688-VII and was enlarged in 1954 to 19 members. However, its activity came to an end in 1957 because it proved impossible to reach an agreement. Only in 1967, with res. no. 2330-XXII which created a new Committee composed of 35 members ("Special Committee for the Definition of Aggression") was work resumed. The work's successful conclusion in 1974 was due also to the fact that many controversial points were eliminated rather than resolved and that, ultimately, the Declaration defines and specifies only the most simple, although the most serious, form of aggression, i.e., armed aggression. The final report of the Special Committee appears in GAOR, 29th sess., Suppl. no. 19.

Is the Council's broad discretion unlimited? Perhaps some limits may be deduced from the overall system. Let us distinguish between a situation characterised by military operations and, more in general, by the use of military force — whether this occurs abroad (international war) or within a country (civil war) does not matter — and a situation characterised by conduct which, although serious, does not involve armed violence (for example, the violation of human rights).

In the first case, since the use of military force is in itself at least a threat to the peace, the only limit that the Council may meet can be drawn *implicitly* from the principle of individual or collective self-defence provided for by Article 51. The Council may not consider as a threat to the peace, a breach of the peace, or an act of aggression the use of armed force in individual or collective self-defence, and intervene against a State which is defending itself or against States which are helping it to defend itself. This, however, is a rather theoretical limit if self-defence is restricted, as Article 51 restricts it, to the hypothesis of a reaction to an "armed attack" ["aggression armée" in the French text]. It is unthinkable, and it has never happened, that the Council has taken action against States... which had been attacked and had defended themselves. It would be a different matter if we were to accept the view favourable to preventive self-defence, or the view that every State could resort to the use of force against grave violations of international law such as gross violations of human rights (humanitarian interventions) or complicity in terrorist activities or in drug traffic. Similar views, usually upheld by the stronger States, in particular by the United States and their closest allies, but never accepted by the weaker ones, are unfounded in the light of Article 51.

Article 51 restricts, without possibility of misunderstanding, the use of force in self-defence to the very specific case of the reaction to an armed attack; that is, of an attack that has already been launched by one State (with regular forces, or, under the above-cited 1974 Declaration on the definition of aggression, with irregulars or mercenaries of equivalence strength) against another State. Only in this case could an act of self-defence not be considered as a threat to the peace or breach of the peace for purposes of the application of enforcement measures.

Article 51 speaks of both individual and *collective* self defence. The latter refers to cases in which the reaction to an armed attack comes not only from the State that has been attacked but also from third States. Collective self defence was introduced at San Francisco to give room to the reciprocal assistance agreements that at the time were being drawn up on the American continent (cf., the Act of Chapultepec of March 3, 1945, in AJ 1945, Suppl. p. 108 ff.) and that later were to proliferate with the establishment of regional organizations such as NATO, OAS, and so on. (The organized collective self-defence action under Article 51 must not be confused, however, with the collective measures that a regional organization may take under the direction of the Security Council in accordance with Article 53, para. 1; see, on this point, § 67).

The views that self-defence would justify preventive attacks, or attacks aimed at saving human lives (attacks with humanitarian purposes) or at counter-acting States encouraging terrorism (for example, the bombing of Libya by the United States in 1986, the air war of NATO against the Republic of Yugoslavia during the Kosovo crisis in 1999, which lasted about three months, the war against Afghanistan in October/November 2002, the war against Iraq in 2003) or illegal drug traffic (the invasion of Panama by the United States in 1989 and the resulting removal of General Noriega), have no basis in the Charter. The prohibition of the use of force, in fact, is expressed by Article 2, para. 4, in a way such as not to tolerate exceptions beyond the ones in Article 51. Moreover, at San Francisco, the absolute character of the prohibition of the use of force was clearly confirmed, apart from the exceptions provided by other rules of the Charter (see U.N.C.I.O., vol. 6, p.

334 and 400). Also the practice is against such theories. For example, in 1951 the Security Council, pointing out the absence of an armed attack, rejected Egypt's view that its measures restricting the passage of ships directed toward Israel through the Suez Canal were justified as self-defence (see SCOR, 6th year, 550th meet., ff.). Likewise, it has always rejected Israel's and South Africa's attempts to justify attacks against neighbouring States with the view that such attacks were reactions to *threats* to their territorial integrity. UN practice, in short, has never endorsed a notion of self-defence other than the one in Article 51 (cf., on this point, COMBACAU, *op. cit.*, p. 22 ff. and see, especially, res. no. 487 of 19 June 1981, condemning Israel for the bombing of nuclear plants in Iraq)), and recourse to this notion in the other above-mentioned cases has always been used by States which, for however powerful, remain a minority group.

> For the full discussion in the Council on the possibility of interpreting the American bombing of Libya in 1986 as self defence, cf. the documents S/PV.2674 of April 15, 1986 and S/PV.2674, 2680 and 2682. A draft resolution condemning the bombing obtained the majority of nine votes necessary for the adoption of a resolution, but it was blocked by the veto of the U.S., Great Britain and France (cf. S/PV.2682). On the Kosovo, Afghanistan and Iraq wars, see §§ 60 and 67.

The doctrine of preventive self-defence is now contained in the document entitled "The National Security Strategy of the United States of America" (the so-called Bush Doctrine) officially presented by the President of the United States to the Congress in September 2002 and conceived as a reaction to the brutal terrorist attack on the Twin Towers on September 11, 2001. According to this document, preventive self-defence will be exercised by the United States whenever it is deemed necessary in order to prevent an imminent threat of attack with weapons of mass destruction or terrorist acts. The Bush doctrine has been condemned or criticised by many States and also by the Secretary General of UN before the General Assembly (see GAOR, 58th sess., Pl. Meet., September 23, 2003). It is not law but a rough and arrogant expression of force.

The reaction against terrorism should not consist of the use of armed force *against a State*, involving the death of innocent people but rather in the adoption of preventive and repressive measures against the individuals committing or organizing such crimes. Worth noting is the fact that, even after September 11, the Security Council, acting in the framework of Chapter VII, only requested the States to take a series of measures, including financial measures, against individuals and groups of individuals, like Al Qaida. The Council never authorised the war conducted by the Unites States and their allies in Afghanistan (see § 60). It is true that in some resolutions which adopted such measures (particularly in res. no. 1368 of September 12, 2001 and no. 1373 of September 28, 2001) it is stated, among the "whereas", that the Council "reaffirms the inherent right of individual or collective self-defence as recognised by the Charter of the UN..."; however, this statement must be read in the context of the measures against terrorists as listed in the resolutions; it cannot be interpreted as authorising a war, since any time the Council has wanted to authorise the use of armed force by States it has done so expressly.

Regarding the "imminent" threat of the use of weapons of mass destruction, it is known that this *casus belli* was relied upon by the United States and United Kingdom at the time of the war to Iraq in 2003. However, it is also well known that the war was condemned by the overwhelming majority of the other States, even when it had not yet been ascertained that the weapons of mass destruction...did not exist.

> Those who tend to extend the lawfulness of the use of force beyond the case of self defence against armed attack usually emphasise the deficiencies in the collective security system provided for by Chapter VII. In particular, they emphasise the possibility that the Security Council can be paralysed by the exercise of the veto. They say that if the Charter guarantees such paralysis by allowing the right of veto, it cannot be interpreted in the sense of prohibiting a State from using any other possibility of defending itself beyond the provision of Article 51. In fact such an observation is not decisive for purposes of increasing the cases of self defence but rather gives us the opportunity to ask whether there can be drawn from Article 2, para. 4, on the prohibition of the use of armed force, and from Article 51 itself, real obligations and rights that can be invoked by the States between themselves, outside of the institutional framework of the United Nations. In other words, it seems to us that in such a vital subject, as is maintenance of the peace, the Charter must be seen *only* as a set of rules regulating certain powers of the organs. In this perspective, Article 51 should not come into play as a norm sanctioning a right of the States, but rather as a norm which places a limit on the power of the Security Council to adopt enforcement measures against a State on the basis of Chapter VII. If, then, the Council is paralysed, this means that the Charter, including Article 51, has exhausted its function.

More interesting, from a legal viewpoint, is the other hypothesis, that is, the one in which the situation brought to the attention of the Council is not characterised by military operations, whether international or internal. Considering the vague and elastic nature of the notion of threat to the peace, and taking into account the fact that the enforcement measures of Chapter VII fall outside the exception of domestic jurisdiction, the Council could consider, as a threat to the peace and therefore subject to enforcement measures, any conduct whatsoever, either within or outside a State, such as the adoption of a certain political regime, a treatment of the economic interests of aliens that is not in conformity with international standards, the closing of ports to foreign ships, the refusal to extradite criminals, and the like. All this does not make much sense. Then, what is the criterion for establishing the limit beyond which the Council cannot go? In our view the conduct of a State cannot be condemned by the Council, and cannot therefore be subject to enforcement measures, *when the condemnation is not shared by the opinion of most of the States and their peoples*. A limit of this kind can be implicitly found in Article 24, para. 1, which provides that the Security Council acts "in the name" of all UN members. Even if this provision does not place any limit on the mandate given to the Council, it cannot be thought that the UN members wanted to give the Council carte blanche. Mainly, however, such limit can be found in those principles in the preamble to the Charter and in Article 1 which bind the United Nations to pursue justice and co-operation among people. Justice alone, as an absolute value, does not say much when it is referred to an organ such as the Council which is a political and not a judicial organ. It acquires, by contrast, an unquestionable relevance if it is anchored in something real such as the opinion of the majority of States.

The possibility that the Security Council can consider certain situations as a threat to the peace which are not so considered by the majority of States can more easily occur today owing to the present hyper-activity of the Council. During the Cold War things were different. Indeed, at that time, only twice did the Council take action, with enforcement measures under Chapter VII, in situations not characterised by military operations. We are referring to res. no. 232 of December 16, 1966 and no. 253 of May 5, 1968 against Southern Rhodesia and no. 418 of November 4, 1977 against South Africa. These resolutions were adopted to penalise the apartheid policy of these two States (see § 58). In both cases it certainly cannot be said that the decisions of the Council did not correspond to the common opinion of the majority of the States especially if we consider the numerous resolutions adopted by the General Assembly specifically to induce the Council to take decisive action.

As for the new phase which opened with the end of the Cold War and which began with the resolutions against Iraq, some doubt may already arise regarding the legality of some of the decisions or parts of the decisions taken by the Council. This is the case of res. no. 687 of April 3, 1991, which put an end to the Gulf War, establishing a series of conditions for the cease-fire between Iraq on one side and Kuwait and its allies on the other. Resolution no. 687 was based expressly, as nearly all the other resolutions against Iraq, on Chapter VII. Since it was passed when the Iraqi armed aggression had been driven back, all the decisions contained in it postulate that a threat to the peace is implicit in the subsequent conduct of Saddam Hussein's government. For some parts of the resolution, it is doubtful whether this ascertainment corresponds to the general opinion of the States. In particular, Part E of the resolution which requires Iraq to pay compensation for the damage caused by the invasion and the unlawful occupation of Kuwait, and to accept that this damage be evaluated by a special Commission encharged with managing a compensation fund (cf. also subsequent res. no. 692 of May 20, 1991, which set up the Fund and the Commission and res. no. 705 of August 15, 1991, which set the minimum amount due from Iraq at 30% of the annual value of its oil exports). Part F, para. 22, of the resolution concerns the obligation to pay the compensation. Under this part, Iraq's failure to accept this would result in maintenance of the embargo (under Article 41 of the Charter) on Iraqi exports ordered by previous res. no. 661 of August 6, 1990 (see § 58). The only possible interpretation of Part E and Part F, para. 22, of the resolution is that refusal to pay compensation for war damages — compensation which, incidentally, finds little precedent in practice — constitutes a threat to the peace. Exactly such an interpretation does not seem to correspond to what is generally thought in the international community.

Another action of the Council over which there may arise some doubt as to the legality of the Council's own ascertainment of the existence of a threat to the peace, is contained in res. no. 748 of March 31, 1992. This imposed on the States the blocking of air communication with Libya and an embargo on the supplying of aircraft and weapons to that country. The resolution, expressly based on Chapter VII (and coming within the framework of Article 41: see § 58), justified these enforcement measures both by the fact that Libya had not agreed to the request of the United States, Great Britain and France to hand over two of its citizens accused of having taken part in acts of terrorism which led to the destruction in flight of two planes belonging to PAN AM (flight 103) and UTA (flight 772) and by the fact that Libya had not yet completely ended its participation in terrorist acts or in giving assistance to groups of terrorists. The resolution also provided (at para. 3) that sanctions were to be applied until the Council had ascertained that Libya had put an end to its refusal to hand over the two suspected terrorists and to its involvement in terrorist activities. It is evident that the resolution (subsequently reaffirmed and enlarged by res. no 883 of November 11, 1993) started (as it would have to start, under Article 39) from the assumption that participation in terrorist acts and the refusal to hand over presumed terrorists constitutes a threat to the peace. The first point meets no objection: a State which encourages international terrorism may well be considered, according to international *communis opinio* (various times also expressed by the General Assembly), as threatening the peace among nations, and may well be subject to sanctions until it has shown that it has changed its mind. By contrast, serious doubts may arise over the part of the resolution which considered the failure to extradite Libyan citizens as a threat to the peace, and made the ending of sanctions contingent upon the ending of this behaviour of the Libyan government. It is questionable whether the failure to extradite two criminals may actually, according to general opinion, be considered a threat to the peace. This is all the more so in that, under the Montreal Convention of September 23, 1971 on the suppression of unlawful acts against the safety of civil aviation, which was applicable to the case and under international customary law, a State which detains a person presumed responsible for acts of terrorism is free to choose between extradition to other States for punishment or to prosecution and trial before its own judicial authorities (the *aut dedere aut judicare* principle). The sanctions were suspended in 1999, after the transfer of the accused to Netherlands to appear before a Scottish court setting there (see res. of the Security Council no. 1192 of August 27, 1998 and the Statement by the President of the Security Council on Lockerbie suspects of April 8, 1999, in ILM, 1999, p. 949) and were abolished in 2003 (res. no. 1506 of September 12, 2003) after the settlement of the dispute between Libya, the United States and the United Kingdom.

The same must be said of res. no. 1054 of April 26, 1996 which decides that all States must significantly reduce the Sudanese diplomatic and consular staff in their territories and restrict the entry to, or the transit through, their territories of Sudanese officials, due to the refusal of Sudan to extradite to Ethiopia three suspects wanted in connection with the assassination attempt against the President of Egypt (see § 58). See also res. no. 1070 of August 16, 1996 which, for the same reasons, imposes to all States an air traffic blockade against the Sudanese airlines. All these measures have been terminated once the Sudan decided to comply with the said resolutions (see res. no. 1372 of September 28, 2001).

The discretionary power of the Security Council has no other limitations. The opinion has been expressed in legal literature that the Council must abide by general international law, in particular by the rules of *jus cogens*. In our opinion no such limit exists as far as the determination of a threat to the peace, a breach of the peace or an act of aggression is concerned. The framer of the Charter did not express such a view; on the contrary, Article 1, par. 1 of the Charter limits the respect of international law to the UN function of settlement of disputes. A different question is whether the application of enforcement measures under Articles 41 and 42 of the Charter must comply with general international law (on this question see §§ 58 and 59). The same question arises with regard the measures of governance of territories (see § 60 *bis*). .

56. *The measures provided for by the Charter. A) Recommendations under Article 39.*

BIBLIOGRAPHY: see § 55. *Adde*: STARITA, *Processi di riconciliazione nazionale e diritto internazionale*, Napoli, 2003.

Article 39 provides that, when faced with a threat to the peace, a breach of the peace or an act of aggression, the Council may either decide what enforcement measures to take under Articles 41 and 42 or (alternatively or simultaneously) "make recommendations". As can be very clearly deduced from the preparatory works, these recommendations may be identical to the recommendations under Chapter VI. In other words, the intention in Article 39 is to confirm that, also in situations coming under Chapter VII, the Council may exercise its peaceful settlement function, indicating to the States concerned procedures and methods of settlement (like those regulated by Article 33, para. 2 and Article 36) or terms of settlement (like those regulated by Article 37). The only difference between the peaceful settlement function in Chapter VI and the one under Article 39 is procedural, in that only in the first case does the obligation exist that a directly concerned Council member must abstain from the vote (Article 27, para. 3, last part).

The content and the nature of recommendations under Article 39 were discussed in Committee 3 of Commission III of the San Francisco Conference, which was concerned with Chapter VII, sec. B, of the Dumbarton Oaks proposals (present Chapter VII of the Charter). In the final report of the Committee we read:
"In using the word 'recommendations' in Section B, as already found in paragraph 5, Section A [the latter corresponds to the present Chapter VI], the Committee had intended to show that the action of the Council so far as it relates to the peaceful settlement of a dispute or to situation giving rise to a threat of war, a breach of the peace, or aggression, should be considered as governed by the provisions contained in Section A. Under such an hypothesis, the Council would in reality pursue simultaneously two distinct actions, one having for its object the settlement of the dispute or the difficulty, and the other, the enforcement or provisional measures, each of which is governed by an appropriate section in Chapter VII" (see U.N.C.I.O., vol. 11, p. 19 and vol. 12, p. 507).
Committee 3 did not raise the problem of the voting procedure for the adoption of recommendations under Article 39. This problem was raised by the Netherlands in Committee 1 of Commission III, to which questions regarding procedure had been referred, including the so-called Yalta formula, that is, the present Article 27. The Netherlands proposed, with an

amendment to the whole of Chapter VIII, sections A and B (the amendment is reproduced in U.N.C.I.O., vol. 3, p. 325 f.), that the provision corresponding to the present Article 39 be inserted in Sec. A (today, Chapter VI) instead of in Sec. B (today Chapter VII), specifically in order to guarantee that both in deciding the existence of a threat to the peace, a breach of the peace or an act of aggression and in making recommendations, the Council would be bound by the rule, set out only with regard to Sec. A, that an interested Member State must abstain from the vote. However, the Dutch amendment was not even put to the vote, because the provision of the present Article 27, the provision agreed upon at Yalta by the Great Powers (see § 1 A), was considered unchangeable. Cf. U.N.C.I.O., vol. 11, p. 327 ff., p. 455 and p. 517. Considering the preparatory works and considering the very clear text of Article 27, para. 3, last part, which limits the obligation to abstain of the interested member to decisions under Chapter VI, it is to be excluded that the same obligation exists with regard to Article 39.

In order to establish whether a resolution which recommends procedures or terms of settlement comes under Article 39 rather than Chapter VI, the following criteria must be evaluated. First, the principle that acts of the Council must be identified mainly on the basis of their operative part (see § 49), should be applied. This means that Article 39 comprises of those resolutions which, in indicating procedures or terms of settlement, simultaneously adopt one of the other measures governed by Chapter VII (provisional measures under Article 40, measures involving or not involving the use of armed force under Articles 41 and 42). If the operative part does not allow an unambiguous identification, one must look at the reasoning and refer to Article 39 those resolutions which expressly declare that they concern a threat to the peace, a breach of the peace or an act of aggression. Lastly, one can look at the objective situation and consider Article 39 as applicable if the resolution refers to a crisis provoked by the use of military force (it does not matter whether it is in a situation of international war or of civil war) and thus objectively qualifying as a breach of the peace.

For recommendations under Article 39, as for the recommendations governed by Chapter VI, the domestic jurisdiction clause, which is excluded by Article 2, para. 7, last part, only with regard to the enforcement measures, is applicable. Obviously, the erosion that this limit has undergone in practice (see § 45 III), an erosion that has been shown specifically in civil war situations, has to be taken into account. As far as civil wars are concerned, the peaceful settlement of disputes on the basis of Article 39 particularly covers cases where some form of national conciliation is going on. The Security Council intervenes in these procedures, through the Secretary-General, in order to promote, and monitor the execution of, agreements among the different factions which have participated in the war. Normally such agreements contain provisions on the future constitutional regime of the country, the assistance of the United Nations in the democratic orientation of local institutions, in the monitoring and organizing of political elections, in the economic reconstruction of the country, and so on.

In so far as they refer to a situation that can be qualified objectively as a threat to the peace or a breach of the peace, Article 39 covers, first of all, the resolutions (on "terms of settlement") with which the Council has condemned acts of armed reprisal or actual invasions, inviting the States (or the factions) responsible not to repeat them and threatening (but then not implementing) enforcement measures in case of repeated offences. There have been a great many resolutions of this kind adopted against Israel: cf., for example, res. no. 171 of April 9, 1962, no. 228 of November 25, 1966, no. 248 of March 24, 1968, no. 256 of August 16, 1968, no. 262 of December 31, 1968 (in this case the Council also invited Israel, which had attacked the Beirut airport and destroyed several civilian aircraft, to pay appropriate compensation to Lebanon), no. 265 of April 1, 1969, no. 270 of August 26, 1969, no. 280 of May 19, 1970, no. 316 of June 26, 1972, no. 337 of August 15, 1973, no. 347 of April 24, 1974, no. 509 of June 6, 1982. Cf. also the following resolutions: no. 178 of April 24, 1963 and no. 204 of May 19, 1965, relating to armed actions of Portugal in Senegalese territory; no. 290 of December 8, 1970, which condemned Portugal for having "invaded" Guinea, and requested it to pay compensation for damage caused to the lives and to the property of the local inhabitants; no. 384 of December 22, 1975 and no. 389 of April 22, 1976, containing the invitation to Indonesia to withdraw its armed forces which had invaded East Timor; no. 387 of March 31, 1976, no. 393 of July 30, 1976, no. 428 of May 6, 1978, no. 447 of March 28, 1979, no. 454 of November 2, 1979, on South Africa's invasion of the territories of neighbouring States (Angola, Zambia, etc.); no. 1177 of June 26, 1998, urging Ethiopia and Eritrea to cease hostilities and to achieve a peaceful settlement of their dispute; no. 1339 of January 31, 2001 (on a comprehensive settlement of the conflict in Abkhazia, Georgia).

As examples of recommendations under Article 39 combined with one of the other measures governed by Chapter VII, cf., among many, res. no. 50 of May 29, 1948 and no. 338 of October 22, 1973, which, concerned with the armed conflicts between Israel and the Arab States, invited the parties to a cease-fire (a measure under Article 40) and to have recourse to mediation; res. no. 186 of March 4, 1964 which, considering the situation in Cyprus a threat to the peace, authorised the Secretary-General to establish a UN force for the purposes of preventing fighting on Cyprus territory and invited him to appoint a mediator in agreement with the Cypriot, British, Greek and Turkish governments; res. no. 425 of March 19, 1978 which, besides deciding to send a United Nations force in Southern Lebanon, requested Israel to end its military action against Lebanon; res. no. 450 of June 14, 1979, again on the Lebanese situation, containing the same request to Israel as well as an invitation to the parties to negotiate within the Armistice Commission; res. no. 502 of April 3, 1982 relating to the Falklands/Malvinas war, which "demanded" an end to hostilities and "asked" Argentina and the United Kingdom to seek a diplomatic solution to their dispute; res. no. 514 of July 12, 1982 and no. 522 of October 4, 1982 on the ending of hostilities, on the sending of observers and on recourse to the mediation of the Secretary-General, with regard to the war between Iran and Iraq; res. no. 660 of August 2, 1990 which, expressly referring to Article 39 and Article 40 of the Charter, condemned the invasion of Kuwait by Iraq, and, for the part that can be referred to Article 39, "obliged" the two countries to settle their disputes by negotiation; res. no. 674 of October 29, 1990, on the treatment of foreign citizens by Iraq; res. no. 687 of April 3, 1991 which, besides maintaining the embargo (under Article 41) against Iraq after the Gulf War, contains (in para. 3 of part A) an invitation to the Secretary-General to co-operate in the delimitation of the frontier between Iraq and Kuwait; res. no. 713 of September 25, 1991, which, besides decreeing the embargo on arms export to Yugoslavia, requested the Secretary-General to offer his assistance in reaching a definitive end to hostilities in that country; res. no. 773 of August 26, 1992, which contains an invitation to Iraq and Kuwait to co-operate fully with the Commission for the delimitation of the boundary, appointed by the Secretary-General in May 1992; res. no 1160 of March 31, 1998 (reiterated by res. no. 1199 of September 23,

1998, no. 1203 of October 24, 1998 and some others) on the achievement of a political solution of the Kosovo crisis; res. no. 1337 of March 12, 2002 and no. 1435 of September 24, 2002 (cessation of acts of violence and acts of terrorism in Palestine and in Israel; withdrawal of Israel forces from Palestinian cities occupied after September 2000); res. no. 1515 of .November 19, 2003 (endorsement of the roadmap to a Two-States solution to the conflict between Israel and Palestine).

For examples of indications of "terms of settlement" to factions in post- civil war situations, see the pertinent parts of res. no. 788 of November 19, 1992, on the situation in Liberia; of res. no. 797 of December 10, 1992, and no. 863 of September 13, 1993, on the situation in Mozambique; of res. no. 804 of January 29, 1993, no. 811 of Mars 12, 1993, no. 823 of April 30, 1993, no. 834 of June 1, 1993, no. 851 of July 15, 1993, no 922 of May 31, 1994, no. 932 of June 30, 1994, no. 945 of September 29, 1994, and no. 966 of December 8, 1994, on the situation in Angola; of res. no. 861 of August 27, 1993, on the situation in Haiti; of res. no. 1234 of April 9, 1999, no.1273 of November 5, 1999, no. 1279 of November 30, 1999, no. 1291 of February 24, 2000, and no. 1304 of June 16, 2000, on the situation in the Democratic Republic of Congo; of res. no. 1245 of June 11, 1999, no. 1270 of October 22, 1999, on the situation in Sierra Leone; of res. no. 1491, of July 7, 2003 (situation in Bosnia Herzegovina).

For the consideration of these, and other similar cases concerning the function of settlement of disputes, see STARITA, *op. cit.*, p.200 ff.

It has been maintained in legal doctrine and in practice that Article 39 authorises the Council also to recommend measures like those regulated by Articles 41 and 42 (measures involving and not involving the use of armed force). Indeed, some observers hold that the power of recommendation set forth in Article 39 would exactly and exclusively serve this purpose. Aside from this last view, which must be immediately rejected in that it is clearly belied by the above cited preparatory works, the examination of the problem can be postponed to when Articles 41 and 42 will be discussed, as the interpretation of these two articles is indispensable for reaching a correct solution.

57. B) *Provisional measures (Article 40).*

BIBLIOGRAPHY: see § 55. *Adde*: FABBRI, *Le misure provvisorie nel sistema di sicurezza delle Nazioni Unite*, in *RDI*, 1964, p. 186 ff.; BAILEY, *Cease-Fires, Truces and Armistices in the Practice of the UN Security Council*, in *AJ*, 1977, p. 463 ff.; FROWEIN, in SIMMA (ED.), *Charta der Vereinten Nations*, München, 1991, p. 571 ss.

The provisional measures in Article 40 constitute the *typical* measures of Chapter VII, together with measures not involving (Article 41) or involving (Article 42) the use of armed force. Their provisional nature is related both to the aim pursued, which is only that of preventing a worsening of a situation, and to the limits placed on their content, since they must not prejudice "the rights, claims or positions of the parties concerned".

Given these characteristics, the provisional measures were meant to be emergency measures preliminary to any other resolution adopted on the basis of Chapter VII. This is why Article 40 provides that the Council resort to them "before making the recommendations or deciding upon the measures provided for in Article 39". However, it would be out of place to say that the Council is rigidly bound from a chronological point of view. Indeed, a crisis *which is considered* as a threat to the peace, breach of the peace or act of aggression can develop over long periods of time, and with alternating turns of events, so that interventions of different intensity may be necessary at different times. The Council thus could be compelled both to adopt several measures at the same time and to again take up provisional measures also after having adopted other resolutions on the basis of Chapter VII, for example, after having recommended settlement procedures on the basis of Article 39 or after having decided upon measures not involving, or even involving, the use of armed force. Taking into account the spirit and purposes of the collective security system under Chapter VII, it does not seem that such conduct of the Council (recurrent in the practice) should be considered illegal.

Likewise, the opinion must be rejected that provisional measures are an *indispensable stage* before passing to the measures in Articles 41 and 42. The San Francisco Conference which drew up Article 40 (which does not appear in the Dumbarton Oaks proposals) unanimously agreed that neither provisional measures nor recommendations under Article 39 were to be considered as a necessary prerequisite to enforcement measures (see the already cited report of Committee 3 of Commission III, in U.N.C.I.O., vol. 11, p. 19).

The provisional measures form the object of recommendations by the Council ("The Council", Article 40 states, may "*call upon* the parties concerned to comply with such provisional measures... etc."). Once again, then, we are in the presence of acts that do not bind the parties to keep to the prescribed conduct. In legal doctrine and in practice, an attempt has been made to give a binding nature to the "invitation". Such view is linked, first of all, to a more general tendency to maintain the obligatory nature of any resolution of the Council, and especially those envisaged by Chapter VII. This is a tendency, however, that, as we shall see when we examine the acts of the United Nations in general, is not acceptable (see § 90). The same view is also based on a specific argument that would be offered by Article 40, specifically in the last part of the article, which states, "The Security Council shall duly take account of failure to comply with such provisional measures". In other words, the last part of Article 40, referring to the possibility of sanctions (under Articles 41 and 42) would make the requested conduct obligatory. Also this reasoning is not acceptable as it casts too wide a net: in fact the Security Council may duly take account of *any* conduct of a State. Neither does it seem that the terminology that the Council uses in adopting resolutions regarding provisional measures affects their non-binding nature. Especially in recent times, this terminology denotes the intention of the organ to give its invitations an urgent nature: "The Council... urgently requests...", "... the Council... urges...", "The Council... demands..." are the formulas which occur in many resolutions coming under Article 40. It would be risky to try to take from these formulas, which certainly can be connected to the *threat of sanctions* contained in the last part of the article, an unwritten rule on their obligatory nature.

A typical provisional measure under Article 40 is the *cease-fire,* or, more generally, the cessation of acts of violence requested by the Council during international or civil wars. Considering the objective circumstances and the nature of the measure, the invitation to cease fire falls *in any case* in the realm of Article 40. If, occasionally, some of the Member States of the Council have said they were acting in the framework of Chapter VI, such intention has been necessitated by political reasons, that is, by the desire to alienate their partners involved in the crisis as little as possible. It would be absurd to maintain this from the viewpoint of a correct interpretation of the Charter.

Examples of resolutions containing a cease-fire, or the cessation of acts of violence, in international or civil wars: res. no. 27 of August 1, 1947 (Indonesian war of independence); no. 50 of May 29, 1948 and no. 54 of July 15, 1948 (Arab-Israeli conflict); no. 63 of December 24, 1948 (Indonesia); no. 92 of May 8, 1951 (Middle East); no. 104 of June 20, 1954 (Guatemala); no. 164 of July 22, 1961 (Franco-Tunisian conflict); no. 205 of May 22, 1965 (Dominican Republic); no. 210 of September 6, 1965 (Indo-Pakistani conflict); nos. 233, 234, and 235 of June 6, 7 and 9, 1967 (Israeli Six-Day War); no. 307 of December 21, 1971 (India-Pakistan); no. 338 of October 22, 1973 (Middle East); no. 353 of July 20, 1974 and no. 357 of August 14, 1974 (Cyprus); no. 502 of April 3, 1982 (Falklands-Malvinas war); no. 508 of June 5, 1982 (Lebanon); no. 514 of July 12, 1982 (war between Iran and Iraq); no. 517 of August 4, 1982 (Lebanon); no. 582 of February 24, 1986 (war between Iran and Iraq); no. 812 of March 12, 1993 (Ruanda); no 1052 of April 18, 1996 (Lebanon); no. 1097 of February 18, 1997 (Eastern Zaire and Great Lakes region); no. 1397 of March 12, 2002 and no. 1435 of September 24, 2002 (cessation of acts of violence between Israel and Palestine).

After the end of the Cold War, a cease-fire has been requested several times, together with the adoption of measures within the framework of Articles 41 and 42. Cf., for example, res. no. 713, para. 2, of September 25, 1991, no. 724, para. 7, of December 15, 1991, no. 743, para. 8, of February 21, 1992, and no. 762, para. 2, or June 30, 1992 (all on the war in the former Yugoslavia); no. 733, para. 4, of January 1, 1992, no. 746, para. 2, of March 17, 1992, and no. 767, para. 9 of July 27, 1992 (all on the civil war in Somalia); no. 788, para. 6 of November 19, 1992 (civil war in Liberia); no. 1076 of October 22, 1996, 1193 of August 27, 1998 and 1214 of December 8, 1998 (civil war in Afghanistan); no 1199 of September 23, 1998 (civil war in Kosovo); no. 1227 of February 10, 1999 (war between Ethiopia and Eritrea).

It is not always easy to distinguish between an invitation to apply a provisional measure and a recommendation on "terms of settlement" (within the meaning of Article 39 or Article 37), as the former may consist in a partial settlement of the question which set off the crisis. A framing within Article 40 should be preferred when the predominant purpose of the resolution is not to aggravate the situation.

Aside from resolutions on cease-fires, the following resolutions can be considered as indicating provisional measures: those which, in the case of civil wars or wars of independence, urge the liberation of political prisoners (for example, res. no. 63 of December 24, 1948 on the war in Indonesia); or those which invite States not involved in an international or domestic conflict not to support the parties in conflict and not to furnish them with armed troops or war materials (for example, res. no. 50 of May 29, 1948 on the Middle East, no. 104 of June 20, 1954 on the domestic situation in Guatemala, no. 61 of February 21, 1961 and no. 169 of November 24, 1961 on the domestic situation in the Congo and inviting the States not to send mercenaries and not to introduce weapons in Congolese territory); or those which request the withdrawal of foreign troops from territories in a state of civil war (for example, res. no. 143 of July 14, 1960 with a request to the Belgian government to withdraw its troops from the Congo); or, lastly, those which request one of the States involved in a war to withdraw its own troops to certain positions (for example, res. no. 660 of August 2, 1990, expressly based on Articles 39 and 40, which "demanded" that Iraq withdraw its forces to the positions occupied on August 1, 1990).

Sometimes the Council has made only a general appeal, addressed to all the States, which also can be referred to Article 40, to... not aggravate a situation. It did so, for example, in 1971 in relation to the Indo-Pakistani conflict (res. no. 307, para. 2, of December 21, 1971).

As a provisional measure can also be considered the one contained in res. no. 250 of April 27, 1968, which requested Israel, in order not to aggravate tension with Jordan, not to hold a military parade set for the following May 2 in Jerusalem. The reason Israel relied upon in order to justify, in this specific case, non-performance, is unacceptable. According to its view the resolution involved a matter of Israeli domestic jurisdiction (cf. SCOR, 23rd year, 1417th meet.). As we have already seen, measures under Article 40 in any case fall outside the exception of domestic jurisdiction (see § 47).

58. C) *Measures not involving the use of armed force (Article 41).*

BIBLIOGRAPHY: see § 55. *Adde*: RUZIÉ, *Les sanctions économiques contre la Rhodésie*, in *Journal du droit international*, 1970, p. 20 ff.; DOXEY, *Economic Sanctions and International Enforcement*, London, 1971; SKUBISZEWSKI, *Recommandations of the UN and Municipal Courts*, in *BYB*, 1972-73, p. 353 ff.; BROWN-JOHN, *Multilateral Sanctions in International Law. A Comparative Analysis*, New York, 1975.; ZICCARDI CAPALDO, *Le situazioni territoriali illegittime nel diritto internazionale*, Naples, 1977, p. 99 ff.; DAVID, *Les sanctions économiques prises contre l'Argentine dans l'affaire des Malouines*, in *RBDI*, 1984/85, p. 150 ff.; WILLAERT, *Les sanctions économiques contre la Rhodésie (1965-1979)*, ivi, p. 216 ff.; JOYNER, *Sanctions, Compliance and International Law: Reflections on the UN Experience Against Iraq*, in *Vanderbilt Journal of International Law*, 1991, p. 1 ff.; CONFORTI, *Non-Coercive Sanctions in the UN Charter: Some Lessons from the Gulf War*, in *EJIL*, 1991, p. 110 ff.; BURCI, *L'azione del Consiglio di Sicurezza delle N.U. nella crisi del Golfo*, in *CI*, 1991, p. 278 ff.; MARTIN-BIDOU, *Les mesures d'embargo prises à l'encontre de la Yougoslavie*, in *AF*, 1993, p. 262 ff.; LOPEZ MARTIN, *Embargo y bloqueo aéreo en la práctica del Consejo de Seguridad: del conflicto del Golfo al caso de Libia*, in *ReD*, 1994, p. 39 ff.; DAHMANE *Les measures prise par le Conseil de Sécurité contre les entités non-étatiques*, in *Afr J*, 1999 p. 55 ff; ALABRUNE, *La pratique des comites des sanctions du Conseil de Sécurité depuis 1990*, in

AF, 1999, p. 226 ff; STARCK, *Die Rechtsmässigkeit von UNO-Wirtschafssanktionen, ecc,* Berlin, 2000; De HOOG, *Attribution or Delegation of (Legislative) Power by the Security Council ? The case of the UNTAET*, in *International Peacekeeping*, 2001, p. 7 ss.; CRAVEN, *Humanitarianism and the Quest for Smarter Sanctions*, in *EJIL*, 2002, p. 43 ff.; ELLEN O'CONNELL, *Debating the Law of Sanctions, ibid.*, p. 63 ff.; BENNOUNA, *Les sanctions économiques des Nations Unies*, in *RC*, 2002, vol. 300, p. 13 ff.

These measures definitely have the nature of sanctions and therefore are imposed *against* a State which, in the judgement of the Security Council, has broken or threatened the peace or is to be considered an aggressor. They are adopted by the Member States of the United Nations (all the members or even only some of them: see Article 48, para. 1), at the request of the Council. Article 41 speaks of complete or partial interruption of economic relations and of rail, sea, air, postal, telegraphic and other means of communication, as well as the severance of diplomatic relations. However, this list is not exhaustive, as the Council may order any other measure whose purpose is to provide a sanction and which does not involve the use of armed force. It is obvious that the *cumulative* application of all the measures listed will result in the total isolation of the State they are issued against.

Also conduct occurring only within a State may lead the Council to have recourse to the measures under Article 41, since such measures are not subject to the exception of domestic jurisdiction (see § 47). Indeed, it is especially in internal conflicts, and for the purpose of protecting the civilian population, that the Council usually intervenes. Sometimes the sanctions are even imposed by the Council against *armed* political groups. In recent times, measures not involving the use of force have been imposed on all States with regard to the fight against groups committing acts of terrorism. International terrorism is an offence against the international community as a whole, being widespread around the world. This is why the action of the Security Council is to be considered as justifiable.

Economic sanctions were also set out by the Covenant of the League of Nations, at art, 16, para. 1. However, they were, first of all, restricted to a very specific possibility, the possibility that a Member State had resorted to *war* in contempt of the Covenant provisions. Secondly, they were to be *applied automatically* by the Member States, without any decision (and therefore without exercising any discretion) by the League organs. As is well known, such sanctions were adopted against Italy during the Ethiopian war in 1936.

By definition, measures not involving the use of armed force are the object of a Council *decision*, that is, of an act which binds the Member States to adopt them (although the possibility exists that a State may inform the Council, under Article 50, if it has "special" economic difficulties). This can be drawn from Article 39 which provides that decisions under Article 41 are binding and which contrasts them to recommendations ("The Council... shall make recommendations, or decide what measures *shall* be taken in accordance with Articles 41 and 42"). It can also unambiguously be found in the preparatory works, if we consider that Article 41, together with Article 42, were conceived of at Dumbarton Oaks and were accepted by the San Francisco Conference as the most important innovation in the Charter as compared to the Covenant of the League of Nations. This innovation was characteristic of the broad decision-making powers attributed to the Council (cf. U.N.C.I.O., vol. 12, p. 278). Given these elements, no weight should be given to an apparent contradiction in the wording of Article 41 which, on one hand, provides that "The Security Council may decide what measures not involving the use of armed force *are* to be employed to give effect to its decisions....", and, on the other hand, adds that the Council may *call upon* the Member States to apply such measures.

Art. 41 deals with sanctions and with sanctions only. The Council may take measures not listed, since the list is not exhaustive, provided that they are sanctions not involving the use of armed force. The opinion has been held (by Hoogh) according to which Article 41 gives the Council a double power, one implied, the other express: on the one hand, the (implied) power to make "decisions" for maintaining or restoring peace and, on the other hand, the power to "decide what measures not involving the use of armed force are to be employed to give effect to its decisions". Using the first power, the Council could take no matter what decision provided that it is aimed at maintaining or restoring the peace; using the second one, the Council could impose the sanctions listed, or sanctions not listed, in Article 41. This opinion, which has been upheld in order to justify the institution of international criminal courts, like the International Criminal Tribunals for the former Yugoslavia and Rwanda, has no basis in the preparatory works of the Charter and in the Article 41 read in conjunction with Article 39. Art. 39 is clear in the sense that, after the determination of a threat to, or a breach of, the peace, the measures that shall be taken "to maintain or restore international peace and security", are either recommendations or decisions taken in accordance with Article 41 and 42. It would be very strange if Chapter VII empowered the Council to take decisions of such importance as to be assisted by sanctions without saying a word about their content and limits: for instance, are these decisions subject to the domestic jurisdiction exception, an exception which indeed is excluded by Article 2, n. 7, with regard the "enforcement measures under Chapter VII " only ? As we have seen, the doctrine of implied powers must be used with caution (see § 5), and this is especially true in a sensible matter as the one we are dealing with now. Having said that, the formulation of Article 41 ("The Security Council may decide what measures ...are to be employed to give effect to its decisions..."), is certainly redundant, but not more redundant than the last part of the first sentence of Art. 41 ("...call upon the members...to apply such measures") and many other articles of the Charter. Regarding the institution of criminal tribunals, it must be simply recognized that it is a measure not considered by the Charter (see § 60 *bis*).

During the Cold War period, there were not a great many binding decisions made by the Council under Article 41. More generally, there were not many measures of an enforcement nature, truly able to discourage breaches of the peace. In fact, there were only two cases that came within the framework of Article 41 as binding decisions! This is the case of resolutions no. 232 of December 16, 1966 and no. 253 of May 29, 1968 (confirmed by subsequent decisions; cf. res. no. 277 of March 18, 1970, no. 314 of February 28, 1972, no. 320 of September 29, 1972, no. 333 of May 22, 1973, no. 388 of April 6, 1976, no. 409 of March 27, 1977) against Southern Rhodesia and res. no. 418 of November 4, 1977 (also confirmed, and extensively interpreted, in subsequent decisions: cf., particularly, res. no. 591 of November 28, 1986) against South Africa because of the two countries' apartheid policies. The resolutions against Southern Rhodesia, repealed with res. no. 460 of December 21, 1979, following the forming of a government representing the majority of the people, imposed a series of measures (prevention of import and export, interruption of air services, closing of borders to Rhodesian citizens or to residents in Rhodesia, and so on) and aimed at the *total isolation* of the Rhodesian government at the time. In the case of South Africa, the 1977 resolution was restricted to imposing an embargo on any supplying of weapons to the South African government.

After the end of the Cold War, Council resolutions coming under Article 41 have proliferated. The Council has intervened with measures not involving the use of armed force (in addition to those involving such use) in many important international and domestic crises that have occurred in recent times. In so far as these crises were characterised by violence and by gross violations of human rights, they have interested the international community as a whole. This is the case of the Gulf crisis, the crisis in Yugoslavia, the one in Somalia and many others. The same can be said of the measures adopted against groups committing acts of terrorism.

Beginning with the Gulf crisis (a crisis which, as we shall see, mainly provoked the adoption of measures involving the use of force), the fundamental resolution was no. 661 of August 6, 1990, which was adopted against Iraq immediately after its invasion of Kuwait. Res. no. 661 obliged all States to break off all economic relations with Iraq, and, in particular, placed an embargo on imports and exports from and toward this country and prohibited all financial operations with the Iraqi government (excluding operations necessary for payment of medicines) and with firms under its control. Worth mentioning are also, among the many resolutions that are linked to res. no. 661: res. no. 670 of September 25, 1990, binding the States to the so-called air blockade, that is, to prohibiting in their territory (and therefore in the exercise of normal policy activity under territorial sovereignty) the taking off, landing and flying over of aircraft suspected of breaking the embargo; and res. no. 687 of April 2, 1991, which established, at sec. F, that the measures provided by res. 661 shall be maintained until Iraq has carried out what has been required by the resolutions, such as payment of compensation, elimination of military arsenals, and so on. All prohibitions related to trade with Iraq, with the exception of prohibitions related to the sale or supply of arms and related material, and all economic and financial measures against Iraq, have been abolished by res. no. 1483 of May 22, 2003, adopted after the fall of Saddam Hussein's regime.

With regard to the Yugoslav crisis, the first resolution, no. 713 of September 25, 1991, adopted when the civil war still seemed to be a war of secession, was restricted to providing an embargo on weapons intended for (all of) Yugoslavia. Later, an important decision among those which come under Article 41, was res. no. 757 of May 30, 1992 which, after having reiterated condemnation of the intervention of the Yugoslav Republic (Serbia-Montenegro) in Bosnia-Herzegovina, already expressed in a previous resolution (res. no. 752 of May 15, 1992), bound all States to adopt a series of economic sanctions against this Republic, from the embargo on imports and exports, to the blocking of financial operations, to the suspension of all co-operation in scientific and technical fields, as well as to prohibit aircrafts coming from or directed towards Serbia-Montenegrin territory from taking off, landing and flying over their territory. In turn, res. no. 820 (part B) of April 17, 1993 extended the embargo to the territories of Croatia and to those of Bosnia-Herzegovina controlled by the Serbs, and also provided for the prohibition of commercial traffic with the Republic of Yugoslavia along the Danube; the interruption of land traffic and the obligation of the States where there were ships in port which had broken the embargo to confiscate the ships and their loads.

The economic sanctions against the Republic of Yugoslavia (Serbia-Montenegro) were terminated by res. no. 1074 of October 1, 1996. During the Kosovo crisis, in 1998-1999, the Security Council was unable to take any decisions against this country with the exception of an embargo on arms and related material (res. no. 1160 of March 31, 1998, reiterated by res. no. 1199 of September 23, 1998 and no. 1203 of October 24, 1998).

In the case of the crisis in Somalia — another crisis which saw the Council take measures mainly involving the use of armed force — res. no. 733 of January 23, 1992, prohibited the export of arms to Somalia.

Among those resolutions by which the Security Council has decided a number of measures in order to prevent and repress acts of terrorism, see especially res. no. 1373 of September 28, 2001. See also res. no 1377 of November 12, 2001, no. 1455 of January 17, 2003, no. 1456 of January 20, 2003.

For other recent examples of decisions containing measures under Article 41, cf. the already cited resolutions no. 748 of March 31, 1992 and no. 883 of November 11, 1993 against Libya which, in so far as the Libyan government had refused to hand over two Libyan citizens accused of grave acts of terrorism (a handing over requested with prior resolution no. 731 of January 23, 1992, within the framework of Chapter VI: see § 55 *bis*), ordered the interruption of air traffic and of the supplying of aircraft or parts of aircraft as well as of weapons to that country and a series of other economic restrictions (the sanctions were suspended in April 1999 an abolished in September 2003: see § 55 *bis*). Cf. also res.: no. 788 of November 19, 1992 (confirmed by subsequent res. no. 813 of March 25, 1993) on the embargo on the sale of arms to Liberia, because of the civil war underway there; no. 841 of June 16, 1993, no. 873 of October 13, 1993, no. 875 of October 16, 1993, and no. 917 of May 6, 1994, against the military regime in Haiti, no. 864 of September 15, 1993 on the embargo on the sale of arms and oil products to UNITA, the Angolan armed political party; no. 1054 of April 26, 1996, ordering the reduction of the Sudanese diplomatic and consular staff and the restriction of the entry into, or the transit through, the territory of all States of Sudanese officials, due to the refusal of the Sudan to extradite to Ethiopia the suspects wanted in connection with the assassination attempt on the life of the President of Egypt occurred in Addis Abeba; all these measures have been abolished in September 2001 (see § 55 *bis*); no. 1127 of August 28, 1997, sect. B (closure of the territory of States to officials, adults members of their families, air-crafts, vessels, etc., of the Angolan UNITA); no. 1132 of October 8, 1997 (sanctions against the military junta in Sierra Leone: the sanctions were terminated by res. No. 1156 of March 16, 1998, due to the restoration of a democratic government in this country); no. 1171 of June 5, 1998 (*embargo* on arms to be sent to non-governmental forces in Sierra Leone); no. 1173 of June 12, 1998 (again against UNITA); no. 1306 of July 5, 2000, no. 1385 of December 19, 2001 and 1446 of December 4, 2002 (on illicit traffic in rough diamonds in Sierra Leone); no. 1333 of December 19, 2000 (against the Taliban faction in Afghanistan); no. 1343 of March 7,

2001 (against Liberia); no. 1390 of January 16, 2002 (against the Taliban faction and Al Qaida); no. 1478 of May 6, 2003 (again against Liberia); no. 1556 of July 30, 2004 (embargo on the sale and supply of arms to non-governmental entities and individuals in Sudan).

A weak point in the measures governed by Article 41 lies in the fact that, once the Council has imposed an obligation on the States to adopt such measures, this obligation must be fulfilled in practice. In other words, if it is true that the States are obligated by the United Nations Charter to carry out the decisions regarding measures not involving the use of armed force, it is also true that often various States, for political or economic reasons, tend to disregard this legal obligation. Usually when the Council orders sanctions under art, 41, it appoints a Committee to see that the sanctions are carried out (cf., merely as examples, para. 6 of the cited res. no. 661 of August 6, 1990 against Iraq and paragraphs 12 and 13 of the cited resolution no. 757 of May 30, 1992 against the Yugoslav Republic). However it is not difficult to get around this supervision, since it is mainly carried out through reports sent by the States themselves. We see reflected in this matter the perpetual problem of international law, that is, law within whose sphere rules are created, but are often not applied.

With reference to the past, the vicissitudes regarding the implementation of sanctions against Southern Rhodesia within the legal systems of Member States, particularly the Western Powers, were not exemplary. The most striking — and openly carried out — case of the non-application of economic sanctions concerned the United States. Between 1971 and the end of 1976 a special law in the United States authorised the import of Rhodesian chromium (the law was justified by the U.S. delegate in the Council with the claim... that it was identical to the practice of some other States! Cf., for example, SCOR, 27th year, 1645th meet., no. 29 ff.). Only at the beginning of 1977, under pressure from the Carter Administration was this law abrogated (the relevant acts appear in *ILM*, 1972, p. 178 ff., and 1977, p. 425 ff.). Aside from those of the United States, there were many violations by the States of the economic blockade which, if not authorised, were at least tolerated. In one of the various reports to the special Committee appointed by the Council to investigate them, about 135 were mentioned (cf. the 5th Report of the Committee, in SCOR, 27th year, *Special Suppl.* no. 2, p. 27 ff.). Still in 1998 the Security Council, in a resolution couched in very general terms, was forced to urge all States and other organizations to report on possible violations of arms embargoes established by the Council (see res. no. 1196 of September 16, 1998).

Also regarding the embargo on arms intended for South Africa, violations were often denounced, even in General Assembly resolutions. For an interesting list of the loopholes devised by various States to elude the spirit, if not the letter, of cited res. no. 418 of November 4, 1977, cf. the Report of the Committee for Sanctions against South Africa (doc. S/14179 of September 19, 1980), examined by the Security Council in its sessions of September 20 and 23, 1982.

For more recent violations of Article 41, see, for instance, res. no. 1407 of May 3, 2002, no. 1425 of July 22, 2002, no. 1474 of April 8, 2003 and no. 1519 of December 16, 2003 (denouncing the continued flow of weapons and ammunition supplies to Somalia).

The violation of Council resolutions is facilitated by the view that such acts, like, moreover, all binding acts of an international organization, would become operational only after the issuance of specific domestic implementing acts. This view is quite widespread in the legal doctrine and the case law of various countries, and was confirmed, for example, precisely with regard to Security Council resolutions under Article 41, in a judgement of the Australian Supreme Court of September 10, 1973 (in *UNJY* 1974, p. 208 f.), as well in a decision of the District Court for the District of Columbia, United States, of May 13, 1975 in *Diggs* v. *Dent* (in *ILM*, 1975, p. 803 ff.). In our opinion, a firm stand must be taken against this view. If a State has undertaken to respect the UN Charter (a commitment usually made with the agreement of the legislative organs) and if Article 41 of the Charter requires the observation of Security Council decisions, we cannot see why the administrative and judicial organs of the country should not be considered authorised to demand similar compliance by its citizens. Obviously a different situation exists when a domestic law expressly states the intention not to apply Council decisions (see the American law on the import of Rhodesian chromium, cited above). In that case, and only in that case, nothing can be done at the level of the administrative and judicial bodies.

The monitoring of the applications of sanctions is also necessary to ensure that no useless suffering is inflicted by economic measures to the population of the target State, a necessity which has become increasingly evident especially in recent years and particularly in the framework of the action against Iraq during and after the Gulf war. In various resolutions the Security Council has authorised derogation on the duty of States to apply economic or others sanctions. Derogations had been already authorised at the time of Cold War, in the case of sanctions against Rhodesia (for the practice, see CRAVEN, *art .cit.*, p. 49). For the more recent practice, see, for instance,: res. no. 666 of September 13, 1990 which provided the possibility that, through the United Nations, in agreement with the International Red Cross or other entities with humanitarian purposes, foodstuffs could be delivered to Iraq; res. no. 986 of April 14, 1995, which authorised the States to derogate in some circumstances to the *embargo* on petroleum and petroleum products originating in Iraq, for humanitarian reasons; res. no. 1111 of July 4, 1997 (*idem*); res. no. 1127 of August 28, 1997, para. 5 of sect. B (derogation to the air-traffic embargo against UNITA in Angola); res. no. 1143 of December 4, 1997 and no. 1153 of February 20, 1988 (again on derogation to the petroleum embargo against Iraq).

The practice quoted above shows a clear trend towards the duty of the Security Council to comply with general international law, at least with international humanitarian law, when deciding on *economic* sanctions.

A third State whose economy is linked to the economy of the target State may also be damaged by economic sanctions. According to Article 50 of the Charter, it has the right to consult the Security Council for taking appropriate measures. In 1995 attention has been drawn to this matter by the General Assembly (see res. no. 50/51 of December 11, 1995).

On the monitoring of the humanitarian aspects of the sanctions attention was also called by the UN Secretary-General B. Boutros Ghali in his *Supplement to an Agenda for Peace* (Doc. A/50/60 and S/1995/1, of January 3. 1995, para. 69 ff.). The Secretary-General suggests setting up a mechanism in order *inter alia:* to measure the effects of the sanctions in order to enable the Security Council to take decisions with a view to maximising their political impact and minimising collateral damages; to ensure the delivery of humanitarian assistance to vulnerable groups within the target State; and to explore ways of assisting third States that are suffering collateral damages.

May the Council restrict itself to *recommending* measures not involving the use of armed force, and thereby leave the States free to adopt them or not? Even if the measures were conceived at Dumbarton Oaks and at San Francisco as the expression of a true decision-making power of the Council with regard to the Member States, it seems to us that the possibility of adopting recommendations must be recognised according to the spirit of Article 41. In fact, the power to recommend is included within the larger power to decide. Since Article 41 lists measures of various kinds and intensity (from the very bland sanction of severing diplomatic relations to the strong measures of economic blockade), it implicitly allows the Council to soften the intensity of one of its decisions by giving it the mere nature of a recommendation.

In our opinion, recommendations on measures not involving the use of armed force may be considered lawful only if they are covered by Article 41. This is so even if achieved through a broad interpretation of the article. On the contrary, in legal doctrine and in practice there is a widespread tendency to seek a different basis for the recommendations on the assumption that Article 41 (just like the following Article 42) is concerned *only* with binding decisions, as only binding decisions are adequate for the effective collective security system that is the core of Chapter VII. Reference is sometimes made to Article 39, but more often to Chapter VI as the chapter characterised by the Council's power to recommend, or Article 24 which confers on the Council "primary responsibility for the maintenance of the peace". Aside from the fact that Article 39 was conceived solely with regard to the peaceful settlement function, that neither the letter nor the spirit of Chapter VI justify any resolution intending to impose sanctions, and that Article 24 cannot be the basis for specific powers (see § 60 *bis*), the tendency of the doctrine clearly contradicts itself. If Article 41 were to picture the system of sanctions not involving the use of armed force as inextricably tied to the full decision-making power of the Council; if, in other words, Article 41 were to recognise as indispensable for purposes of collective security the fact that the power to decide sanctions is centralised in the Council so as to guarantee both the objectivity of a decision and the general applicability of measures involving sanctions, then it seems there would be no alternative. The act with which the organ makes only a recommendation, deferring the final decision to the individual State, should logically be considered unlawful. Actually, for the reasons we have given before, Article 41 does not demand as much and it is this article which furnishes the legal basis for sanctions which are recommended as well as for those which are imposed as mandatory.

In order to determine whether a measure under Article 41 is a recommendation or a decision, the Council's intention is decisive. The intention is made evident, first, by the rest of the resolution, and, secondly, from the discussions and the vote which came before and after the resolution was adopted.

The view held by the International Court of Justice in this matter is unacceptable. According to this view the reference, in the preamble to a resolution, to Article 25 of the Charter ("The members of the United Nations agree to accept and to carry out the decisions of the Security Council in accordance with the present Charter"), would constitute positive proof of the Council's intention to issue a binding decision. This view, contained in the opinion of June 21, 1971 on the *Legal Consequences for States of the Continued Presence of South Africa in Namibia (Southwest Africa) Notwithstanding Security Council Resolution 276 (1970)*, in ICJ, *Reports*, 1971, p. 53, no. 115, will be discussed later on (see § 90), since it was put forward by the Court with reference not to Article 41 but to the problem of the meaning of Article 25 with regard to Council acts in general.

Examples of *simple recommendations* within the framework of Article 41 are seen mainly, but not exclusively, in the practice relating to the Cold War era. At that time the Council was not able to take *decisions*.

Cf. resolutions no. 180 of July 31, 1963 and no. 218 of November 23, 1965 against Portugal for its colonialist policy and no. 181 of August 7, 1963 against South Africa for its apartheid policy, all inviting the States to prohibit the sale of weapons, or of certain types of weapons to the two countries. Cf. also resolutions no. 276 of January 30, 1970, no. 283 of July 29, 1970 and no. 301 of October 20, 1971 on Namibia, confirmed by subsequent resolutions, in the parts in which they invited the States to sever diplomatic and commercial relations with South Africa "as far as they extend to Namibia", a territory held by South Africa since the time of the League of Nations and now independent (see § 81).

No serious doubts can be raised about the nature of a mere recommendation of all these acts. This nature can been seen from the formulation of the text, as compared to the text of binding decisions, and also from statements made at the time of the vote by some Western permanent members, members who would have been able to prevent the adoption of decisions with their veto. The statements meant to emphasise the non-binding effect of the acts. All the above recommendations avoided speaking, in their statement of reasons, of a threat or breach of the peace, or acts of aggression and used terms that were somewhat more toned down, such as "disturbance of the peace", "very grave situation", and so on. This does not affect their coming within the framework of Article 41 since, as we have often repeated, it is not the reasoning but rather the operative part which characterises a decision (see § 49).

Lastly, it should be recalled that some permanent (and non-permanent) members of the Council, the Western powers, used to declare that they held these resolutions to be extraneous to Article 41 and to Chapter VII. We have already discussed the fallacy of this point of view and need not return to it here. Actually, the statements of the Western States essentially had the purpose of confirming the non-binding nature of the resolution and their intention to vote for them (or, at least, not to prevent their adoption with a veto) on the condition that they were not considered binding. In short, all that can be obtained from these statements is the certainty that they were mere recommendations. For references, cf., for example, the statements of the US and British delegates regarding res. no. 181 of August 7, 1963 against South Africa, in SCOR, 18th year, 1056th meet., p. 6 f. and p. 8 f.; of the British delegate in reference to res. no. 191 of June 18, 1964, again against South Africa, in SCOR, 19th year, 1135th meet., p. 10; of the Belgian delegate in reference to res. no. 218 of November 23, 1965 against Portugal, in SCOR, 29th year, 1268th meet, p. 5, no. 23; again of the British delegate after the adoption of resolution no. 282 of July 23, 1970 against South Africa, in SCOR, 25th year, 1549th meet.; of the French, British and Belgian delegates regarding res. no. 301 of October 20th, 1971 on Namibia, in SCOR, 26th year, 1588th, 1589th and 1994th meets.

As examples of recommendations in more recent practice see: res. no. 1076 of October 22, 1996, para. 4, where the Security Council calls upon all States to end the supply of arms to all parties to the conflict in Afghanistan; res. no. 1227 of February 10, 1999, urging all States to end immediately all sales of arms and munitions to Ethiopia and Eritrea.

As we have noted, the list of measures which do not involve the use of armed force, is not exhaustive in Article 41. Therefore, any decision or recommendation of the Security Council which calls upon the States, explicitly or implicitly, to take actions which have the outward character of sanctions with regard to a certain State, or to an armed political group within a State, come within the framework of this article. Such an atypical measure can be found in those resolutions often used by the Council in order to declare certain domestic acts "invalid". This is the case, for example of: res. no. 252 of May 21, 1968, adopted against Israel and confirmed in subsequent decisions (cf., for example, res. no. 478 of August 20, 1980) which stated that the Council "considers that all legislative and administrative measures and actions taken by Israel, including expropriation of land and properties thereon, which tend to change the status of Jerusalem, are invalid..."; res. no. 276 of January 30, 1970, concerning Namibia, also reiterated in the following years but now obsolete owing to the independence acquired by the country, which "declared" the entire presence of South African authorities in Namibian territory "invalid and illegal"; res. no. 446 of March 22, 1979, which considered the Israeli practice of establishing colonies in occupied Arab territories to be without any "legal validity"; res. no. 554 of August 17, 1984, which declared invalid the South African constitution enacted in November 1983; res. no. 662, now obsolete, of August 9, 1990, which declared Iraq's proclaimed annexation of Kuwait "null and void". Such statements could appear *ultra vires*, since invalidity inflicted by the Council has no possibility of being effective within the legal orders of the target States. In fact, they can be given only the implicit value of a request made to the Member States to *refuse to recognise* the "invalid" measures, and therefore not to apply them if in any way they acquire relevance before their State organs, for example, legal actions before their Courts involving expropriated property, and so on. In this sense, they are acts coming within the framework of Article 41.

Also for atypical measures, it will be necessary to establish case by case, with the usual methods of interpretation, whether the Council has intended to make them the object of binding decisions or of recommendations. With regard to the resolutions we have just cited, it seems that, with the exception of res. no. 662 of 1990 against Iraq, the hypothesis of a recommendation is the correct one. To be persuaded of this, it is sufficient to examine the discussions that preceded the resolutions and to bear in mind the atmosphere of compromise in which they were carried out.

Even if it is now a closed matter, worthy of mention is the already cited advisory opinion of June 21, 1971 of the International Court of Justice, which was concerned with res. no. 276 of January 30, 1970 on Namibia. The opinion does not frame the Council resolution within Article 41, but considers it (cf. ICJ, *Reports* 1971, p. 51 f., partic. no. 110) as the expression of a presumed residual power of the Council, supported by Article 24 of the Charter, on the maintenance of the peace (for a critique of this opinion, see § 60 *bis*). When it goes on to establish the legal consequences of the declaration of "invalidity" and "illegality" of South Africa's presence in Namibia, however, the opinion ultimately identifies such consequences in the *non-recognition* of the situation by the other States (CIJ, *Reports*, cit, p. 54 ff.), that is, in sanctioning measures that are clearly based, in our view, on Article 41.

59. D) *Measures involving the use of armed force (Articles 42 ff.). Peacekeeping Operations.*

BIBLIOGRAPHY: see § 55. *Adde*: MILLER, *Legal Aspects of the UN Action in the Congo*, in *A.J*, 1961, p. 1 ff.; RAID, *The UN Action in the Congo and its Legal Basis*, in *REgDI*, 1961, p. 1 ff.; BOWETT, *UN Forces*, London, 1964, p. 153 ff. and p. 552 ff.; SEYERSTED, *UN Forces in the Law of Peace and War*, Leiden, 1966.; BOYD, *UN Peace-Keeping Operations: A Military and Political Appraisal*, New York, 1972; THEODORIDES, *The United Nations Peace-Keeping Force in Cyprus (UNFICYP)*, in *ICLQ*, 1982, p. 765 ff.; RZYMANEK, *Some Legal Problems of UN Peacekeeping: UNEF-2 and UNDOF Experiences*, in *Polish Yearbook of International Law*, 1987, p. 85 ff.; LE PELLET, *Les bérets bleus de l' ONU: à travers 40 ans de conflit israelo-arabe*, Paris, 1988; SUY, *Legal Aspects of UN Peace-keeping Operations, ivi*, p. 318 ff..;SIEKMANN, *National Contingents in UN Paecekeeping Forces*, Dordrecht, 1991; HAGELSOM, GERT-JAN, *The Law of Armed Conflict and UN Peace-Keeping and Peace-Enforcing Operations*, in *Hague Yearb. of International Law*, 1993, p. 45 ff.; MAIJER, *UN Peace-Keeping Forces: The Conditions of Change, in LJIL*, 1994, p. 63 ff.; WARNER (ed.), *New Dimensions of Peacekeeping*, Dordrecht, 1995; PICONE, *Il peacekeeping nel mondo attuale etc.,* in *RDI*, 1996, p. 5 ss.; PINRSCHI, *Le operazioni di peacekeeping delle Nazioni Unie per il mantenimento della pace*, Padova, 1998, Part. 1, Chapt. 1 and 2; CELLAMARE, *Le operazioni di peeace-keeping multifunzionali*, Torino, 1999; SAROOSHI, *The UN and the Development of Collective Security: The Delegation by the UN Security Council of its Chapter VII Powers*, Oxford, 1999; RONZITTI, *Comamdo e controllo nella Carta delle Nazioni Unite*, in RONZITTI, *Comando e controllo nelle forze di pace e nelle coalizioni militari*, Milan, 1999, p. 31 ff.; BENVENUTI, *Forze multinazionali e diritto internazionale umanitario, ibid.,* p. 222 ff.; GARGIULO, *Il controverso rapporto tra Corte penale internazionale e Consiglio di Sicurezza per la repressione dei crimini di diritto internazionale*, in *CI* 1999, p. 428 ff.; *Wundeh Eno*, UN *Peacekeeping Operations and Respect for Human Rights*, in *SAYB*, 1999, p. 76 ff: FRULLI, *Le operazioni di peacekeeping delle Nazioni Unite e l'uso della forza*, in *RDI*, 2001, p. 347 ff.; SAROOSHI, *Aspects of the relationship between the International Criminal Cour and the UN*, in *NYIL*, 2001, p. 27 ff.; ARCARI, *Quelques remarques à propos de l'action du Conseil de Sécurité dans le domaine de la Justice pénale internazionale*, in *ADe*, 2002, p. 207 ff.; HESELHOUS, *Resolution 1422 (2002) des Sichereitsrates zur Begrenzung der Tätigkeit des Internationalen Strafgerichtshofs*, in *ZöRV*, 2002, 907 ff; KATAYANAGI, *Human Rights Functions of UN Peacekeeping Operations*, New York, 2002; ORAKHELASHVILI, *The Legal Basis of the UN Operations*, in *Virg JIL*, 2003, p. 485 ff:

Articles 42 and those following concern the possibility that the Security Council may decide to use force *against* a State responsible for aggression, or responsible for a threat to the peace or for a breach of the peace. Or it may decide to use force *within* a State by intervening in a civil war, where it deems that the domestic situation constitutes a threat to the peace (as often occurs in the case of civil war with its tragic consequences for the local population). The domestic nature of a situation does not constitute an obstacle to Council action, since the enforcement measures under Chapter VII do not come under the limit of domestic jurisdiction (Article 2, para. 7, last part). Indeed, as we have often said, it is exactly in domestic crises, and mainly for humanitarian purposes, that the Council today has the most opportunity to intervene.

Resort to military measures by the Security Council is clearly seen by Article 42 as an international police action. ("The Council... *may take such action* by air, sea or land forces as may be necessary to maintain or restore... peace"). The decision of the Council thus belongs to the kind of operational measure through which the Organisation does not order or recommend something to the States, but acts directly (see § 92). As specified by Articles 43 and following and in line with what was decided at the San Francisco Conference as the principal characteristic of the United Nations collective security system (cf. U.N.C.I.O., vol. 12, p. 279), direct action consists of the use of national armed contingents which are under an international command depending on the Security Council.

It is easy to understand the purpose pursued by Articles 42 and those following when they concentrate not only the power to decide that force is to be used but also the supervision of the military operations in the hands of the Security Council. This is, on the one hand, to guarantee the objectivity and impartiality of the operation as well as to see that such action remains within the limits strictly necessary for maintenance of the peace, and, on the other hand, to remove any military initiative from the individual States which is not justifiable, under Article 51, for reasons of individual or collective self-defence (on this, see § 55 *bis*).

As for the ways in which, under the Charter, the Security Council may take action, Articles 43, 44 and 45 lay down the *obligation* on the Member States to enter into agreements with the Council in order to establish the number, the degree of readiness, the deployment, and so on, of the armed forces to be utilised, totally or partially, by the organ (cf. also Article 48, para.

1) as the necessity arises. Under Articles 46 and 47, the actual use of the various national contingents is to be decided by a Military Staff Committee, composed of the Chiefs of Staff of the five permanent members and under the authority of the Council. The special agreements to be concluded between the UN Member States and the Council are considered by the Charter as the pre-conditions and the cornerstone of the system. These agreements are, moreover, the subject of a true *de contrahendo* obligation on the States. Indeed, it was clearly and expressly said at San Francisco that the Council would never be able to demand any assistance from the States, with weapons and with soldiers, which was not provided for by the special agreements (see U.N.C.I.O., vol. 12, p. 508).

Articles 43 ff. have never, from 1945 until today, been applied. The agreements for making national military contingents available to the Council, under Article 43, which were to be concluded "as soon as possible" (the Charter dates from 1945!), have never seen the light, nor has the Military Staff Committee of the Council ever functioned. In previous editions of this book we consequently held the view that Articles 43 ff. and the *de contrahendo* obligation on the Member States had been abrogated by custom. Now, the revitalisation of the Council after the end of the Cold War entails a reappraisal of this view in the sense that a "revival" (which has not yet taken place) of these articles cannot be excluded. It is indicative that the "Agenda for Peace" Report presented by the Secretary-General B. Boutros-Ghali to the Security Council in June 1992 (in *ILM*, 1992, p. 956 ff.), a Report dealing with the strengthening of the UN role in the area of maintenance of the peace (see § 8), provides that the agreements under Article 43 of the Charter may be concluded in the future (cf., para. 43 of the Report).

Up until today, and especially after the end of the Cold War, the Council has usually intervened in international or domestic crises with measures of a military nature in two different ways, sometimes combining them. It either has created United Nations Forces who are engaged, although with very limited tasks, in peacekeeping operations or it has authorised the use of force by the Member States, either individually or within regional organizations. The use of force by regional organizations will be discussed later, in Section V (see § 65). Here, we will deal firstly with peacekeeping operations and then with the authorisation of the use of force by Member States. In our opinion, peacekeeping actions can be traced back to Article 42 although broadly interpreted. The authorisation of the use of force by States - a matter dealt with in the next paragraph as an enforcement measure not provided for in the Charter - largely departs from Article 42.

As far as peacekeeping forces are concerned, there were very few between 1945 and 1987 and many more in the years after 1988. The principal ones are, or have been, the following: ONUC, which was active in the Congo in the sixties to help the Congo out of its state of civil war and anarchy; UNEF II (United Nations Emergency Force), established in 1973, as a buffer between Egypt and Israel, and dissolved in 1979 (not to be confused with UNEF I, set up by the General Assembly in 1956: see § 64); UNFICYP, created in 1964 and still operating as a buffer force between the tow Cypriot States; UNDOF (United Nations Disengagement Observation Force), stationed since 1974 in the Golan Heights between Israel and Syria; UNIFIL (United Nations Interim Force in Lebanon), established in 1978 and operating in Southern Lebanon; UNAVEM II and III, operating since 1991 in Angola; UNPROFOR, established in 1992 in the former Yugoslavia and operating particularly in Bosnia-Herzegovina until December 1995; UNOSOM, which has been operating, between 1992 and 1995, in Somalia; UNOMOZ, set up with res. no. 797 of December 16, 1992 and stationed in Mozambique; UNOMSIL, operating in Sierra Leone between 1998 and 1999; MINURCA, operating in the Central Africa Republic since 1998; UNAMSIL, created in 1999 and operating in Sierra Leone, MONUC, created in 1999 and operating in the Democratic Republic of Congo since 2000; UNMEE, operating in Ethiopia and Eritrea since 2000; UNMISET, created in 2002 and operating in East Timor; UNMIL, operating in Liberia since 2003; MINUSTAN, operating in Haiti since June 2004; ONUB, operating in Burundi since June 2004.

Aside from the case of the Congo, the practice followed by the Security Council in the other cases has been to limit the duration of the mandate of the Forces it has established, and then to gradually extend it, always for limited periods (usually six, nine or twelve months). This practice has its roots in the disagreements which occurred in the Council at the time of the Congo action when, since the Council had not set any limit and could not decide for a certain period of time, the Secretary-General (who is appointed by the Council to head the Forces) in the end had to decide what to do (see § 65.). With the system of extension and therefore of automatic expiration of the mandate of the Force in the event of the Council's inactivity, the intention is to strengthen the principle (strenuously defended by the Socialist States of East Europe in the Cold War period) that the Forces' operations, even if they are carried out under the direction of the Secretary-General, remain entirely under the "authority" of the Council. The observation of the principle is also assured by continual close contact between the Secretary and the Council, contact maintained through periodic reports, request for approval of the appointment of high-level officers, and so on.

The principal characteristic of the peacekeeping operations is the Security Council's delegation to the Secretary General of both provision and command of the UN Forces, through agreements with the Member States. According to common opinion, another characteristic is that the UN Forces, which normally intervene in internal crises, operate with the consent of the State, or States, on whose territory they are stationed. Actually, this is a pure legal fiction since often either no local government has existed since the beginning of the operations or it has ceased to exist during the operations. This could be the case in civil wars or in a situation of anarchy, for example the Congo in 1960-61 and Somalia in 1992. Yet, according to common opinion, the peacekeeping forces are not meant to use force. They are simply buffer forces, meant only to divide adversaries and to help them in re-establishing and in maintaining conditions of peace and security without being allowed to use arms, except for self-defence, even though they are fully equipped. In other words, they should be considered, to use current terminology, as peacekeeping and not peace-enforcing forces. Moreover, they are often combined with UN civil personnel in order to provide humanitarian assistance, to monitor the execution of agreements concluded by different factions within the framework of procedures of national conciliation (sec § 56), and to assist the local authorities in acts of civil administration, in post-conflict situations (so called multidimensional or multifunctional peacekeeping).

No doubt the task of these forces is always very limited, and was particularly limited in the Cold War period. However, this is not enough to conclude that the UN Forces have nothing to do with the use of armed force, even if it is limited. Moreover some of them have been established with the task of peace-enforcing or have transformed from peacekeeping forces to peace-enforcing forces. The case of the Congo, as well as the cases of the former Yugoslavia and Somalia, are indicative in this sense.

In the case of the Congo, the Security Council, in res. no. 143 of July 14, 1960, "authorised" the Secretary-General to provide military assistance to the Congolese government until the Congo was able to maintain domestic order by itself. Subsequently, the United Nations Force (ONUC) was set up with contingents offered voluntarily by the Member States and was placed under the authority of the Secretary-General. In the meantime, a series of very serious events had occurred, such as the establishment of various centres of power in the country, the killing of the leader Lumumba, the secession of the Katanga province, and the death of the then Secretary-General Hammarskjold. The Council then adopted other resolutions confirming the purposes of the Force and authorising the use of weapons to prevent civil war (res. no. 161 of February 21, 1961) and to eliminate the presence of foreign mercenaries in the country, particularly in the Katanga province (res. no. 169 of November 24, 1961). As a result, ONUC carried out what was a real, although brief, war of liberation in the Katanga province.

In the case of Yugoslavia, the first resolution concerning UNPROFOR (United Nations Protection Force) was res. no. 743 of February 21, 1992, which decided to establish the Force "under the authority" of the Council in order to "create the conditions of peace and security required for the negotiation of an overall settlement of the Yugoslav crisis" (para. 5) and invited the Secretary to take the necessary measures. A long series of subsequent resolutions then specified, in relation to developments in the crisis, the various tasks of the Force. The main ones were: res. no. 761 of June 29, 1992 and no. 764 of July 13, 1992 which (respectively, para. 1 and para. 2) authorised the Force to "ensure the security and functioning of Sarajevo airport and the delivery of humanitarian assistance"; no. 779 of October 6, 1992, which authorised it to monitor the complete withdrawal of the Yugoslav army from Croatia and the demilitarisation of the Prevlaka peninsula; res. no. 807 of February 19, 1993 which called upon the Secretary-General to equip the Force with suitable weapons for its defence; res. no.836 of June 4, 1993 which entrusted the force with the task of defending several Bosnian cities, and their surrounding areas, which had been declared "safe areas" in previous resolutions; no. 913 of April 22, 1994, which invited the Secretary-General to take all the necessary measures in order to enable the UNPROFOR to control the situation and the respect of the cease-fire in Gorazde. These resolutions provide evidence that even if UNPROFOR was not engaged in true military actions, it cannot be considered a mere instrument of peaceful measures. By res. no. 1031 of December 15, 1995 the Security Council put an end to the mandate of UNPROFOR, following the Dayton Agreement.

With regard to Somalia, ONUSOM was initially established with res. no. 751 (paras. 2 and 7) of April 24, 1992, with the task of "supporting" the Secretary-General's efforts to facilitate the cease-fire between the factions at war in the country and to furnish humanitarian assistance to the population. However, subsequently, with res. no. 814 (part B, paras. 5 and 14) of March 26, 1993, it took on the functions that had formerly been exercised by a groups of States under United States unified command. In particular, it took on the function of consolidating, extending and maintaining the security of the whole country. Res. no. 837 of June 6, 1993, adopted after a Somali attack on a group of Pakistani blue helmets, entrusted the Force (now called ONUSOM II) with the task of taking "any measure against all those responsible for the armed attacks". Unfortunately, this resolution constituted the legal grounds for a brutal attack against the districts controlled by the Somali General Aidid, an attack which, in the name of the United Nations, provoked the killing of innocent victims and was thus deplored by the civilised world. Nobody can deny that this action constitutes use of force. In March 1995 ONUSOM was withdrawn from the territory of Somalia, as demanded by res. no. 954 of November 4, 1994.

By res. no. 1327 of November 13, 2000 with Annex, the Security Council has laid down some general "decisions and recommendations" on the establishment and behaviour of the peacekeeping forces. This was with the aim of strengthening the peacekeeping operations and giving them "clear, credible and achievable mandates" as well as "a credible deterrent capability". Worth noting is the recommendation contained in Part IV of the Annex, according to which the peacekeeping operations should be deployed within 30 days, and in case of complex operations, within 90 days of the Security Council resolution establishing its mandate.

In Part I of the Annex, the Council urges the parties to a "prospective peace agreement" where a peacekeeping operation is envisaged, to bear in mind the need for any provision regarding such operation "for the...compliance with the rules and principles of international law, in particular international, humanitarian, human rights and refugee law". Needless to say that the peacekeeping forces have to comply with these rules even more closely. The above cited case of the attack of the ONUSOM II in 1993 is a clear case of non compliance with humanitarian law and should never be repeated.

The above resolutions show a clear trend towards the duty of the Security Council to comply with international law when a peacekeeping operation is set up. This duty is parallel to the Council's duty with regard to those measures not involving the use of force (see § 58).

One question needs to be treated here since it is mainly linked to the status of the UN Forces. It concerns the relation between the Security Council and the International Criminal Court whose Statute, approved by the Rome UN Conference of Plenipotentiaries, entered into force on 1 July 2002. By res. no. 1422 of July 12, 2002 (and then by the identical res. no. 1487 of June 12, 2003), the Security Council, referring to Article 16 of the Rome Statute and acting under Chapter VII, has requested the Court not to commence or proceed with investigation or prosecution against current or former officials or personnel involved in UN operations for acts relating to such operations, unless the Security Council decides otherwise. The immunity is requested for a period of twelve months starting from 1 July 2003, but the Council "expresses the intention" to renew the request for further 12-month periods, if necessary. According to Article 16 of the Rome Statute "No investigation or prosecution may be commenced or proceeded with under this Statute for a period of 12 months after the Security Council has requested the Court to that effect; that request may be renewed by the Council under the same conditions". In fact, the request has not been reiterated on June 2004, due to the events in Iraq and the gross violation of humanitarian rules by US soldiers. A draft resolution drawn up by United States has not been presented since it would not have the required majority within the Council.

In legal doctrine the question of whether res. no. 1422 and 1487 are compatible with the powers of the Security Council under the Charter is the object of sharp debate. Doubts about the legality of the resolutions have been raised, as Chapter VII does not deal with the relations between the Security Council and international tribunals. Doubts have also been raised about the possibility of considering the activity of the Court as a threat to the peace, the previous determination of such threat being indispensable for any decision of the Security Council under Chapter VII. In particular, the general immunity requested for all members of peacekeeping forces coming from non-Member States of the Statute of the Court, instead of a request made on a case by case basis, has been considered *ultra vires*. In our opinion, leaving aside the sad impression created by resolutions imposed by only one Member State of the Council, the United States, and the setback thus suffered by International justice, the decision of the Security Council cannot be considered contrary to the Charter. It is not a question of finding a special provision of the Charter which deals with this specific case. It is not a question of the lack of determination about a specific threat to the peace in order to justify the request of immunity. The Security Council has not only the power to create military forces but also the power to enact all regulations governing them and their status: the immunity granted to the members of these forces is exactly the expression of the latter .

Having said that, the resolutions on immunity have to be evaluated from another point of view. No doubt the Council is bound by humanitarian and human rights law, as well as some other international rules of *jus cogens*. Moreover, in the already quoted res. no 1327 of November 13, 2000 with Annex,, as we have seen, the Council has recognised the importance of humanitarian and human rights rules by committing the UN Forces to their observance. We can consequently wonder whether the general request for immunity, contained within res. no. 1422 and 1487, does comply with such rules. Indeed, the power granted to the Security Council by Article 16 of the Statute of the Court has been considered as contrary to humanitarian law by some Non Governmental Organizations, during the preparatory works of the Statute (see AMNESTY INTERNATIONAL, *The International Criminal Court Making the Right Choise - Part I*, London, 1997, p. 95 ff.; HUMAN RIGHTS WATCH, *Commentary for the August 1997 Preparatory Committee Meeting on the Establishment of an International Criminal Court*, 1997, p. 9 f.). However, even if this is the way of dealing with the question of the legality of the resolutions on immunity, the answer to the question is still positive. In fact, the resolutions do not grant an absolute immunity, since it notes that "States not party to the Rome Statute will continue to fulfil their responsibilities in their national jurisdictions in relation to international crimes". What is at stake, therefore, is not immunity but simply *international* immunity.

In light of the above, in what framework can peacekeeping operations be put? We have always held, and we continue to hold that the peacekeeping Forces carry out the international police action spoken of in Article 42. This is in spite of their usually limited tasks, and in spite of the fact that their provision and their command are ensured *case by case* by the Secretary-General (but under the authority and continuous supervision of the Security Council) and not, as Articles 43 ff. prescribe, directly by the Council and with contingents *permanently* available to the Council. When Article 42 says that the Council "... may take such action by air, sea or land forces as may be necessary to maintain or restore international peace and security...", we do not see why by action only war or action involving the spilling of blood is meant. On the other hand, the nature of international police action under Article 42 is not diminished because the blue helmets are usually forbidden to fire (except in self-defence), just as the action of national police forbidden to fire on demonstrators is no less considered police action. Nor the absence of the Military Staff Committee under the direct authority of the Security Council, provided for by Articles 46 and 47, has a decisive weight. The command being entrusted to the Secretary-General, it is sufficient to remind that, according to Article 98, this organ may perform all the functions the Council deems advisable to delegate to him.

> The delegation with which Article 98 deals ("The Secretary-General...shall perform such functions as are entrusted to him by [the Security Council]...") is not a true delegation as this is intended in domestic law, i.e. as a mandate given by a person to another person. Since the Secretary-General is the chief administrative officer of the Organization, one of his institutional task is exactly to execute the decisions of the Security Council. The relationship with the Security Council is always an inter-organic relationship within the framework of the Charter (see § 65). Quite different is the relationship between the Council and a Member State when the latter is called by the former to act on its behalf (see § 60).

We must recognise that our view is not shared in legal literature. Most commentators hold the opinion that only peace-enforcing forces (i.e. forces enabled to make war) were taken into consideration by the Founders of the United Nations when drafting Article 42 ff.; they either tend to bring peacekeeping operations under Charter provisions other than Chapter VII, especially under the norms on peaceful settlement in Chapter VI, or speak of the formation of unwritten rules which have now taken root with the agreement of all the Member States. Some scholars even say that peacekeeping operations...come between Chapters VI and VII.

The first of these views is absurd, as the peaceful settlement function also belongs to the General Assembly and no one any longer today dares to hold that the Assembly (which only in one remote case created a Force for maintenance of the peace: see § 64) is competent in this matter. The second view seems more convincing and seems to be shared by the above cited *Agenda for Peace* of the Secretary-General B. Boutros-Ghali (cf. *ILM*, 1992, p. 967, para. 46, where peacekeeping operations are defined as an "invention" of the United Nations; see also the Secretary-General' s *Supplement to an Agenda for Peace, Doc.* A/50/60 and S/1995/ 1, January 3, 1995, para. 33 ff.*).* One could say, at this point, that whether one holds our view or holds that an *ad hoc* customary rule has been formed, the substance does not change. Actually, there is a difference, and it is not a negligible one, when we consider that peacekeeping operations are very costly, that all the Member States are called upon to participate, according to Article 17, in the expenses for carrying them out, and that, for reasons which will be discussed later (see § 86), it would be difficult to say that there exists an obligation to contribute to expenses that cannot be brought within a specific Charter provision.

Even if their functions are limited, the UN Forces, in so far as they arc actual military forces operating in permanent crisis situations, must be distinguished from UN observer corps, which come under the function of investigation (see § 51). However, the two forces sometimes tend to overlap. In fact, the difference lies more in quantity than in quality, the military presence being normally assured by *single* armed persons in the case of observer corps.

60. *Measures not provided for by the Charter. A) The authorization of the use of force by States.*

BIBLIOGRAPHY: See § 55. *Adde*: GAJA, *Il Consiglio di Sicurezza di fronte all'occupazione del Kuwait: il significato di un'autorizzazione,* in *RDI*, 1990, p. 380 ff.; VERHOEVEN, *Etats alliés ou Nations Unies? L' ONU face au conflit entre l'Irak et le Kuweit,* in *AF*, 1990, p. 145 ff.; BURCI, *L'azione del Consiglio di Sicurezza delle N.U. nella crisi del Golfo,* in *CI*, 1991, p. 278 ff.; AA.VV., *Agora: the Gulf Crisis in International and Foreign Relations Law,* in *AJ*, 1991, p. 63 ff. and p. 506 ff.; PYRICH, *UN: Authorisations of Use of Force — Security Council Resolution 665 and Security Council Resolution 678,* in *HILJ*, 1991, p. 265 ff.; DOMINICÉ, *La sécurité collective et la crise du Golfe,* in *EJIL*, 1991, p. 85 ff.; SCHACHTER, *UN Law in the Gulf Conflict,* in *AJ*, 1991, p. 452 ff.; VILLANI, *Lezioni su l'ONU e la crisi del Golfo,* Bari, 1991; MAJID, *Is the Security Council Working? "Desert Storm" Critically Examined,* in ., 1992, p. 984 ff.; LOBEL and RATNER, *Bypassing the Security Council: Ambiguous Authorisations to Use Force, Ceasefires and the Iraqui Inspection Regime,* in *AJ*, 1999, p. 124 ff. ; BENVENUTI, *Forze multinazionali e diritto internazionale umanitario,* in RONZITTI, *Comando e controllo nelle forze di pace e nelle coalizioni militari,* Milan, 1999, p. 222 ff. SAROOSHI, *The UN and the Development of Collective Security: The Delegation by the UN Security Council of its Chapter VII Powers,* Oxford, 1999; BLOKKER, *Is the Authorization Authorized ? Powers and Pracice of the UN Security Council to Authorize the Use of force by Coalitions of the Able and Willing,* in *EJIL*, 2000, p.541 ff.; SICILIANOS, *L'autorisation par le*

Conseil de Sécurité de recourir à la force: une tentative d'évaluation, in *RGDIP*, 2002, p. 5 ff.;
PICONE, *La guerra contro l'Iraq e le degenerazioni dell'unilateralismo*, in RDI, 2003, p. 39 ff..

Notwithstanding frequent resort to the use of UN Forces after the end of the cold war, things have now changed. The deployment of UN Forces has proved almost unfeasible for many reasons (political, military, logistic, etc.). The experience of ONUSOM in Somalia and UNPROFOR in the former Yugoslavia testify to this.

The failure of the action of the Council is very well illustrated by the part of the above cited res. no. 954 of 1994 on the withdrawal of UNOSOM from Somalia, where the Council recognises that "the lack of progress in the Somali peace process and in national reconciliation, in particular the lack of sufficient co-operation from the Somali parties over security issues, has fundamentally undermined the United Nations objectives in Somalia..." and that "the people of Somalia bear the ultimate responsibility for achieving national reconciliation and bringing peace in Somalia".

It is understandable, then, that the Council is now oriented to confer the task of conducting military operations for the maintenance of peace and security to the Member States, acting individually or through regional organizations (on regional actions see § 67).

Twice during the Cold War and several times since the beginning of the nineties, instead of acting directly, as prescribed in Article 42, or through the Secretary-General in peacekeeping operations, the Council has authorised or recommended or delegated (the three terms are used interchangeably here) Member States to use force *against* a State or *within* a State and placed the command and the supervision of military operations in their hands.

We are speaking here of actions of States authorised, or recommended, or delegated, etc., by the Council, therefore, of actions in which the individual States are free to participate or not to participate. The problem of Council decisions which *obliges* Member States to use force has never arisen. In the absence of practice and in the light of the Charter text, this type of decision would certainly be illegal.

In two cases authorisation was given to conduct a full-fledged war to counteract outside aggression. The first was the Korean War, which took place in 1950 when the Member States were "invited" to help South Korea defend itself from an attack by North Korea. The second case was the Gulf War, carried out in 1991 by a coalition of Member States "authorised" by the Council to help the Kuwait government take back its territory occupied by Iraq.

In the case of Korea, in a first resolution, no. 83 of June 27, 1950, the Council recommended that the Member States furnish assistance to South Korea. In a subsequent resolution, no. 84 of July 7, 1950, it expressed satisfaction with the support given by a certain number of States to the recommendation of June 27, and accepted that the command of the forces operating against North Korea be undertaken by the United States, authorising use of the UN flag. The two resolutions were contested by the Soviet Union but only regarding their procedural aspect, as they had been adopted in its absence (see § 25).

In the case of the Gulf crisis, after having taken several decisions under Article 41, the Council passed res. no. 678 of November 29, 1990 in an effort to induce Iraq to leave Kuwait. This resolution authorised the Member States, if Iraq were not to have retreated within January 15, 1991, to use "all necessary means" to reach this aim and to restore peace and security in the Gulf area. Among the necessary means — according to the terminology which thereafter became standard in order to indicate also the use of armed force — military action was included and it punctually began on the date set.

In other cases Member States have been authorised to use military force in internal crises. One important example is INTERFET (International Force for East Timor), a multinational force led by Australia and entrusted by the Security Council (res. no. 1264 of September 15, 1999) with the task of restoring peace and security in East Timor. The action of the Force, which faced serious troubles following the result of the referendum in favour of the independence of this country from Indonesia, was very successful and lasted until the replacement of the Force by the military personnel of the UNTAET, the UN Transitional Administration in East Timor, created by res. no. 1272 of October 25, 1999 (see § 60 *bis*).

Recently, the use of military forces by Member States has been authorised as far as the (tragic) situation in Iraq is concerned, after the unauthorised International war conducted by the coalition led by the United States. By res. no. 1511, of October 16, 2003, the Security Council, at para. 13 "authorises a multinational force under unified command [the forces of occupying Powers were already on the spot!] to take all necessary measures to contribute to the maintenance of security and stability in Iraq" and at para. 14 "urges Member States to contribute assistance under this mandate, including military forces, to the multinational force referred to in para. 13 above". The authorisation has been reiterated by res. no. 1546 of June 8, 2004. This time, the mandate of the multinational force will be reviewed after twelve months from the date of resolution and will terminate earlier at the request of the Interim Government of Iraq (par. 12 of the res.) a Government installed on June 2004 - and whose true independence from the multinational force could be called into question!.

There are numerous other examples of authorisation of the use of force in internal crises. As far as the war in Bosnia Herzegovina, see, for instance: res. no. 816 of March 31, 1993, which authorised the Member States to use their air forces individually or within the framework of a regional organizations; res. no. 1031 of December 15, 1995, which acknowledged the transfer of functions from UNPROFOR (see § 59) to the Multinational Implementation Force (IFOR) created by the Dayton Agreement; res. no. 1087 of December

11, 1996, para. 18, which authorises the Member States to establish a Multinational Stabilisation Force (SFOR) as a successor of IFOR. With regard to the Somali crisis, the res. no. 794 of December 3, 1992 can be cited. By it the Council authorised the Member States to co-operate in carrying out the "offer" of a UN member (read: the United States) to use the necessary means (read: use of force) in order to establish "a secure environment for humanitarian relief operations" by providing their military forces. As we have already had occasion to note, the functions thus entrusted to the Member States were subsequently transferred to the United Nations Force operating in Somalia, which absorbed the national military contingents (see § 59).

For other examples see: res. no. 929 of June 22, 1994, authorising a French force to intervene in Rwanda; res. no. 940 of July 31, 1994, authorising the USA to intervene in Haiti and lead the Multinational Force in Haiti (MFH); res. no. 998 of June 6, 1995, authorising the constitution of a "Rapid Reaction Force" (RRF) in the former Yugoslavia with contingents from France, the Netherlands and the United Kingdom; res. no. 1080 of November 15, 1996, authorising the creation of a temporary multinational force to intervene for humanitarian reasons in the Eastern Zaire; res. no. 1101 of March 28, 1998 (Multinational Protection Force for Albania, leaded by Italy; res. no. 1264 of September 15, 1999 (Multinational Force in East Timor); res. no. 1386 of November 20, 2001 and no. 1444 of November 27, 2002 (International Security Assistance Force in Afghanistan; res. no. 1464 of February 4, 2003 (French forces, together with ECOWAS forces, in Ivory Coast); res. no. 1484 of May 30, 2003 (Interim Emergency Multinational Force in Bunia, Democratic Republic of Congo); res. no. 1497 of August 1st, 2003 (Multinational Force in Liberia); res. no. 1529 of February 29, 2004 (Multinational Interim Force in Haiti)..

Measures short of war, but still definable as measures involving the use of armed force, have been authorised or recommended to Member States. Among them are those authorising the establishment of naval blockades, which, also through the use of force, are designed to prevent trade by ships of any nationality (and in derogation of the principle that on the high seas a ship is subject only to the flag State) with certain ports. A precedent of a naval blockade, at the time of the Cold War, can be found in res. no. 221 of April 9, 1966, which, to strengthen the prohibition on the sale of oil to Southern Rhodesia (see § 58), "called upon" Great Britain to prevent "by the use of force if necessary" the arrival of oil in the port of Beira (Mozambique) which was intended to continue by land for Rhodesia. Much larger naval blockades have been set up more recently, and precisely during the Gulf crisis, before the outbreak of hostilities against Iraq, and during the Yugoslav crisis.

In the first case, res. no. 665 of August 25, 1990 "called upon" the Member States to prevent any ship coming from or directed towards the coasts of Iraq and occupied Kuwait from violating the embargo established by previous res. no. 661 of August 6, 1990. In the case of the Yugoslav crisis similar measures were ordered against the Yugoslav Republic (Serbia-Montenegro) with res. no. 787, para. 12, of November 16, 1992.

Is the delegation of the use of force by the Council to the States lawful?

The question of the legality of the delegation of the use of force to States has been considered in legal doctrine, in the light of general principles of domestic law regarding the mandate. The opinion has been held that Article 24 of the Charter ("...Members *confer* on the Security Council primary responsibility for the maintenance of international peace and security...") embodies a delegation of power from Member States to the Security Council. The consequence - we say - should be the impossibility for the Council itself to delegate, since a well established general principle of law states that delegatus *non potest delegare.*

We do not believe that Article 24 can be interpreted as containing a true delegation in the meaning this term has in domestic law. The terminology used in the article cannot be read in a literal sense. It is rather a way of stating that the Security Council has the monopoly of the use of military force, with the exception of self-defence. If Article 24 were interpreted in the sense of the delegation theory, then the Member States, at least collectively, could decide to use force whenever they wanted, since the *delegans* can always resume the power conferred to the *delegatus*. Such a consequence is manifestly absurd. Worthy of note is also that Article 24 has not only been interpreted as containing a delegation of power, with the consequence of the applicability of the principle *delegatus non potest delegare*, but also in the quite opposite sense, i.e. as a rule which, being couched in very general terms, could justify all actions of the Security Council not expressly set forth by the Charter provided that they are necessary in order to maintain international peace and security!

The attempt has been made (by SAROOSHI, *op. cit.*, pp.22-46) to reconcile the principle "*delegatus non potest delegare*", with the delegation of the use of force by the Security Council to States. This author also starts from the assumption that Article 24 of the Charter embodies a true delegation to the Council. However, he holds that the principle does not prevent the (sub)delegation to States, but only implies that the (sub)delegation is subject to certain conditions, namely that it does not include: the determination of the threat to the peace, the breach of the peace or an act of aggression; an unrestricted power of command; broad powers of discretion; the exercise of powers in a way other than that specified by the Charter. Moreover, the terms of the (sub)delegation should be construed narrowly. The attempt is not convincing, since the principle "*delegatus non potest delegare*" as a general principle of law suffers no other exception than the express authorization on the part of the *delegans* to proceed with a sub-delegation.

In our opinion, it is correct to say that the Charter does not permit the delegation of military force by the Council to the States. However, the reason for that is simply because the founders of the United Nations wanted to concentrate the international police power in the hands of the Organisation with the consequent guarantee of objectivity and impartiality of military actions. As time went by, as the original idea of the framers of the Charter was revealed as Utopian, the practice of delegation begun. Now the Council tends more and more to follow this practice, while maintaining its control over operations. This being the case, and due to the lack of a serious opposition to such practice among the great majority of Member States, delegation has to be considered as permissible under an unwritten rule which has taken root in recent times. On the basis of this rule, the Council is assuming more and more functions that are *directive* rather then *operative*.

In previous editions of this book, and specifically with regard to the Gulf War, we held the opinion that the intervention of States "authorised" by the Council could come within the framework of Article 51 when, as in this case, it was an intervention aimed at repelling an armed attack in the exercise of collective self-defence (see § 55 *bis*). However, especially in the light of more recent practice, this framing seems unsatisfactory and not much in keeping with reality, since delegation to States also concerns interventions in civil war situations which it is impossible to define as collective self-defence., not being a reaction to an armed aggression.

The delegation to States must be couched in express terms. No resolution of the Council can be interpreted as implicitly authorising the use of force by States if it does not contain a clear authorisation. The events which preceded the second war in Iraq by a coalition led by the United States in 2003 are very meaningful in this sense. Res. no. 1441 of November 8, 2002, authorised UN inspectors to be sent to Iraq to investigate possible weapons of mass destruction. It deplored the continuous violations by Iraq of its obligations vis-à-vis the United Nations, and warned Iraq once again "that it will face serious consequences" as a result of these violations. In the opinion of the Member States of the coalition, such a warning was sufficient to justify the subsequent war. However, it is well known that the opposite view was upheld by the overwhelming majority of the UN members.

The resolutions adopted by the Security Council at the time of the war in Afghanistan also cannot be interpreted as authorising this war. Some of these resolutions (particularly res. no. 1368 of September 12, 2001 and no. 1373 of September 28, 2001) after having requested the States to take a series of measures, including financial measures, against terrorists and terrorist organizations, like Al Qaida, embodied a "whereas" reaffirming "the inherent right of individual and collective self-defence" . References to self-defence, made in resolutions whose operative parts were clearly applying measures not involving the use of military force, do not seem sufficient to justify military actions by States.

According to the rule on authorisation which has emerged from practice, the control on the way operations are carried out by States must remain in the hands of the Security Council. This is clearly a *minimum* which is necessary in order to say that military action is still carried out in the framework of the United Nations. In fact, the Council is constantly kept informed, directly or through the reports of the Secretary-General, about the conduct of operations, so that it is able to give those directives it deems appropriate.

Since the military action of States has to be carried out under the supervision and control of the Security Council, the illegality of a war conducted without authorisation by the Council cannot be removed by a subsequent (implied) ratification, for instance by providing a post-war administration of the territory wherein the war took place. The case of the Kosovo crisis can be cited in this regard. After three months of the unauthorised air war by Nato forces in 1999 (see § 67), by res. no. 1244 of June 10, 1999 the Council established UNMIK, the UN Interim Administration in Kosovo (see § 60 *bis*) still in charge, with some of the NATO forces (the KFOR) ensuring the external security of the territory. The resolution clearly governs the post-war situation and has been welcome within the Security Council as a way of restoring the authority of the Council (See Doc. S/PV. 4011 of June 10, 1999). However, it does not embody any express ratification of the air war; nor it could be interpreted as entailing an implied ratification precisely because the Security Council had no control of operations during the war. The same must be said of resolutions (for instance res. no. 1483 of May 22, 2003, no. 1511 of October 16, 2003) concerning the post-war situation in Iraq and recognising the "authority" of the occupying coalition forces led by the United States.

What we say about unauthorised military actions is strictly linked to the United Nations system including customary rules which have emerged within the system. In our opinion, the question can be put differently from the point of view of general (customary) international law. When the UN system does not work, then general international law is by itself unable to govern the *jus ad bellum*, showing a "lacuna" which opens the way to discussion of the problem of war in the context of natural law as a problem of "just" or "unjust" war. See on this point, CONFORTI, *The Doctrine of "Just War" and Contemporary International Law*, in IYIL, 2002, vol. XII, p. 3 ff.

According to another view (Picone), when the UN system of collective security does not work or works imperfectly, unauthorised military action by Member States can be permitted on the basis of customary international law, provided that countries react against violations of obligations *erga omnes*, in particular International crimes. The Member States are then acting *uti universi*, i. e. in the name of International community as a whole. In some cases, namely when it is evident that the intervention of the Security Council has no other aim but to legitimize an action already decided by single States, the UN Organization is in these States' service and becomes itself an organ of the International community. This view is not convincing since the equation International crimes with the right of every State to react with the use of force is not persuasive.

Lastly, the forces of Member States whose creation is authorised by the Security Council must comply with general International law, especially Humanitarian law. Such compliance is imposed by the Council on the peacekeeping forces (see § 59) and it is even more understandable that it is incumbent on forces set up by States. Moreover, all Sates must abide by international law, and it would be strange if they were exempted when using force for the maintenance of peace and security.

In fact, the boundary between action of the States, under the supervision and authority of the Council, and action of the Secretary-General, under the supervision and authority of the Council, tends to vanish. Besides, even if the first kind of action is legal, its superiority, in terms of impartiality and objectivity, with respect to the other kind should not be exaggerated. The violent operations carried out by ONUSOM in Somalia (see § 59) show that the use of military force, even on the part of the United Nations, should always be discouraged. In other words, use of force always has odious consequences, no matter who is behind it. How, then, can the fundamental problem of maintaining peace be resolved? In our view, the only solution would be to provide the United Nations with effective instruments to *prevent* crises from breaking out, and this could be done only by giving the United Nations the means to carry out serious, continuous and effective arms control. This is obviously a utopian solution in light of the actual behaviour of States, but it is one worth striving for.

As we have already noted in discussing revision of the Charter (see § 8), General Assembly res. no. 46/36 of December 12, 1991 established at the United Nations a "Register of conventional weapons" in which, beginning from January 1, 1992, there were to be registered data, *provided by the Member States*, relating to the import and export of conventional arms as well as the size of national stocks. A system of control by the United Nations over the production and sale of arms, instead of being based only on data provided by the States, should involve *direct* means of information and inspection, as well as enforcement measures of the kind governed by Article 41 to compel if necessary the States to tolerate them. The need for preventive disarmament in order to reduce the sale and the number of small arms and light weapons in conflict-prone regions is stressed in the Report of the Secretary-General to the 54 th sess. of the General Assembly in 1999 (see Doc. A/54/1 of August 31, 1999, para. 37 ff.). However, up to now nothing very serious has occurred regarding this matter.

60. *bis*. B) *Measures on governing territories.*

BIBLIOGRAPHY: HIGGINS, *The Advisory Opinion on Namibia: Which UN Resolutions Are Binding under Article 25 of the Charter* ?, in *ICLQ*, 1972, p. 270 ff.; CRAWFORD, *The ILC's Draft Statute for an International Criminal Tribunal*, in *AJ*, 1994, p. 140 ff.; OELLERS-FRAHM, *Das Statut des Internationalen Strafgerichtshofs zur Verfolgung von Kriegsverbrechen im ehemaligen Jugoslawien*, in *Bruns'Z*, 1994, p. 416 ff.; HOCHKAMMER, *The Yugoslav War Crimes Tribunal: The Compatibility of Peace, Politics and International Law*, in *Vanderbilt Journal of International Law*, 1995, p. 119 ff.; VIERUCCI, *The First Steps of the International Criminal Tribunal for the Former Yugoslavia*, in *EJIL*, 1995, p. 134 ff.; CARELLA, *Il Tribunale penale per la ex Jugoslavia*, in PICONE (ed.), *Interventi delle Nazioni Unite e diritto internazionale*, Padua, 1995, p. 463 ff.; GUILLAUME, MARBICH AND ETIENNE, *Le cadre juridique de l'action de la KFOR au Kosovo*, in *AF*, 1999, p. 308 ff.; CAHIN, *L'action internationale au Timor oriental, ibid.*, 2000, p. 139 ff.; De Hoog, *Attribution or Delegation of (Legislative) Power by the Security Council ? The case of the UNTAET*, in *Int.PK*, 2001, p. 7 ff.; Irmischer, *The Legal Framework for the Activities of the UN Interim Administration Mission in Kosovo: Te Charter, Human Rights and the Law of Occupation*, in *GYIL*, 2001, p. 353 ff.; Matheson, *United Nations Governance of Postconflict Societies,* in HJIL, 2001, p. 76 ff.; Shustov, *Transitional Civil Administration within the Framework of UN Peacekeeping Operations: A Strong Mechanism ?,* in Int PK, 2001, p. 417 ff.; Strohmeyer, *Collapse and Reconstruction of a Judicial System*, in *Ath and J*, 2001, p. 46 ff.; Abline, *De l'indépendence du Timor-Oriental*, in *RGDIP*, 2003, p. 349 ff.; Korhonen, *International Governance in Post-Conflict Situations*, in *LJIL*, 2001, p. 495 ff.; Von Carlowitz, *UNMIK Lawmaking between Effective Peace-Support and Internal Self-determination*, in *AV*, 2003, p. 336 ff.

Sometimes the Security Council, acting in the framework of Chapter VII and invoking the necessity to maintain or restore peace and security, has organized the governance of territories. Such territories might have been the object of contrasting claims by neighbour States or have been the battlefield of a civil war. Single acts of governance have also been decided and executed.

The establishment of administrations of territories has also been decided in some cases by the General Assembly, for a transitional period, in the framework of de-colonisation. See § 80 *bis.*

Very often the Security Council has participated, through the Secretary-General and his staff, in constitutional procedures of national conciliation. We have considered this function as a kind of peaceful settlement of disputes according to Article 39 (see § 56).

Already at the beginning of the United Nations' life the Security Council was called on to participate in the government of disputed territories. This was the case of the Free Territory of Trieste established by the peace treaty of 1947 between the Allied Powers and Italy. According to Annex VI, the Free territory was conceived as a small State ruled by a Governor appointed by the Security Council together with independent local legislative, judicial and executive authorities. The example of Trieste is not very meaningful, since the Free Territory was never instituted and the territory of Trieste was successively divided up between Italy and Yugoslavia.

More recently two examples of administration set up by the Council, with express reference to Chapter VII, and entrusted to the Secretary-General with full legislative and executive authority deserve a particular mention. One is the case of UNMIK (UN Interim Administration in Kosovo), the other is UNTAET (UN Transitional Administration in East Timor).

UNMIK, established by res. no. 1244 of June 10, 1999 immediately after the end of NATO's air war, is still operative. Its function is to organize and oversee the development of provisional institutions for democratic and autonomous self-government pending a political settlement, and, at a final stage, to oversee the transfer of authority from provisional institutions to institutions established under the said political settlement. UNMIK is headed by a Special Representative of the Secretary-General, who is assisted by the OSCE (see § 68) in matters of democratisation and institution building, by the European Union in matters of reconstruction and economic development and by NATO forces (KFOR) as far as the external defence is concerned. A "Constitutional Framework for Provisional Self-government in Kosovo" has been adopted by UNMIK regulation n.° 9/2201 of May 15, 2001, according to which a Parliamentary Assembly, a President of Kosovo and other representative institutions have been created and are now in function. Although the UN administration is considered to be provisional, its end is not easily foreseeable due to the difficulties of combining the Kosovar Albanians' claim for independence, the protection of the Serb minority and the claim for territorial integrity of Serbia and Montenegro.

UNTAET was created by res. no. 1272 of October 25, 1999 to provide security and maintain order throughout the territory of East Timor, to support capacity-building for self-government, to ensure the co-ordination and delivery of humanitarian assistance to the population which had been the target of massacres on the part of the guerrilla sustained by Indonesia following the referendum of August 1999 in favour of the independence of the territory. The UN administration lasted until May 20, 2002 when the territory became independent and was admitted to the United Nations as Timor-Leste. The new State is now assisted by UNMISET (UN Mission of Support in East Timor), a multifunctional peacekeeping force (see § 59), which is composed of civil and military personnel headed by a Special Representative of the Secretary-General, and whose mandate is to assist the local authority in promoting stability, democracy, justice, public security, law enforcement, external security and border control for a period of two years.

Although anomalous, the case of the post-conflict administration of Iraq by the United States' led coalition deserves mention here. By res. no. 1483 of May 2003, after having recognised "the specific authorities, responsibilities, and obligations under applicable International law, of these States as occupying powers under unified command (the Authority)", the Security Council at para 9 "supports the formation...of...a transitional administration run by Iraqis, until an internationally recognised, representative government is established by the people of Iraq and assumes the responsibilities of the Authority ". In fact, at the moment we are writing, the transitional administration is mainly run under the control of the coalition led by the United States. The case is anomalous since the coalition administration has not been created but only recognised by the Security Council and - as in the case of the use of military force dealt with above (see § 60) - the action is carried out by Member States instead of the Secretary-General.

The case of UNTAC (UN Transitional Authority in Cambodia) created by res. no. 745 of February 28, 1992 on the basis of an agreement between the interested States promoted by the five permanent Members of the Security Council, can also be cited. For a period of more than one year UNTAC was entrusted with the task of assisting the civil administration, preparing political elections and protecting human rights in Cambodia. Worth noting is the fact that in this case - a case which does not differ in substance from the subsequent cases of UNMIK and UNTAET, indeed - the Security Council did not mention Chapter VII..

The institution of tribunals dealing with crimes committed by individuals can be considered as single acts of governance. The first two well known examples are the International Criminal Tribunal for the former Yugoslavia (ICTY), established by res. no. 827 of May 25, 1993, and the International Criminal Tribunal for Rwanda (ICTR), established by res. no. 955 of November 8, 1994. The first was created for the prosecution of serious violations of International Humanitarian law committed in the former Yugoslavia after January 1992; the second for the prosecution of violations of International Humanitarian law and genocide committed by Rwandan citizens between January 1 and December 31, 1994. Although the two Tribunals do not sit in the territory where their jurisdiction is exercised (the seat of the first is in The Hague, of the second in Arusha) they may be considered assisting in the governance of such territories.

The Security Council has also played a role in the establishment of the Special Court for Sierra Leone. The creation of the Court was envisaged by res. no. 1315 of August 14, 2000 and set up by an agreement signed by the Secretary-General and the Government of Sierra Leone on February 27, 2002. It has one Trial Chamber and one Appeals Chamber. The first consists of three judges, two appointed by the Secretary-General and one appointed by the Government; the Appeals Chamber consists of five judges, three appointed by the Secretary-General and two appointed by the Government. The Court has jurisdiction to hear crimes of war, crimes against humanity and other serous violations of humanitarian law committed in Sierra Leone since November 30, 1996.

The measures of governance we are dealing with do not find an express ground in the Charter. Many attempts have been made in legal doctrine and in practice to bring these measures within the "enforcement measures" set forth by Articles 41 and 42. The creation of criminal tribunals in particular has been the object of speculation. The most wide spread opinion in this regard is that Article 41 applies. The fact that Article 41 deals with behaviours which the Security Council can impose on States has not be considered as decisive. What States can be requested to do - it has been said - the Council can also do. Such opinion has been held by the International Criminal Tribunal for the former Yugoslavia (see the decision of the Trial Chamber, of August 10, 1995, *case no IT-94-I.T/ Defendant: Dusko Tadic*, para. 27-32, and the decision of the Appeals Chamber of October 2, 1995, in the same case). According to a more sophisticated opinion (De HOOG),

Article 41 should be split in two parts, one allowing the Security Council to take whatever decision it deems necessary to maintain or restore peace and security (in this case, the decision to create a tribunal), the other allowing the Council to call upon the States to co-operate with the tribunal. We have already criticised the last opinion (see § 58) and there is no need to deal with this again here. The first opinion is also unconvincing, since the jurisdiction of the Tribunals - and the same can be said of the administration of territories - is exercised upon individuals, while the enforcement measures set forth by Article 41 are clearly conceived as measures against States or armed factions within a State.

Another view which cannot be accepted, although it is upheld by some principal organs of the United Nations, is that measures not set forth by one or the other article of Chapter VII can be grounded on Article 24, para. 1. According to this view, paragraph 1 of Article 24, by stating that the Security Council has the primary responsibility for the maintenance of international peace and security, allows the Council to take whatever measure, provided that it is necessary for maintaining or restoring peace. In other terms, the Council could exercise a kind of general, residual power. This view is contradicted by the second paragraph of Article 24, wherein the "specific powers" granted to the Council with reference to Chapters VI, VII, VIII, and XII are enumerated. And, indeed, why should Chapter VII specify, in Articles 40, 41, and 42 ff., the measures the Council could adopt, if the Council can take any other action in order to maintain peace and security? In fact, the theory of residual powers, although apparently progressive, was used, during the Cold war, to provide a legal basis for those Council resolutions characterised by compromise, basic disagreement among the members of the organ, and near total incapacity to deal effectively with the substantive issues of a dangerous situation. Article 24, in other words, was invoked for resolutions which clearly betrayed its spirit in as much as they involved the circumvention of the Council's responsibilities rather than the earnest undertaking of them.

This can be said, for instance and with respect, with regard to the advisory opinion of June 21, 1971 of the International Court of Justice, which applied the theory of residual powers under Article 24 (cf. ICJ, *Reports*, 1971, p. 51, no. 110) to Council resolution no. 276 of January 30, 1970 on the Namibia question. This resolution had been limited to declaring South Africa's presence in Namibia (today independent) as "invalid", and it had been adopted after ascertaining that it was impossible for the Council to proceed against South Africa with effective and decisive sanctions, as the majority of the Member States and civilised peoples wished to do.

The opinion of the Secretary-General B. Boutros Ghali, an opinion expressed in a Report concerning the International Criminal Tribunal for the former Yugoslavia (cf. Doc. S/25704 of May 3, 1993, paras. 18-30) is close to the theory of residual power. In the Report, this kind of organ was considered a subsidiary organ of the Council under Article 29 of the

Charter ("The Security Council may establish such subsidiary organs as it deems necessary for the performance of its functions"). In the same Report, the functions of the Tribunal were deemed to be covered by Chapter VII without further specification.

In our opinion it must be recognised that the practice of the Security Council has largely deviated from the letter and the spirit of the Articles in Chapter VII. As for all other acts of the United Nations which cannot be grounded in the Charter the question must be asked whether a customary rule has emerged from practice. The answer is yes, even adopting the rigorous method we pleaded for in the introduction to this book (see § 4). The lack of opposition to the participation of the Council to the government of post-conflict areas, together with the *communis opinio* among the generality of the Member States that the intervention of the Council is necessary in order to restore peace and security in these areas, testify in favour of the existence of such a custom.

Accordingly, we revise the opinion expressed in preceding editions of this book, according to which the administration of territories and the creation of International criminal tribunals were to be included among the measures set forth in Article 42 as a kind of belligerent measure. Indeed, it must be recognised that such an opinion was unable to explain cases wherein no previous armed actions had been carried out by UN Forces or with the authorisation of the Security Council, such as the administration of Kosovo or the creation of the Tribunal for Rwanda.

It has been asked whether the administrators of territories under the control and the directives of the Security Council must abide by rules of international law. As we have seen, a trend going in such a direction is developing in practice regarding all measures involving and not involving the use of forces (see §§ 58 and 59). By analogy, the same must be said of UN administrations of territories, particularly as regard respect for human rights and humanitarian law as well as the compliance with the principle of self-determination of governed people.

Section III

MAINTENANCE OF THE PEACE: THE FUNCTIONS OF THE GENERAL ASSEMBLY

BIBLIOGRAPHY: HAVILLAND, *The Political Role of the General Assembly*, New York, 1951; VALLAT, *The General Assembly and the Security Council of the United Nations*, in *BYB*, 1952, p. 79 ff.; GENTILE, *Competenza del Consiglio di Sicurezza e dell'Assemblea Generale in materia di mantenimento e ristabilimento della pace*, in *CS*, vol. V, 1953, p. 312 ff.; BRUGIÈRE, *Les pouvoirs de l'Assemblée Générale des Nations Unies en matière politique et de securité*, Paris, 1955; ANDRASSY, *Uniting for Peace*, in *AJ*, 1956, p. 563 ff.; ZICCARDI, *L'intevento collettivo delle Nazioni Unite e i nuovi poteri dell'Assemblea Generale*, in *CI*, 1957, p. 211 ff. and p. 415 ff.; GOODRICH and ROSNER, *The United Nations Emergency Force*, in *Int. Org.*, 1957, p. 413 ff.; SOHN, *The Authority of the United Nations to Establish and Maintain a Permanent United Nations Force*, in *AJ*, 1958, p. 229 ff.; VALLAT, *The Competence of the United Nations General Assembly*, in *RC*, 1959, II, p. 244 ff.; BAILEY, *The General Assembly of the UN*, London, 1960; SEYERSTED, *United Nations Forces — Some Legal Problems*, in *BYB*, 1961, p. 351 ff.; POIRIER, *La force internationale d'urgence*, Paris, 1962; SEYERSTED, *Can United Nations Establish Military Force and Perform Other Acts Without Specific Basis in the Charter?*, in *ZöR*, 1962, p. 188 ff.; EL DIN ATTIA, *Les forces armèes des Nations Unies en Corée et au Moyen Orient*, Paris, 1963; ALESSI, *L'evoluzione della prassi delle Nazioni Unite relativa al mantenimento della pace*, in *RDI*, 1964, p. 519 ff., partic. p. 533 ff.; SCHACHTER, *The Quasi-Judicial Role of the Security Council and the General Assembly*, in *AJ*, 1964, p. 960 ff.; PETERSEN, *The Use of the Uniting for Peace Resolution since 1950, ibid.*, p. 255 ff.; SEYERSTED, *UN Forces in Law of Peace and War*, Leiden, 1966, p. 44 ff.; SHEIKH, *UN Peace-Keeping Forces — A Reappraisal of Relevant Charter Provisions*, in *RBDI*, 1971, p. 469 ff.; PFEIFENBERGER, *Die Vereinte Nationen Ihre politische Organe in Sichereitsfragen*, Salzburg-München, 1971; BOYD, *UN Peacekeeping Operations: A Military and Political Appraisal*, New York, 1972; RUDA, *Drafting History of Articles 10 and 11 of the Charter of the UN on the Function and Powers of the General Assembly*, in *Festschrift für W. Wengler*, I, Berlin, 1973, p. 375 ff.; GUILHAUDIS, *Considérations sur la pratique de l'« Union pour le maintien de la paix »*, in *AF*, 1981, p. 382; CHEBELEU, *Role of the UN General Assembly in the Settlement of International Disputes. Some Rumanian Proposals*, in *Rev. Roum. d'Etudes Internat.*, 1981, p. 443 ff.; REICHER, *The Uniting for Peace Resolution on the Thirtieth Anniversary of its Passage*, in *Columbia Journ. of Transn. Law*, 1981, p. 1 ff.; CATALDI, *L'Assemblea Generale delle Nazioni Unite e la controversia sulle Falkland-Malvinas*, in RONZITTI (ed), *La questione delle Falkland-Malvinas nel diritto internazionale*, Milan, 1984, p. 75 ff.;.; PETERSON, *The General Assembly in World Politics*, Boston, 1986; WHITE, *Keeping the peace*, Manchester, 1993, p. 117 ff.; DURCH, *UN Temporary Executive Authority*, in DURCH (ed), *The evolution of UN Peacekeeping*, New York 1993, p. 285 ff.; PINESCHI, *Le operazioni delle Nazioni Unite per il mantenimento della pace,,* Padova, 1998, Part 1, Chapt. 3; TOMUSCHAT, *"Uniting for Peace" - ein Rückblick nach 50 Jahren*, in *Friedens Warte*, 2001, p. 289 ff.

61. *Discussions and recommendations on general questions.*

In the field of maintaining peace, as in nearly all other fields (economic, social and cultural co-operation, etc.) in which the General Assembly is called upon to intervene, this body may issue only recommendations, that is, acts without binding force.

Since it is the organ in which all States are represented, the Assembly's power to discuss any question of a general nature regarding maintenance of the peace, and to possibly issue recommendations on such issue, has noteworthy importance. This power, which appears first in Article 10, is specifically provided by Article 11, para. 1 ("The General Assembly may consider the general principles of co-operation in the maintenance of international peace and security... and may make recommendations with regard to such principles to the members or to the Security Council or to both"). In looking through the proceedings of the various sessions of the organ it is noticeable how much space is dedicated to "general discussions" which touch upon all the most important political and international topics of the period in which the session is held. It is with reference to such discussions that the United Nation's nature of an "international forum", of a "center of open diplomacy", or of a "mirror of world public opinion" stands out. The number of recommendations — in truth, often wordy and repetitious — of the Assembly on general questions is very impressive.

62. *The peaceful settlement function.*

With regard to specific disputes and questions concerning given States, the Assembly exercises the same identical peaceful settlement function as does the Council on the basis of Chapter VI of the Charter. The peaceful settlement function of the Assembly has a broader scope of application than that of the Council. It covers, under Article 14, any question that touches upon the general welfare or friendly relations among nations ("... the Assembly", Article 14 says, "may recommend measures for the *peaceful adjustment* of any situation... which it deems likely to impair the general welfare or friendly relations among nations, including situations resulting from a violation of the provisions of the present Charter setting forth the Purposes and Principles of the United Nations..."). The provision in Article 14 absorbs the more specific one in Article 11, para. 2, according to which "The General Assembly may discuss any questions relating to the maintenance of international peace and security brought before it by any member of the United Nations, or by the Security Council, or by a State which is not a member of the United Nations in accordance with Article 35, paragraph 2 and... may make recommendations with regard to any such question to the State or States concerned...". Actually, Article 10 would be enough to provide a basis for the peaceful settlement function of the Assembly. This article gives the organ a general power to discuss "any questions... within the scope of the present Charter" and to "make recommendations... on any such questions...".

With regard to the procedure by which the Assembly is entrusted with a dispute or question, see Articles 12 ff. of the organ's rules of procedure. These articles provide that the proposal to place a given question on the agenda of a session may be made by the other principal organs of the United Nations (those indicated by Article 7 of the Charter) as well as by any Member State or by a non-Member State. However, this is only if it is made under Article 35, para. 2, that is, if the State brings to the attention to the Assembly a dispute to which it is a party that is likely to threaten the peace. The rules of procedure thus confirm, with regard to any kind of dispute or question, the rules that Article 35, paras. 1 and 2, and Article 11, para. 2, formulate only in relation to the field of maintenance of the peace.

As we saw regarding the Security Council (see § 43), the limitation concerning non-Member States has no practical relevance.

The very general terms of Article 14 ("... recommend *measures for the peaceful adjustment*...") allow the peaceful settlement function of the Assembly to cover all the measures which could be adopted by the Security Council under Articles 33, para. 2, 36, 37 and 38 of the Charter. The Assembly may therefore use any instrument, as long as it is non-binding, that may bring about agreement between the parties involved in an international dispute or crisis or directly concerned in a situation. It may recommend recourse to one of the procedures under Article 33, or indicate terms of settlement (that is, solutions on the merits) or provide for the establishment or directly establish (making use of Article 22 on subsidiary organs) organs of good offices, mediation, conciliation, and so on. On the other hand, the absence of detailed provisions such as those provided for the Security Council by Chapter VII, an absence to be appreciated, eliminates any problem of interpretation.

For some few examples of resolutions, see *UN Rep. and Supplements, sub* Article 14, (however, many resolutions coming under the peaceful settlement function appear in the lists under Articles 10 and 11) and: res. no. 1947-XV of October 31, 1960 (recommendation to Italy and Austria to negotiate a settlement of the Upper Adige question); no. 1599-XV of April 15, 1961, relating to the presence of foreign troops in the Congo; no. 1616-XV of April 21, 1961 (the Cuba-United States conflict); no. 1855-XVII of December 19, 1962 (on the re-unification of Korea); no. 1964-XVIII of December 13, 1963 (*idem*); no. 2077-XX of December 18, 1965 (observance of the territorial sovereignity of Cyprus); no. 2453-XXIII (*A*) of December 19, 1968 (Middle East question); no. 2504-XXIV of November 19, 1969 (on the agreement between Indonesia and the Netherlands for Western Irian); no. 2516-XXIV of November 25, 1969 (on the re-unification of Korea); no. 2535-XXIV,B, of December 10, 1969 (on the Middle East question); no. 3160-XXVIII of December 14, 1973 (on the dispute between Great Britain and Argentina over the Falklands/Malvinas Islands); no. 3333-XXIX of December 17, 1974 and no. 3390 A-XXX of November 18, 1975 (again on the re-unification of Korea); no. 3395-XXX of November 20, 1975 (negotiations for Cyprus); no. 34/412 of November 21, 1979 (negotiations between the United Kingdom and Guatemala for Belize); no. 34/412 of November 21, 1979 (negotiations for Gibraltar); no. 37/9 of November 4, 1982 (Falklands/Malvinas); no. 38/12 of November 16, 1983 (*idem*); no. 38/10 of November 11, 1983 (support for the Contadora group's mediation activities in Central America); no. 38/77 of December 15, 1983 (Antarctic regime); no. 39/6 of November 1, 1984 (Falklands/Malvinas); no. 40/188 of December 17, 1985 (invitation to revoke the unilateral embargo ordered by several countries against Nicaragua); no. 41/31 of November 3, 1986 (invitation to apply the decision of the International Court of Justice of June 27, 1986 on the United States intervention in Nicaragua); no. 41/31 of November 3, 1986 (bombing of Libya by the United States); no. 42/124 of December 7, 1987 (torture and cruel treatment of children in South Africa); no. 43/177 of December 15, 1988 (Arab-Israeli conflict); no. 44/2 of October 6, 1989 (*idem*); no. 44/10 of October 23, 1989 (peace process in Central America); no. 44/124 B of December 14, 1989 (Antarctic regime); no. 44/240 of December 28, 1989 (armed intervention of the United States in Panama); no. 45/68 of December 6, 1990 (Arab-Israeli conflict); no. 46/7 of October 10, 1991 and no. 46/138 of December 6, 1991 (human rights situation in Haiti); no. 46/18 of November 29, 1991 (situation in Cambodia); no. 46/75 of December 11, 1991 (Arab-Israeli conflict); no. 47/19 of November 24, 1992 and various others up until res. no. 58/7 of November 4, 2003 (request to the United States to lift the embargo against Cuba); no. 47/20 of November 24, 1992 (human rights situation in Haiti); no. 47/21 of November 25, 1992 (withdrawal of foreign military forces from the Balkans); no. 47/57 of December 9, 1992 (Antarctic regime); no. 47/63 of December 11, 1992 (Middle East); no. 47/118 of December 18, 1992 (peace process in Central America); no. 47/139 of December 18, 1992 (human rights situation in Cuba); no. 47/140 of December 18, 1992 (human rights situation in El Salvador); no. 47/141 of December 18, 1992 (human rights situation in Afghanistan); no. 53/94 of February 11, 1999 (peace in Central America); no. 53/164 of February 25, 1999 (human rights in Kosovo); no. 54/42 (peaceful settlement of the question of Palestine); no. 57/113 A of December 6, 2002, with reference to previous resolutions (situation in Afghanistan); no. 57/228 of December 18, 2002 (Khmer Rouge trials in Cambodia); no. 57/234 of December 18, 2002 (human rights in Afghanistan).

Aside from the substantial limit of domestic jurisdiction, the peaceful settlement function of the Assembly meets only the procedural limit under Article 12: "While the Security Council is exercising in respect of any dispute or situation the functions assigned to it in the present Charter, the General Assembly shall not make any recommendation with regard to that dispute or situation unless the Security Council so requests". The limit of domestic jurisdiction has been lost in practice with regard to human rights and other matters (see § 45 III). The provision of Article 12 is a corollary of the principle affirmed by Article 24 under which the Council has *primary* responsibility for maintenance of the peace. The phrase "while the Security Council is exercising the functions assigned to it by the present Charter..." is to be understood restrictively, so as not to compromise the aim of the peaceful settlement of the dispute or situation. The exception founded on the fact that the case is pending before the Security Council may therefore be legitimately raised before the Assembly, independently of circumstances of mere form such as the registration of the dispute or situation on the agenda of the

Council, only if the Council or its subsidiary organs are discussing or are actively concerned with the question, or if there is a reasonable probability that they will be so in a short time.

According to the International Court of Justice (Advisory Opinion of July 9, 2004, on *The Legal Consequences of the Construction of a Wall in the Occupied Palestinian Territories,* para. 27-28), the practice has evolved, showing "an increasing tendency over time for the General Assembly and the Security Council to deal in parallel with the same matter concerning the maintenance of international peace and security" . Moreover, the Court holds the opinion that such a practice "is consistent with Article 12, para. 1, of the Charter (sic!)" and this is sufficient for concluding, in the specific case, that the General Assembly could deal with the construction of the wall by Israel. With due respect, this opinion of the Court seems to be excessive from a general point of view and unnecessary in order to solve the problem of "*lis alibi pendens*" in the specific case, since the Security Council neither discussed, nor adopted any resolution on the construction of the wall.

> The Assembly practice initially seemed to favour a formalistic interpretation of Article 12, and therefore the necessity that a question be cancelled from the Security Council agenda so that the Assembly could make it the subject of recommendations (cf. UN Rep., *sub* Article 12, nos. 23-54). Then, there was a tendency to take an excessively restrictive view, by interpreting the phrase in Article 12 "while the Council is exercising..." in the sense of "while the Council is contemporaneously exercising..." (cf. *UNJY*, 1964, p. 229 ff. and, especially, 1968, p. 185). The reservations that were occasionally presented in the Assembly (for example: by Belgium, Holland and Norway in 1970 concerning the discussion of the question of apartheid in South Africa, with which the Council was seized, in GAOR, 25th sess., Spec. Pol. Comm., 69th meet., nos. 7 and 43, and Pl. meet., 1864th meet., no. 84 ff.; by Holland in 1971 regarding the Middle East question, also before the Council, in GAOR, 26th sess., Pl. meet., 2009th meet., no. 83 and 2016th meet., no. 221; by Iraq in 1990 in relation to the Gulf crisis, in A/45/PV.3 of September 25, 1992) usually fall on deaf ears. See also UN Rep., Suppl. No. 6, par. 16 ff.
>
> Since there are no other limits to the peaceful settlement function of the Assembly, besides those of domestic jurisdiction, under Article 2, para. 7, and of "*lis alibi pendens*", under Article 12, the view held by the United States in the session of November 6, 1986 (doc. A/41/PV.53) after the adoption of the above-cited resolution no. 41/31 of November 3, 1986, which invited the U.S. to give effect to the judgment handed down on June 27 of the same year by the International Court of Justice in the Nicaragua-United States case, cannot be shared. According to this view, Article 94, para. 2 (which provides that the Security Council may make recommendations or decide upon measures to give effect to a judgment of the Court if one of the parties fails to do so voluntarily) would prevent the General Assembly from making recommendations on the matter.

Does the Assembly have a power of investigation more or less similar to the one granted to the Security Council in Article 34? The answer must be yes. It is a power that is implicit in the peaceful settlement function, indispensable to the organ in establishing what measures of peaceful adjustment are to be recommended for a specific case, and it unquestionably can be deduced from the broad formulation of Article 14. It is obvious that, thus defined, the investigation must be preparatory to the peaceful settlement function. It becomes illegitimate if it is connected to the exercise of functions that the Assembly does not have, for example, functions which belong exclusively to the Security Council, such as those governed by Articles 41 and 42.

63. *The problem of General Assembly powers regarding "action".* A) *The solutions given by the Charter.*

There was much discussion and, and much quibbling, in the past over the General Assembly's power to take action for the protection of the peace and, more specifically, to decide measures of the kind set out by Chapter VII of the Charter. This power has been affirmed by some observers in light of the Charter and by many on the basis of rules taking shape by custom. The topic was the subject of heated discussions in the doctrine between 1950 and 1960, a period when the Assembly, under pressure from the United States, expressed the wish to replace the Security Council in maintaining the peace, once it was clear that the Council was paralysed by the use of the veto power. Later, the subject became less important owing to the Assembly's incapacity to continue this course as a result of the enormous increase in the number of members and of the Great Powers' reluctance to allow effective action by an enlarged organ that they were increasingly less able to control. With the Security Council's recent hyper-activism, the topic has lost importance even more.

From the point of view of the Charter, the meaning of Article 11, para. 2, is the crucial point. After having recognised the Assembly's power to discuss and to make recommendations on any question concerning mainte-nance of the peace, this provision adds "any such question *on which action is necessary* shall be referred to the Security Council...". Can it be said that this confirms the Assembly's lack of competence with regard to *all* measures provided under Chapter VII, a chapter entitled "*action* with respect to threats to the peace, etc." and which speaks only of the Security Council? Or is it possible to adopt a view that is more favourable to the Assembly?

In our opinion, there cannot be any doubt about the Assembly's abso-lute and complete lack of competence to resort to measures involving the use of armed force. First of all, it is to be excluded that the Assembly may impose or even only recommend to the States resort to the use of armed force.. Secondly, it is to be excluded that the Assembly may undertake actions such as those governed by Article 42, that is, establish and direct armed forces for international police operations (even for "buffer zone" operations or operations to be carried within a State) or authorise their establishment and direction by the Secretary-General. If the reservation in Article 11, para. 2, in favour of the Security Council, has a meaning, it must be referred to actions of this kind.

In the light of the Charter, therefore, the Assembly resolutions adopted during the 1956 Suez crisis, and which were at the basis of the first *United Nations Emergency Force* (UNEF I), were illegal. This has been the only important operation carried out by the General Assembly regarding maintenance of the peace.

The Force (not to be confused with UNEF II which was to be established by the Security Council in 1973: see § 59) was set up by the Secretary-General with contingents offered by the Member States. It had the task of "ensuring and monitoring" the cessation of hostilities between Egypt, on one side, and Israel, Great Britain and France on the other (cf. res. no. 998-ES I of November 4, 1956, res. no. 1000-ES I of November 5, 1956, and res. no. 1001-ES I of November 7, 1956). The Socialist countries expressed their view that the Suez action was unlawful, given the Assembly's lack of competence on the matter. They stated (cf., for example, GAOR, 1st Em. Spec. Sess., Pl. meet., 567th meet., no. 292-297; cf. also GAOR, 11th sess., Pl. meet., 591st meet., no. 40, 592nd meet., no. 53, 595th meet., no. 170) that they approved the UNEF resolutions from a political viewpoint but abstained from voting for them specifically to stress their reservations of a legal nature. These reservations led in the following years to their refusal to contribute to the UN's expenses for maintaining the Force: see § 86).

Those who affirmed the legality of the Suez action used arguments that were very similar to the ones adopted with regard to the subsequent actions of the Security Council in the Congo, in Cyprus and in the Middle East (see § 59). It was said that the UNEF action differed from the action under Article 42 of the Charter, since it had been organized with the consent of the territorial government, with forces not exactly directed against a State and with the intent not to use arms except in self-defence. In this way, an attempt was made to overcome the obstacle of the Assembly's lack of competence. The International Court of Justice (advisory opinion in the case *Certain Expenses of the United Nations* of July 20, 1962) chose this route when it was called to give an opinion on the refusal of some States to contribute to the expenses for the maintenance of the Force, a refusal which was also justified by the illegality of the relevant Assembly decisions (on the financial aspects of the case, see § 86). According to the Court, the measures taken in respect of Suez by the Assembly would not constitute one of the enforcement actions under Article 42 and reserved for the Security Council, but would come within Article 14, specifically among the measures that the Assembly may "recommend" for the "peaceful adjustment of situations..." (cf. ICJ, *Reports*, 1962, p. 171 f.).

The above views are unfounded and the Assembly's lack of competence remains if, as we have previously sought to demonstrate (see § 59), it is held that Article 42 is not to be restricted to actions undertaken *against* one specific State but covers any UN operation of a military nature. As for the opinion of the International Court of Justice, with all due respect, it seems to us that reference to Article 14 is absurd. Article 14 gives the Assembly the power to make recommendations to the States, whereas the UNEF resolutions belong to the category of operational decisions, that is, decisions through which the Organization itself undertakes action (see § 92). Moreover, since Article 14 is concerned with measures for the "peaceful adjustment" of situations, it seems quite far-fetched to bring under it the establishment of a military force, even if it is a buffer force such as UNEF. In fact, the opinion of the Court was not complied with by many States (*ibid.*).

Once the Assembly's power to carry out military operations is excluded, may the organ at least order measures of the kind governed by Article 41? It is on the basis of this article that the Security Council may impose or also only recommend that the Member States adopt the so-called measures not involving the use of force, such as the severance of diplomatic relations, economic sanctions, and so on, against a given State. In so far as the Assembly certainly does not have binding powers regarding the maintenance of the peace, the only problem that can arise is whether it may recommend measures not involving the use of force.

Examples of Assembly resolutions recommending sanctions: no. 39-I of December 12, 1946, which called upon the States to recall their heads of diplomatic missions accredited with the Fascist government in Spain (a measure then revoked with res. no. 386-V of November 4, 1950); no. 500-V of May 18, 1951, relative to the embargo on certain goods intended for North Korea and the People's Republic of China; no. 1761-XVII of December 6, 1962, reconfirmed, specified and broadened several times in the following years (cf., for example, res. 37/69 A of December 9, 1982 and 39/72 A of December 13, 1984) on the severing of economic relations with (and on the total isolation of) South Africa because of its policy of apartheid; res. no. 2949-XXVII of December 8, 1972, no. 2203-XXVIII of December 17, 1973, no. 3336-XXIX of December 17, 1974, no. 35/122 B of December 11, 1980, no. 37/88 C and E of December 10, 1982, no. 37/123 A of December 20, 1982 and various others, up until res. no. 54/37 of December 1, 1999, on the non-recognition of Israeli acts of government in the Arab territories; res. no. 42/23 F of November 20, 1987, no. 43/50 J of December 5, 1988 and various others, up until res. no. 47/116 D of December 18, 1992, recommending an oil embargo against South Africa.
Are these resolutions lawful under the Charter?

An objective interpretation of the Charter leads to the conclusion that the Assembly also lacks competence in this case. Consequently, its relevant resolutions are not in conformity with the Charter. An exception to this conclusion is that of resolutions limited to confirming the sanctions already decided or recommended by the Security Council. This has occurred, for example, regarding the non-recognition of Israeli acts of government in the occupied Arab territories.

The view here expressed is supported by the following reasons: first, the provision which explicitly concerns sanctions, Article 41, envisages only the competence of the Security Council; second, the sanctions, even if only recommended, are strictly part of the collective security system culminating in operations of a military nature; third, as a result, the reservation under Article 11, para. 2, relating to Security Council "action", could not be referred to measures under Article 42 unless it is held that it concerns also measures under Article 41; and, lastly, the provisions on the functions of the Assembly, particularly in Articles 10, 11 and 14, seem to concern decisions inviting co-operation among the States and the peaceful adjustment of disputes rather than resolutions having the nature of sanctions.

The view has been expressed that the measures under Article 41, or at least some of them (for example, the severance of diplomatic relations), could always be recommended by the Assembly as lawful measures under customary international law and therefore that a State could also adopt them on its own initiative. This opinion was expressed, for example, by some delegates in the Assembly with regard to the cited resolution on the recall of heads of mission from Franco's Spain (cf. GAOR, 1st sess., Pl. meet., 58th meet., pp. 1193 and 1220). This view cannot be accepted. Any form of unfriendly, or even hateful, conduct of one State towards another, even if in itself lawful under international law, acquires the clear nature of a sanction if it is ordered by an international organ in the exercise of its functions, and must therefore be sustained by the competence of the organ that orders it. A different problem — which is fashionable today but which, as it does not concern the United Nations lies outside our treatment — is whether sanctions against States responsible for serious violations of international law may be adopted also by States not directly injured by such violations. It is certain, however, that the Assembly could not itself endorse or authorise such sanctions (even if they are lawful under customary international law) since the Assembly is bound by the powers attributed to it by the Charter.

With regard to the third type of measures under Chapter VII, the provisional measures governed by Article 40 (see § 57), it is possible to recognise the Assembly's competence to adopt them. It is certainly true that the provisional measures are linked to the collective security system culminating in the military operations under Article 42 and that they in fact constitute the first, even if not indispensable, stage for Security Council "action" in the case of a threat to the peace or a violation of the peace. However, it is also true that, exactly because they constitute the first stage, these measures do not have, neither by definition must they have, the nature of sanctions. Thus, they tend to blur with the measures for the peaceful adjustment of situations, which certainly do come under the (peaceful settlement) function of the Assembly. The Assembly may therefore recommend a cease-fire or the liberation of prisoners or call upon the States not to introduce arms into areas where hostilities are underway, and so forth.

Cf., for example, res. no.107-S I of May 15, 1947 (invitation to the Middle East governments and to the Arabs and Jews of Palestine to abstain from using weapons or from any other action "which might create an atmosphere prejudicial to an early settlement of the question of Palestine"); res. no. 193-III of November 27, 1948 (invitation to bordering States not to support the guerrilla forces in Greece); res. no. 997-ES I of November 2, 1956 (cease-fire between France, Great Britain, and Israel on one side and Egypt on the other, during the Suez crisis, and recommendation to all the Member States not to send war material into the hostilities zone); res. no. 37/3 of October 22, 1982 (cease-fire between Iran and Iraq); res. no. 53/200 of February 12, 1999 (cease-fire in Afghanistan).

Lastly, on the basis of Article 39 (see § 56), both the General Assembly, as well as the Security Council may intervene in procedures of national conciliation.

The Assembly has very rarely acted in this way. For an example, see res. no. 48/267 of September 19, 1994, on the situation in Guatemala.

64. B) *The alleged formation of customary rules on the subject.*

If military action (Article 42) and sanctions not involving the use of armed force (Article 41) are prohibited to the Assembly by the Charter, the question has been asked whether a customary rule has emerged on this subject. One part of legal doctrine holds that practice supports a positive answer. The first example used is usually the well-known Assembly resolution no. 377/V of November 3, 1950 "Uniting for Peace". This resolution, adopted during the Korean crisis at the most acute stage of the Cold War, explicitly established that, in the case of the Security Council's inability to act when confronted with a breach of the peace or an act of aggression, the General Assembly could order appropriate measures, including the establishment of UN armed forces (cf. Part. A of the resolution, partic. nos. 1 and 8). It provided, from a procedural point of view, that the Assembly could be convoked for this purpose in a special emergency session upon the request of the Security Council (voting without the right of veto) or of a majority of the members of the Organization. As a proof of a customary rule on the full power of the Assembly to recommend and to undertake measures for the maintenance of the peace, the "Uniting for Peace" resolution and other resolutions we have already reported in the previous section are indicated.

Serious doubts can be raised over the customary basis of the Assembly's power. Two facts are decisive on this. The first is that the opposition by a group of States, the Socialist States, against the Assembly's having this power was persistent and effective during the Cold War period. This opposition was shown in vehement form against the Uniting for Peace resolution, against the embargo measures ordered by the Assembly with regard to North Korea and Communist China, against the Assembly's appointment of certain subsidiary organs, such as the Committee for Collective Measures, which were in some way related to measures for maintenance of the peace, and, lastly, against entering expenditures relating to these organs in the UN budget.

The second fact is that even those countries, and particularly the Western powers, which had advocated the adoption of the Uniting for Peace resolution changed their position when they lost control of the General Assembly.

With regard to Communist opposition, cf.: against Uniting for Peace, GAOR, 5th sess., 1st Comm., 357th meet., no. 39 ff.; against res. no. 500-V of May 18, 1951 on the embargo on goods intended for China and North Korea, GAOR, 5th sess., Pl. meet., 330th meet., no. 37 ff., 64 ff., 69 ff., 85 ff., 101 ff.; against the creation of subsidiary organs, UN

Rep., *sub* Article 22, no. 51 ff. and Suppl. no. 1, no. 9, note 5; against expenditures for subsidiary organs, GAOR, 7th sess., Pl. meet., 410th meet., no. 23 ff., 10th sess., Pl. meet., 559th meet., n. 148 ff., 11th sess., 5th Comm., 551st meet., no. 1 ff., 12   th sess. , PL. meet., 731st meet., no. 71. The Socialist States also expressed their view of the illegality of the Uniting for peace resolution in the case of the Soviet invasion of Afghanistan, with regard to the Security Council's convening of the Assembly in a special emergency session at the beginning of the 1980's.Cf., for the protests made in the Council in the sessions between January 5 and 9, 1980, doc. S/PV.2185-S/PV.2190. For the protests in the Assembly, see the statements by Afghanistan, Mongolia and Czechoslovakia, in GAOR, 6th   Em. Sp. Sess. (January 10-14, 1980), 1st meet., no. 26 and no. 39, 6th mett., no. 92.

For the position of the United States and of the other States which in 1950 had strongly supported the Uniting for peace resolution, the reservations expressed during the adoption of res. No. 2107-XX of December 21, 1965, recommending economic sanctions against Portugal for its colonialist policies, are significant. These reservations were based on the Assembly's lack of competence to order sanctions. Cf. GAOR, 20th sess., 4th Comm., 1591st meet., no. 1 (Canada), 1592nd meet., no. 10 (United States), no. 44 f. (Bolivia).

Cf. also the reservations expressed by Australia, in 1976 regarding one of the many resolutions on the embargo against South Africa, in GAOR, 31st. sess., Pl. meet., 58th meet., no. 64 and the ones of various Western States, again based on the Assembly's lack of competence to order sanctions and again concerning the resolutions adopted against South Africa, in GAOR, 35th sess. (1980), Pl. meet., 98th meet., no. 10 (EEC countries) and no. 26 (New Zealand), 37th sess. (1982), Pl. meet., A/37/PV.98, p. 2 (Japan), 38th sess. (1983), Pl. meet., A/38/PV.83, p. 20 (EEC countries); 43th sess (1988), Pl. meet., A/43/PV.68; 44th sess. (1989), A/44/PV.63 (Belgium).

The case of West Irian has also been considered as an example of peacekeeping operations grounded in practice,. This was a (single) case of temporary administration by the United Nations organized by the General Assembly in 1963 and concerning a former colony of the Netherlands. In our opinion, the Assembly was rather acting at the time in the framework of de-colonizaton (see § 78).

Section IV

MAINTENANCE OF THE PEACE. THE FUNCTIONS OF THE SECRETARY-GENERAL

BIBLIOGRAPHY: SCHWEBEL, *The Secretary-General of the United Nations, His Political Powers and Practice*, Harvard University Press, 1952; VIRALLY, *Le rôle politique du Secrétaire général des Nations Unies*, in *AF*, 1958, p. 360 ff.; SIOTIS, *Essai sur le Secrétariat international*, Genève, 1963, p. 168 ff.; BAILEY, *The Secretariat of the United Nations*, New York, 1964; GORDENKER, *The UN Secretary-General and the Maintenance of Peace*, New York, 1967; SMOUTS, *Le Secrétaire général des Nations Unies; son rôle dans la solution des conflits internationaux*, Paris, 1971; RAMCHARAN, *The Good Offices of the United Nations Secretary-General in the Field of Human Rights*, in *AJ*, 1982, p. 130 ff.; JORDAN, *Dag*

Hammarskjöld Revisited: The UN Secretary-General as a Force in World Politics, Durham, 1983; EL ARABY, *The Office of Secretary-General and the Maintenance of International Peace and Security*, in *REgDI*, 1986, p. 1 ff.; BOURLOYANNIS, *Fact-Finding by the Secretary-General of the UN*, in *New York Univ. Journal of International Law and Politics*, 1990, p. 641 ff.; LAVALLE, *The « Inherent » Powers of the UN Secretary-General in the Political Sphere: A Legal Analysis*, in *NILR*, 1990, p. 641 ff.; SZASZ, *The Role of the UN Secretary-General: Some Legal Aspects*, in *New York Univ. Journal of International Law and Politics*, 1991, p. 161 ff.; RIVLIN and GORDENKER (eds.), *The Challenging Role of the UN Secretary-General. Making the "Most Impossible Job in the World" Possible*, Westport, 1993; MURTHY, *Th Role of the UN Secretary-General since the End of the Cold War*, in *The Indian Journal of International Law, 1995, p. 181 ff.*; FRANK and NOLTE, *The Good Offices Function of the UN Secretary General*, in ROBERTS AND KINGSBURY, *United Nations Divided World,*, 2nd ed., 1996, p. 143 ff.: NEWMAN, *The UN Secretary-General from the Cold War to the New Era: A Global Peace and Security Mandate ?*, New York, 1998; SAROOSHI, *The UN and the Development of Collective Security (The Delegation by the UN Security Council of its Chapter VII Powers)*, Oxford, 1999, Chapter .

65. *Delegated functions and executive functions.*

The most important power of the Secretary-General in the area of maintenance of the peace (as in every other field of UN activity) is drawn from Article 98, under which the Secretary performs the functions that are "entrusted" to him by the General Assembly or the Security Council. The delegation of powers so provided by Article 98 is not subjected to any special condition or even to the setting of any guidelines. An objective limit, however, may be implied in the UN system, especially in the provisions which attach the responsibility for maintenance of the peace to the Security Council and, secondarily, to the General Assembly. These provisions make it unthinkable that there could be any transfer of functions that does not pertain to *specific* cases. It is also obvious that the only functions that can be transferred are the ones held by the delegating organ.

As occurs in any case of delegation, the Secretary enjoys wide autonomy in carrying out the functions entrusted to him. In the exercise of such autonomy the personality of the holder of the office plays a decisive role. Autonomy must, however, be exercised in compliance with limits and instructions imposed by the delegating organ as well as with the observance of the Charter provisions. However, it includes the decision-making power and also the implied powers that are necessary for fulfillment of the task.

As we have already noted in the context of peacekeeping operations (see § 59) Article 98 does not envisage the type of delegation as provided for in domestic law, i.e. as a mandate given by a person to another person. The delegation can be better explained as "instructions". The Secretary-General being the chief administrative officer of the Organization, the relation with the Security Council is always an inter-organic relationship within the framework of the Charter. It is obvious that the functions entrusted to the Secretary-General can be exercised by his representatives. A "sub-delegation" of powers (SAROOSHI) is also obvious. The relationship between the Secretary-General and his representative is a hierarchical one and the delegation of powers by the Security Council to the Secretary-General always covers the staff under his jurisdiction.

Many examples of delegation can be seen in practice. There are various resolutions in which the Secretary was entrusted with powers pertaining to the Security Council or the General Assembly, particularly powers of investigation, of mediation and, more in general, of conciliation. However, the most striking cases concern operations for the maintenance of the peace, especially the establishment, as requested by the Security Council, of military forces entrusted with peacekeeping functions (see § 59). These cases are to be noted precisely because of the Secretary-General's exercise of a series of powers expressly coming within the tasks entrusted to him. Examples can be seen in the conclusion of agreements with States on whose territories the Forces have been operating and with the States that have contributed to their establishment, the decision concerning the specific use of such Forces, the issuance of all the rules governing the service relationship between the solders and the Secretary, and so on.

In the last decade the cases of delegation by the Security Council or the General Assembly are numerous especially as far as powers of conciliation and mediation are concerned. See, for instance, regarding the Security Council, res. no 788 of November 19, 1992. para. 7, which authorizes the Secretary-General to support the process of national conciliation in Liberia; and res. no. 811 of March 12, 1993, para. 8, on the national conciliation in Angola. Regarding the General Assembly, see, for instance, res. no. 46 of October 11, 1991, entrusting the Secretary-General with powers of mediation between the *de facto* Government of General Cedras and the Government of President Aristide in Haiti.

The delegation may be subject to a specific directive or not. As an example of a delegation free from conditions or restrictions the Security Council resolution no. 1511 of October 16, 2003 may be quoted. Para. 7 and 8 of the resolution authorizes the Secretary-General to participate in the political process in Iraq, on the request of occupying States. On the basis of this resolution, the Secretary-General and his Special Advisor were able to formulate various proposals on the transfer of powers from the occupying States to the Iraqi people (see Doc. S/2004/140 of February 23, 2004 and the Statement of the President of the Security Council of April 27, 2004, in Doc. S/PRST/2004/11)

The delegation may always be revoked by the delegating organ. However, what will happen if the organ in question, after having transferred certain powers and issued certain directions on a specific question, no longer is able to take decisions on subsequent developments in the matter? Must the Secretary-General in this case continue in the exercise of the delegated functions, or will the delegation terminate because of the change in circumstances? A question of this kind arose during the Congo action when, between August 1960 and February 1961, the chaos existing within the

Congo made the carrying out of the task (which had no time limit) entrusted to the Secretary by Security Council res. no. 143 of July 14, 1960 very problematic. The task was to assist the Congolese government in maintaining order (see § 59). Dag Hammarskjold, who was Secretary at the time (and who was subsequently to give his life through service to the United Nations), on one hand had requested, to no avail, instructions from the Security Council and the General Assembly (both were paralyzed by conflicts between their members), and on the other was harshly criticized by the Soviet Union and the other Socialist countries (who reached the point of asking for his resignation) for his initiatives. Hammarskjold's view that the Secretary had the duty to continue an operation he had undertaken, even at the cost of making independent decisions, should be shared in this particular case. Perhaps it is correct to say that a delegation ceases only when there has been such a radical change of circumstances as to make any decision impossible in the light of what were the instructions. And this cannot be said about the Congo.

Cf., for the criticism and the defence in the Security Council of the Secretary-General's actions: SCOR, 15th year, 888th-889th meets., 901st-916th meets., and 16th year, 928th-932nd meets.

The purely administrative functions of the Secretary-General must be kept distinct from the delegated functions, although this distinction is more quantitative than qualitative and has had no important repercussions. The executive functions (Article 97: "The Secretary-General... shall be the chief *administrative* officer of the Organization") include any kind of activity necessary to give effect to the decisions of the General Assembly or of the Security Council which does not involve, or which involves to a very limited extent, the exercise of decision-making power by the Secretary. An example which is typical and which often occurs is given by resolutions which, after having recommended certain conduct to the States, request the Secretary-General to make inquiries and to keep the organ informed as to whether the recommendation has been carried out.

66. *Autonomous initiatives for peaceful settlement.*

Even without specific delegation by the Assembly or the Council, the Secretary-General has often carried out peaceful settlement functions by offering his role as a mediator to those States involved in an international or domestic crisis. The Charter does not expressly envisage such initiatives. Nor the view that they implicitly come within the power attributed to the Secretary by Article 99 ("The Secretary-General may bring to the attention of the Security Council any matter which…may threaten the maintenance of international peace…") cannot be accepted. The provision of Article 99 deals with a procedural matter, the convening of the Council, and it cannot serve to solve a question of substance. Rather, it seems that the Secretary's initiatives must be placed outside of the formal institutional framework of the United Nations. In practice, doubts may be cast about the compatibility of the Secretary-General's general power of mediation and conciliation in an *International* crisis (a crisis involving States) with the Charter.

> The practice regarding international crises is poor. Moreover, the lack of competence of the Secretary-General to take autonomous initiatives has been stressed by some States with regard the Kosovo crisis, during the three months' air war against the Republic of Yugoslavia in 1999. The United States Secretary of State, in particular, warned the Secretary-General to confine himself to execute the resolutions adopted by the General Assembly and the Security Council, i.e. to co-ordinate the humanitarian aids to the Kosovo refugees (see the newspaper *Le Monde* of May 8/9, 1999).

As far as domestic crises are concerned, the conclusion is perhaps somewhat different. The autonomous initiatives of the Secretary-General within the framework of national conciliation have never been met by objections from Member States. On the contrary, they have ex post gained the support of the Security Council or the General Assembly.

> See, for instance, SC resolutions no. 782 of October 13, 1992 (situation in Mozambique), no. 1216 of December 21, 1998 (wherein the Security Council "welcomes the agreements between the Government of Guinea Bissau and the Self Proclaimed Military Junta", an agreement concluded with the mediation of the Secretary-General), no. 1234of April 9, 1999 (wherein the Council "expresses its support for the Special Envoy of the Secretary-General for the peace process in the Democratic Republic of Congo). Regarding the General Assembly, see, for instance, res. no. 38/10 of November 11, 1983, para. 8 and 9, and no. 39/4 of October 20. 1994. para. 3 and 4.

It is to be excluded that the Secretary may proceed independently with *formal* investigations of the kind envisaged by Article 34. Neither can the power of investigation be held to be implicit in Article 99, because of the merely procedural nature of this provision. On the other hand, it is a power whose exercise would be unthinkable outside of the institutional framework of the United Nations.

> The power to conduct investigations was claimed by the Secretary-General in the UN's first year. However, it was done only in an incidental and very general manner. During a Security Council meeting where the question of infiltration through Greek borders during the civil war was being discussed, the then Secretary Trygie Lie asserted his own "right to make such enquires or investigations" in order to establish whether a question should or should not

be brought to the attention of the Council (cf. SCOR, 1st year, 70th meet., p. 404). However, his statement did not have any specific consequences.

The problem was again proposed in 1970 when the Secretary-General, at the invitation of Great Britain and Iran, conducted an investigation aimed at ascertaining the wishes of the inhabitants of the Bahrein Islands regarding a possible relationship of protection or of union with either State, or the acquisition of full independence. The results of the investigation, favourable to independence, were communicated by the Secretary to the Security Council (see doc. S/9772 in SCOR, 25th year, Suppl. for April-May-June 1970, p. 166), and the Council adopted them with res. no. 278 of May 11, 1970. During the debate, however, both the Soviet Union (see doc. S/9737, in SCOR, 25th year, Suppl. cit,, p. 143, and 1536th meet., no. 73) and France (ivi, 1536th meet., no. 156) protested over the procedure adopted and over the "independent" action of the Secretary. France in particular said that such a procedure should not be meant to constitute a precedent. The position of France and the USSR, opposed in an opinion of the Secretariat (in *UNJY*, 1973, p. 162 ff.) which resorted to the theory of implied powers (on this, see § 5), is, for the reasons we have given, correct.

Section V

MAINTENANCE OF THE PEACE AND REGIONAL ORGANIZATIONS

BIBLIOGRAPHY: YEPES, *Les accords régionaux et le droit international*, in *RC*, 1947, II, p. 235 ff.; VELLAS, *Le régionalisme international et l'ONU*, Paris, 1948; BOUTROS-GHALI, *Contribution à l'étude des ententes régionales*, Paris, 1949, p. 122 ff.; VAN KLEFFENS, *Regionalism and Political Pacts*, in *AJ*, 1949, p. 666 ff.; KULSKI, *The Soviet System of Collective Security Compared with the Western System*, in *AJ*, 1950, p. 453 ff.; SABA, *Les accords régionaux dans la Charte de l'ONU*, in *RC*, 1952-I, p. 635 ff.; VIGNES, *La place des pactes de défense dans la société internationale actuelle*, in *AF*, 1959, p. 37 ff.; FERNANDEZ-SHAW, *La Organizacion de los Estados Americanos*, Madrid 1963; THOMAS and THOMAS, *The Organization of American States*, Dallas, 1963; QUADRI, *Diritto internazionale pubblico*, Naples, 1968, p. 373 ff.; THARP (ed.), *Regional Organizations, Structures and Functions*, New York, 1971; PERNICE, *Die Sicherung des Weltfriedens durch Regionale Organisationen und die Vereinten Nationen*, Hamburg, 1972; BOUTROS-GHALI, *La Ligue des Etats arabes*, in *RC*, 1972, II, p. 1 ff.; MOUSSA, *Rapports entre les Nations Unies et la Ligue des Etats arabes*, in *REgDI*, 1973, p. 67 ff.; LEWIN, *The OAS and the UN: Relations in the Peace and Security Field*, New York, 1974; CHAYES, *The Cuban Missile Crisis*, London, 1974; TIEWUL, *Relations Between the UN Organization and the Organization of African Unity in the Settlement of Secessionist Conflicts*, in *HILJ*, 1975, p. 259 ff.; WILSON, *The Settlement of Conflicts Within the Framework of Relations Between Regional Organizations and the UN: the Case of Cuba 1962-64*, in *NILR*, 1975, p. 282 ff.; LEITA, *Il sistema di sicurezza interamericano nel Protocollo di emendamento del Trattato di Rio de Janeiro*, in *CI*, 1977, p. 26 ff.; FRANCIS, *Treaty Establishing the Caribbean Community, an Analysis*, in *IJIL*, 1982, p. 278 ff.; BAKHSHAB, *The Concept of Regional Arrangements*, in *REgDI*, 1984, p. 195 ff.; ACEVEDO, *The Right of Members of the Organization of America States to Refer their « Local » Disputes Directly to the UN Security Council*, in *Am. Univ. Journal of International Law and Policy*, 1989, p. 25 ff.; ACEVEDO, *Relationship between the Organization of American States and the*

United Nations with Regard to Settlement of Regional Disputes, in *Thesaurus Acroasium*, 1991, p. 61 ff.; FARER, *The Role of Regional Organizations in International Peace-making and Peace-keeping: Legal, Political and Military Problems*, in *Blauhelme in einer turbulenten Welt*, Baden-Baden, 1993, p. 275 ff.; THEUERMANN, *Regionale Friedenssicherung im Lichte von Kapitel VIII der Satzung der Vereinten Nationen: Juristische und politische Probleme*, in *Blauhelme in einer turbulenten Welt*, Baden-Baden, 1993, p. 231 ff.; WOLFRUM, *Der Beitrag regionaler Abmachungen zur Friedenssicherung: Möglichkeiten und Grenzen*, in *Bruns'Z*, 1993, p. 576 ff.; WALTER, *Vereinte Nationen und Regionalorganisationen. Eine Untersuchung zur Kapitel VIII der Satzung der Vereinten Nationen*, Berli,, 1996; BLOKKER and MULLER, *NATO as the UN Security Council's Instrument: Question Marks from the Perspective of International Law ?*, in *Leiden JIL*, 1996, p. 411 ss.; GIOIA, *The UN and Regional organizations in the Maintenance of Peace and security*, in BOTHE, RONZITTI and ROSAS (EDS), *The OSCE in tne Maintenance of Peace and Security. Conflicts Prevention, Crisis Management and Peaceful Settlement of Disputes,* The Hague, 1997, p. 191 ss.; IOVANE, *La NATO, le organizzazioni regionali e le competenze del Consiglio di sicurezza in tema di mantenimznto della pace, ibid.,* p. 43 ss.; HENKIN, *Kosovo and the Law of "Humanitarian Intervention,* in *AJ*, 1999, p. 824 ff.; CHARNEY, *Anticiptory Humanitarian Intervention in Kosovo, ibid.,* p. 834 ff.; REISMAN, *Kosovo's Antinomies, ibid.,* p. 860 ff.; SIMMA, *NATO, the UN and the Use of Force: Legal Aspects,* in *EJIL*, 1999, p. 1 ff.; TUZMUKHAMEDOV, *The Legal Framework of CIS Regional Peace Operation,* in *Int Pk*, 2000, p. 1 ff.; Deen-Racsmáni, A Redistribution of Authority Between the UN and Regional Organizations in the Field of the Maintenance of Peace and Security, in LJIL, 200o, p. 297 ff.; VILLANI, *Les rapports entre l'ONU et les organisations régionales dans le domaine du maintien de la paix,* in *RC* 2001, vol. 290, p. 225 ff.; PISTOIA, *Le operazioni militari c.d. non-Article 5 nella nuova dottrina strategica della NATO,* etc., in SCISO (ed.), *L'intervento in Kosovo. Aspetti internazionalistici e interni,* Milan, 2001, p. 139 ff.; ÖSTERDAHL, *The Continued Relevance of Collective Security Under the UN: The Security Council, Regional Organizations and the General Assembly,* in *Finnish Yearbook of Int. Law,* 2002, p. 103 ff.; DE WET, *The relationship between the Security Council and Regional Organizations during Enforcement Actions under Chapter VII of the UN Charter,* in *Nordic Journal of Int. Law,* 2002, p. 1 ff.

67. *Regional actions "authorized" by the Security Council.*

As the opening article in Chapter VIII on regional arrangements, Article 52 recognizes international organizations that are created at a regional level and emphasizes their task in the settlement of local disputes between the countries who are member of them. This is an almost superfluous provision, since resort to regional agencies is already mentioned in Article 33 as one of the means for the peaceful settlement of disputes.

The importance of regional organizations in preventing conflicts among their members is more and more referred to by the Security Council in recent practice. As a model see, for instance, res. no. 1170 of May 28, 1998 on the role of the Organization of the African Unity.

Article 53 is much more important. It concerns regional agencies organized for its members' defense and mutual assistance in the event of war or crises short of war. It provides that the Security Council may utilize "regional agreements or agencies for enforcement action under its authority", and adds that "no enforcement action shall be taken under regional arrangements... without the authorization of the Security Council...". This provision is linked with Article 51 which permits *collective* self-defense in the event of armed attack and which was formulated with regional organizations in mind (see § 55 *bis*). Such organizations thus may act with the use of force on the authorization of the Security Council, or without the authorization of the Council but only to counteract an armed attack.

Article 53 envisaged another possibility of action by regional agencies that could be carried out without the authorization of the Council. That is the case of war against a country which, during the Second World War, had been an "enemy" of one of the signatories of the Charter. This part of the article has been now abrogated as a consequence of a fundamental change of circumstances (*rebus sic stantibus*).

Since enforcement action against a State, or within a State, requires the authorization of the Security Council, the regional agencies appear, under this respect, and as has been correctly noted (QUADRI) as "decentralized United Nations organs".

We must stress that, according to the UN Charter, the authorization of the Security Council is always needed when force is used by a regional organization. In fact, the cases of regional organizations acing without authorization have increased in recent times, but cannot be considered as supported by a customary rule due to the reactions they still meet.

With regard to unauthorized actions, the 1962 Cuban crisis should be mentioned first of all. At that time the United States set up a naval blockade of the Cuban coasts in order to prevent the installation on the island of missile-launching ramps coming from the Soviet Union. The blockade, which nearly set off a war between the two superpowers, was preceded by a decision of the OAS (Organization of American States), adopted on the basis of Article 8 of the Treaty of Reciprocal Assistance (Rio de Janeiro, 1947). The resolution, requested by the United States, recommended that the Member States use any measure, including the use of force, to avoid Cuba receiving military supplies of any kind from the URSS and to prevent the use of the missile ramps that had already been installed.

The United States' action, in that it was contrary to Article 2, para. 4 (which prohibits the *threat* or the use of force), clearly departed from the Charter principles. It could not be justified as self-defence under Article 51 as it was not directed against an armed attack (see § 55 *bis*); and neither could it come within Article 53, since the OAS resolution lacked the authorization of the Security Council. In defending the United States, it was said that the rule on the authorization in Article 53 had lost its efficacy, owing to the *rebus sic stantibus* clause, given the impotence and paralysis of the Council at that time. Following what we have already concluded concerning self-defence (see § 55 *bis*), it must be said that whoever holds such view must coherently conclude that the whole Charter and not only its individual provisions has lost its function. The truth of the matter is that the United States' action, not supported by any Charter provision, could have been justified under the Charter only if had had the nature of self-defence under Article 51. On the Cuban crisis, both for a description of the events and for the legal views held, cf. the articles by various authors in *AJ*, 1963, p. 515 ff.

The United States' action in the Dominican Republic in 1965, when troops landed during the civil war, is also to be considered contrary to the Charter. The view, held by the United States delegate in the Security Council (and vehemently challenged by the USSR and Cuba), that the action was lawful in so far as it was authorized by the OAS Council of Ministers and its purpose was solely to protect and evacuate foreign civilians without supporting any of the parties involved in the conflict, cannot be shared. This is because the OAS did not have the authorization of the Security Council under Article 53 and because an action using armed force, for reasons similar to those we spoke of regarding United Nations Forces (see § 60), is always to be considered as an "enforcement action" under this article. For the lengthy debate in the Security Council, see SCOR, 20th year, 1196th-1204th, 1207th-1209th and 1212th-1222nd meets, (for the U.S. thesis, see, especially, 1212th meet., no. 144 f. and 1222nd meet., no. 21).

Neither can the military intervention of the United States, Barbados and Jamaica in Grenada in October 1983 come within the framework of Article 53, although it had been decided by the Organization of Eastern Caribbean States. Also this decision did not have the necessary authorization of the Security Council. For the debate in the Council, see SCOR, October 25-28, 1983 (S/PV.2489). In legal literature, see the articles by various authors in *AJ*, 1984, p. 131 ff.

The same must be said of the intervention of ECOMOG, the peacekeeping force of the Economic Community of West African States (ECOWAS) in Liberia in 1990. The intervention was not authorized by the Security Council which only later commended the efforts of ECOWAS in restoring order to the country (see resolution no. 866 of September 22, 1993. The resolution cannot be interpreted as an *ex post* ratification, for the reasons we have explained when dealing with unauthorized actions of single States (see § 60). For other cases of unauthorized actions of ECOMOG, see DEEN- RACSMÁNY, *art. cit.*, p. 316 ff.

Last but not least, the three months' air war by NATO forces against the Republic of Yugoslavia in 1999 during the Kosovo crisis must also be considered as a clear violation of the Charter. Quite different is the problem whether this kind of actions, and of any other armed actions for humanitarian reasons, can be justified from a moral point of view.

As we have already noted (see § 60) when the United Nations fail in controlling a crisis, then general international law is by itself unable to govern the *jus ad bellum*. This reveals a "lacuna" which opens the way to discussion of the problem of war in the context of natural law as a problem of "just" or "unjust" war.

The re-vitalization of the Security Council after the end of the Cold War had repercussions on the relationships between the Security Council and regional agencies. In various resolutions adopted on the basis of Chapter VII, the Council, in recommending or authorizing the adoption of enforcement measures by the Member States, addressed the resolutions both to the Member States individually and the Member States as members of regional agencies or arrangements (expressly referring to Chapter VIII), or directly to one regional organization or another.

As far as the first formula is concerned, many resolutions adopted during the Yugoslav crisis can be quoted, and in particular: resolutions no. 770 of August 13, 1992, on the adoption of the measures necessary to ensure that humanitarian assistance reached Sarajevo and other places in the former Yugoslavia; no. 781 of October 9, 1992 and no. 816 of March 31, 1993 on the adoption of the measures necessary to ensure a ban on military flights over Bosnia and Herzegovina; no. 787 of November 16, 1992, on the naval blockade against the Republic of Yugoslavia (Serbia and Montenegro). The appeals by the Council in this case were received and acted upon by the Western European Union and by the North Atlantic Treaty Organization.

Regarding authorization directly addressed to a regional organization, see, for instance, res. no. 504 of April 30, 1982, which endorsed the setting up of a pan-African Force by the OAU (Organization for African Unity) for maintenance of the peace in Chad. The case of KFOR, the NATO forces entrusted with the external defence of Kosovo in the framework of UNMIK (see § 60 *bis*), is also a case of application of Article 53.

68. *Existing regional Organizations.*

The following are the most important regional agencies for the purposes of Chapter VIII.

The *North Atlantic Treaty Organization* (NATO) was established in 1949 to bind Western Europe and the United States together in a common defense alliance. After the end of the Cold War many countries from Eastern Europe have joined the alliance. Its members are now: Belgium, Bulgaria, Canada, Czech Republic, Denmark, France, Germany, Greece, Hungary, Iceland, Italy, Latvia, Lithuania, Luxembourg, the Netherlands, Norway, Poland, Portugal, Romania, Slovakia, Slovenia, Spain, Turkey, United Kingdom, and United States. Under Article 5 of the treaty, in the event of armed attack against one of the members, the others agree to assist them and to take such action that *each of them* deems necessary to restore peace (they are therefore not obliged to intervene automatically with military force). In time of peace, the Organization has the purpose of developing military co-operation among the member countries (through military organs, the so-called *Commands*). Its main organs are the *Council*, which brings together the representatives, usually Foreign Ministers but also the Heads of State and Government, of all the members and the *Defence Committee*, composed of the chiefs of general staff, again of all the members. By the Alliance's Strategic Concept of 1991, and especially by the Alliance's New Strategic Concept approved by the Heads of State and Government in 1999, NATO has decided to pursue not only the defense of its members but also to participate in military actions for the maintenance of peace and security. By that, it fully satisfies the requirements of Chapter VIII of the UN Charter. The question of whether the decisions of 1991 and 1999 comply with the North

Atlantic Treaty - a question which has been raised in legal literature – does not have any interest in a discussion on the law of the United Nations.

The *Western European Union* (WEU), established by the Treaty of Brussels of March 17, 1948. Besides developing economic, social and cultural co-operation among the members, the Organization has the purpose of assuring mutual assistance in the case of aggression. Its principal organ is the Council, where the parties may consult one another on any situation that may constitute a threat to the peace (Article 8, para. 3). In a sense it is the defense alliance of the European Union: according to Article 17 (former Article J.7) of the Treaty on European Union as amended by the Treaty of Amsterdam of 1997, the WEU "is an integral part of the development of the Union providing the Union with access to an operational capability", particularly in performing humanitarian tasks, peacekeeping tasks and tasks of combat forces in crisis management. The Union may also avail itself of the WEU to elaborate and implement decisions and actions of the Union which have defense implications.

The *Organization of American States* (OAS), which joins together the United States and the countries of Latin America, and which was established in 1948 by the Treaty of Bogotà. Among the purposes of the Organization, besides co-operation in the economic, social, legal and cultural fields, there is "strengthening the peace and security of the American continent", "pacific settlement of disputes among the members", and a collective security system through "common action on the part of the Member States in the event of aggression". The OAS has many organs, and among them the most important are: the *General Assembly*, consisting of the representatives of all the Member States, the *Meeting of Consultation*, where the Foreign Ministers of the members meet; the *Permanent Council of the Organization*, composed of a representative of each member.

The *League of Arab States*, formed in 1945. This Organization does not only have the purpose of military alliance but also aims at the development of co-operation in various sectors, from politics to economics, communications to health and social security, and so on. The principal organ is the *Council*, consisting of representatives of all the members. Its decisions are binding only on the States which agree by their affirmative vote to adopt them. Article 6 of the constitutive treaty provides that, in the event of aggression against a member, the Council must decide (by unanimity) what measures to take to repel it.

The *Organization for African Unity* (OAU), created in 1963, has as its principal purpose "to promote the unity and security of the African States", eradicating from the continent all forms of colonialism and of foreign economic and political interference. The OAU Charter does not contain any specific provision on reciprocal defense, and only indicates, among the purposes of the Organization, "defending the sovereignty, territorial integrity and independence of the Member States". The main organs are: the Assembly of Heads of State and Government, the Council of Ministers, the Secretary-General, and the Commission of Mediation, Conciliation and Arbitration, which, under Article XIX of the Charter and in accordance with a procedure to be defined by a separate Protocol, is to settle disputes among the Member States.

The *Commonwealth of Independent States* (CIS) was created in 1991 from among the former Republics of the URSS after the dissolution of this State. The main organs of the CIS are the Council of Heads of State, the Council of Heads of Government, the Council of Foreign Ministers, the Council of Defense Ministers, the Council of Board Troops Commanders. The goals of the Organization, as they are stated in the Commonwealth Charter of January 22, 1993, are, *inter alia*, the strengthening of relations of friendship, good neighborhood and cooperation between States, particularly when the sovereignty and territorial integrity of a Member State is threatened. The participation of peacekeeping forces within the territory of the CIS has been envisaged by the Kiev Agreement of 1992, the Charter and various subsequent agreements.

The Warsaw Pact Organization, established in 1955 by the countries of Eastern Europe to counterbalance NATO, was also a regional organization, dissolved when the Socialist regimes in those countries fell. The Warsaw Pact, as the Atlantic Pact, provided that the contracting States would consult one another and assist one another in the event of armed attack against one of them and also provided for military co-operation in time of peace. The basic organs of the Pact were the *Political Committee*, where consultation and consideration of matters of interest to the alliance took place and the *United Command*, to which a part of the armed forces of the Member States were assigned.

The *Economic Community of West African States* (ECOWAS) is a further example. Although this organization is mainly devoted to economic cooperation among its members, in its framework a non-standing military force (ECOMOG) also operates as a peacekeeping force in the region.

The *Organization of Eastern Caribbean States* (OECS) was established in 1981 by several States in the area and its constitutive treaty includes reciprocal defense among the purposes of the union (Article 3, para. 2).

The *Organization for Security and Co-operation in Europe* (OSCE) is one of the largest regional organizations in Europe with Member States from Europe, Central Asia and North America. The Organization succeeded the Conference on Security and Co-operation in Europe (CSCE) issued from the historical Helsinki Agreements of 1975 concluded by Western and Eastern European countries during the Cold War. The OSCE's tasks have been fixed by various Declarations of the Head of States and Governments of Member States since it is not based on a true treaty. The last and most important one is the Charter for European Security issued by the Conference of Istanbul of November 19, 1999. The Charter reaffirms the OSCE as a regional arrangement under Chapter VIII of the UN Charter and, *inter alia*, commits the Organization, in co-operation with other organizations and institutions, to develop its role in peacekeeping operations, in particular providing support for the supremacy of law and democratic institutions and for the maintenance and restoration of law and order, assisting in the organization and monitoring of elections, verifying and assisting in fulfilling agreements on the peaceful settlement of conflicts, and providing support in the rehabilitation and reconstruction of various aspects of society. The participation of OSCE in peacekeeping operations, mainly with the function of helping local authorities in civil and political matters, is widespread. To mention only one example, the OSCE is assisting UNMIK in matters of democratisation and institution building (see § 60 *bis*). The fact that the Organization is not based on a true international agreement in the legal sense, and that, consequently, its resolutions do not have a strictly legal character, is not an obstacle to the Security Council making use of the Organisation whenever the occasion arises.

For the text of the Istanbul Declaration of 1999, cf. *ILM*, 1999, p. 255 ff. A previous and also most important Declaration was the Helsinki Declaration of July 10, 1992 (ibid., 1992, p. 1385 ff) wherein the Organization already defined itself as a regional agreement under Chapter VIII of UN Charter. It should be noted, with regard to the conflicts in the former Yugoslavia, that, even before the Declaration of 1992, the Security Council called upon the parties to make use of the CSCE's contribution or in any case to act in accordance with its principles. Cf., for example, resolutions no. 713, para. 1, of September 25, 1991, no. 740, para. 7, of February 7, 1992, no. 743, para. 10, of February 21, 1992, no. 762, para. 11, of June 30, 1992.

Section VI

ECONOMIC CO-OPERATION AND ACTION FOR DEVELOPMENT

BIBLIOGRAPHY: ASHER, *The United Nations and Promotion of the General Welfare*, Washington, 1957; DOMERGUE, *Technical Assistance: Theory, Pratice and Policies*, London, 1968; EL-NAGGAR, *The UNCTAD*, in *RC*, 1969, III, p. 241 ff.; GRAY, *Resource Flows to Less-Developed Countries*, New York, 1969; GUTTERIDGE, *The United Nations in a Changing World*, 1969, Dobbs Ferry, N.Y., p. 72 ff.; SEN, *UN in Economic Development*, New York, 1969; SHARP, *The United Nations Economic and Social Council*, New York-London, 1969; EPPLER, *Wenig Zeit für die dritte Welt*, Stuttgard, 1971; FOIGHEL, *Development Aid. A Legal Analysis*, Copenaghen, 1971; DICKE, *Die administrative Organisation der Entwicklungshilfe durch die Vereinten Nationen*, Frankfurt a.M., 1972; GOSOVIC, *UNCTAD, Conflict and Compromise*, Leiden, 1972; JORDAN, *Multinational Co-operation: Economic, Social and Scientific Development*, London, 1972; MARTIN, *Development Assistance*, Paris, 1972; HEIDUK, *Die weltwirtschaftlichen Ordnungsprinzipen von GATT und UNCTAD*, Baden-Baden, 1973; JENKS, *Economic and Social Change and the Law of Nations*, in *RC*, 1973, I, p. 455 ff.; BOHNET (cd.), *Das Nord-Süd Problem, Konflikte zwischen Industrie- und Entwicklungsländern*, München, 1974; FLORY, *Souveraineté des Etats et Coopération pour le Developpement*, in *RC*, 1974, I, p. 255 ff.; PLASIL-WENGER, *UNIDO: Problem Child of the United Nations Family*, in *Journal of World Trade Law*, 1974, p. 186 ff.; VIRALLY, *La Charte des droit et devoirs économiques des Etats*, in *AF*, 1974, p. 57 ff.; FEUER, *Réflexions sur la Charte des droits et devoirs économiques des Etats*, in *RGDIP*, 1975, p. 273 ff.; MCWHINNEY, *The International Law-Making Process in the New International Economic Order*, in *CYIL*, 1976, p. 57 ff.; TOMUSCHAT, *Die Charte der wirtschaftlichen Rechte und Pflichte der Staaten*, *Bruns'Z*, 1976, p. 444 ff.; VILLANI, *Conciliation and Consensus in UNCTAD*, in *IYIL*, 1976, p. 61 ff.; KOUL, *The Legal Framework of UNCTAD in World Trade*, Leiden, 1977; MARCHISIO, *Là cooperazione per lo sviluppo nel diritto delle Nazioni Unite*, Naples, 1977; ID., *Organizzazione delle Nazioni Unite per lo sviluppo industriale*, in *Enciclopedia del diritto*, 1981, vol. XXXI, p. 329 ff.; RUCZ, *Le Conseil Economique et Social de l'O.N.U. et la coopération pour le développement*, Paris, 1985; COLLIARD, *L'adoption par l'Assemblée générale de la Declaration sur le droit au développement (4 déc. 1986)*, in *AF*, 1987, p. 614 ff.; ABI-SAAB, *Le droit au développement*, in *Annuaire suisse de droit international*, 1988, p. 9 ff.; KIWANUKA, *Developing Rights: The UN Declaration on the Right to Development*, in *NILR*, 1988, p. 257 ff.; FLORY, *La quatrième décennie pour le développement: la fin du Nouvel ordre économique international?*, in *AF*, 1990, p. 606 ff.; BARSH, *A Special Session of the UN General Assembly Rethinks the Economic Rights and Duties of States*, in *AJ*, 1991, p. 192 ff.; WILLIAMS, *Third World Co-operation: the Group of 77 in UNCTAD*, London, 1991; MARCHISIO, *Gli atti di Rio nel diritto internazionale*, in *RDI*, 1992, p. 581 ff.; DAUDET (ed.), *Les Nations Unies et le developpement: le cas de l'Afrique*, Paris, 1994; BELHADJ, *Le droit de l'homme au developpement*, Rabat, 1995; BASSIN, *The United Nations in Global Economic and Social Policy-Making*, in Hüfner, *Klaus Agenda for Change*, Opladen, 1995, p. 229 ff.; JAIN, *La seguridad ambiental y la Naciones Unidas*, in Deara Wasquez, *Las Naciones Unidas a los cincuenta años*, México, 1995, p. 223 ff.; TROMP, *Las Naciones Unidas y la seguridad ambiental, ibid.*, p. 241 ff.; BEIGBEDER, *Reforming the Economic and Social Sectors of the United Nations: An Incomplete Process, ibid.*, p. 239 ff.; SILVEIRA, *UN Commission on Sustainable Development (CSD)*, in *Yearbook of International Environmental Law*, 1996, p. 374 ff.; MARCHISIO, *Carta dell'ONU, cooperazione e sviluppo sostenibile*, in *Rivista della cooperazione giuridica internazionale*, 1999, 11 ff.; SOCIÉTÉ DE DROIT INTERNATIONAL, *Les Nations Unies et la protection de l'environment. La promotion d'un développement*. Septième rencontre d'Aix-en-Provence, Paris, 1999.

On the UN Specialized Agencies *adde*: SHARP, *The Specialized Agencies and the United Nations*, Carnegie Endowment for International Peace, 1949; LABEYRIE-MENAHEM, *Des Institutions Specialisées*, Paris, 1953; SABA, *L'activité quasi legislative des institutions specialisées des Nations Unies*, in *RC*, 1964, I, p. 607 ff.; YEMIN, *Legislative Powers in the United Nations and Specialized Agencies*, Leiden, 1969; ALEXANDROWICZ, *The Law-Making Functions of the Specialized Agencies of the UN*, South Hackensack, 1974; LUARD, *International Agencies (The Emerging Framework of Interdipendence)*, London, 1977; ZARB, *Les Institutions Spécialesées du Systéme des Nations Unies et leurs membres*, Paris, 1980; DI BLASE, *Nazioni Unite e istituti specializzati: La rilevanza giuridica del coordinamento*, Naples, 1982; AMERI, *Politics and Process in the Specialized Agencies of the United Nations*, Brookfield, 1982; CAILLOUX, *Aspects juridiques de la vie des institutions spécialisées de l'ONU*, in *AF*, 1983, p. 533 ff.; DOUGLAS, *The Specialized Agencies and the UN: The System in Crisis*, New York, 1987; AA.VV., *International Development Agencies (IDA's) Human Rights and Environmental Considerations*, in *Denver Journal of International Law and Policy*, 1988, p. 29 ff.; GHEBALI, *The International Labour Organisation: A Case Study on the Evolution of UN Specialized Agencies*, Dordrecht, 1989; SAULLE, *Istituti specialzzati delle Nazioni Unite*, in *Enciclopedia giuridica Treccani*, vol. XVII, 1989.

69. *Political de-colonization and economic de-colonization. Co-operation for "sustainable" development.*

As is stated in Article 1 on the purposes and principles of the United Nations and is then specified in Chapters IX and X, which are dedicated to the subject, the United Nations is to promote international co-operation in the economic and social field. This is a field which has assumed considerable importance in the life of the United Nations owing to the great effort that the Organization is making, and which goes under the name of co-operation for development, in its intention to reduce the serious and dramatic inequalities existing among the States. The pressure coming from the General Assembly is very strong, and it is supported, obviously, by the fact that the developing countries which have the most interest in the success of the effort, hold the majority in the Assembly. In other words, the Organization is facing the same thrust and the same ethos which in the fifties underlay the process of de-colonization. However, the obstacles and the delays are much greater now, not only and not so much because of the seriousness and the complexity of the problems to be resolved but because, unlike political de-colonization, with respect to which the Great Powers did not have a united front, the process of economic de-colonization has as a backdrop a clear contrast between the interests of the rich countries and those of the poor countries. In a situation of this kind, the negative aspect represented by the lack of effective powers of the Organization toward the Member States cannot be under-estimated. And, unfortunately, it cannot be said that as of today, United Nations action has had great success.

Within the United Nations, the problems of development were first considered in an isolated form, that is, mainly in their economic aspects. Toward the middle of the 80's, under pressure from the Western World, they were connected to the problem of respect for human rights. From the beginning of the 90's, they have been intertwined with ecological problems, an intertwining which is leading to the notion, still with uncertain boundaries, of "sustainable development", that is to say, of a development compatible with the preservation of the environment and of resources for present and future generations.

70. *The organs charged with economic co-operation.*

Under Article 60 of the Charter, the principal organs dealing with economic co-operation are the General Assembly and, under its authority, the Economic and Social Council. As it has already be seen (§ 38) these two organs head a whole set of subsidiary organs appointed by them. There is a hierarchy of all such organs with the Assembly at the top. The activity of the Assembly, the Economic and Social Council, and the dependent organs is coordinated with the specialized agencies, autonomous international organizations also functioning in the field of economic co-operation (see § 73). Worth mentioning are also the functions of the Secretariat, functions to which the conclusions we made with regard to the maintenance of the peace (see § 65) are applicable *mutatis mutandis.*

71. *Normative functions.*

United Nations action for economic co-operation and development has consisted mainly in the preparation of a series of *rules* which the Organization believes should regulate relationships between the States in this sector. These rules, which are often drawn up after in-depth studies (carried out on the basis of Articles 13 and 62, para. 1, of the Charter) are contained in solemn *Declarations of Principles* of the General Assembly, in *recommen-dations* addressed to the States by the General Assembly or by the Economic and Social Council (as foreseen in Articles 10, 13, and 62) or by their re-spective subsidiary organs, or in *draft conventions* to be submitted for ratifi-cation by the Member States (see Article 62, para. 3). All these rules, from the viewpoint of the Charter, do not have binding force. Neither the Assembly nor the Economic and Social Council, and, consequently, not even their subsidiary organs, have binding powers. Also the declarations of principles cannot be otherwise defined, again from the viewpoint of the Charter, except as the expression of the power of the Assembly to recommend (see § 94). Moreover, at least for the time being, no unwritten customary rules have emerged which strengthen the organs' powers in this field (unlike what it has happened in the field of de-colonization: see § 79). A different problem, which has not to be dealt with here, consists in asking whether some of the rules drawn up by the United Nations have been transformed into legally binding norms through the instruments of classic international law, that is, custom and agreement. Such transformation, as far as draft conventions are concerned, is obviously envisaged by the Charter and takes place when the Member States ratify them.

The fact that normative acts of the United Nations in the field of economic co-operation do not have legally binding force must not be interpreted as discounting their value and their usefulness. They have (just as Assembly declarations and recommendations had at the time of de-colonization) the force that is conferred on them by the great ideals that they pursue, by the tenacity with which these ideals are pursued, and by the correspondence that such ideals find in the collective conscience.

The general (non-binding) rules of economic co-operation, and, in particular, of co-operation for development, are first of all contained in several "historical" and a little old fashioned resolutions of the General Assembly. Among them, there are the Declaration and the Program of Action on the Establishment of a New International Economic Order (res. no. 3201 and no. 3202 S-VI of May 1, 1974) and the Charter of Economic Rights and Duties of States (res. 3281-XXIX of December 12, 1974). The Declaration, the Program and the Charter, on the one hand, have a synoptic character in that they reproduce certain rules, now considered cornerstones in the normative role of the Assembly, of previous declarations and resolutions (as, for example, res. no. 1803-XVII of 1962 on permanent sovereignty over natural resources, no. 2625-XXV of 1970 on friendly relations and co-operation between States, no. 2626-XXV of 1970 on international strategy for development, and no. 2749-XXV, again of 1970, on the sea-bed and the ocean floor, and the subsoil thereof, beyond the limits of national jurisdiction). On the other hand, they outline their own "philosophy" regarding the growth of the developing countries. This, essentially, is the idea that such growth should not only consist of assistance provided by individual States or groups of States (with the related political and economic conditioning, and sought under the form of request for aid) but should rather develop through a general mobilization of the community of States. Within this mobilization the countries with developing economies should be able to assert their negotiating power which derives from their own particular positions and especially from their full, inviolable and permanent sovereignty over their own resources. In particular, the Declaration, the Program and the Charter, having restated such permanent sovereignty, recognize *inter alia*: the right of every State to adopt the economic and social system which it believes to be the most adequate for its needs; the right to nationalize foreign property; the right to regulate the activity of multinational companies within its territorial limits and to see that such activity is supervised and regulated at the international level; the right to form associations of producing States of primary commodities; the right to participate in the exploitation of the seabed and ocean floor, and the subsoil thereof, beyond national jurisdiction, through the mechanisms that ensure an equal distribution of the relative benefits, taking into account the interests and needs of the developing countries. A similar philosophy can be seen in the rules which, again under the above-mentioned acts, are to regulate international trade and the agreements on economic co-operation Examples are those which advocate negotiation which is free from any political or military conditioning, carried out under the supervision of the international community; the necessity of a correct and fair balance between the prices of the products imported and exported by developing countries; the granting to these countries, in trade agreements, of *preferential* rather than *reciprocal* treatment, as well as any other advantage suitable to guarantee an increase in their monetary reserves, the diversification of their exports, the acceleration of the growth rate of their trade, the betterment of the conditions for access to markets, the stability and the remunerativity of the prices for goods; the conclusion of long-term multilateral commodity agreements; the access of developing countries to scientific and technology reports and to the transfer of technologies, and so on. All this is, as expressly stated in the Charter of Economic Rights and Duties of States (Preamble (m)), for reaching "international social justice".

Despite the fact that the developed countries have never stopped raising reservations regarding the content of many of the rules contained in the three above mentioned acts, such rules have continued to be an important reference point for the UN organs, particularly for the General Assembly. Under pressure from the developed countries, and in a certain sense as a condition for the participation of these countries in co-operation for development, these rules have been integrated, or rather, inserted into a broader framework of social needs and actions, in which economic development, social development and environmental protection are considered as interdependent. This integration can be seen, in particular, in several subsequent acts of the General Assembly, such as the Declaration on the right to development (res. no. 41/128 of December 4, 1986), the

Declaration of international economic co-operation and the re-launching of economic growth and development (res. S-18/3 of May 1, 1990), the Rio Declaration on environment and development of June 14, 1992 (Declaration issued, together with the Agenda 21, a plan of action in the same subject, by the UN Conference on the Environment and Development, and adopted by the General Assembly with res. no. 47/190 of December 22, 1992) and the Declaration on the occasion of the 50th anniversary of the United Nations (res. no. 50/6 of October 24, 1995). Without prejudice to the idea that the growth of the developing countries is first of all linked to international co-operation, the protection of human rights as an element in every national plan for development is emphasized by res. 41/128. It is mainly the 1992 Rio Declaration that is concerned with the environment, besides some references in the Declaration S-18/3. The Rio Declaration reconciles the positions of the developing countries, concerned with their growth, and the developed countries, determined to consider protection of the environment as the priority. Principle 3 of the Declaration states that the right to development must be fulfilled "so as to equitably meet developmental and environmental needs of present and future generations" (the so-called sustainable development); in turn, principle 4 states that "environmental protection shall constitute an integral part of the development process and cannot be considered in isolation from it". In any case, responsibility for the conservation, protection and restoration of the environment, a responsibility that is commensurate to the "contribution" to degradation, should mainly be up to the developed countries (principles 7). Finally, a restatement of the principles governing economic development, social development and environmental protection is contained in the Declaration on the 50th anniversary: democracy, respect for human rights, including the right to development, the participation of all countries in the process of globalization and its benefits, avoidance of the marginalization of least developed countries from this process, promotion of appropriate demographic policies, co-operation on reducing natural disasters, etc., are reaffirmed by this Declaration.

In more recent times, the General Assembly, while reaffirming the above mentioned goals, has focused its normative function on the impact of globalization on developing countries, the strength of partnership with the private sector and with civil society organizations in order to involve them in the development process and the eradication of poverty, the latter being a *conditio sine qua non* for the promotion of respect for human rights. Detailed rules on these issues are contained, *inter alia*, in the Millennium Declaration (res. no. 55/2 of September 8, 2000), in res. no. 55/102 of December 4, 2000 on globalization and its impact on the full enjoyment of all human rights, in res. no. 56/76 of December 11, 2001 on global partnership, in the

Johannesburg Declaration on sustainable development (issued from the World Summit on sustainable development, held in South Africa from August 26 to September 4 2002 and endorsed by res. no. 57/253 of December 20, 2002), in the Monterrey Consensus of the International Conference on Financing for Development, held in Mexico from March 18 to 22, and referred to in various resolutions of General Assembly, in res. no. 57/250 of December 20, 2002, which establishes that the "High Level Dialogue", on strengthening international cooperation for development through partnership, must be held biennially and have as its overall theme "The Monterrey Consensus: status of implementation and tasks ahead" (a dialogue based on res. no. 57/250 has been held on October 2003).

Complementary to all the rules contained in the just indicated acts are the ten-year programs that the General Assembly has adopted from 1960 and which indicate the aims and objectives to be reached in co-operation for development. Unfortunately, these programs can be seen as indicative not only for what they propose for the future but also because they usually record the failures of the efforts made to reach the objectives set for the previous ten years. The most recent of them is the Programme of Action for the Least Developed Countries (res. no. 55/279 of July 12, 2001).

In addition to the Assembly (and to a series of subsidiary organs), the United Nations Conference on Trade and Development (UNCTAD) has played an important role in the performance of normative functions. The Conference, which met for the first time in Geneva in 1964, was transformed in the same year by the Assembly, with res. no. 1995-XIX, into a permanent (subsidiary) organ. In fact, it is an organization within the Organization, since its structure is quite similar to that of the specialized agencies (see § 73), and it consists not only of the actual Conference, in which all the UN Member States are represented, and which meets every three or four years, but also of a Council with a limited membership, of various Commissions, and of a Secretariat. UNCTAD's purpose is to promote international trade in the framework of the policy for development of developing countries, preparing studies, setting the rules that must regulate such trade and interrelated areas such as finance, technology and investments and encouraging negotiation of the relative *multilateral agreements*. Among other things, UNCTAD has led to: the preparation of a general system of preferences in trade exchanges in favor of the developing countries; the conclusion of multilateral agreements on some primary products, such as the agreements on rubber of 1979, on cacao of 1980, the agreement for the establishment of a Common Fund for raw materials of 1980, etc.; the drawing up of a code of conduct of "maritime conferences" (and thus of agreements between navigation companies), then adopted as a multilateral convention in 1974; a decisive contribution to the drawing up of a code on the transfer of technologies, which was then negotiated in a special Conference; and so on. However, more than anything, UNCTAD is known for an intense activity of providing incentives, both inside and outside the United Nations, concretely dealing with the problems of development. Its 11th Conference which was held in Rio de Janeiro from 13 to 18 June 2004 had as its theme "Enhancing coherence between national development strategies and global economic processes towards economic growth and development".

    The Executive Committee on Economic and Social Affairs (EC-ESA), created by the Secretary-General in 1997, co-ordinates the organs dealing with the normative function in addition to providing the co-ordination of operational functions (see § 72).

    The various resolutions mentioned so far provide only a few examples out of the great mass of studies, declarations and recommendations which, in all areas of international economic and social co-operation have been issued by the Assembly, the Economic and Social Council, and the myriad subsidiary organs and sub-organs of both, as well as from Conferences convened from time to time by the Assembly and in which all the Member States may be represented. For a more detailed overview one only has to glance through one of the repertories of the resolutions of recent Assembly sessions. Let us only observe here that, notwithstanding this mass of (non-binding) rules, the gap between the rich and those who live under the minimum standard of livelihood is still enormous. Fewer rules and more action is perhaps what is needed!

72. *Operational functions.*

    Within the framework of co-operation for development, there has been an increasing number of initiatives aimed at having the United Nations intervene solving specific social and economic problems, under the form of *deliberation and implementation of programs of technical assistance and other kinds of aid* to developing countries. Also for these operational functions, the Assembly and the Economic and Social Council have gradually created innumerable organs and relative offices. Among the oldest organs and programs are UNICEF (United Nations International Children's Emergency Fund), established in 1946 and the Ordinary Program for Technical Assistance entrusted to the Secretary-General by res. no. 200-III of December 4, 1948. A series of funds and programs in the most diverse areas has been established later on: for instance, the United Nations Volunteers Program (UNV), established in 1971, the UN Environment Program (UNEP), begun in 1972, the UN Fund for Population Activities (UNFPA), also of

1972, the Revolving Fund for Natural Resources Exploration, of 1973, the Special Fund for Land-Locked Developing countries, of 1976, the UN Development Fund for Women (UNIFEM), established in 1976, the UN-Habitat, established in 1978, the UN International Drug Control Program (UNDCP). The United Nations Development Program (UNDP) deserves special mention. UNDP, in which two previous programs (the Expanded Program of Technical Assistance, EPTA, of 1949, and the Special Fund, of 1958) have merged, was created, as a subsidiary organ of the General Assembly, by res. no. 2029-XX of November 22, 1965. With regard to operational functions, UNDP is, in a certain sense, what UNCTAD is for normative functions (see § 72), that is, the key organ of the United Nations for promotion of co-operation for development. Its powers, initially set out in general terms (the constitutive resolution speaks of assistance to developing States), were specified by res. no. 688-XXV of December 11, 1970, which introduced a system of planning for individual countries. The task of UNDP is to approve national programs presented by the individual States, to allocate the relative funds, and to supervise the realization of the projects in the program. Such realization is usually entrusted to other agencies, specifically other international organizations, mainly the Specialized Agencies (whose co-operation is regulated by special agreements: see § 73), or other UN bodies working in the aid sector, such as UNICEF, the various special funds, and so on. From the point of view of structure, UNDP, like UNCTAD, is a kind of organization within the Organization. It enjoys a certain autonomy and is composed of a Governing Council (in which 48 UN Member States take part, 27 chosen from developing countries and 21 from the industrialized countries) with decision-making functions, of a Committee (in which there are represented the international organizations and the UN organs which cooperate with UNDP) with consultative functions, and of a Administrator with executive functions. However its formal dependence on the General Assembly, and hence its nature as a subsidiary organ of the Assembly, cannot doubted.

Worth of mention is also the Commission on Sustainable Development (CSD) which was established in 1992 to ensure effective follow-up of the above mentioned UN Conference on Environment and Development, to monitor and report on the implementation of the agreements concluded on the subject at the local, national, regional and international levels.

In 1997 the Secretary-General created the UN Development Group (UNDG) to improve the effectiveness of the UN action for development. The UNDG brings together the operational institutions working on development and is chaired by the Administrator of UNDP. At the same time, the already cited Executive Committee on Economic and Social Affairs EC-ESA, also created by the Secretary-General (see § 71), coordinates the work not only of normative but also of operational agencies.

Unquestionably, the operational activities, particularly activities of technical assistance, can come within the UN's sphere of competence as set by the Charter. The pertinent, even if the only (and with a rather exceptional nature in the context of the Charter), provision on the subject is Article 66, para. 2, under which the Economic and Social Council "may, with the approval of the General Assembly *perform services* at the request of the Members of the United Nations and at the request of specialized agencies". The fact that the services, as has usually occurred up to now, are performed not by the Council but by organs dependent on the Assembly does not seem to give rise to difficulties from a legal viewpoint. The quasi-hierarchical relationship linking the Council to the Assembly (see § 38) may well explain the substitution of the former by the latter without resorting to the view (see MARCHISIO, *La cooperazione*, cit., p. 58 ff. and 152 ff.) of a customary extension of Assembly powers.

However, the most relevant practical problem raised by the operational activities for development is that of *obtaining the funds* necessary for carrying them out. In our view, one must reject the idea that provision of funding can be defined as "Organization expenses" and therefore be *obligatorily* apportioned among the Member States by the two-thirds majority of the Assembly under Article 17 of the Charter (see § 86). In fact, Article 66, para. 2, in using a very vague and all-encompassing formulation ("...perform services...") and in concerning assistance agreed upon on a case-by-case basis ("...services... at the request of the members of the United Nations and at the request of specialized agencies"), means that each assistance program has its own autonomous source of financing and thus requires an *ad hoc* provision of funds. Practice is in conformity with this when we consider that all the Funds, Programs, etc., that have been established up to now have functioned on the *voluntary* contributions of the States, with the exception of the above-mentioned Ordinary Program for Technical Assistance, created in 1948 and still functioning, whose expenses are entered in the ordinary UN budget and obligatorily apportioned according to Article 17; that this Program has always had a very modest importance, being limited to the setting up of fellowships, of research centers, and of missions of experts; that in spite of its entry in the ordinary budget, for very many years, it gave rise to reservations and protests of principle on the part of the group of Socialist countries; that the rule of voluntary contribution has often been reiterated by the capital-holding countries (for example, by the United States), that is, by the countries on which the financing ultimately depends; and that, therefore, the entering of small amounts intended for aid activities in the ordinary budget, far from being evidence of a rule in force, can only rest on the tolerance and the acquiescence of the Member States. It is also clear that if the principle was affirmed in practice that the Member States had an *obligation* to contribute to the operational activities for development through the ordinary budget, all the growth problems of the developing countries, that is, of the countries that hold the majority in the Assembly necessary for... approving the budget, could be resolved at once!

On the reservations of the USSR and the other Socialist countries of Eastern Europe at the time of the establishment of the Ordinary Program for Technical Assistance, see GAOR, 3rd sess., Pl. meet., 170th meet., p. 700s. For later reservations, again of the USSR, see GAOR, 25th sess., 1970, Pl. meet., 1933rd meet., no. 19 f.; 28th sess., 1973, doc. A/PV 2206; 30th sess., 1975, doc. A/PV 2444; 31st sess., 1976, Pl. meet., 107th meet., no. 104 f. For the positions taken by the capital-holding countries in favor of the voluntary nature of contributions, see, for example, GAOR, 26th sess., 1971, Pl. meet., 2031st. meet., no. 20 (USA); 28th sess., 1973, doc. A/PV 2206 (France).

Anyone who cares about the future of the developing countries can only hope for a massive increase in the number of operational activities of the United Nations. In fact, if technical assistance and aid come from a universal organization such as the United Nations, if, in other words, the flow of capital coming from wealthy countries and intended for poor countries is "filtered" by such an Organization, the assistance becomes neutral in that it is freed from political, or even military, conditioning. Unfortunately, precisely owing to these characteristics, the operational activities of the United Nations represent only a modest fraction of the over-all volume of international assistance, most of which is still covered by *direct* aid and by contributions granted on a bilateral or multilateral scale. In other words, the multiplication, inexplicable under various aspects, of United Nations organs intended for operational functions has unfortunately not been matched, owing to the lack of funds, by real and effective action for development. Since this is the present situation, it is impossible to agree with those observers who hold that the United Nations is being transformed into a large operational agency. In fact, the Organization is and remains, as it was conceived of at San Francisco, an entity whose powers are predominantly normative, an entity intended not to act, but to dictate rules to the States.

73. *Relations with Specialized Agencies.*

There are many international organizations that operate in the economic and social field apart from the United Nations. They are both universal and regional organizations. The most important of the universal organizations are called the Specialized Agencies of the United Nations, as they are related to the United Nations and to a certain degree come under its power of coordination and supervision. They are, however, autonomous organizations, created by agreements completely separate from the Charter, and their members only generally speaking are also UN members. Their functions are more or less similar to those of the UN organs in that they operate for purposes of social and economic co-operation. They issue and prepare normative acts, mainly *recommendations* and multilateral *draft conventions* (very rarely *binding decisions* for the Member States), or they carry out operational tasks in the field of assistance and international aid. With few exceptions, their structure consists of a plenary organ in which all the Member States are represented, of a Council with a more restricted membership, and a Secretariat. For some specialized agencies concerned with international monetary problems (such as the International Monetary Fund and the International Bank for Reconstruction and Development), agencies where decision-making power, through the weighed-vote system, is firmly in the hands of the developed countries, the demand for greater "democratization", coming from the developing countries, has up to now not been answered.

Existing specialized agencies: FAO (Food and Agriculture Organization) which absorbed the activities and property of the old International Institute of Agriculture created in 1905; ILO (International Labor Organization), already existing at the time of the League of Nations, whose plenary organ has the peculiarity of consisting not only of government delegates but also of representatives from employers and workers, and which has been responsible for an important contribution to job protection through the preparation of multilateral agreements on the subject; UNESCO (United Nations Educational, Scientific and Cultural Organization); ICAO (International Civil Aviation Organization); WHO (World Health Organization); IMO (International Maritime Organization); ITU (International Telecommunication Union); WMO (World Meteorological Organization); UPU (Universal Postal Union); IMF (International Monetary Fund), whose plenary organ consists of the Board of Governors in which each Member State is represented by the Governor of its own central bank or by a substitute; IBRD (International Bank for Reconstruction and Development) with a structure similar to that of the IMF; IFC (International Finance Corporation); IDA (International Development Association); WIPO (World Intellectual Property Organization); IFAD (International Fund for Agricultural Development); United Nations Industrial Development Organization, UNIDO, formerly a subsidiary organ of the UN General Assembly and transformed into a specialized agency in a 1979 treaty.

Worthy of mention is also IAEA (International Atomic Energy Agency), the Organization whose purpose is to promote the development and enlarging of peaceful uses of atomic energy. IAEA does not qualify as a specialized agency, in that, because of the matter it is concerned with, it has ties with both the Assembly and the Security Council, and not, as the agencies, with the Assembly and the Economic and Social Council. However, it has a liaison agreement with the United Nations, concluded in 1957, which puts it in a condition not very different from that of the Agencies.

The relationship between each specialized Agency and the United Nations stems from an agreement which is entered into by the two organizations (see Article 57 of the Charter) and which is negotiated by the Social and Economic Council and approved by the General Assembly. Up to now the content of each liaison agreement linking the two organizations has usually conformed to a model set in 1946 when agreements were concluded by the UN with ILO, UNESCO and FAO. This model provides for an exchange of representatives, observers, documents, resort to consultation if necessary, coordination of their respective technical services, the commitment of the specialized agency to at least consider UN recommendations, and so on. However, the importance of the liaison agreement and of the related attribution of the qualification of a specialized Agency mainly lies in the resulting applicability of the Charter rules regarding the agencies. These provisions subject them, within certain limits, to the UN's power of coordination and supervision. Among these provisions, there are Article 58 which (together with Article 60) qualifies the General Assembly and the Economic and Social Council to make recommendations "for the coordination of the policies and activities of the specialized agencies" (in the same sense, cf. also Article 62, para. 1, and Article 63, para. 2); Article 64, which gives the Council the right to request "regular reports" from the Agencies; and Article 17, para. 3, under which the Assembly "shall examine the administrative budgets of such specialized agencies with a view to making recommendations to the agencies concerned".

The relations between the United Nations and the Agencies have become more intense in the framework of co-operation for development, especially after the setting up of UNDP. As we have seen, the Agencies are represented in an organ of the Program, the Consulting Committee, and can carry out projects, within the framework of the planning for a specific country, that have been commissioned by the Program itself (see § 73). This is a matter of co-operation on an equal basis which is grounded in agreements and not in relationships of subordination. Since (with the exception of the 1974 UN-WIPO agreement), the above-mentioned liaison agreements are not recent and they do not contain precise provisions on the operational co-operation and in particular on the coordination of technical assistance activities, co-operation and coordination can be found in special agreements between UNDP and the individual Agencies. These agreements were already concluded in the 60's by the Special Fund, an entity established in 1958 and then merged into UNDP.

The fact that the relations between the UN and the Agencies are on an equal basis and that there is not a dependent relationship is the only important characteristic that makes the Agencies different from entities such as UNCTAD, UNICEF, etc., which are subsidiary organs of the Assembly. The difference, however, is becoming less and less important owing to the

UN's tendency to exercise more control over the Agencies. This tendency is inevitable in that it is based on objective needs of co-ordination and on the elimination of duplication and waste.

The nature of the liaison agreements between the United Nations and the Agencies has given rise to debates in legal doctrine. Some authors, the present writer among them, have raised doubts about the possibility and the usefulness of defining such conventions as true international legal agreements, producing rights and obligations for the parties and revealing their international legal personality. We think that they are rather a set of rules which, as intended by the Charter and the constitutive treaties of the Specialized Agencies, have become an integral part of both and, specifically, can be included among the provisions which regulate the functions of the respective organs. Therefore, their violation by the General Assembly or by the Economic and Social Council or by an organ of the Specialized Agency should not be seen in the same way as the non-fulfillment of treaty obligations but as the cause of the illegality of the resolutions of one of these organs. *Mutatis mutandis*, the same considerations are to be made concerning the UNDP-Agencies liaison agreements.

Section VII

THE PROTECTION OF HUMAN RIGHTS

BIBLIOGRAPHY: LAUTERPACHT, *The Universal Declaration of Human Rights*, in *BYB*, 1948, p. 354 ff.; BRUNET, *La garantie internationale des droit del'homme dans le cadre des Nations Unies*, Paris, 1949; GUGGENHEIM, *Die völkerrechtliche Schutz der Menschenrechte*, in *Friedenswarte*, 1949, p. 177 ff.; LAUTERPACHT, *International Law and Human Rights*, London, 1950; SPERDUTI, *La Dichiarazione universale dei diritti dell'uomo*, in *CI*, 1950, p. 216 ff.; DROST, *Human Rights as Legal Rights*, Leiden, 1951; ROBINSON, *The Universal Declaration on Human Rights; its Origin Significance and Interpretation*, New York 1958; MOSKOWITZ, *Human Rights and World Order*, London, 1959; GANJI, *International Protection of Human Rights*, Genève, 1962; HALASZ, *Socialist Concept of Human Rights*, Budapest, 1966; EICHELBERGER, *The UN and Human Rights*, New York, 1968; MOSKOWITZ, *The Politics and Dynamics of Human Rights*, New York, 1968; ROBERTSON, *Human Rights in the World*, Manchester, 1972; CASSESE, *The New UN Procedure for Handling Gross Violations of Human Rights*, in *CI*, 1975, p. 49 ff.; SCHREIBER, *La pratique récente des Nations Unies dans le domaine de la protection des droit de l'homme*, in *RC*, 1975, II, p. 297 ff.; MARIE, *La Commission de droit de l'homme de l'ONU*, Paris, 1975; ID., *La situation des droits de l'homme au Chili: enquête de la Commission des droits de l'homme des Nations Unies*, in *AF*, 1976, p. 305 ff.; MEISSNER, *Die Menschenrechtsbeschwerde vor der Vereinten Nationen*, Baden-Baden, 1976; ALAIMO, *L'Italia e le convenzioni internazionali in materia di diritti dell'uomo*, in *RDI*, 1976, p. 291 ff.; TENEKIDES, *L'action des Nations Unies contre la discrimination raciale*, in *RC*, 1980, III, p. 269 ff.; GAJA, *I patti internazionali sui diritti economici, sociali e culturali e sui diritti civili e politici*, in VITTA and GREMENTIERI, *Codice degli atti internazionali sui diritti dell'uomo*, Milan, 1981, p. 47 ff.; EL-SHEIKH, *UN and Violations of Human Rights*, in *REgDI*, 1980, p. 133 ff.; FISCHER, *Reporting under the Covenant on Civil and Political Rights: The First Five Years of the Human Rights Committee*, in *AJ*, 1982, p. 142 ff.; HUMPHREY, *Human Rights and the United Nations: A Great Adventure*, Dobbs Ferry, 1984; VIJAPUR, *The UN Mechanisms for the Promotion and Implementation of Human Rights*, in *IJIL*, 1985, p. 576 ff.; MERON, *Human Rights Law-Making in the UN: A Critique of Instruments and Process*, Oxford, 1986; CANÇADO TRINDADE, *Co-Existence and Co-Ordination of Mechanisms of International Protection of Human Rights*, in *RC*, 1987, II, p. 9 ff.; KAMMINGA, *The Thematic Procedures of the UN Commission on Human Rights*, in *NILR*, 1987, p. 299 ff.; DORMENVAL, *Procédures onusiennes de mise en oeuvre des droits de l'homme: limites ou défauts?*, Paris, 1991; MCGOLDRICK, *The Human Rights Committee: Its Role in the Development of the International Covenant on Civil and Political Rights*, Oxford, 1991; NOWAK, *Country-Oriented Human Rights Protection by the UN Commission on Human Rights and its Sub-Commission*, in *Netherland Yearbook of International Law*, 1991, p. 39 ff.; ALSTON (ed.), *The United Nations and Human Rights: A Critical Appraisal*, Oxford, 1992, GHERARI, *Le Comité des Droits économiques, sociaux et culturels*, in *RGDIP*, 1992, p. 75 ff.; PASTOR RIDRUEJO, *Les procédures publiques spéciales de la Commission des droits de l'homme des Nations Unies*, in *RC*, vol. 228, 1991-III, p. 183 ff.; KENNY, *Formal and Informal Innovations in the United Nations Protection of Human Rights: The Special Rapporteur on the Former Yugoslavia*, in *ZöRV*, 1995, p. 19 ff.; ALSTON and CRAWFORD (eds.), *The Future of Human Rights Treaty monitoring*, Cambridge,2000, pp. 1-198; BAYEFSKY (ed.), *The UN Human Rights Treaty System in the 21th Century*, The Hague, 2000; ID., *The UN Human Rights Treaty System. Universality at the Crossroads*, New York, 2001; ID., *How to Complain in the UN Human Rights Treaty System*, NNew York, 2002; RAMCHARAN, *The UN High Commissioner for Human Rights*, The Hague, 2002; YOUNG, *The Law and Process of the UN HolmströHuman Rights Committee*, The Hague, 2003 .

74. *General aspects of United Nations action.*

Another purpose of the United Nations is that of "promoting and encouraging respect for human rights and for fundamental freedoms for all without distinction as to race, sex, language or religion" (Article 1 of the Charter). The General Assembly and, under its direction, the Economic and Social Council, are competent on the matter of the protection of human rights, just as they are on economic co-operation (Chapters IX and X of the Charter). Both these organs have in turn created a series of subsidiary organs, the most important being the Commission on Human Rights which constitutes one of the so-called technical or functional Commissions of the Council (see § 38).

The competence of the General Assembly, of the Economic and Social Council, of the Commission on Human Rights and of other subsidiary organs is exercised through the issuance of *normative* acts that are *not binding*, such as recommendations, declarations of principle, and multilateral draft conventions. By contrast, there are some organs which are entrusted with *operative* functions. The most important one is the UNHCR (UN High Commissioner for Refugees) which was created by the General Assembly in 1950. Since then it has helped about 50 million people to restart their lives, giving a fabulous contribution to one of the most dramatic problems of the world to-day. Of a special mention is also the action of the High Commissioner for Human Rights, an independent office from the Secretary-General. The High Commissioner was established by the General Assembly in 1993. The main task of the High Commissioner is to monitor, and collect information on, violations of human rights and refer this information to the appropriate UN organs

As in the field of co-operation for development, so to in the subject of human rights, the Organization's efforts focus on creating equal standard of living in the world, on protecting the weakest, whether they are individuals or entire groups, and on awakening recalcitrant or reactionary governments. The protection of human dignity, in the very broad sense that we saw in discussing domestic jurisdiction (see 45 III), constitutes one of the fundamental values of today's international society. The resolutions of a general nature which pursue this value are very numerous.

Human rights are felt to affect the very growth of the developing countries, as is stated in various and already cited General Assembly Declarations and recommendations (see § 72).

The promotion of democracy and democratic institutions is also considered as an important aspect of human rights protection. We prefer to treat it in the framework of self-determination of peoples (see § 79).

75. *Action regarding individual countries.*

As has been seen in discussing domestic jurisdiction, there is no longer any limit to UN action regarding individual countries. The General Assembly, the Economic and Social Council. Their subsidiary organs and other UN bodies may therefore address any kind of resolution to them.

Of course, the attention of the Organization is more attracted by the gross violations committed by a given country, i. e. by most inhuman practices, such as apartheid, torture, cruel and degrading punishment, and so forth, against individuals or against categories of individuals, and by *generalized* violations of other rights. On the other hand, these gross violations of human rights, are increasingly dealt with by de Security Council as a threat to international peace and security claiming for action under Chapter VII (see § 55 *bis*).

Res. no. 1235-XLII of June 6, 1967 and no.1503-XLVIII of May 27, 1970 of the Economic and Social Council are still fundamental with regard to gross violations. These resolutions authorized the Sub-Commission on Prevention of Discrimination and Protection of Minorities (a subsidiary organ of the Commission on Human Rights) to appoint working groups and through them to examine communications received by the Secretary-General on human rights, with a view to singling out those which reliably reveal the existence of gross violations. The Sub-commission makes reports to the Commission on Human Rights which may conduct an in-depth investigation of the matter brought to its attention, or, also, but with the consent of the accused State, appoint an *ad hoc* investigating Committee, and in turn make or propose recommendations to the Economic and Social Council. In this way a procedure is begun which may stop at the Commission or at the Council but may also result in General Assembly resolutions.

The procedures laid down by the above mentioned resolutions has been used a number of times and there have been various resolutions adopted by the Commission on Human Rights to denounce gross violations and to call upon the States responsible to halt them. The Commission has been concerned, for example, with the violation of human rights in South Africa, in the Arab territories occupied by Israel, in Equatorial Guinea, in Chile, in Cambodia, in Bolivia, in El Salvador, in Guatemala, in Iran, in the Democratic Republic of Congo, in Sudan, in Sierra Leone, etc. etc. In turn, the General Assembly, which obviously may also proceed independently of the Commission's initiatives, periodically addresses recommendations to most of the States that do not have a good human rights record.

In many resolutions, the Commission or the Assembly has requested the discontinuance not only of cruel and degrading treatment but also of practices that deny to the population the enjoyment of civil and political or economic, social and cultural rights. These practices range from the establishment of concentration camps to armed repression and mass arrests, or to forced labor and the "enforced disappearance" of members of the opposition, to restriction on freedom of expression, information, association and so on, to the refusal to allow elections with the free participation of all the political forces, and even to the refusal to carry out agricultural reforms which would remove the limits to the exercise of economic and social rights.

In recent years, the role of the above mentioned High Commissioner for Human Rights, and its function of enhancing respect for human rights in individual countries, has become very important. In the case of Rwanda, for example, the High Commissioner has made valuable contributions towards the improvement of the situation in the country, after the genocide which occurred there.

Other Committees which have been established by some of the Conventions listed in the following paragraph also monitor the respect for human rights. Among them are: the Committee on the Elimination of Racial

Discrimination, the Committee on the Elimination of Discrimination against Women. the Committee against Torture and the Committee on the Rights of the Child. Normally these Committees receive reports from the Contracting States and, in turn, submit reports to the General Assembly, directly or through the Economic and Social Council, with suggestions about recommendations to be addressed to the interested State. Following special consent given by a contracting State, communications from individuals or groups of individuals can also be received by some of them (see § 77).

76. *Resolutions of a general nature.*

Among the resolutions worth of mention that are not addressed to individual States but to the States in general, and that have more than others made a significant contribution to the development of the subject, are, first, the numerous declarations of principle adopted by the Assembly, from the well-known Universal Declaration on Human Rights (res. no. 217-III of December 10, 1948) to those concerning specific sectors such as the Declaration on the Rights of the Child (res. no. 1386-XIV of November 20, 1959), on racial discrimination (res. no. 1904-XVIII of November 20, 1963), on discrimination against women (res. no. 2263-XXII of November 11, 1967), on religious intolerance (res. no. 36/55 of November 25, 1981), and, more recently, on the treatment of prisoners (res. no. 45/111 of December 14, 1990), on the protection of juveniles deprived of their liberty (res. no. 45/113 of December 14, 1990); on the protection of persons against forced disappearances (res. no. 47/133 of December 18, 1992), and so on. These are acts that do not have a binding nature (aside from certain limited legal effects that they produce: see § 94) but that have great moral force.

Then, there are various multilateral draft conventions, also adopted by the General Assembly and open for ratification by the Member States, in particular: the International Covenant on Civil and Political Rights and the one on Economic, Social and Cultural Rights (approved with Assembly res. no. 2200-XXI of December 16, 1966), which entered into force in 1976 after reaching the minimum required number of ratifications and which constitute, together with the Universal Declaration on Human Rights, the most important and fundamental standard that has been set by the international community regarding human rights; the Convention on the Elimination of All Forms of Racial Discrimination, adopted in 1965 and entered into force in 1969; the Convention the Convention on the Elimination of All Forms of Discrimination Against Women, adopted in 1979 and entered into force in 1981; the Convention Against Torture and Other Cruel, Inhuman or Degrading Treatment or Punishment, adopted in 1984 and entered into force in 1987; the Convention on the Rights of the Child, adopted in 1989 and entered into force in 1990.

Worth of mention is also the Vienna Declaration on human rights of June 25, 1993 which, although not adopted by the General Assembly but by a special Conference of States convoked by the General Assembly, summarises the contents of the previous Assembly declarations.

77. *The Human Rights Covenants and the Human Rights Committee.*

It is outside the scope of this study to deal with problems regarding the interpretation of the two Covenants on Civil and Political Rights and on Economic, Social and Cultural Rights of 1966 (as well as of the other Conventions mentioned in the preceding section), their relationships with other international agreements (for example, the European Convention on Human Rights), and the constitutional and legislative mechanisms provided for their implementation in the legal systems of the contracting States. These problems would be better dealt with in a work on international law. There is no doubt, however, that the two Covenants, although endowed with an autonomous life, are closely linked to the United Nations system, especially as far as the very soft international mechanisms for guaranteeing their observance are concerned. For this reason, they need to be treated briefly.

Both Covenants have been ratified by a large number of countries belonging to a variety of geo-political areas, from the Western countries to the States of Eastern Europe, from the Arab countries, to the States of Africa, Asia and Latin America. Under the two Covenants, the rights which the States are obliged to recognize as belonging to all individuals within their jurisdiction, without distinction as to sex, race, religion, political opinion, etc. (cf. Article 2, para. 2, and Article 3 of the Covenant on Economic Rights and Article 2, para. 1 and Article 3 of the Covenant on Civil and Political Rights) are very broad and very detailed. Among the economic rights, there are the rights to work, to fair wages, to social security and to other forms of social assistance, to form trade unions, and to strike. With regard to civil and political rights, the usual catalogue of individual freedoms is repeated and, under many respects, widened and further specified in a way as to include personal liberty, freedom of thought, conscience and religion, and association.

The two Covenants have also been adhered to by States which notoriously do not have a record of compliance with, or consideration for, such a broad notion of human dignity. There is a suspicion that many countries have adhered for merely window-dressing purposes, without seriously intending to fulfill the relevant obligations.

The *international* machinery of supervision provided by the Covenants is not very strong and this is another fact which... explains the high number of adhesions. The Covenant on Civil and Political Rights created a Human Rights Committee (Article 28 ff.) which began functioning in 1977 and consists of 18 members, elected, in their personal capacity, by the contracting States for a four-year period. The Committee, however, may consider claims presented *against* a contracting State by other States or by individuals only if the accused State has, for inter-State claims, declared that it has accepted the competence of the Committee on the matter (Article 41), or, for individual claims, has ratified an *ad hoc* optional protocol. Otherwise, the competence of the Committee is to receive reports from the States on the implementation of the Covenants in their respective territories, to study them and to transmit to the States parties and to the Economic and Social Council "such general comments as it may consider appropriate" (Article 40, para. 4).

Even if the acts of the Committee do not have much value from a legal point of view since they do not have binding nature, the contribution being made by the Committee to the building of a body of principles and rules applicable to individual claims is an important one. This is particularly true with regard to the principles on admissibility of communications, those on *locus standi*, on the prior exhaustion of local remedies, on the simultaneous pendency of other suits before international bodies, and so on. For the Committee's activity, cf. the reports that this organ annually presents to the General Assembly (GAOR, Suppl. no. 40).

Some of the already cited Committees set up by other conventions on human rights (see § 75), like the Committee on the Elimination of Racial Discrimination (art. 14 of the Convention) , the Committee against torture (art. 22 of the Convention) and the Committee on the Elimination of Discrimination against Women have a similar function to that of the Human Rights Committee. In respect of the Committee on the Elimination of Discrimination against Women, the relevant rules are contained in an Optional Protocol to the Convention, which has been elaborated inside the Economic and Social Council and has been opened by the General Assembly for signature and ratification by the States on October 6, 1999.

The Covenant on Economic, Social and Cultural Rights provides that the States send reports on measures adopted to ensure observance in their territories (Article 66 ff.) but it does not establish *ad hoc* organs to do so. The reports are sent to the Economic and Social Council through the Secretary-General, and the Council may in turn transmit them to the Commission on Human Rights "for study and general recommendations" (Article 19). In 1985 the Economic and Social Council created the Committee on Economic, Social and Cultural Rights to assist it in its tasks, as stated by the Covenant.

Section VIII

DE-COLONIZATION AND SELF-DETERMINATION
OF PEOPLES

BIBLIOGRAPHY: VAN LANGENHOVE, *Les territoires non autonomes d'après la Charte des Nations Unies*, Bruxelles, 1952; EAGLETON, *Self-Determination in the UN*, in *AJ*, 1953, p. 592 ff.; WENGLER, *Le droit de libre disposition des peuples comme principe de droit international*, in *Revue Hellenique du droit international et étranger*, 1957; ANDRASSY, *Le droit des peuples à l'autodétermination*, in *Revue de la Politique Internationale*, 1965, p. 7 ff.; STARACE, *La questione dei territori portoghesi d'oltremare dinanzi alle Nazioni Unite*, in *CS*, vol. XII, 1966, p. 477 ff.; VISMARA, *Le Nazioni Unite per i territori dipendenti e per la decolonizzazione*, Padua, 1966; MIAJA DE LA MUELA, *La emancipation de los pueblos coloniales y el derecho internacional*, Madrid, 1968; MARTINE, *Le Comité de decolonisation et le droit international*, in *RGDIP*, 1970, p. 357 ff.; EMERSON, *Self-Determination*, in *AJ*, 1971, p. 459 ff.; MUSTAFA, *The Principle of Self-Determination in International Law*, in *The International Lawyer*, 1971, p. 479 ff.; YASSIN EL-AYOUTY, *The UN and De-colonization: the Role of Afro-Asia*, The Hague, 1971; FINGER, *A New Approach to Colonial Problems at the United Nations*, in *Int. Org.*, 1972, p. 143 ff.; CALOGEROPOULOS-STRATIS, *Le droit des peuples à disposer d'eux-mêmes*, Bruxelles, 1973, p. 105 ff.; SINHA, *Is Self-Determination Passé*, in *Columbia Journal of Transn. Law*, 1973, p. 260 ff.; SUREDA, *The Evolution of the Right of Self-Determination. A Study of UN Practice*, Leiden, 1973; MATHY, *L'autodétermination de petits territoires revendiqués par des états tiers*, in *RBDI*, 1974, p. 167 ff. and 1975, p 129 ff.; TRANGERS, *The Legal Effect of United Nations Action in Support of the PLO and the National Liberation Movements of Africa*, in *IIILJ*, 1976, p. 561 ff.; ENGERS, *From Sacred Trust to Self-Determination*, in *NILR*, 1977, p. 85 ff.; WITKIN, *Transkei: An Analysis of the Pratice of Recognition — Political or Legal?*, in *HILJ*, 1977, p. 605 ff.; POMERANCE, *Self-Determination in Law and Pratice: The New Doctrine in the United Nations*, The Hague, 1982; IOVANE, *Le Falkland/Malvinas autodeterminazione o decolonizzazione*, in *La questione delle Falkland-Malvinas nel diritto internazionale* (edited by N. Ronzitti), Milan, 1984, p. 85 ff.; GUARINO, *Autodeterminazione dei popoli e diritto internazionale*, Naples, 1984; BLAY, *Self-Determination Versus Territorial Integrity in De-colonization Revisited*, in *IJIL*, 1985, p. 386 ff.; LATTANZI, *Autodeterminazione dei popoli*, in *Digesto (dir. pubbl.)*, vol. II, 1987, p. 4 ff.; ARANGIO-RUIZ, *Autodeterminazione (Diritto dei popoli alla)*, in *Enciclopedia giuridica Treccani*, vol. IV, 1988; CRAWFORD, *The Rights of Peoples*, Oxford, 1988; HANNUM, *Autonomy, Sovereignty and Self-Determination: The Accomodation of Conflicting Rights*, Philadelphia, 1990; TWINING (ed.), *Issues of Self-Determination*, Aberdeen, 1991; HALPERIN, MORTON, SCHEFFER, SMALL, *Self-Determination in the New World Order*, Washington, 1992; TOMUSCHAT (ed.), *Modern Law of Self-Determination*, Dordrecht-Boston-London, 1993; DURCH, *UN Temporary Executive Authority*, in DURCH (ed), *The evolution of UN Peacekeeping*, New York 1993, p. 285 ff.; KIRGIS JR., *The Decrees of Self-Determination in the United Nations Era*, in *AJ*, 1994, p. 304 ff.; CASSESE, *Self-Determination of Peoples. A Legal Reappraisal*, Cambridge, 1995; PINESCHI, *Le operazioni delle Nazioni Unite per il mantenimento della pace,*, Padova, 1998, Part 1, Chapt. 3, p. 144 ff.; MOORE (ed), *National Self-Determination and Secession*, Oxford, 1998; RAIČ, *Statehood and the Law of Self-Determination*, The Hague, 2002.

78. *UN competence to decide on the independence of peoples under colonial domination.*

United Nations activity in favor of the independence of colonial peoples, an activity which has managed to produce effects of great political significance and of high moral value, is known to everyone. On the legal plane, it has led to the abrogation of most of the Charter provisions on the subject and to their substitution with customary norms whose applicability should be extended to those territories still subject to colonial domination.

There is no doubt that, strictly following the intention of the framers of the Charter (and aside from the provisions on the trusteeships which will be discussed shortly), the colonial Powers would have had no obligation to bring their colonies to independence. Article 73, dedicated to the "non-self-governing territories", an article which can be considered abrogated, only calls upon the colonial powers to promote the political, economic, social and educational advancement of the peoples of the territories under their responsibility, to protect them... against abuses, and to promote self-government. The UN's power to see that all this be done was then very limited. The only relevant provision on the matter was Article 10, under which the Assembly may discuss and make recommendations "on any questions or any matters within the scope of the present Charter". Given the reservation on domestic jurisdiction under Article 2, para. 7 (another provision now obsolete with regard to colonial relations: see § 45 III), the power under Article 10 should have been considered limited to questions of a general nature, with the consequent prohibition for the Assembly to be concerned with situations in *individual* non-self-governing territories. This prohibition was, moreover, confirmed in Article 73 (*e*), which, on the one hand, obliged the colonial powers to transmit to the Secretary-General "statistical and other information of a technical nature relating to economic, social and educational conditions in the territories for which they are respectively responsible" and, on the other, specified that this transmission had only "information purposes".

The practice in the early, but not very early, years of the United Nations was dominated by the conflict between the Assembly majority which was determined to claim competence in the colonial sector, and the colonial Powers determined to oppose them. The view of the latter was that the information transmitted to the Secretary-General, being only information, could not be discussed by the Assembly. The opposing view resulted in the appointment, with res. no. 332-IV of December 2, 1949, of a Committee for the examination of the information, to which there were to belong eight States administering territories and eight elected by the Assembly. The illegality of the appointment of this Committee was denounced on a number of occasions by France, the United Kingdom, Belgium, etc., with the refusal, sometimes threatened, sometimes carried out (for example, by Belgium beginning from 1953), to participate in the Committee proceedings or to co-operate with it (for the discussions and the protests of the colonial powers, cf., for example, GAOR, 5th sess., Suppl.

no. 17, *Report of the Committee on Information from Non-Self-Governing Territories*, p. 1 f.; 7th sess., Pl. meet., 402nd and 403rd meet.; 8th sess., Suppl. no. 15, *Report of the Committee*, etc., p. 1; 9th sess., Suppl. no. 18, *Report of the Committee*, etc., p. 1 f.).

It can safely be said that the United Nations practice, in sweeping away Article 73, gave birth to a rule which binds the States still holding colonial territories not to hinder their independence. As early as 1960, the General Assembly took a position in this sense, solemnly affirming that "the subjection of a people to alien domination" was to be considered contrary to the Charter (res. no. 1514-XV of December 14, 1960, containing the Declaration of the independence of colonial peoples). Whatever the value of this Declaration was at the time it was issued, it today corresponds to the *communis opinio* of the international community and is therefore confirmed by custom.

It can similarly be held, with regard to UN competence, that, with the limit of domestic jurisdiction removed on the subject, and with the unconditioned support of national liberation movements in the colonies having prevailed in the Assembly, customary practice has consolidated the power of the Assembly to adopt measures with regard to individual non-self-governing territories in order to ensure their independence and, more generally, has recognized the power of the Assembly to be concerned with any colonial matter. As we noted in discussing domestic jurisdiction, this power no longer raises any notable objections.

Lastly, the view is not unfounded that the resolutions, by which the Assembly lays down the modalities and the agenda for the granting of independence to non-self-governing territories, have, again by virtue of custom, binding force.

> Custom does not have objective limits. It may produce rules that not only widen the sphere of the subjects with which an international organ may be concerned, but may also widen express powers. For a contrary view, cf. the opinion of Judge FITZMAURICE attached to the advisory opinion of the International Court of Justice of June 21, 1971, on Namibia, in ICJ, *Reports*, 1971, p. 282.
>
> It is, moreover, indicative that the Assembly decisions on the territories still subject to colonial rule appeared for various years in officials records under the heading "decisions" and not under "resolutions".

The competence of the Assembly on de-colonization is not, however, boundless. First, there is a general limit deriving from the principle of self-determination of peoples, the principle that underlay the practice which overwhelmed Article 73. This principle, which will be dealt with shortly, obliges the Assembly to decide on the future of a non-self-governing territory by taking account of the aspirations of the local population. According to the opinion expressed by the International Court of Justice in the Western Sahara case of October 16, 1975 (ICJ, *Reports*, 1975, p. 33, no. 59), the Assembly may decide, if special circumstances so require, without consulting the inhabitants of the territory and as long as the aim of respecting their wishes is in some way satisfied. Then, there is the principle of "territorial integrity", according to which consideration must be given to the historical-geographical ties between the territory to be de-colonized and a bordering State which has previously come into being through de-colonization. The content of this principle is not entirely clear. It is, doubtlessly, a rule that is able to *derogate* from the principle of self-determination only when, as for example, in the case of the Falkland/Malvinas Islands or of Gibraltar under British rule, the majority of the local population is not native but "imported" from the mother country. Also in these cases, one must ask, however, in what sense, and up to what point, the claims of the bordering State are to be satisfied. It has convincingly held in legal doctrine (IOVANE) that the practice seems to indicate that the Assembly, which certainly does not have the power to transfer the territory of the colonial power to the contiguous State, may, however, ask that these States agree between themselves on a solution favoring de-colonization.

> Cf. in IOVANE, *art. cit.*, p. 108 ff., a list of territories (Western Irian, Ifni, Goa, Sao, Joao Batista de Ajuda, the Gloriose Islands, Gibraltar, etc.) that have been claimed, and sometimes obtained, by the contiguous States. At the end of 2003 a number of territories were still under colonial domination. Among them: New Caledonia (see GA res. no. 58 /106 of December 17, 2003), Tokelau (see GA res. no. 58/107 of December 17, 2003), American Samoa, Anguilla, Bermuda, the British Virginia Islands, the Cayman Islands, Guam, Montserrat, Pitcairn, Saint Helena (see GA res. no. 58/108 of December 17).
> For an example of the application of the principle of territorial integrity by the Assembly, cf. res. no. 47/9 of October 27, 1992 (which confirms similar resolutions adopted in the previous years) on assigning the island of Mayotte, under French domination, to the Islamic Republic of Comore. This resolution was contested by France.

The case of West Irian, a former colony of the Netherlands, is also indicative of the competence of the General Assembly to take decisions on matters of de-colonization. In this case the Assembly decided, following an agreement between Indonesia and the Netherlands subject to its approval, that the territory of West Irian should be administered by the United Nations until its transfer to Indonesia in conformity with the principle of territorial integrity. See AG res. no. 1752-XVII of September 21, 1962. The UN administration (UNTEA), headed by an Administrator appointed by the Secretary-General, lasted from October 1st, 1962 to May 1st, 1963. In our opinion, the consideration of this case in the framework of de-colonization is the proper one, even if legal doctrine tends to qualify it as a case of peacekeeping.

79. *The self-determination of peoples.*

The practice that has given rise to new rules in the field of de-colonization was avowedly inspired by, and continues to be inspired by, the principle of self-determination of peoples. This principle is mentioned in Article 1, para. 2, of the Charter (and in identical words in Article 55), as well as in a series of resolutions and solemn declarations of the General Assembly. In addition to the resolutions on de-colonization, it is stated in the 1970 Declaration on Friendly Relations and Co-operation between States (see § 94). Also the two United Nations Covenants on Human Rights (see § 77) and other international conventions contain rules that confirm respect for the principle. Self-determination is now, especially as a consequence of the practice that has developed in the UN, a general principle of customary law. What its content is? It is not easy to give an exact answer to this question, the contents of the principle being in evolution. In fact, self-determination from a legal point of view has not the meaning that it has in ordinary language. It would be misleading to say that the international Community can require that all Governments of the earth must have the consent of the majority of their subjects and have been freely chosen by them (so called domestic self-determination). International law is still far from prescriptions of this kind, even if it is undeniable that the overwhelming majority of States, as is also expressed in many resolutions and declarations of the General Assembly (see, among them, the already quoted Millennium Declaration contained in res. no. 55/2 of September 8, 2000, para. 6) *tend* to consider self-determination as synonymous with democracy, and of democracy meant in the sense of democratic legitimacy of Governments. Even after the fall of the Communist regimes in Eastern Europe, the countries that do not conform to this tendency, and although they may enjoy the favor of powerful States (for example, some Arab countries in the Middle East or some African States), are not few. In fact, the declarations in favor of democracy are not followed by a serious and generalized fight against undemocratic States. Moreover, a genuine inclination for democracy on the part of the International Community should imply its own democratization; however it remains a community largely ruled by an oligarchy. It would be equally misleading to interpret the principle of self-determination as allowing the secessionist aspirations of regions and autonomous provinces, even if they are regions that are ethnically distinct from the rest of the country. Even in the recent

Kosovo crisis, notwithstanding the systematic terrorization of ethnic Albanians, the massive torture and summary executions and mass forced displacement of ethnic Albanian, the General Assembly (see for instance res. no. 53/164 of February 25, 1999) and the Security Council (see for instance res. no. 1244 of June 10, 1999), after having condemned such tragic violations of human rights, have not put into question the territorial sovereignty of the Republic of Yugoslavia (Serbia and Monenegro) on the Kosovo region, reaffirming every time the call for "substantial autonomy and meaningful self-administration" for the Region.

Having said that, a rigorous analysis of the problem which takes into account the actual behavior of the States - what the States do as opposed to what the States say - shows that the principle of self-determination has a rather limited sphere of application. It applies only in territories under a domination of a *foreign* Government (so called external self-determination) and, therefore, besides colonial territories, in those which have been conquered and occupied by force (for example, the territories occupied by Israel in 1967 or the territory of Iraq, occupied by the coalition forces in 2003). In short, it obliges the Government controlling a territory that is not its own to allow either independence or the possible association or merger with another State, that is, the people's free choice of their own international status and their own political system. In the UN system, the principle of self-determination enables the organs, particularly, the General Assembly, to undertake action so that these objectives can be reached. Such action, in the case of colonial territories (and only in this case), may consist, as we have seen, in the adoption of binding decisions.

This is the meaning that the principle of self-determination has up to now assumed in the practice. It is difficult to say what its meaning was at the beginning, when reference to the principle was inserted in Articles 1 and 55 of the Charter (with a modification of the Dumbarton Oaks proposals desired by the sponsoring Powers at the San Francisco Conference: cf. UNC.I.O., vol. 3, p. 622). In fact, no one was able to clarify, during the Conference, what exactly was to be meant by "friendly relations among nations based on the principle... of self-determination of peoples" (cf. IOVANE, *art. cit.*, p. 89, partic. nos. 13 and 14). It is very probable that self-determination was meant at the time not as the obligation of a Government occupying a territory to allow the territory itself to decide its own destiny (otherwise the Charter's acceptance of the colonial situation could not be explained) but simply as an obligation of all the States not to interfere in the free choices, concerning setting up of the Government, the Constitution, laws and so forth, which are made in foreign States (indications in this sense may be found in the concise and rather ambiguous Report of Commission I, which at San Francisco was concerned with Article 1, para. 2. See particularly the passage in the Report which mentions the Axis Powers' practice of exploiting for their own aggressive purpose "alleged expressions of the popular will": cf. UNC.I.O. vol. 6, p. 455.) Meant in this way, the principle of self-determination easily blends with the principle of non-intervention in the internal affairs of others (such characterisation is still evident in some interpretations of Article 1, para. 2, for example, in JOYNER and GRIMALDI, *The United States and Nicaragua: Reflections on the*

Lawfulness of Contemporary Intervention, in *Virg. JIL*, vol. 25, 1985, p. 643), and obviously had a much narrower meaning than what it has come to assume in the practice.

The exact determination of the material sphere of application of the principle of self-determination, that is, of cases of territories under a *foreign* Government, presents considerable difficulty when it involves territories in which the foreign Government, although present with its own armed forces, relies on a local Government. Sometimes, the local Government is formed before the foreign invasion and seeks to be legitimized with a request for more or less fraternal "help". Sometimes the local Government is obviously created by the occupying State or States. In cases of this kind, unless the presence of the foreign Government is such as to have the local Government become a mere puppet Government, that is, a Government which acts in practice as an organ of the occupying State and is without international personality, it must be said that the principle of self-determination applies to both Governments, obligating both to end the foreign occupation. It seems to us that it is in this sense that the United Nations practice, especially the resolutions of the General Assembly which usually condemn foreign occupation in the name of the principle of self-determination, is to be interpreted.

Among the resolutions which, besides condemning armed intervention of foreign Powers as contrary to the ban of use of force, appeal to the principle of self-determination in occupied territories, and notwithstanding the real or the sham existence of local Governments, see the many resolutions adopted in the case of Afghanistan during the Soviet occupation between 1980 and 1989 (cf., for example, res. no. 39/13 of November 15, 1984, affirming "the right of the Afghanistan people to establish their own form of Government and to chose their own economic, political and social system without outside interventions...". See also the various resolutions on the occupation of Cambodia by Vietnam between 1979 and 1990: cf., for example, res. no. 39/5 of October 30, 1984. Cf. also res. no. 38/7 of November 2, 1983 against the intervention of the United States in Grenada and including the request to allow the people of this State "to choose its government democratically".

The situation in Iraq after the creation of the so called Interim Government in 1994, a Government very close to the United States, can also be quoted. Res. no. 1546 of June 8, 2004 of the Security Council was mainly concerned with issues related to the maintenance of peace and security (see § 60); however, it also compels both the Iraqi Interim Government and the States of the so-called Coalition to put an end to the occupation as quickly as possible, with the consequence of leaving the Iraqi people to decide on their own destiny.

80. *Trusteeship.*

BIBLIOGRAPHY: DUNCAN HALL, *Mandates, Dependencies and Trusteeship*, London, 1948; VEDOVATO, *Les accords de tutelle*, in *RC*, 1950, I, p. 613 ff.; RAGGI, *L'amministrazione fiduciaria internazionale*, Milan, 1950; CONFORTI, *Sovranità sui Paesi in amministrazione fiduciaria e rapporti tra gli ordinamenti dell'amministrante e dell'amministrato*, in *RDI*, 1955, p. 13 ff.; CAPOTORTI, *Natura e caratteri degli accordi di amministrazione fiduciaria*, in *RDI*, 1955, p. 185 ff. and 457 ff.; TOUSSAINT, *The Trusteeship System of the United Nations*, London, 1956; QUADRI, *Diritto coloniale*, 4th ed., Padua, 1958, p. 106 ff.; BADIALI, *La struttura dell'accordo di amministrazione fiduciaria e il problema degli « Stati direttamente interessati »*, in *CS*, vol. IX, 1958, p. 75 ff.; LEROY, *La nature juridique des accords de tutelle*, in *RGDIP*, 1965, p. 977 ff.; LUCCHINI, *Vers un nouveau statut de la Micronésie ou la disparition prochaine de la tutelle*, in *AF*, 1975, p. 155 ff.; ARMSTRONG and HILLS, *The Negotiations for the Future Political Status of Micronesia*, in *AJ*, 1983, p. 484 ff.; HINCK, *The Republic of Palau and the United States: Self-Determination Becomes the Price of Free Association*, in *California Law Review*, 1990, p. 915 ff.; MCKIBBEN, *The Political Relationship Between the United States and Pacific Islands Entities: The Path to Self-Government in the Northern Mariana Islands*, Palau and Guam, in *HILJ*, 1990, p. 257 ff.; RADIVOJEVIC, *United Nations Reform and the Position of the Trusteeship Council*, in *Review of International Affairs*, 1998, p. 27 ff.

The evolution that has taken place in the United Nations system regarding the non-self-governing territories has absorbed and made obsolete the trusteeship system, a system which by itself has exhausted its function. This system was introduced in the Charter by Chapters XII and XIII, along the model of (and for the continuity of) the mandate system in force at the time of the League of Nations. Its purpose was to give the territories under trusteeship a more advantageous regime than the one of ordinary non-self-governing territories. For the former, in fact, and not for the latter (cf. Article 76), the word "independence" was used, and a special organ of supervision over the administering powers, the Trusteeship Council, operating under the authority of the General Assembly, was created.

Under Article 22 of the Covenant of the League of Nations, the areas placed under mandate after the First World War were the African possessions and the Pacific islands taken away from the German Empire, as well as the Middle East territories that had been part of the Ottoman Empire. On the basis of agreements made by the winning powers, the following were designated Mandatory Powers: Great Britain (Iraq, Palestine, Transjordan, part of Togo and of Cameroon, the island of Nauru); France (Syria, Lebanon, part of Togo and of Cameroon); Belgium (Rwanda Urundi); South Africa (South West Africa or Namibia); Australia (New Guinea); Japan (the Marianne, Marshall and Caroline islands in the South Pacific) and New Zealand (Samoa). The assigning of these territories as mandates and not as mere territorial extensions as a consequence of the war involved, at least in theory, the obligation to govern in the interest of the local populations and to be subject to a certain supervision by the League. The mandates were, then, divided by Article 22 into categories according to the stage of development of the various territories, with the competence of the Mandatory Powers correspondingly graded. In the case of the Middle East countries, France and Great Britain should have been limited to functions of "advice and assistance".

At San Francisco, the trusteeship ("tutelle" in French) system was foreseen for territories already held under mandate (provided that they had not become independent), for territories taken from enemy States during the Second World War, and for any other colonial territory that the mother country had decided to administer as a trusteeship (Article 77, para. 1). In all cases, the trusteeship system would have been applied under an agreement concluded between the States directly concerned and approved by the UN (Article 77, para. 2, and Article

79), assuming, therefore, the consent of the Power which held the territory as a mandate, as a war conquest or by other title.

Subsequent acts subjected to trusteeship all the territories already held under mandate, except for the Middle East countries which had in the meantime become independent and except for Southwest Africa (Namibia) because the Mandatory Power, South Africa, had always refused to establish a new system in that territory. In addition to the former mandates, the one and only other case of trusteeship was that of Somalia, a territory coming under, as a former Italian colony, the second of the categories indicated by Article 77, para. 1, and assigned in trusteeship to Italy.

All the territories under trusteeship have reached independence. Hence the Trusteeship Council has no work to perform any more. A proposal aiming at giving it the new function as a "guardian and trustee of the global commons" in order to watch at the sustainibility of the environment, the protection of human rights and the safeguard of peoples in situation of complete breakdown of the States, was submitted by Malta to the General Assembly, in 1996, during the 50th session of the Assembly (see Doc. A/50/142). In 1998 a similar proposal has been made by the Secretary-General in a "note on a new concept in trusteeship" (Doc. A/52/849). According to the note, the Trusteeship Council should be a forum through which States exercise their action "for the integrity of the global environment and common areas, such as the oceans, atmosphere and outer space". It should also serve "to link the Organization and civil society in addressing areas of global concern, which require active contribution by public, private and voluntary sectors". Up to now, the proposal has not found strong supporters among the Member States (see, for instance, the contrary views expressed by the United States, India, Japan, and others during the 52nd session of the General Assembly, 83rd meet.).

81. *The case of Namibia.*

BIBLIOGRAPHY: FERRARI BRAVO, *La questione dell'Africa Sud-occidentale,* in *DI,* 1960, p. 34 ff.; DUGARD, *The Revocation of the Mandate for South West Africa,* in *AJ,* 1968, p. 78 ff.; LUCCHINI, *La Namibie, une construction de l'ONU,* in *AF,* 1968, p. 355 ff.; DUGARD (ed.), *The South West Africa/Namibia Dispute, Berkeley-Los Angeles-London, 1973;* OBZUWA, *The Namibian Question: Legal and Political Aspects,* Benin City, 1973; HERMANN, *The Legal Status of Namibia and of the UN Council for Namibia,* in *CYIL,* 1975, p. 306 ff.; BARSOTTI, *In tema di amministrazione diretta di territori non autonomi da parte dell'ONU: il caso della Namibia,* in *CS,* 1980, vol XVI, p. 53 ff.; ZACKLIN, *The Problem of Namibia in International Law,* in *RC,* 1981, II, p. 225 ff.; KAMTO, *L'accession de la Namibie à l'indépendence,* in *RGDIP,* 1990, p. 577 ff.; ABI-SAAB, *Namibia and International Law: An Overview, in AYIL,* 1993, p. 3 ff.; SINJELA, MPAZI, *The Role of the United Nations Transition Assistance Group (UNTAG) in the Independence Process of Namibia, ivi,* p. 13 ff.

In 1990 Namibia (South West Africa) also became independent. This territory had been assigned to South Africa as a mandate after the First World War (see § 80) and for a very long period of time the South African Government had refused to give it independence, to submit it to trusteeship, or to administer it under the supervision of the United Nations. The conflict between the UN and South Africa over the fate of Namibia, besides having some very dramatic moments, gave rise, especially in the first twenty-five years of the Organization, to heated debates of a legal nature.

The view held by the South African Government, and which the latter used to practically annex Namibia after 1945 and to extend there also its policy of apartheid was that the administration of the territory had remained completely free from international control once the controlling entity, the League of Nations, had dissolved. This view was always tenaciously opposed by the General Assembly and also by the International Court of Justice in a series of advisory opinions. The first of these, issued in 1950 at the request of the General Assembly, is the fundamental one.

In the 1950 opinion (cf. ICJ, *Reports*, 1950, p. 128 ff., partic. p. 133 ff. and p. 136 f.), the Court mainly went back to a kind of transitory provision in Chapter XII of the Charter, in Article 80, para. 1 ("Except as may be agreed upon in individual trusteeship agreements... and until such agreements have been concluded, nothing in this chapter shall be construed in or of itself to alter in any manner the rights whatsoever of any states or any peoples or the terms of existing international instruments to which Members of the United Nations may respectively be parties"). It inferred from Article 80, para. 1, that South Africa's obligations concerning the mandate over Namibia still existed. It held that since these obligations consisted in administering the territory prevalently in the interests of the local population and mainly in the administration's reporting... to the League of Nations, it was natural that after the dissolution of the League an international body with similar functions and structure would undertake the supervision over the Mandatory Power. It concluded, although it is unclear whether on the basis of Article 80, para. 1, or on other bases, in the sense that the UN was the League's successor in this matter. The Court asked itself what was to be, within the United Nations system, the specific organ competent for supervision (at the time of the League, the Council was competent with regard to mandates; it was the organ which roughly corresponded in structure, but not in its functions, to the present Security Council), and decided that the General Assembly, as the holder under Article 10 of the Charter of wider and more comprehensive powers, was competent.

The 1950 advisory opinion (followed in 1955 and 1956 by two opinions on specific questions, that of the majority on which to decide on South West Africa and that of the possibility of hearing Namibians presenting petitions, a possibility that had been excluded at the time of the League of Nations: cf. ICJ, *Reports*, 1955, p. 67 ff. and 1956, p. 23 ff.) provided the General Assembly with the legal arguments for issuing a whole series of resolutions aimed at putting pressure on South Africa so that Namibia would not be excluded from the de-colonization process. As fundamental stages in this action, two resolutions deserve mention: res. no. 2145-XXI of October 27, 1966 with which the Assembly, after having contested the persistent violation by South Africa of the obligations incumbent on it as a Mandatory Power and as a UN member, "decided" to end the mandate, arrogating to the United Nations the responsibility for the administration of Namibia in view of its independence and inviting the Security Council to keep watching the situation; and res. no. 2248 S-V of May 19, 1967 which created an organ for governing the territory, the United

Nations Council for Namibia, an organ whose first act was to confiscate all the resources of the country in the interest of the Namibian people (decree no. 1 of September 27, 1974)

The Security Council supported the General Assembly, without however exercising the enforcement powers given it by the Charter but by limiting itself to recommending a series of measures. For the purposes of subsequent developments, res. no. 435 of September 29, 1978 was very important. It approved a plan of the Secretary-General to ensure the independence of Namibia by holding free elections under UN supervision. South Africa for a long time boycotted this plan (which was accepted by SWAPO, the liberation movement in Namibia), and the boycotting was deplored many times by the Council (cf., for example, res. no. 532 of May 31, 1983). It was only in 1990, after various negotiations, and as implementation of the plan envisaged in res. no. 435 of 1978, that Namibia finally acquired independence.

In light of the above, there were two problems which deserve consideration from a legal viewpoint. The first is what was the legal basis of the Assembly "decision" to terminate the South African mandate. The second is what value could be given to the creation of the United Nations Council for Namibia and the acts issued by it, given that this organ of administration was not actually able to exercise effective power with the territory owing to the continual South African presence.

The first problem was examined in another advisory opinion, of June 21, 1971 (in ICJ, *Reports*, 1971, p. 16 ff.) handed down by the International Court of Justice on the Namibian question. Briefly, the Court took up again, and enriched with new arguments, the view it held in the 1950 opinion, based on the survival of the South African mandate and the UN succession to the League of Nations. However, it warned that the terms of the mandate should have been interpreted in an evolutionary way, taking into account the practice and present circumstances, instead of those at the time of the League (*Reports*, cit., p. 28 ff., partic. p. 31). Considering that the Covenant had not conferred upon the League Council the power to terminate mandates (a proposal in this sense had even been rejected during the preparatory works), the Court held that the termination ordered by the Assembly was justified on the basis of general principles of International law valid both then and now, i. e. the principle that... a party may terminate a treaty for material breach by the other party (*ibid*, p. 45 ff.).

In our view, termination of the mandate could have been justified on less complicated legal grounds. Namibia should have simply qualified as a non-self-governing territory; therefore, the Assembly resolution of October 27, 1966, having terminated the South African mandate, was to be considered, and to be fully justified by law, as the expression of the Assembly's power to decide in a binding way on the independence of all territories still under colonial domination (see § 78).

As for the problem of the legal value to be assigned to the creation of the United Nations Council for Namibia, since the Council for Namibia lacked effective power (from the point of view of international law it could be considered as a sort of government in exile or as a national committee operating abroad, that is, as an entity devoid of international personality: see § 20), the relevant resolutions could only have the meaning of invitations calling upon the States to *deny recognition to the acts of government adopted by South Africa with respect to Namibian territory*.

Section IX

REGISTRATION OF TREATIES

BIBLIOGRAPHY: DEHOUSSE, *L'enregistrement des traités*, Paris, 1929; DELBEZ, *Manuel de droit international public*, Paris, 1951, p. 211 ss.; BRANDON, *The Validity of Non-Registered Treaties*, in *BYB*, 1952, p. 186 ss.; ID., *Analysis of The Terms «Treaty» and «Internatinal Agreement» for Purpose of Registration*, in *AJ*, 1953, p. 49 ss.; ROSENNE, *United Nations Treaty Practice*, in *RC*, 1954, II, p. 426 ss.; ZEMANEK, *Die Entwicklung des völkerrechtlichen Vertragsrechtes*, in *ZöR*, 1955, p. 391 ss.; BROCHES and BOSKEY, *Theory and Practice of Treaty Registration*, in *Nederland Tijdschrift voor International Recht*, 1957, p. 159 ss.; MCNAIR, *The Law of Treaties*, Oxford, 1961, p. 178 ss.; HIGGINS, *The Development of International Law Through the Political Organs of the UN*, London, 1963, p. 328 ss.; LILLICH, *The Obligation to Register Treaties and International Agreements with the UN*, in *AJ*, 1971, p. 771 ss.; TABORY, *Recent Developments in United Nations Treaty Registration and Publication Practices*, in *AJ*, 1982, p. 350 ss.; HAN, *The UN Secretary-General Treaty Depositary Function: Legal Implications*, in *Brooklyn Journal of International Law*, 1988, p. 549 ss.; FLEISCHAUER, *The United Nations Treaty Series*, in *Essays in Honour of S. Rosenne*, Dordrecht, 1989, p. 131 ss.; HUTCHINSON, *The Significance of the Registration or Non Registration of an International Agreement in Determining Whether or Not it is a Treaty*, in *Current Legal Problems*, 1993.

82. *Effects of registration.*

Article 102 of the Charter provides: "1. Every treaty and every international agreement entered into by any Member of the United Nations after the present Charter comes into force shall as soon as possible be registered with the Secretariat and published by it. 2. No party to any such treaty or international agreement which has not been registered in accordance with the provisions of paragraph 1 of this Article may invoke that treaty or agreement before any organ of the United Nations".

Article 102 has a precedent in Article 18 of the Covenant of the League of Nations and is linked to the idea of the abolition of "secret diplomacy", an idea championed by President Wilson after the First World War.

As is clearly established by para. 2 of Article 102, the only consequence of registration is the possibility of invoking the treaty before a United Nations organ. Under this aspect, Article 102 moves away from the old Article 18, which said that non-registered treaties were not binding. Actually, this provision which was the product of the initial tendency to consider the Covenant of the League of Nations as a Constitution rather than as an agreement between States remained an only theoretical proposition. Already at that time, it was being interpreted by many States as clearly bending its literal meaning, i. e. in the sense that non-registered treaties could not be invoked before the League organs.

Aside from the possibility to invoke a registered treaty within the United Nations, registration does not have other effects. As has been confirmed in the practice, it is not a form of confirmation which ascertains once and for all the existence and the validity of the agreement and its binding force.

When between 1955 and 1956 the Secretary registered a certain number of agreements entered into by UN members with the Korean Democratic Republic, with the German Democratic Republic and with the People's Republic of China, the United States, the United Kingdom and Nationalist China, which had not rrecognized those countries or had not rrecognized some of them, hastened to declare that registration could not effect the problem as to whether or not the agreements entered into by non-recognized Governments had an international character. This was in conformity with the view held by the Secretary-General in a Statement of 1955, which reads: "The registration of an instrument submitted by a Member State does not imply any judgement as to the nature of the instrument itself or the status of one of the parties or any similar questions". Cf. *UN Rep.* Suppl. no. 1, *sub* Article 102, no. 12 ff.

Also, after the registration of an Egyptian statement of April 24, 1957 on the Suez Canal, several States declared in the Security Council that, in spite of it being registered, the statement itself remained a unilateral act, and as such, was always revocable. Cf. *UN Rep.*, Suppl. no. 2, *sub* Article 102, no. 8.

The possibility to invoke non-registered agreements before bodies different from those of the United Nations was reaffirmed by the decision of July 31, 1989 of the arbitral tribunal for the setting of the Guinea-Bissau-Senegal maritime boundary, in *RDI*, 1991, p. 662 f., paras. 77-78.

The registered acts are published in the *United Nations Treaty Series*.

83. *Effects of non-registration.*

Are non-registered international agreements *never* referred to before UN organs? The answer is related to the problem of what agreements are actually subject to registration.

The problem is usually put in the following terms. What does Article 102 mean exactly when it requires registration for "every treaty and every international agreement"?

Put in this way, the problem does not have an easy answer. The expression "every treaty and agreement", which would seem simple, causes considerable difficulty of interpretation. The notion of international agreement is already quite problematic, as it reflects the uncertainty of the notion of subject of international law. There are a great many entities (international organizations, non-governmental international associations, multinational companies, and so forth) which often enter into agreements with the States but whose personality, and thus whose capacity to conclude true international agreements, can be put in doubt. Are such agreements subject to registration? Also with regard to international agreements concluded by States, doubts can arise whether the letter of Article 102 ("*every* agreement") actually corresponds to its object and purpose, and whether, therefore, registration is required also for agreements with very limited or insignificant content, such as those, for example, which prepare for the visit of a head of State or the exchange of trade information. It is clear that the answer has to be negative, but what, then, does Article 102 exactly require?

A clear solution is not provided by the implementing regulations of Article 102, adopted by the General Assembly with res. no. 97-I of December 14, 1946 and subsequently modified with resolutions no. 364 B-IV of December 1, 1949, no. 482-V of December 12, 1950 and no. 33/141 A of December 19, 1978. Article 1 of the regulations is limited to repeating the formula "every treaty or international agreement", and this is owing to the fact that the Assembly, in drawing up the regulations, attempted but did not succeed in coming to any understanding as to how to better define or to delimit the category of agreements subject to registration (UN Rep., loc. cit, no. 18 ff.). In the debates over Article 1, it was affirmed that Article 102 was not meant to refer only to treaties of a political nature but also concerned those with a "financial, commercial or technical" nature (*ivi*, no. 22), which is obvious. Nor can any light be shed on the problem by Article 12 of the regulations, as modified by the cited res. no. 33/141 A of 1978. This article does not concern *registration*, and even less the decision as to which agreements are subject to it, but the *publication* of agreements in the *Treaty Series*. To avoid the serious delays that always occur in the publication, it provides that the Secretariat has the authority not to publish *in extenso* the bilateral agreements belonging to certain less important categories (assistance and co-operation, the organization of conferences, seminars and meetings, and so on), although interested States and international organizations have the right to ask for copies.

On the other hand, it would be too bold to hold the view that the Secretariat (the Secretary-General) enjoys a discretionary power to decide case by case whether or not a given agreement is to be registered. However, such a view is untenable, due to the terms adopted in Article 102, para. 1, which speak of registration "with" the Secretariat and of the latter's obligation ("shall") to publish it. Without doubt, the Secretariat may question whether a given act constitutes an agreement within the meaning of Article 102 and may decide not to proceed with registration if its conclusion is negative. Without doubt, it may decide once and for all that, in its view, certain categories of agreements cannot be registered. However, as the registration says nothing about the nature of the act registered, so also the refusal to register is not decisive for the purpose of establishing such nature and may even be illegal.

The Secretariat has always acted with a certain broad-mindedness, and followed the principle of generally complying with the requests of the contracting parties, registering also (in accordance with an opinion dating from the San Francisco Conference: UNC.I.O., vol. 13, p. 705) unilateral "commitments", for example, the already cited Egyptian statement in 1957 on the Suez Canal (cf. UN Rep., Suppl. no. 2, *sub* Article 102, no. 5 ff.). It has also registered treaties which had already exhausted their effect prior to registration on the basis of the argument that they were (as emerged in a note by the Secretary General published in *UNJY*, 1975, p. 194 f.) agreements that could eventually be invoked before UN organs and whose publication could therefore have useful effects. Among the categories of agreements or understandings for which the Secretary has excluded registration, there are: agreements between States and certain international entities such as the International Committee for Military Medicine and Pharmacy, the International Patent Institute, and so on; agreements between States and dependent units of the State; the resolutions of international organs; etc. (see UN Rep., *sub* Article 102, no. 31). Sometimes registration has been first denied and then carried out: for example, in the case of the Three-Party Declaration annexed to the Washington agreement of April 5, 1951 between the United States, France and the United Kingdom on the gold of the Bank of Albania disputed between Albania and Italy (cf. BROCHES and BOSKEY, *art. cit.*, p. 285). For other examples in the practice, see *UNJY*, 1967, p. 332 ff., and 1970, p. 185 ff.

In our view, it is useless, as well as difficult, to try to identify all the categories of agreements that can come under Article 102. The rationale of the article, which is to discourage secret diplomacy, makes it possible to follow a different approach. One could, in fact, interpret Article 102 in the sense that an act that is not registered could all the same be invoked before UN organs when the parties have shown good faith as far as registration was concerned. Good faith could certainly be shown when registration has been requested and not obtained. It would also have to be recognized in all cases in which anomalous acts or acts of dubious nature were involved, and the parties had no intention of keeping them hidden.

If good faith exists, the parties *shall have the right* to invoke the non-registered agreement before the UN. A different view (BRANDON, BROCHES and BOSKEY) holds that it is the organ before which the agreement is invoked that would have the discretionary power to decide on the invokability; this view does not take into consideration the question of good faith.

On the basis of the above considerations one should evaluate the few cases in which United Nations organs (especially the International Court of Justice and also the General Assembly) have not raised objections, on the basis of Article 102, regarding non-registered agreements. For these cases, see BROCHES and BOSKEY, *art. cit.*, p. 277 ff. and HOGGINS, *op. cit.*, p. 344 f.

Section X

THE JUDICIAL FUNCTIONS

84. *The judicial settlement of disputes between States.*

BIBLIOGRAPHY: STARACE, *La competenza della Corte Internazionale di Giustizia in materia contenziosa*, Naples, 1970; LACHS, *La Cour Internationale de Justice dans le monde d'aujourd'hui*, in *RBDI*, 1975, p. 548 ff..; GROSS (ed.), *The Future of the International Court of Justice* (2 vols.), Dobbs Ferry, 1976.; FRANK, *Judging the World Court*, New York, 1986; DAMROSCH (ed.), *The International Court of Justice at a Crossroad*, Dobbs Ferry, 1987; BLOED and VAN DIJK (eds.), *Forty Years of International Court of Justice Jurisdiction, Equity and Equality*, Utrecht, 1988; McWHINNEY, *Judicial Settlement of Disputes. Jurisdiction and Justiciability*, in *RC*, vol. 221, 1990, p. 9 ff.; ABI-SAAB, *De l'évolution de la Cour internationale — Réflexions sur quelques tendances récentes*, in *RGDIP*, 1992, p. 273 ff.; SZAFARZ, *The Compulsory Jurisdiction of the International Court of Justice*, Boston, 1993; ROSENNE, *The World Court. What it is and how it Works*, 5th ed., Dordrecht, 1995; BODIE, *Politics and the Emergence of an Activist International Court of Justice*, Westport, 1995; JENNINGS, *The International Court of Justice after Fifty Years*, in *AJ*, 1995, p. 493 ff.; MULLER (ed.), *The International Court of Justice: Its Future role after Fifty Years,* The Hague, 1997; MEYER, *The World Court in Action*, New York, 2002.

The judicial functions belong to the International Court of Justice whose Statute is annexed to the Charter and forms an integral part of it (Article 92). The Court performs the same functions that had been performed by the former Permanent Court of International Justice created at the time of the League of Nations. Its Statute closely follows the one of the old Court.

Article 92 defines the Court as the "principal" judicial organ of the United Nations. The only other judicial organ is the Administrative Tribunal which was created by the Assembly to settle employment disputes between the Organization and its staff. On this, see p. 103 ff.

The Court has, first of all, the function of settling disputes among States, by applying international law (Article 38, para. 1, of the Statute) and handing down decisions with which the parties have undertaken to comply (Article 94, para. 1, of the Charter). This activity (so-called contentious jurisdiction), however, is firmly anchored in a principle that is considered characteristic of international law and which hardly offers a constructive role for purposes of achieving justice in the relations between peoples. It is the principle that, for however it may be formed, an international court may never adjudicate if its jurisdiction has not been previously accepted by all the

States parties to a dispute. Article 36 of the Statute of the Court is inspired by this principle both at para. 1 ("The jurisdiction of the Court comprises all cases which the parties refer to it and all matters specially provided for... in treaties and conventions in force") and at para. 2 ("The States parties to the present Statute may at any time declare that they recognize as compulsory *ipso facto* and without special agreement, in relation to any other State accepting the same obligation, the jurisdiction of the Court...").

The problems relating to the Court's jurisdiction in contentious matters, coming within the subject matter of international process, lie outside our topic.

85. *The advisory function of the International Court of Justice.*

BIBLIOGRAPHY: DUBISSON, *La Cour Internationale de Justice*, Paris, 1964, p. 277 ff.; GREIG, *The Advisory Jurisdiction of the International Court and the Settlement of Disputes Between States*, in *ICLQ*, 1966, p. 325 ff.; KEITH, *The Extent of the Advisory Jurisdiction of the International Court of Justice*, Leiden, 1971; PUENTE, *Consideraciones sobre la Naturaleza y Efectos de las Opiniones Consultivas*, in *Bruns'Z*, 1971, p. 730 ff.; PRATAP, *The Advisory Jurisdiction of the International Court*, Oxford, 1972; POMERANCE, *The Advisory Function of the International Court in the League and UN Eras*, Baltimore-London, 1973; SUGIHARA, *The Advisory Function of the International Court of Justice*, in *Japanese Annual of Int. Law*, 1974, p. 25 ff.; LUZZATTO, *La competenza della Corte Internazionale di giustizia nella soluzione delle controversie internazionali*, in *CS*, vol. XIV, 1975, p. 479 ff.; RADICATI DI BRÒZOLO, *Sulle questioni preliminari nella procedura consultiva davanti alla Corte Internazionale di Giustizia*, in *RDI*, 1976, p. 677 ff.; ZICCARDI CAPALDO, *Il parere consultivo della Corte Internazionale di Giustizia sul Sahara Occidentale: un'occasione per un riesame della natura e degli effetti della funzione consultiva*, in *CS*, XV, 1978, p. 557 ff.; SOHN, *Broadening the Advisory Jurisdiction of the International Court of Justice*, in *AJ*, 1983, p. 124 ff.; SCHWEBEL, *Authorizing the Secretary-General of the UN to Request Advisory Opinions of the International Court of Justice*, in *AJ*, 1984, p. 869 ff.; BENVENUTI, *L'accertamento del diritto mediante i pareri consultivi della Corte Internazionale di Giustizia*, Milan, 1984; AGO, *I pareri consultivi « vincolanti » della Corte internazionale di giustizia. Problemi di ieri e di oggi*, in *RDI*, 1990, p. 5 ff.; ESPOSITO, *La juridicciòn consultativa de la Corte Internaiconal de Justicia*, Madrid, 1996; FRANCK, *Fairness and the General Assembly Advisory Opinion*, in BOISSON DE CHAZOURNES and SAND (eds.), *International Law. The International Court of Justice and Nuclear Weapons*, Cambridge, 1999, p. 511 ff.; TCHIVOUNDA, *La fonction consultative de la Cour Internazionale de Justice dans le cadre de l'application des traités internationaux*, in *RHDI*, 1999, p. 1 ff.; GAJA, *Diseguaglianza tra le parti nella soluzione di controversie per mezzo di un parere della Corte internazionale di giustizia*, in *RDI*, 1999, p. 138 ff.

The advisory function of the International Court of Justice under Article 96 of the Charter and Articles 65 ff. of the Statute of the Court can be considered a judicial function in a broad sense since it is aimed at *stating* the law.

The advisory function has up until today been carried out in a series of important opinions, many of which had been discussed along this book.

Under Article 96, advisory opinions may be requested by the General Assembly and the Security Council as well as, upon the authorization of the General Assembly, by other UN organs and the Specialized Agencies (for example, with res. no. 89-I of December 11, 1946, the Assembly once and for all authorized the Economic and Social Council to address the Court).

The opinions are optional and non-binding, in so far as the organs have not an obligation to request them nor, once the request has been made, are they obligated to comply with them. This lack of binding force, which is characteristic of the opinions, finds confirmation in United Nations practice. Its contrast with the binding force of judgments on disputes among States has also often been confirmed by the Court itself. The fact is significant that various times the opinions, despite the "respect" rendered them in the resolutions of the requesting organ, have remained ineffectual. In view of this, it does not seem possible to say that the advisory function has been put at the same level as the contentious function. This was attempted at the time of the League of Nations with regard to the Permanent Court of International Justice and has been taken up again recently in legal doctrine. Another view (ZICCARDI CAPALDO) which raises perplexity is that the opinions would produce an *effect of lawfulness* similar to what is produced by General Assembly and Security Council recommendations (see § 89). What is true rather is that the Court opinions may contribute, and sometimes have contributed in large, to the formation or to the confirmation of international customary rules. They are then to be seen as demonstration of a kind of *opinio juris ac necessitatis* which, in that it corresponds, and only in that it corresponds, to the real behaviour of the majority of States, gives rise to binding principles for all States. For example, the opinion of May 28, 1951 on the reservations to the Convention for the Punishment of Genocide (in ICJ, *Reports*, 1951, p. 15 ff.) was at the basis of an important change in customary law regarding reservations in international treaties.

Sometimes although advisory opinions are issued under Article 96, they acquire binding force. This is because with treaty norms, or with other appropriate acts, a party beforehand undertakes the obligation to observe them. Cf., for example, Article VIII, sec. 30, of the Convention on the Privileges and Immunities of the United Nations of February 13, 1946 (see § 36) and Article IX, sec. 32, of the analogous Convention on Privileges and Immunities of the Specialised Agencies. Both articles provide that, in the event of a dispute between the UN, or a Specialised Agency, and one or more of the Member States, a request shall be made for an advisory opinion to the Court in accordance with the procedure prescribed by Article 96 of the Charter, with the parties being obligated to accept it. These are, in substance, true arbitration clauses, similar to those that provide the jurisdictional grounds in contentious matters. They refer to the advisory function in that they are stipulated between States and international organizations and thus aim at circumventing Article 34, para. 1, of the

Statute under which only States may be parties in cases before the Court. The same aim was pursued, before 1995 (see § 35), by Article 11 of the Statute of the Administrative Tribunal, established by the General Assembly to settle disputes between the UN and its staff. This article (and a similar provision is still contained in the Statute of the Administrative Tribunal of the International Labor Organization) foresaw the Court's competence to review the Tribunal decisions.

In its opinions of October 23, 1956 and July 12, 1973 (on the review of Administrative Tribunal judgements, respectively of the ILO and of the UN), the Court held that prior acceptance of the binding nature of its advisory function does not constitute an obstacle to the exercise of such function. Cf. ICJ, *Reports*, 1956, p. 84 and 1973, p. 182 f. As an example of advisory opinion given pursuant sect. 30 of the UN Convention on Privileges and Immunities see the opinion already cited (see § 35) of April 29, 1999 in *Cumaraswamy case* (ICJ, Reports, 1999). In this case the Court held that the subject of requested opinion was the one indicated by the requesting organ (the Economic and Social Council) without taking into account the view of the State which had previously agreed on submitting the question to the Court. The finding of the Court seems to be correct, since the jurisdiction of the Court is grounded on Article 96 and only on this article. For a different view, see the dissenting opinion of judge Koroma (ivi, para. 24 of the dissenting opinion) and Gaja, *art. cit.*

Also Article 66, para. 2 (*b*) and (*c*), of the Vienna Convention on the Law of Treaties between States and international organizations and between international organizations (the Convention which codified this matter) provides that the advisory function of the Court, requested through the General Assembly or the Security Council, may be accepted as obligatory in disputes in which the UN or other international organizations are parties.

The opinions requested by the Assembly and by the Security Council may touch upon "any legal question" (Article 96, para. 1). Those requested by the other organs and by the Specialized Agencies may concern "legal questions arising within the scope of their activities" (Article 96, para. 2).

In its opinion of July 8, 1996 on the legality of the use by a State of nuclear weapons in armed conflicts (ICJ, *Reports*, 1996) the Court refused to give an advisory opinion on the request of the Health World Organization, notwithstanding the authorization given once and for all by the General Assembly in the liaison agreement between HWO and UN (see § 73). The refusal was due to the fact that the question of the legality of the use of nuclear weapons was not "a question arising within the scope" of HWO activities.

As can be seen, aside from this last limitation, the object of the advisory function is indicated in such broad terms that it would be arbitrary not to accept any question pertaining to the application of interpretation of legal norms.

Various views expressed both by the States in the General Assembly or before the Court and in legal doctrine, which tend to take away certain legal questions from the advisory jurisdiction of the Court must be rejected.

Only the main views are discussed here. Some minor quibbles, which have been often advanced before, and rejected by, the Court, deserve a mention. Many of them have been recently raised in the case of *The Legal Consequences of the Construction of a Wall in the Occupied Palestinian Territories*: see the Advisory opinion of July 9, 2004, par. 29-35 (irregularities of the procedure followed in the course of the deliberation on the request submitted to the Court), par. 38-39 (lack of clarity of the terms of the question), par. 40 (abstract nature of the question). Another, and very important, objection raised in this case – the objection founded on the "*lis alibi pendens*" embodied in Article12, par. 1, of the Charter – has been dealt with in connection with the function of the General Assembly with regard to the maintenance of peace and security (see § 62).

First, it must and it has been rejected the view, which was held only in the early years of the UN, that opinions should not be issued with regard to interpretation of the Charter. As the Court pointed out in its opinion of May 28, 1948 (*Reports*, 1947-48, p. 61) on admission to the United Nations, and as can be found in the preparatory works (cf. UNC.I.O., vol. 13,p. 719), and in the practice, it is exactly on this subject that the advisory function, coming from the "principal judicial organ of the United Nations", is meant to give crucial contributions in keeping with the spirit of Article 96.

Secondly, no merit can be seen in the view that would remove from the advisory function all questions that can be resolved in legal terms but that have political importance due to the circumstances in which they arise.

Cfr. the already cited opinion of May 28, 1948 on admission in ICJ, *Reports*, 1947-1948, p. 61 (in this case the Court was asked to establish whether the "package" admission proposed by the Soviet Union and opposed by the Western powers was in conformity with the Charter: see § 13). Cf. also the opinions of March 3, 1950 (also on admission), *ivi*, 1950, p. 6 ff., of July 20, 1962 (on Expenses of the United Nations in the Middle East and in the Congo), *ibid.*, 1962, p. 155, of December 20, 1980 (on the interpretation of the agreement between WHO and Egypt), *ibid.*, 1980, p. 87; of July 8, 1996 (on the legality of the threat or use of nuclear weapons) *ibid.*, 1996, p. 8 f.; and of July 9,2004 (on the construction of the wall in the occupied Palestinian territories, par. 4

Lastly, nothing prevents that a question submitted to the Court can be the subject of a dispute between States or between a State and the UN For example, the Assembly or the Security Council, faced with a dispute with which they are dealing, may address the Court even against the wishes of the parties or of one of them, in order to know what is the *legal* solution to the dispute. This results not only from Article 96 which speaks of legal questions in general, but also from Articles 14 and 37 of the Charter which authorize, respectively, the Assembly (see § 61) and the Security Council (see § 54) to recommend to the parties to a dispute solutions in the merits without excluding legal solutions. Nor should it be held, to the contrary, that the issuance of the opinion would circumvent the principle that contentious jurisdiction of the Court may not be established without the consent of all parties and the settlement of the dispute may not take place without the full participation of all parties involved in the judicial proceedings. To this objection one can answer that contentious jurisdiction leads to a judgment binding for the disputing parties, whereas the advisory function, which simply brings about co-operation between the judicial organ and the other United Nations organs, is devoid of any binding effect either for the requesting organ or for the States.

In favour of this view the advisory opinion of March 30, 1950 on the interpretation of peace treaties with Bulgaria, Hungary and Rumania can be cited. Here the Court states "... Another argument that has been invoked against the power of the Court to answer the questions put to it in this case is based on the opposition of the Governments of Bulgaria, Hungary and Romania to the advisory procedure. The Court cannot, it is said, give the Advisory Opinion requested without violating the well-established principle of international law according to which no judicial proceedings relating to a legal question pending between States can take place without their consent. This objection reveals a confusion between the principles governing contentious procedure and those which are applicable to Advisory Opinions. The consent of States, parties to a dispute, is the basis of the Court's jurisdiction in contentious cases. The situation is different in regard to advisory proceedings *even where the request for an Opinion relates to a legal question actually pending between States*. The Court's reply is only of an advisory character: as such, it has no binding force. It follows that no State, whether a Member of the United Nations or not, can prevent the giving of a Advisory Opinion which the United Nations considers to be desirable in order to obtain enlightenment as to the cause of action it should take. The Court's opinion is given not to the States, but to the organ which is entitled to request it; the reply of the Court, itself an 'organ of the United Nations', represents its participation in the activities of the Organization, and, in principle, should not be refused" (Cf. ICJ *Reports*, 1950, p. 71; our italics).

Also the opinion of December 15, 1989 on the Applicability of Article VI, Section 22, of the Convention on the Privileges and Immunities of the United Nations can be cited. Here the Court was called upon to express an opinion, at the request of the Economic and Social Council, on the applicability of the provisions of this Convention to Mr. *Mazilu*, a Rumanian citizen and member of the United Nations subcommittee on discrimination and the protection of minorities, whom the Rumanian Government had prevented from leaving the country (see § 36). Section 30 Article VIII of the Convention, as we have just seen, provides that, in the event of a dispute between the UN and a Member State, an advisory opinion of the Court may be requested, and the parties are *obligated* to comply with it. However, in this case Rumania had formulated a reservation to the Convention, excluding the *a priori* acceptance of such obligation. It was a matter, then, of establishing whether, notwithstanding the reservation, the Court could all the same issue the opinion, obviously without binding effects but as a function normally performed on the basis of Article 96 and therefore as a mere advisory function aimed at indicating to a United Nations organ (in this case the Economic and Social Council, on the authorization of the General Assembly) the solution to a legal question. The Court correctly answered in the affirmative, referring to its opinion of 1950 (cf. ICJ, *Reports*, 1989, p. 188 ff., paras. 29-32).

If the advisory function can extend, without exceptions, to any other legal question, may the Court refuse to perform it anyhow? In other words, does the Court, when confronted with a legal question, have the power to decide, at its own discretion, whether or not to issue an opinion? The answer which is usually given to this question is affirmative and is based on the text of Article 65 of the Statute, under which "the Court may [in French, "peut"] give an advisory opinion...".

The discretionary power under Article 65 has often been invoked before the Court in order to seek to persuade it not to express an opinion in some of the cases that have just been mentioned here. It has been said that even if it is true that the Charter does not exclude the issuance of opinions when the legal question submitted by a UN organ has considerable political importance or is the subject of a dispute between States (or between States and an international organization), and specifically between States which do not agree in requesting the intervention of the highest judicial organ in the organization, nevertheless the latter would make correct use of its discretionary power if, in the presence of such circumstances, it did not express an opinion.

How has the Court behaved in this regard? Its position, as it results from various opinions, is the following: it has as a principle adopted the view that it had a discretionary power on the subject, asking on various occasions whether there were "urgent reasons" for not answering the legal questions put to it by the General Assembly or by other organs. However, it has then carefully avoided applying such view. More specifically, with regard to highly political legal questions, the Court has always denied that political importance was a sufficient reason for refusing to intervene. By contrast, on questions that were the subject of disputes, it has affirmed in principle the appropriateness of not issuing an opinion when the parties were not all in agreement, but in the end it has issued an opinion all the same, sometimes holding that the question submitted did not affect the main subject of the dispute, sometimes denying that a dispute existed, sometimes resorting (as it did in the cited December 15, 1989 opinion in the *Mazilu* case) to subtle and perhaps rather incomprehensible arguments.

For the view that the discretionary power to express or not to express an opinion comes from Article 65 of the Statute, and for the assertion that this power is not, however, to be used to refuse the issuance of an opinion in the event of legal questions having considerable political importance, cf., for example, ICJ, *Reports*, 1962, p. 155 (opinion on the question of expenses for UN actions in the Middle East and in the Congo), 1971, p. 23, no. 28 f. and p. 27, no. 41 (opinion on Namibia), 1996, p. 8 f. (on the legality of the threat or use of nuclear weapons).

On the problem whether the advisory function can be refused at the Court's discretion when the question is the subject of a dispute between States, the Court expressed its view in the already cited opinion of March 30, 1950 on the peace treaties with Bulgaria, Hungary and Rumania. In this case, the request for an opinion from the Assembly concerned the interpretation of certain arbitration clauses of these treaties. Such interpretation was, without doubt, the subject of dispute between the parties, and, moreover, the three States had repeatedly said they were against the issuance of an opinion by the highest UN judicial organ. As we have just recalled (see § 85), the Court in this opinion claimed that it was fully competent to be concerned in an advisory capacity also with questions that were the subject of disputes, given the separation between advisory functions and contentious jurisdiction. Then, right after having made this claim, the Court went on to ask if, however, in the specific case, it should refuse to express a view (because of the opposition of several parties to the dispute) in the exercise of its discretionary power under Article 65. It recalled that in similar circumstances the Permanent Court of International Justice had refused to give an opinion. This was the case of the Status of Eastern Carelia (PCIJ, Series B, no. 5). It stated, although implicitly, that it agreed in principle with the former Court in the sense that opinions should not be issued if they touch upon "essential points" of dispute between Governments, in order not to circumvent the principles on contentious jurisdiction. However, it concluded that in this particular case "essential points" were not involved, and therefore in the end it decided to express an opinion (cf. ICJ, *Reports*, 1950, p. 72).

Cf. also the opinion of June 21, 1971 on Namibia (ICJ, *Reports*, 1971, p. 23 f., no. 30 ff. and p. 27, no. 41) in which the Court, recalling here also the opinion of the Permanent Court in the case of the Status of Eastern Carelia, denied that the question submitted by the Security Council on the status of South West Africa (see § 81) was the subject of dispute between South Africa and other States.

Also in the *Western Sahara* case (opinion of October 16, 1975, in *Reports*, 1975, p. 25, no. 33) the Court began by recalling the principle expressed by the old opinion on the Status of Eastern Carelia, and said: "... in certain circumstances, therefore, the lack of consent of an interested state may render the giving of an advisory opinion incompatible with the Court's judicial character. An instance of this would be when the circumstances disclose that to give a reply would have the effect of circumventing the principle that a state is not obliged to allow its disputes to be submitted to judicial settlement...". In light of this affirmation, one would expect that the Court would have refused to give an opinion, since in this particular case there had been a precise proposal by Morocco to submit the same question which formed the object of the opinion to the contentious procedure before the Court and since Spain had refused this proposal, requesting the Court not to express an advisory opinion. The Court, on the contrary, decided to render an opinion, holding (*ivi*, p. 25, no. 34) that it was not a matter of a pure and simple dispute born "independently in bilateral relations", but of a dispute "that arose during the debates in the Assembly and concerned problems it is involved in". With all due respect, the Court's view was very captious (every question submitted to the Court in its advisory capacity is discussed by the Assembly or by the Security Council, or by other organs authorized to request opinions) and the easier approach to take in this case should have been to finally abandon the old principle in the opinion of the Status of Eastern Carelia.

Similar considerations must be made with regard to the often cited opinion of December 12, 1989 in the *Mazilu* affair, where, as we have just seen, the Court was also faced with a specific dispute between the UN and a Member State, Rumania, as well as with the refusal of the latter to submit the dispute to the judgement of the Court. In this case, the Court overcame the question by holding that the dispute concerned the "application" of the Convention on the Privileges and Immunities of the United Nations, while the request for the opinion concerned the "applicability" of the same Convention (sic!). Cf. ICJ, *Reports*, 1989, p. 190 ff., paras. 37-39, partic. para. 38.

Again, in the opinion of July 9, 2004 on The Construction of a Wall in Palestinian Territories, the Court, quoting the *Western Sahara* opinion, expressed the view that "in certain circumstances . . . the lack of consent of an interested State may render the giving of an advisory opinion incompatible with the Court's judicial character". However, again in this case, the Court found that no such circumstances existed. Why? Essentially because, given the powers and responsibilities of the United Nations in questions relating to international peace and security "the subject-matter of the General Assembly's request cannot be regarded as only a bilateral matter between Israel and Palestine" (paras. 48-50).

In our view, the idea of discretionary power, even if it is moderated by the safeguards found in the Court's jurisprudence, is puzzling. The textual argument on which it is based (the "may" in Article 65 of the Statute) is very weak and should yield to the spirit of the provision on the advisory function which testifies to the *obligatory co-operation of the Court* with the UN organs in the solution of legal questions. It is clear that the most delicate point of the whole matter is that of the connection between the advisory function and contentious or binding jurisdiction. However, it is exactly on this point that the Court should, rather than quibbling as it has done up to now, once and for all, say that the existence of a dispute does not limit *in any way* its competence to render an opinion. Why should the Court be authorized to sacrifice, at its discretion, the advisory function to the contentious function and therefore sacrifice co-operation between the organs to respect for the desire of an individual State to avoid the opinion (even the non-binding opinion!) of the judicial organ? Such a sacrifice could have been justified at the time of the League of Nations and the advisory function of the old Permanent Court, but it seems anachronistic to day. In fact, the case- law of the Court is moving exactly in this direction, particularly if the above mentioned reasoning in the *Construction of a Wall* case is taken into account.

Section XI

FINANCING THE ORGANIZATION

BIBLIOGRAPHY: MARCANTONIO, *L'administration financiére de la Société des Nations*, Paris, 1938; SOMMER, *Les finances de l'ONU*, Zürich 1951; SINGER, *Financing International Organizations: The UN Budget Process*, The Hague, 1951; SAR, *Le financement des activités de l'ONU 1945-1961*, Ankara, 1963; GROSS, *Expenses of the UN for Peacekeeping Operations* ecc., in *Int. Org.*,1963, p. 1 ff.; SIMMONDS, *The UN Assessments Advisory Opinion*, in *ICLQ*, 1964, p. 584 ff.; STOESSINGER, *Financing the UN System*, Wash., 1964; CONFORTI, *La funzione dell'accordo nel sistema delle Nazioni Unite*, Padua, 1968, p. 130 ff. and p. 143 f.; TESAURO, *Il finanziamento delle Organizzazioni internazionali a carattere universale*, in *CI*, 1970, p. 559 ff.; PELLET, *Budgets et programmes aux Nations Unies. Quelques tendances récentes*, in *AF*, 1976, p. 242 ff.; MARTINEZ, *Le financement des opérations de maintien de la paix de l'ONU*, in *RGDIP*, 1977, p. 102 ff.; HÜFNER, *Die freiwilligen Finanzleistungen an das UN-System*, in *GYIL*, 1983, p. 29 ff.; PARISI, *Il finanziamento delle organizzazioni internazionali*, Milan, 1986; ZOLLER, *The "Corporate Will" of the UN and the Rights of the Minority*, in *AJ*, 1987, p. 610 ff.; TAYLOR, GROOM, JENSEN, MORPHET and CHAN, *The Financing of the UN*, in *Review of International Studies*, 1988, p. 289 ff.; DANELIUS, *UN Voluntary Funds*, in *Nor. Journal of International Law*, 1989, p. 185 ff.; DUKE, *The UN Finance Crisis: A History and Analysis, in International Relations*, 1992, p. 127 ff.; ABRASZEWSKI, *Financing the Peace-Keeping Operations of the United Nations*, in *International Geneva Yearb.*, 1993, vol. VII, p. 79 ff.; DORMOY, *Les opérations de maintien de la paix de l'Organisation des Nations Unies. Aspects récents de la question de leur financement*, in *AF*, 1993, p. 131 ff.; SCHOETTLE, ENID, *Kein Geld für den Frieden? Die Finanzierung der UN-Friedenserhaltung*, in *Europa Archiv*, 1993, p. 453 ff.; DURCH, *Paying the Tab: The Financial Crises*, in DURCH (ed.), *The Evolution of UN Peace-Keeping*, New York, 1993; FRANCIONI, *Multilateralism à la Carte: The Legality of Unilateral Withholdings of UN Assessed Contributions*, in *EJIL*, 2000, p. 43 ff.; GERSON, *Multilateralism à la Carte: The consequences of Unilateral "Pick and Pay Approaches"*, ibid., p. 61 ff.; Cardenas, *UN Financing: Some Reflections*, ibid., p. 67 ff.; DELLA FINA, *Il bilancio nel diritto delle Nazioni Unite*, Milan, 2004.

86. *Obligatory contributions of the Member States.*

The UN obtains its own financial means through contributions of the States, contributions that are either *voluntary* (see 87) or *owed* by the Member States.

Article 17, paras. 1 and 2, of the Charter is concerned with the latter.

Under Article 17, the General Assembly approves the budget of the Organization and apportions the expenses among the members. The decision that provides for the apportionment is taken by a two-thirds majority (Article 18, para. 2) and must take into account, approximately, the capacity of each State to contribute (Article 160 of the Assembly rules of procedure). As can be deduced from Article 17, it binds all members. This, then, is one of the few cases in which the Assembly has a power of decision rather than of recommendation.

The obligation to contribute to the expenses, apportioned in accordance with Article 17, finds a specific sanction in Article 19, under which a Member State in arrears with its contributions by two years shall have no vote in the Assembly (see § 15).

Given that the States have the duty to contribute to expenses, what limits does the General Assembly meet in its assessment power? In other words, what is meant by "expenses" that must be apportioned among the members under Article 17? The question was dramatically discussed in the United Nations between 1961 and 1965, when several countries refused to contribute (for reasons that were not economical but rather political) to UN expenses for the maintenance of UNEF (the Force established by the General Assembly in 1956) in the Middle East (see § 64) and of ONUC in the Congo (see § 59), expenses that were to be apportioned by the Assembly. These countries (among them, the USSR, numerous other Socialist States, and France) held that their refusal was *legally* grounded. They maintained that it was not a matter of ordinary but of *extraordinary* expenses, and as such not covered by Article 17, and that at least some of the resolutions that led to the expenses, specifically the Assembly decisions establishing UNEF, were illegal owing to the organ's alleged lack of competence. They also held that by giving the Assembly the power to decide upon and then to allocate any kind of expense, one would have to recognize its functions as a world super-government, in clear contrast with its nature of an organ competent only to make recommendations. Their refusal to contribute was maintained despite censure by the majority in the Assembly, despite the threat of recourse to Article 19 on the suspension of voting rights of members in arrears, and despite the advisory opinion of July 20, 1962 of the International Court of Justice, issued at the request of the Assembly and clearly unfavorable to the view of the contesting States. Moreover, in the end, they substantially were victorious when, to end the dispute which even seemed to be threatening the existence of the Organization, the Assembly (which nearly had not held a session in 1964 so that Article 19 would not have to be applied) unanimously decided that the expenses for UNEF and ONUC would be covered by *voluntary* contributions (resolution of September 1, 1965).

The 1965 decision marked a turning point of great importance in the life of the Organization in that it caused the final loss of any illusion about the possibilities of the UN to assert its authority over individual Member States.

In some other cases the refusal to contribute has occurred with regard, however, to expenses that were not so conspicuous. This is the case, for instance, of the refusal, maintained for a number of years by the Soviet Union and by other Socialist States, to participate in the expenses for the coining of medals in memory of the Korean War or the maintenance of war cemeteries in Korea, a refusal justified by the illegality of the decisions on which the Korean War was based (see § 60). In turn, the United States have always refused to contribute to the expenses of all treaty body activities, i. e. activities of organs created by treaties promoted by the United Nations and certainly not characterized by an institutional link with the United Nations system. Reductions or selective withholdings of a more substantial nature have been occasionally decided by the United States, the major contributor to the UN budget, for political rather than legal reasons and particularly in order to exert pressure so that reforms would be introduced in the UN system, like, for instance, the changing of the voting system within the General Assembly.

With regard to the expenses for UNEF and ONUC, the position of the States that challenged the Assembly resolutions regarding their apportionment (the USSR, the Socialist States, France and some Latin American and Afro-Asiatic countries) can be deduced from their official statements made in the Assembly, some of which date from 1957, the year after the establishment of UNEF. Cf., for example, GAOR, 11th sess., 5th comm., 545th meet. ff., partic. 555th meet., no. 20; 15th sess., 5th comm., 803rd meet., no. 39 ff., no. 53 ff. and Pl. meet., 960th meet., no. 93ff, 122 ff.; 16th sess., Pl. meet., 1086th meet., no. 138 ff., no. 153 ff., 184 ff.; 17th sess., Pl. meet., 1199th meet., no. 54 ff.; 4th spec. sess., 1205th meet., no. 118. Cf. also the USSR memorandum presented to the International Court of Justice during the procedure for the issuance of an advisory opinion in 1962, in ICJ, *Pleadings (Certain Expenses of the United Nations)*, 1962, p. 271 ff., and the remarks of the French Government before the Court (*ivi*, p. 130 ff.). For the cited opinion of July 20, 1962 of the International Court of Justice, see ICJ, *Reports*, 1962, p. 151 ff. The Assembly resolution of September 1, 1965, which put an end to the matter, was taken in the form of approval of a statement by the President (contained in the report of the "Special Commission for operations relating to maintenance of the peace"), and can be found in GAOR, 19th sess., Pl. meet., 1331st meet. It is a resolution that does not come within the framework of Charter norms and which can better be seen as an agreement between States (cf. CONFORTI, *La funzione,* cit., p. 143 f.).

For the refusal of the Soviet Union and of the other States to contribute to the expenses for Korean War cemeteries, cf. CONFORTI, *La funzione*, cit., p. 109.

The practice concerning the United States is reported in ZOLLER, *art. cit.*, p. 610 ff. and MURPHY, in *AJ*, 2000, p. 348 ff.

What, then, is the exact content of Article 17? To refer to the most striking case, that of expenses for UNEF and ONUC, did the claims (which succeeded on the political level) of the USSR, France and the other States not to contribute to these expenses have a legal basis? In seeking an answer, it is useful to start with the cited opinion of July 20, 1962 of the International Court of Justice.

On two points the opinion is certainly correct. The first is that Article 17, in speaking of the UN budget and expenses, does not mean to refer only to expenses of ordinary administration (salaries and allowances of staff members, maintenance of offices). As the Court correctly notes (ICJ, *Reports*, 1962, p. 159), if the Charter wanted to distinguish in general between ordinary activities and extraordinary activities, between "administrative" budget and "operational" budget, it would have had to say so, and it would have had to establish precise rules on the adoption of the second type of budget and the apportionment of the relative expenses. This is all the more true in that the distinction between administrative budget and operational budget is not unknown to the Charter; on the contrary, it assumes this distinction in Article 17, at para. 3, in connection with the expenses of the specialized Agencies. On the other hand, the San Francisco preparatory works show no trace of a limitation of Article 17, paras. 1 and 2, to the administrative budget. The Conference discussed only whether it was preferable to speak of "budget" or "budgets" but in relation to the existence of a separate budget of the Court of Justice in addition to the UN budget (cf. UNC.I.O., vol. 19, p. 43 f. and 62, and vol. 20, p. 395). In conclusion, all that can be said is that from Article 17 there can be excluded only those expenses for which it can be proven that in a special Charter provision a special source of financing is indicated. This is the case of technical assistance programs and, more generally, of operational activities for development, coming under Article 66, para. 2 (see § 72).

The other point on which it would be impossible to differ with the Court (*Reports*, cit., p. 165 ff.) concerns the absence in the UN Charter of special provisions which (similar to the above mentioned provision on economic co-operation) derogate from Article 17, with regard to the function of maintenance of the peace. No merit, in fact, can be seen in the opinion, tenaciously defended before the Court by the USSR and the other Socialist States, that the financing of international armed forces comes within the framework of Article 43 and not of Article 17 of the Charter, thereby falling within the scope of the agreements to be entered into between the Security Council and the Member States under this article. Aside from the fact that the founders of the UN, in contemplating such agreements, hardly intended to deal with the financial aspects but were very much concerned with the military aspects of the Council actions for maintenance of the international order, it would be clearly contrary to the spirit of the Charter and of the collective security system to say that the principal function of the UN, which is that of maintenance of the peace, should be constrained, from the financial viewpoint, within the limits of Article 43. This view is all the more untenable to-day in that Article 43 has never found application (see § 59).

If, up to now, the opinion of the Court can be agreed upon, it cannot be accepted the extreme conclusion it reaches in saying that the Assembly would have a nearly unlimited budgetary authority (power of assessment) under Article 17. In its view, indeed, the Assembly could apportion any expenditure, as long as it involved action *coming within the purposes of the Charter*. With all due respect, this conclusion is absurd and does not even deserve rebuttal. The purposes of the UN, under Article 1, are very elastic and all-encompassing, ranging from maintenance of the peace to international co-operation for solving economic, social, cultural and humanitarian problems. Faced with such broad purposes, how could the Assembly or any other UN organ be prevented from deciding to undertake initiatives capable of committing, without any restraint, the economic resources of the member Governments? And would not this situation amount to realizing a world super-Government which is not recognized by the Charter nor could it in any way be permitted as things stand today?

On this part of the advisory opinion, which thus upholds the illegality of refusing to contribute to the expenses for UNEF and ONUC, cf. ICJ, *Reports*, cit., p. 167-170. The Court uses the theory of implicit powers (see § 5). After affirming that the Organization's expenses under Article 17, "must be tested by their relationship to the purposes of the United Nations", it gives the UN the power to take any measure, and to make any expenditures, necessary for fulfilling these purposes ("... when the Organization takes action which warrants the assertion that it was appropriate for the fulfilment of one of the stated purposes of the United Nations, the presumption is that such action is not *ultra vires*".

In our opinion, the expenses the members have to contribute to on the basis of Article 17 are only those that are generated by activity that has been *legally* decided upon, that is, by activity specifically foreseen by the Charter. In other words, the obligation to contribute exists with regard to all expenditures, as long as the decisions of the Assembly, the Security Council and the other UN organs whose implementation generates such expenditures are fully legal. This can be evinced from the very fundamental concept that UN organs are bound by the rule of law that requires full observance of the Charter (see § 7; see also § 97).

If the obligation to contribute is conditioned by the legality of the decisions which generate the expenses, the Assembly's power to assess is brought within tolerable limits that are coherent with the structure and the functions of the Organization. It should be remembered in fact that resolutions able to generate large expense are only those that can be classified as operational, that is, the resolutions in which the United Nations decides to undertake actions (see § 92). By contrast, resolutions of a normative character, such as recommendations and binding decisions, do not have this capacity. Such resolutions, recommending conduct or imposing conduct *on the States*, do not certainly place economic problems *on the UN* Even a superficial study of the Charter reveals that the power of UN organs to undertake actions is very exceptional with respect to the power to issue resolutions of a normative nature, especially recommendations. The UN is an entity whose fundamental task is to provide norms for the States, and not to take action. This is the reason why the drafters of Article 17 did not think about distinguishing between ordinary and extraordinary expenses, between administrative and operational expenses, and so on. However, this is also the reason why, without prejudice to the obligation to contribute to expenses in the few cases involving the actions envisaged by the Charter (cf. Article 34 on investigation, Article 42 on actions to maintain the peace, Article 87 on visits to trust territories, and some other articles), it cannot be said that an organ's action is legal if the relative power has not been given to it by the Charter provisions. Nor is it possible to infer the power to take action from the power to make recommendations, at least where its exercise involves *considerable* financial consequences.

Besides operational resolutions, the only other decisions able to generate expenditure are the "organizational" resolutions, specifically those establishing organs and thus involving the necessity of financing their functioning (on organizational resolutions, see § 92). However, particularly when such resolutions are not accompanied by operational decisions, that is, when the organ has not been established to undertake actions, it is usually a matter of expenses of normal administration and of limited size.

In the light of these considerations, one can correctly evaluate the refusal of the USSR, France and other countries to contribute to the expenses
for UNEF and ONUC. The refusal had a legal basis in the UNEF case, given
the lack of competence of the Assembly to undertake military actions and
therefore given the illegality of the relative resolutions (see § 63). On the
contrary, it should have been held inadmissible in the case of ONUC, since in
this case the action came under Article 42 of the Charter (see § 159).

It is indicative that although the International Court of Justice in the above opinion
had adopted the theory of implied powers as decisive in the case brought before it, it felt the
need to undertake an in-depth investigation to establish whether the resolutions setting up
UNEF and ONUC were in conformity with the specific Charter provisions on maintenance of
the peace. The Court took care to make it known that it wanted to undertake this investigation
only *ad abundantiam*. For this part of the opinion, cf. ICJ, *Reports*, cit., p. 170 ff.

The subsequent practice concerning the setting up of peacekeeping
forces, forces now always set up by the Security Council and never by the
General Assembly, has clearly tended to be that the relative expenses (which,
incidentally, are so enormous as to sometimes go over the total amount of the
ordinary budget) must be apportioned in accordance with Article 17. The
only peculiarity of the apportionment is that it must be done with criteria
somewhat different from those adopted for ordinary expenses, not excluding
the possibility of larger contributions of a voluntary nature.

Since the forces have been lawfully created, this practice must
certainly be considered as well-founded, and it confirms the correctness of
the view been expressed.

The Assembly began deciding that apportionment should be on the basis of Article
17 when the Security Council set up UNEF-II in 1973 and UNDOF in 1974 (see § 59). Cf., for
example, Assembly resolutions no. 3101-XXVIII of December 11, 1973, no. 3211-XXIX of
November 29, 1974, no. 3374-XXX of November 28, 1975, no. 31/5 of December 22,1976,
no. 32/4 of December 2, 1977. Acceptance of the principle of an obligatory contribution under
Article 17 was also pointed out, with regard to UNEF-II, in an opinion of the Secretariat of
October 23, 1974, published in UNJY, 1974, p. 159 ff. For the more recent practice, cf., for
example, the following resolutions, again of the Assembly: no. 47/71 of December 1, 1992
(UNOSOM: see p. § 59); no. 47/204 of December 22, 1992 (UNDOF); no. 47/205 of
December 22, 1992 (UNIFIL: see § 59); no. 47/210 of December 22, 1992 (UNPROFOR: see
§ 59). All these resolutions confirm, in their preambles, that the expenses for the Force to
which they refer are to be considered as expenses of the Organization in accordance with
Article 17, that the developed countries, considering their financial capacity, must sustain
greater expenses than the developing countries, and that it is important that voluntary
contributions be made.

An exception to the application of Article 17 are the expenses of UNFICYP (see §
59) which, having been set up in 1964, when the protest over the expenses for UNEF-I and
ONUC were still going on, was and still is today financed by voluntary contributions and by
contributions of the States providing the armed contingents.

As far as reductions and selective withholdings in the United States practice or in the practice of other States are concerned, they can be considered admissible if grounded on legal reasons and inadmissible if not. It has been convincingly held (by FRANCIONI) that even withholdings legally grounded should be assisted by the good faith of the opponent and a principle of consistency according to which he opponent soul not be in contradiction with its previous behaviour.

In conclusion, the refusal to contribute to expenses is to be evaluated in the same way as any challenge to an Assembly decision, a challenge which, since the UN does not have suitable means for *compelling* a State to fulfill its obligations, may be smoothed out only by agreement or by acquiescence (see § 97). It also should be noted that, since the States are usually in arrears with their payments (arrears which, as can be deduced from Article 19, can legally arrive at an amount equal to two years of contributions), the amounts that are the subject of the refusal usually coincide with the arrears. The arrears, moreover, are the real plague of the Organization's finances, as can be seen from the repeated appeals of the Secretaries-General that the States make their payments on time.

87. *Voluntary contributions.*

Voluntary contributions of States or of entities different from States may be provided for, explicitly or implicitly, by particular norms of the Charter (as occurs for operational activities in the area of economic co-operation: see § 72). They may also be requested by the Organization both to enlarge funds already established with obligatory contributions (as occurs in the case of peacekeeping operations: see § 86) and to finance activities that are related to the Charter's purposes (for example, the fund-raising promoted by the UN for humanitarian purposes).

Nothing prevents a UN organ, in adopting an operational resolution likely to create expenses under Article 17, from making its application dependent on financing through contributions that are either voluntary or previously assessed. This was the position taken by the Security Council immediately after the experience of the protests against ONUC expenses, with regard to peacekeeping actions, and specifically in the case of the UN Force in Cyprus, established in 1964. The resolution which set up UNFICYP (see § 87) and the resolutions that have renewed its mandate over the years have been taken after the necessary funds had been secured. On the contrary, as it has been seen, in other cases of the establishment of forces by the Security Council Article 17. has been applied.

88. *Issuance of loans.*

Sometimes the Organization has turned to the financial market. It is the case, for example, of Assembly res. no. 1739-XVI of June 27, 1961, which authorized the Secretary-General to issue a certain number of UN bonds and res. no. 1878 S-IV of June 27, 1963, which extended the term for their sale. During the period of the Cold War, this method of financing met with the opposition of the Soviet Union and of other countries and was denounced as contrary to Article 17 which foresees only the contributions of Member States as income. Indeed, this view does not seem to be completely unfounded.

For the opposition, see GAOR, 16th sess., Pl. meet., 1086th meet., no. 235 ff.; 4th sp. sess., Pl. meet., 1205th meet.,no. 73, 118 and 129. The USSR stated, also later on, that it would not have contributed to the payment of the interest and to its capital share of the bonds. Cf. GAOR, 4th sp. sess., Pl. meet., 1205th meet., no. 88 (*c*); 25th sess., 1970, Pl. meet., 1933rd meet., no. 19 f.; 26th sess., 1971, Pl. meet., 2031st meet., no. 43 f.; 28th sess., 1973, doc. A/PV 2206; 31st sess., 1976, Pl. meet., 107th meet., no. 104 f.

CHAPTER FOUR

THE ACTS

89. *Recommendations to the States.*

BIBLIOGRAPHY: SLOAN, *The Binding Force of a Recommendation of the General Assembly of the UN*, in *BYB*, 1948, p. 3 ff.; LAUTERPACHT (*diss. op. in the South-West Africa Case*), in *CIJ, Recueil*, 1955, p. 188 ff.; JOHNSON, *The Effects of Resolutions of the General Assembly of the UN*, in *BYB*, 1955-56 p. 97 ff.; VIRALLY, *La valeur juridique des recommandations des organisations internationales*, in *AF*, 1956, p. 66 ff.; FITZMAURICE, *The Law and Procedure of the International Court of Justice*, in *BYB*, 1958, p. 5; MALINTOPPI, *Le raccomandazioni internazionali*, Milan, 1958, partic. Chap. III; QUADRI, *Comment on Article 5*, in *Commentario al trattato CEE*, ed. by Quadri, Monaco and Trabucchi, I, Milan, 1965, p. 54 ff.; DETTER, *Law Making by International Organization*, Stockholm, 1965, p. 207 ff.; CASTLES, *Legal Status of UN Resolution*, in *The Adelaide Law Review*, 1967, p. 74 ff.; PANEBIANCO, *Raccomandazioni delle Nazioni Unite e libertà degli Stati membri*, in *ADI*, 1966, p. 268 ff.; DI QUAL, *Les effets des résolutions des Nations Unies*, Paris, 1967, p. 109 ff.; CONFORTI, *Le rôle de l'accord dans le système des Nations Unies*, in *RC*, 1974, II, p. 262 ff.; SCHREURER, *Recommendations and the Traditional Sources of Int. Law*, in *GYIL*, 1977, p. 103 ff.; REY CARO, *La competencia legislativa de la Asamblea General de las Naciones Unidas. Efectos juridicos de las Resoluciones*, in *Annuario de Derecho Internac.*, 1979, vol. V, p. 111 ff.; THIERRY, *Les résolutions des organes internationaux dans la jurisprudence de la Cour International de Justice*, in *RC*, 1980, II, p. 432 ff.; SKUBISZEWSKI, *Rechtscharakter der Resolutionen der Generalversammlung der Vereinten Nationen, V Deutschpolnisches Juristen-Kolloquium*, Bd. 2, Baden-Baden, 1981, p. 13 ff.; SLOAN, *General Assembly Resolutions Revisited (Forty Years Later)*, in *BYB*, 1987, p. 39 ff.; RINOLDI, *Atti delle Organizzazioni internazionali*, in *Enciclopedia giuridica Treccani*, vol. III, 1988; BIERZANEK, *Some Remarks on "Soft" International Law*, in *Polish Yearbook of International Law*, 1988, p. 21 ff.

As it has been often noted, a recommendation is the characteristic act that the organs of the United Nations (and of international organizations in general) have the power to issue. A recommendation is not binding and specifically does not bind the State, or the States, to which it is directed, to adhere to the conduct that has been recommended. However, it cannot be said that it has no legal consequences at all.

In our opinion, a recommendation produces, under the Charter, the effect of legality: a State does not commit a wrongful act when, in order to carry out a recommendation of a UN organ, it acts in a way that is contrary to commitments previously undertaken by agreement or to obligations deriving from customary international law. The effect of legality is to be allowed only in a relationship between Member States, and only with regard to *lawful* recommendations. Within these limits the effect can be deduced from the obligation to cooperate that the States have undertaken in adhering to the Charter and from the power given to the UN to pursue general purposes, even through non-binding acts. In other words, the possibility for UN organs to indicate to the Member States what conduct is necessary for the common interest would not make sense unless it were to involve the individual States's renouncing the reporting of the possible illegality of recommended conduct, in the light of rules that were different from those of the Charter.

Against the effect of legality, Article 103 of the Charter has been called into question. This article, in sanctioning only the precedence of Charter *obligations* over obligations arising from other agreements, would lead it to be excluded that the same precedence could be assigned to recommendations. This argument can be rejected. In fact Article 103 has the single clear purposes of expecting the Member States to respect at all costs the Charter obligations, while in the case of a recommendation the Member State is free not to adhere to the conduct recommended. In short, the effect of legality does not concern the problem of whether or not the State must carry out the recommendation but the problem (which should be resolved in the affirmative) of whether or not the State which has carried it out is to be protected.

> The area in which the effect of legality may have the most importance is that of Security Council recommendations whose subjects are enforcement measures under Chapter VII of the Charter. The States to whom such measures are requested may, thus, in adopting them, violate treaty norms different from the Charter or rules of general international law. The practice offers an example that might serve to illustrate this. It is Security Council resolution no. 221 of April 9, 1966 (see § 60) which reaffirmed the prohibition on the sale of oil to Southern Rhodesia, a prohibition already recommended in previous acts, and "invited" Great Britain to prevent by any means whatsoever the arrival of oil in the port of Beira (Mozambique) which was intended to be transported by land to Rhodesia. Actually, in the days prior to the resolution British authorities had searched the Greek ship *Joanna-V* on the high seas, off the coast of Beria. This had met very strong opposition on the part of the Greek Government in that it was contrary to international rules on maritime navigation. When, however, after the Council resolution had been adopted, a second Greek ship, *la Manuela*, was stopped and searched, there were no protests from the Greek Government (for an account of the events, see *RGDIP*, 1967, 472 ff.).

Some commentators connect to a recommendation the obligation of the State addressed to take its content into consideration in good faith. In particular, it has been held (LAUTERPACHT) that good faith obligates a State that does not intend to comply with the act to explain its reasons. This view must be shared, and it, too, can be based on the duty to cooperate inherent to the Charter. In providing that any obligations assumed in accordance with the

Charter must be fulfilled in good faith, Article 2, para. 2, confirms its positive value. It could perhaps more precisely to be said that the State to whom a recommendation is addressed (provided that it is a Member State of the UN) must accept the debate on its "merits", and it must intervene and explain, again regarding the merits, the reasons for its non-compliance. In short, it must agree to participate in the broadest discussion of the subject. No one can deny the importance of an obligation of this kind in a system like that of the UN, especially in organs like the General Assembly and the Security Council, where most of the issues dealt with have a political nature and the discussion stage sometimes may have more importance than the decision stage.

No other effects can be attributed to recommendations.

Some observers hold that the behavior of a State is unlawful when the State systematically refuses to observe a number of recommendations. Also this view is based on the principles of good faith and of cooperation. It is however unacceptable in that neither principle can be used up to the point of subverting the nature that the Charter gives to the act, that is, up to the point of making the recommended behavior obligatory, even after a certain period of time and a certain number of resolutions.

A view that was rather widespread in the past but is somewhat less so today, as the result of the fact that recommendations, especially those of the General Assembly are ever more often an instrument of party propaganda, is the one which appeals to the "moral" or "political" authority of the act. These are, however, effects of a non-legal nature that can be omitted here. In fact this authority can also be attributed, as has happened in the practice, to a "nonexistent" resolution, that is, to a draft resolution that did not, by a narrow margin, succeed in obtaining the majority required by the Charter.

Examples of appeals to moral authority can be found in Security Council practice, with regard to resolutions that had wide support but were blocked by a veto. For example, in 1946, France and Great Britain stated that they would have complied with the will of the majority favorable to a plan for the withdrawal of French and British troops from Lebanon and Syria even if the majority had not been sufficient in order to formally adopt the resolution (cf. SCOR, 1st year, 23rd meet., p. 368)). In 1964 Malaysia stated it "agreed to" a Council resolution concerning the Malaysian-Indonesian dispute, not adopted owing to a Soviet veto (cf. SCOR, 19th year, 1152nd meet, no. 102 ff.). In 1980 the President of the United States, Carter, in ordering sanctions against Iran to react to the illegal detention of American citizens in the American Embassy in Tehran, appealed to draft resolution S/373, approved by ten members of the Council but blocked by the veto of the USSR (cf. REISMAN, in *AJ*, 1980, p. 905). Also the draft resolution on the United States' failure to implement the judgement of the International Court of Justice of June 27, 1986 in the Nicaragua-United States case can be cited. The draft was not adopted by the Security Council on October 28, 1986 because of the United States veto, although it had obtained 11 favourable votes and three abstentions (of France, the United Kingdom and Thailand). On that occasion the United Kingdom stated that the resolution was to be held well-founded in law (in fact, Article 94 provides for the Council's competence to take the necessary measures so that the decisions of the Court are carried), but that it was not "politically" expedient (cf. S/PV.2718).

90. Decisions.

BIBLIOGRAPHY: SLOAN, *The Binding Force of a Raccommandation of the General Assembly of the UN*, in *BYB*, 1948, p. 3 ff.; KELSEN, *The Law of the United Nations*, London, 1950, p. 444 ff.; MORELLI, *Nozioni di diritto internazionale*, Padua, 1967, p. 295 ff.; CASTANEDA, *Valor juridico de las resoluciones de las Naciones Unidas*, Colegio de Mexico, 1967, chapters I-IV; DI QUAL, *Les effets des rèsolutions des Nations Unies*, Paris, 1967, p. 47 ff. and p. 75 ff.; QUADRI, *Diritto internazionale pubblico*, Naples, 1968, p. 580 f.; HIGGINS, *The Advisory Opinion on Namibia: Which UN Resolutions are Binding under Article 25 of the Charter?*, in *ICLQ*, 1972, p. 270 ff.; TIEWUL, *Binding Decisions of the Security Council within the Meaning of Article 25 of he United Nations Charter*, in *IJIL*, 1975, p. 195 ff.; KRÖKEL, *Die Bindungswirkung von Resolutionen des Sichereitsrates der Vereinten Nationen*, Berlin, 1977; SONNENFELD, *Resolutions of the UN Security Council, Dordrecht, 1987; SLOAN, General Assembly resolutions Revisited (Forty Years later), in* BYB, 1987,p. 105 ff.

Decisions, as opposed to recommendations, have fully binding force for the States to which they are addressed. There are not many of them in the United Nations system. Among the most important worth of mention are the General Assembly decisions which approve the budget and apportion expenses of the Organization among the Member States (Article 17) and Security Council decisions on measures not involving the use of force (Article 41). Worth of mention are also: decisions of the Security Council in the case of failure to comply with a judgment of the International Court of Justice, decisions which, under Article 94, para. 2, may consist, as preferred by the Council itself, in recommendations or in decisions; the resolutions with which the various collective organs adopt their own rules of procedure (cf. Articles 21, 30, 72, para. 1, and 90, para. 1), creating rules which bind the individual Member States of the body; acts relating to the status of UN members, such as decisions of the Assembly on suspension and expulsion (Articles 5 and 6), which decide, respectively, total or partial suspension and the extinction of the rights and obligations connected with such status.

It is worth dwelling on the power of the Security Council to issue decisions for maintenance of the peace, which bind the States they address. As it has been seen examining the provisions of Chapters VI and VII of the Charter, also the Council normally has the power to make only recommendations and it may resort to binding decisions only within the framework of Article 41, that is, when it is faced with crises that are so serious as to require sanctions. It is certainly not the case of again opening the discussion over Chapters VI and VII and repeating what it has already be said in discussing the functions of the Security Council. Only one point, however, deserves mention. This is the necessity to react to certain opinions in legal doctrine, which, from general and theoretical viewpoints, want to give the Security Council a much broader decision-making power. For example, it has been held that also recommendations, at least those falling within Chapter VII, are binding on the States because the Council may be led, when they are not carried out, to resort to sanctions under Article 41, or even to the use of force on the basis of Article 42 (KELSEN); or it has been held that Article 25, in affirming the commitment of the Member States "to accept and to carry out" the decisions of the Council, entails the binding nature of all Council acts, because all these acts postulate a decision (KELSEN); or, again, that the binding force of the resolutions depends on the force they have from a political point of view and that, from this point of view, also a simple invitation from the Council may be equivalent to an order (QUADRI). The International Court of Justice followed this way of thinking in its advisory opinion of June 21, 1971 on Namibia (see § 58). In its view, the Council could give binding force to any decision regarding maintenance of the peace and could express an opinion of the kind any time it called upon the States to respect a decision under Article 25 (cf. ICJ, *Reports*, 1971, p. 52 ff., nos. 112-116).

With due respect, such opinions cannot be accepted. Not only do they fail to find confirmation in the practice of the organ and in the attitudes of the majority of States, but neither can they be supported by valid textual arguments. In particular, it should be denied that Article 25 can be used to broaden the decision-making power of the Council. This article must be interpreted systematically and therefore by taking into account all the other provisions of the Charter on maintenance of the peace which manifestly use the distinction between recommendation and binding decision. Framed in this way, Article 25 is certainly not able to nullify this distinction but, on the contrary, assumes that the decisions to be accepted and carried out have already been identified. However, could it not be held that Article 25, interpreted systematically and not literally, intends to confirm a general obligation to cooperation with the organ rather than a specific and precise duty to carry out its resolutions?

91. *Organizational resolutions.*

BIBLIOGRAPHY: SLOAN, *The Binding Force of a Recommendation of the General Assembly of the UN*, in *BYB*, 1948, p. 4; JOHNSON, *The Effect of Resolutions of the General Assembly of the United Nations*, ivi, 1955-56, p. 101 f.; FITZMAURICE, *The Law and Procedure of the International Court of Justice*, ibid., 1958, p. 4.

Legal doctrine, particularly the English language authors, classify among the decisions that are binding for all the Member States resolutions of an organizational nature, that is, those that establish organs or provide for the election of their members. They concern, for example, the creation of subsidiary organs (Articles 22 and 29 of the Charter), the election of the members of the Security Council, of the Economic and Social Council, and of the Trusteeship Council by the Assembly, the appointment of the Secretary-General (Article 97), and so on. These resolutions would be binding on all members because they would involve the relationships between the Member States or because the Member States would have the obligation not to raise objections against anyone acting pursuant to them. With regard specifically to electoral acts, one should speak of "an obligation for all Members to recognize those states [the elected States] as having the prerogatives accompanying such membership" (SLOAN).

It does not seem that the immediate effects of organizational resolutions can be defined as obligations of the Member States. In so far as they deal with the functioning of the organization, these decisions concern the structural stage of the UN system, creating an objective right that is difficult to translate in terms of legal relationships, in terms of rights and obligations. What it can be said, in a rather repetitious way, is that their effects consist in the creation and renewal of the organs! Doubtlessly, from this point of view, the organizational acts must be kept separate from mere recommendations. It is actually in a category of its own with respect both to recommendations and to decisions binding on the Member States.

The only aspect under which one can discuss whether the organizational resolutions are capable on the average of producing legal obligations concerns their influence on the UN budget and on the apportionment of expenses among the Member States under Article 17 (see § 86).

92. *Operational resolutions.*

BIBLIOGRAPHY: CONFORTI, *Le rôle de l'accord dans le système des Nations Unies*, in *RC*,1974, II, p. 260 ff.; SLOAN, *General Assembly Resolutions Revisited (Forty Years Later)*, in *BYB*, 1987, p. 112 ff.

Like organizational acts, also operational resolutions must be considered as a special category since they are different from both decisions binding on the Member States and recommendations. Operational resolutions are the resolutions providing for a UN action. When we speak of a UN action, we mean an action *directly* carried out by the Organization, for example by the Security Council or by the General Assembly, or by the Secretary-General as entrusted by these two organs under Article 98, or by a subsidiary organ created by them. The Charter and the practice offer numerous examples of operational resolutions. This is the case of the resolutions setting up UN armed forces under Article 42, the resolutions which order an investigation or those which provide for programs of technical assistance, and so forth. Of course, the same resolution may have at the same time an organizational nature and an operational nature when, instead of providing that certain action be carried out by an already existing organ (for example, by the same organ that issued the resolution or by the Secretary-General), it establishes an *ad hoc* subsidiary organ.

It is evident that operational resolutions do not immediately produce obligations for the Member States and that they cannot be considered as binding decisions. At the same time, however, they are distinguished from recommendations. When the Assembly or the Council decided to undertake an action, such action is outside the sphere of recommendations. In fact, the acting is very different from recommending, since in one case an event occurs and in the other a rule of conduct is laid down; moreover the measure with which the action is decided is not addressed to the Member States, but belongs, as the organizational decisions belong, to the *structural* (*Sein*) dimension and not to the *normative* (*Sollen*) dimension of the United Nations system.

As is the case for organizational decisions, also here the only problem that can be envisaged in terms of obligations is the one of the influence of operational decisions on the UN budget and on the apportionment of expenses under Article 17 (see. § 86).

93. *Proposals, authorisations, delegations of powers or functions, approvals, directives, recommendations between the organs.*

BIBLIOGRAPHY: VIRALLY, *La valeur juridique des recommandations des organisations internationales*, in *AF*, 1956, p. 70 ff.; DI QUAL, *Les effets des rèsolutions des Nations Unies*, Paris, 1967, p. 17 ff.; SAROOSII, *The UN and the Development of Collective Security – The Delegation by the UN Security Council of its Chapter VII Powers*, Oxford, 1999.

In relations between the organs, the Charter provides also for the issuance of acts which are very often patterned, both in terminology and in substance, after the acts of public or private corporations in municipal law. The following are envisaged in the Charter: proposals (for example, proposals of the Security Council to the Assembly on admission, suspension and expulsion of members, improperly called recommendations in the English and French texts of Articles 4, 5 and 6); approvals (Article 66, para. 2, relating to technical assistance programs); directives and delegations (Articles 60, 85, para. 2, and 87 on the relations between the General Assembly on one hand and the Economic and Social Council and the Trusteeship Council on the other; Article 66, para. 3, on the delegation of functions from the Assembly to the Economic and Social Council; Article 98, on the functions delegated to the Secretary-General; authorizations (Article 12, para. 2: "The Secretary-General, with the *consent* of the Security Council, shall notify the General Assembly at each session of any matters relative to the maintenance of international peace..."; Article 53, para. 1, on the necessity of the authorization of the Security Council for enforcement actions decided by regional organizations).

There is not enough legal material to develop a theory of all these acts, similar to the very advanced one regarding corresponding acts in municipal law. On the other hand, the significance of each act can easily be inferred from the interpretation of the rule providing for it.

Worth noting is the effort made by D. SAROOSHI to develop a theory of the delegation of functions from the Security Council to the Secretary-General, Member States, subsidiary organs and Regional arrangements. We have taken into account many aspects of this theory in various parts of this book. Some general aspects deserve attention now, namely the distinction drawn between the delegation of powers and the delegation of a function, and between delegation and authorization (*op. cit.*, p. 10 ff.). In his view, a delegation of power implies a discretionary power of decision-making on the part of the delegated entity. However, what is delegated is in fact just a mere power of implementation. The authorization is more limited than the delegation of powers, since it consists of carrying out a specified objective. It is doubtful whether such subtle distinctions are practically fruitful. In this book we have used all this terms as synonyms.

The organs may also address recommendations to each other. For example, the Assembly may do so regarding the Security Council (Articles 10 and 11, para. 1 and 2), the Economic and Social Council regarding the Assembly (Article 62, para. 1), and so on. These are acts which cannot be given important legal consequences.

94. *Declarations of principles.*

BIBLIOGRAPHY: SCHACHTER, *The Relation of Law, Politics and Action in the UN*, in *RC*, 1963, II, p. 185 f.; BIN CHENG, *UN Resolution on Outer Space: « Istant » International Customary Law?*, in *Indian Yearbook of International Law*, 1965, p. 35 ff.; DECLEVA, *Le Dichiarazioni di principi delle Nazioni Unite*, in *ADI*, 1965, p. 63 ff.; ASAMOAH, *The Legal Significance of the Declarations of the General Assembly of the UN*, The Hague, 1966; VERDROSS, *Kann die Generalversammlung der Vereinten Nationen das Völkerrecht weiterbilden?*, in *Bruns'Z*, 1966, p. 690 ff.; CONFORTI, *La funzione dell'accordo nel sistema delle Nazioni Unite*, Padua, 1968, p. 150 ff.; ARANGIO-RUIZ, *The Normative Role of the General Assembly of the United Nations and the Declaration of Principles of Friendly Relations*, in *RC*, 1972, III, p. 431 ff.; CONFORTI, *Le rôle de l'accord dans le système des Nations Unies*, in *RC*, 1974, II, p. 281 ff.: SCHWEBEL, *The Effect of Resolution of the UN General Assembly on Customary International Law*, in *American Society of Int. Law, Proceedings*, 1979, p. 301 ff.; OSAKWE, *Contemporary Soviet Doctrine on the Source of General International Law*, ivi, p. 310 ff.; GARIBALDI, *The Legal Status of General Assembly Resolutions: Some Conceptual Observations*, ibid., p. 324 ff.; AGRAWALA, *The Role of General*

Assembly Resolutions as Trend-Setters of State Practice, in *IJIL*, 1981, p. 513 ff.; GRÜNINGEN, *Die Resolutionen der Generalversammlung der Vereinten Nationen und ihr Einfluss auf die Fortbildung des Völkerrechts*, in *Festschrift Bindschedler*, Bern, 1980, pp. 187-200; JOYNER, *UN General Assembly Resolutions and International Law: Rethinking The Contemporary Dynamics of Norm-Creation*, in *Calif. W. Internat. Law Journal*, 1981, p. 445 ss,; MACGIBBON, *Means for the Identification of International Law* etc., in *International Law: Theaching and Practice*, London, 1982, p. 10 ff.; HIGRASHI, *The Role of Resolutions of the United Nations General Assembly in the Formative Process of Customary Law*, in *JapAIL*, 1982, p. 11 ff.; BESTELIU, *Quelque réflexion sur le rôle des résolutions adoptées dans le Système des Nations Unies dans la formation du droit international économique*, in *Revue roumaine d'études internationales*, 1986, p. 227 ff.; SKUBISZEWSKI, *Resolutions of the UN General Assembly and Evidence of Customs*, in *Studi in onore di R. Ago*, Milan, 1987, p. 503 ff.; TUNKIN, *The Role of Resolutions of International Organisations in Creating Norms of International Law*, in BUTLER (ed.), *International Law and the International System*, Dordrecht, 1987, p. 5 ff.; HIGGINS, *The Role of Resolutions of International Organizations in the Process of Creating Norms in the International System*, ivi, p. 21 ff.; KOPAL, *The Role of UN Declarations of Principles in the Progressive Development of Space Law*, in *Journal of Space Law*, 1988, p. 5 ff.; ROLDAN BARBERO, *El valor juridico de las resoluciones de la Asamblea General de la ONU en la sentencia Nicaragua contra Estados Unidos de 27 de junio de 1986*, in *ReD*, 1990, p. 81 ff.; SLOAN, *United Nations General Assembly Resolutions in our Changing World*, New York, 1991.

From the early years of life of the UN, the General Assembly has followed the practice of addressing solemn declarations of principles to the States concerning not only international relations but also and especially relations within the different State communities. Beside the well-known Universal Declaration of Human Rights (res. no. 217-III of December 10, 1948), worth of mention are, among many others, the following Declarations: on genocide (res. no. 96-I of December 11, 1946), on the independence of colonial peoples (no. 1514-XV of December 14, 1960), on the prohibition of the use of nuclear and thermonuclear weapons (no. 1653-XVI of December 24, 1961), on sovereignty over natural resources (no. 1803-XVII of December 14, 1962), on the elimination of racial discrimination (no. 1904-XVIII of November 20, 1964), on the elimination of discrimination against women (no. 2263-XXII of November 7, 1967), on territorial asylum (no. 2312-XXII of December 14, 1967), on progress and social development (no. 2542-XXIV of December 11, 1969), on friendly relations and cooperation between States (no. 2625-XXV of October 24, 1970), on the legal principles governing the sea-bed and the ocean floor, and the sub-soil thereof, beyond the limits of national jurisdiction (no. 2749-XXV of December 17, 1970), on the definition of aggression (no. 3314-XXV of December 14, 1974), on measures to eliminate international terrorism (no. 49/60 of December 9, 1994, supplemented by the Annex to res. no. 51/210 of December 17, 1996) on crime and public security (no. 51/60 of December 12, 1996). Special mention should be given the Declaration and Program of action for the establishment of a new international economic order (nos. 3201 and 3202 S-VI of May 1,

1974), the Charter of the Economic Rights and Duties of States (no. 3281-XXIX of December 12, 1974), the Declaration on the right to development (no. 41/128 of December 4, 1986) and the Declaration on international economic cooperation (no. S-18/3 of May 1, 1990), the Declaration on the occasion of the 50th anniversary of the UN (no. 50/6 of October 24, 1996), which are at the basis of UN activity in thc field of cooperation for development (see § 71), the Millennium Declaration (no. 55/2 of September 8, 2000; the Declaration on the new partnership for Africa's development (res. no. 57/2 of September 16, 2002.

Sometimes the Declarations of principles are limited to reproducing already existing international rules, specifically, customary rules or rules already contained in the Charter. This can be said, for example, of the principle of the non-appropriability of resources of the sea-bed and of the subsoil thereof beyond the limits of domestic jurisdiction, a principle formulated by the above-mentioned resolution of December 17, 1970 and constituting a corollary of the customary principle of freedom of the seas. The same can be said, to give another example, of the principle that prohibits the use of force or the principle of good faith, both set out in Article 2 of the Charter and confirmed by the Declaration on friendly relations between the States of October 24, 1970. It is clear that in these cases no one could put in doubt the obligatory nature of the declared principles, but this obligatory nature necessarily has its foundation in customary law or in the Charter.

Aside from reproducing already existing rules, what is the significance of these Declarations? No doubt, in principle, that they are not binding. The Assembly does not have decision-making powers. Under Article 10 of the Charter, it can only discuss subjects coming within the purposes of the Charter and make recommendations in this regard to the States. The Declarations of principles appear, therefore, in the light of the Charter, as mere recommendations, although of a general and solemn nature, and the States remain free to decide to comply with them. It is indicative, moreover, that most times this freedom is expressly claimed and emphasized in the Assembly when the Declaration is adopted even by the Governments giving it their affirmative vote. It is the case, for instance, of the unequivocal reservations on the obligatory nature of the Universal Declaration of Human Rights of 1948 from the same States that were supporting it. The same can be said of the reservations that accompanied the 1974 unanimous adoption (by consensus) of the Declaration and Program of action for the establishment of a new international economic order.

With regard to the Universal Declaration, cf. the reservations of France, the Netherlands, Australia, Mexico, etc., in GAOR, 3rd sess.; Pl. meet., 180th meet., p. 866 and 873; 181st. meet., p. 876 and 885. For the reservations relating to the resolutions on the new economic order, see § 97.

In fact, the Declarations perform a very important role in the development of international law and of its adjustment to the needs for solidarity and for interdependence that are more and more being felt in the world today. It is not a matter of giving them a binding force which on the basis of the Charter they do not have. It is a matter of recognizing the contribution that, with them, the UN Assembly is giving to the formation of international law, although within the framework of the typical sources of this law, such as custom and agreement. Of what does this contribution consist? With regard to customary law, the Declarations play a role in the process of its formation, as *State practice*, as the synthesis of the attitudes of States that adopt them and not as formal acts of the UN This is shown by the fact that, as is generally recognized, their value as elements in the formative practice of customary law is higher when they are adopted by unanimity or by consensus or at least by a very wide majority.

With regard to treaty law, it is possible to say that certain Declarations have the value of true international agreements. This is the case of those Declarations, such as, for instance, the res. no. 1803-XVII of December 14, 1962, on sovereignty over natural resources that not only formulate a principle but *expressly and unequivocably equate its non-observation with violation of the Charter.* Since the Assembly does not have the power to interpret the Charter in a way that is binding on the individual States (see § 6), also Declarations of this kind remain, from the viewpoint of the Charter, mere recommendations. One can say, however, placing them outside the UN system that they have the nature of international agreements (specifically of agreements in a simplified form that is, entered into without a formal act of ratification) and that as such they are binding on the States which voted for them. It seems, in fact, that *by equating the non-observance of a certain principle to non-observance of the Charter, a verbal expedient is being used to purely and simply confirm that such principle is now obligatory.* From this it appears completely correct to assume, at least until there is clear proof to the contrary (*id est*, provided that there are no *express* reservations when the resolution is adopted), that the States that participate by favorably voting for the act intend to bind themselves. Indeed, the alternative is the following: either this presumption is accepted or the Declaration represents, to use a private law term, non-serious declarations or declarations rendered with a mental reservation.

In recent times Declarations of principles have also been adopted by the Security Council. See, for instance: res. no. 1377 of November 12, 2001, containing the Declaration on the global effort to combat terrorism; res. 1467 of March 18, 2003, embodying a Declaration on "proliferation of small arms and light weapons and mercenary activities: threats to peace and securities in .West .Africa". These Declarations, like General Assembly Declarations, have non-binding force, since thy are not adopted under Chapter VII of the Charter. Therefore, the observations above made with regard to the Declarations of General Assembly can be applied to those issued by the .Security Council.

95. *The UN resolutions and the rule of law: The duty of the organs to comply with the Charter and with international law.*

BIBLIOGRAPHY: KOPELMANAS, *L'ONU*, I, Paris, 1947, p. 297 ff.; CHAKSTE, *Justice and Law in the Charter of the UN*, in *AJ*, 1948, p. 158 ff.; GROSS, *The UN and the Rule of Law*, in *Int. Org.*, 1965, p. 538 ff.; HALDERMAN, *The UN and Rule of Law*, Dobbs Ferry, New York, 1966.; HIGGINS, *The Place of International Law in the Settlement of Disputes by the Security Council*, in *AJ*, 1970, p. 1 ff.; CONFORTI, *Le rôle de l'accord dans le système des Nations Unies*, in *RC*, 1974, II, p. 209 f.; GOTTLIEB, *The Legitimacy of General Assembly Resolutions*, in *Isr. Yearbook of Human Rights*, 1987, p. 120 ff.; SAJOSÉ GIL, *Las consequencias juridicas de los actos «ultra vires» de las organizaciones internacionales, en particular de l'ONU*, in *RBDI*, 1990, p. 443 ff. ; OASTHUIZEN, *Playing the Devil's Advocate: The UN Security is Unbound by Law ?*, in *LJIL*, 1999, p.549 ff..; KOROMA, *International Law Limits to the Security Council*, in GOWLLAND DEBBAS (ed), *UN Sanctions and International Law*, The Hague, 2001, p. 71 ff.

As it has already indicated, the UN organs must respect the Charter (see § 7). Also the violation of international customary rules or general principles of law, when they are rules or general principles that Charter provisions do not derogate explicitly or implicitly from entails the illegality of the acts. A clear example of derogation is that deducible from Article 27, para. 3, last part, which removes from the *nemo judex in re sua* principle Security Council resolutions adopted under Chapter VII (see § 27).Another example is that of the power of the Security Council to determine the existence of a threat to the peace, a breach of the peace and an act of aggression, a power which is almost unlimited under Article 39 of the Charter (see § 55 bis). .

The necessity that general international law be respected by the organs finds support in the Charter provisions stating the UN's purposes, at least as far as "adjustment or settlement of international disputes or situations" are concerned (cf. Article 1, para. 1). Similarly, the provisions, also regarding the purpose of the Organization, which make reference to particular parts of general International law like the principle of self-determination or the international protection of human rights (cf. Article 1, para. 2 and 3), may be cited. In any case, the respect for general International law may be deduced from the nature of the United Nations legal system, which constitutes special law in comparison with the law of the Community of States.

The observance of general international law is necessary, for example, regarding decisions which, such as those on credentials, concern State succession and its effects on membership in the Organization (see § 21).

96. *The observance of rules of procedure*

BIBLIOGRAPHY: JESSUP, *International Parliamentary Diplomacy*, in *AJ*, 1957, p. 401; SØRENSEN, *Principes de droit international public*, in *RC*, 1960, III, p. 93; WENGLER, *Völkerrecht*, Berlin, 1964, p. 559; DURANTE, *L'ordinamento interno delle Nazioni Unite*, Milan, 1964, p. 82; CASTAÑEDA, *Valor juridico de las resoluciones de las Naciones Unidas*, Colegio de Mexico, 1967, p. 32 f.; CONFORTI, *Le rôle de l'accord dans le système des Nations Unies*, in *RC*, 1974, II, p. 215 ff.

Can the violation of rules of procedure be cause of illegitimacy of the resolutions of the organs? These rules, adopted on the basis of specific Charter provisions (cf. Article 21 with regard to the General Assembly, Article 30 for the Security Council, Article 72, para. 1, for the Economic and Social Council) without doubt bind the individual Member State (see § 90). However, do they bind also the organs? Or it must be said that the organs, as they are qualified by the above provisions to issue by (simple) majority their own rules of procedure, so they may, by majority, not apply them with regard to *specific individual cases*? At first glance, both views seem plausible. In favor of the latter, there are both an argument of a formal nature, regarding the voting system adopted on the subject, and an argument that a certain flexibility in the application of the rules of procedure may be necessary to meet situations of a special character. In favor of the first view, it could be said that the possibility for the majority to subvert at will the rules of procedure is not very compatible with the purpose of the rules, which is that of an orderly and impartial course in the proceedings of the organ. In conclusion, in the United Nations the same questions arise that have often filled legal doctrine concerning public law in municipal systems, with regard to the rules of procedure of collective bodies, especially of Parliaments.

Both views have been supported in the practice. On various occasions, especially in the Organization's first ten years, the minorities in the organs (especially in the General Assembly and in the Security Council) have raised protests against the non-observance of the rules of procedure, maintaining that it was impossible, for the organs themselves, to subvert the rules in specific cases. These reservations, however, came up against precise stands of the majority which consisted in defending the principle that every organ is "master of its own procedure".

In fact, the protests of individual States have become much weaker in recent times. There have been fewer challenges to the principle that the organ may derogate as it wishes from the rules of procedure (for examples of the unchallenged application of this principle, cf. GAOR, 37th sess., 1982, Pl. meet., 43rd meet. and 110th meet.; 38th sess., 1983, Pl. meet., 34th meet.; 41th sess., 1986, Pl. meet., doc. A/41/PV.51).

The problem must be resolved by seeking to identify the particular features and the relevance that Articles 21, 30, and 72, para. 1, all with the same content, give to the power of the various organs to adopt their own rules of procedure.

It must be said at the outset that the fact that the rules of procedure were adopted by (simple) majority, and that therefore can be modified by majority, is not in itself an argument capable of justifying derogation by the majority from the rules in specific cases. To the contrary, it could be held that the Charter, precisely when it provides in the articles cited that an organ "shall adopt its own rules of procedure", speaks against the possibility of an *ad hoc* derogation. It could be said, that is, that attributing the organs the power to make their own rules of procedure would have not made sense if such power were not exercised by the issuance of generally applicable rules, thereby excluding the possibility that individual rules could be created for individual cases. The conclusion would thus be reached that, under the Charter, any procedure contrary to the rules of procedure could be adopted only after a well-pondered modification of the text of the rules. This conclusion, moreover, could be confirmed by several provisions in the rules of procedure themselves. For example, one could cite Article 163 of the Assembly rules of procedure which provides that "These rules of procedure may be amended by a decision of the General Assembly, taken by a majority of the members present and voting, after a committee has reported on the proposed amendment".

Everybody, however, can see how strained a rigid interpretation of the Charter would be which would exclude any even minimal derogation from the rules of procedure on the basis of norms that provide in a very general manner the power to adopt rules of procedure.

In our view, all that must be derived from the Charter is the general recognition of a principle of objectivity and impartiality in the conduct of activities of the organs. This principle is not so much inferred from the express prevision of a power to adopt rules of procedure, which in itself recalls the idea of a prior objective ordering of the procedures, as by the spirit of the Charter and in particular by the characteristics it assigns to the organs. These are collective bodies called to deal with international problems, situations and disputes that have a predominantly political nature and in which the discussion stage has assumed an importance that is equal, if not superior, to the decision stage. This is the reason why it is necessary that the first stage proceeds according to rules which impartially guarantee the individual State, member of the organ, real participation in the organ's proceedings.

In the light of the principle of objectivity, those derogations or violations of the rules of procedure that suppress or seriously limit the right of the member of the organ, to express its opinion or present its proposals are illegal. In particular a violation of the principle of objectivity will occur whenever a State is unjustifiably excluded from the proceedings (for example, the violation of the provision of Article 29 of the Assembly's rules and Article 17 of the Security Council's rules, which allow the representative of a

Government whose credentials are being challenged to be seated provisionally with the same rights as the representatives), or when a State is not able to know or to become informed about the subject of a discussion (for example, because the subject does not appear on the agenda) or, again, in the case where its representatives are denied the right to speak or to vote.

Again in the light of the principle of objectivity and impartiality, it must be denied the legality of such derogations or violations of the internal rules of procedure which, even without suppressing or compromising the right of the Member State, bring about a appreciable change in a given procedure. In other words, it can be said that a precise and well-thought-out amendment of the rules of procedure is always necessary, pursuant to the principle of objectivity, when the organs intend to adopt procedures *fundamentally* different from the ones provided. It seems truly inconceivable that a change of this kind can correspond to requirements of objectivity and of impartiality if realized in relation to a specific case. Vice versa, when it is a matter of adopting derogations that do not affect, except in a limited and non-essential way, the regulation of the procedure, a prior general amendment of such rules does not seem imposed by the above requirements. It must therefore be held inadmissible, to give some examples, that in specific cases the rules on credentials can be departed from, for instance, by derogating from the rules concerning the organ competent to issue them, or that the terms or the prescribed majorities are changed in drawing up the agenda, or that, with regard to the General Assembly, there is a change in the distribution of functions between plenary assembly and commissions, or that the order of the discussion and the voting is radically changed.

For specific applications of the principle of objectivity and impartiality with regard to cases that have occurred in General Assembly and Security Council practice, see CONFORTI, *op. cit.*, p. 49 ff. note 77 ff.

97. *Illegality of acts and the role of agreement in the United Nations system.*

BIBLIOGRAPHY: TAMMES, *Decisions of International Organs as a Source of the International Law*, in *RC*, 1958, II, p. 337 ff.; ROBINSON, *Metamorphosis of the UN*, ivi, p. 560 ff.; SERENI, *Diritto internazionale*, II, 2, Milan, 1960, p. 980 ff.; MORELLI, *Nozioni di diritto internazionale*, 7th ed., Padua, 1967, p. 221 ff.; CONFORTI, *Le rôle de l'accord dans le système des Nations Unies*, in *RC*, 1974, II, p. 209 ff.; THIERRY, *Les résolutions des organes internationaux dans la jurisprudence de la Cour Internationale de Justice*, in *RC*, 1980, II, p. 385 ff.; FLAUSS, *Les réserves aux résolutions des Nations Unies*, in *RGDIP*, 1981, p. 5 ff.; ZOLLER, *The « Corporate Will » of the UN and the Rights of the Minority*, in *AJ*, 1987, p. 610 ff.; FRANCK, *The "Powers of Appreciation": Who is the Ultimate Guardian of UN Legality?*, in *AJ*, 1992, p. 519 ff.; BEDJAOUI, *Du contrôle de légalité des actes du Conseil de sécurité*, in *Nouveaux itinéraires en droit. Hommage à François Rigaux*, 1993, p. 69 ff.; ID., *Nouvel ordre mondial et contrôle de la légalité des actes du Conseil de sécurité*, Brussels, 1994; BROWNLIE,

The Decisions of Political Organs of the United Nations and the Rule of Law, in *Essays in Honour of Wang Tieya*, 1994, p. 91 ff.; MARTENCZUK, *The Security Council, the International Court and Judicial Review: What Lesson from Lockerbie*, in *EJIL*, 1999, p. 517 ff.; FASSBENDER, *Quis Judicabit? The Security Council. Its Powers and Its Legal Control, ibid.*, 2000, p. 219 ff.; DUGARD, *Judicial Review of Sanctions*, in GOWLLAND DEBBAS (ed), *UN Sanctions and International Law*, The Hague, 2001, p. 83 ff.; Schweigman, *The Authority of the Security Council under Chapter VII of the UN Charter. Legal Limits and the Role of the International Court of Justice*, The Hague, 2001; MARCHI, *Accord de l'Etat et droit des Nations Unies*, Paris, 2002.

One of the most important but also very contradictory characteristics of the United Nations system is that, on the one hand, the organs are compelled to observe the law and especially the Charter, but on the other the Charter does not provide any review mechanism over the legality of their resolutions, and especially it does not envisage effective review of a judicial nature. What happens then if a Member State challenges the legitimacy of a decision and states its intention to refuse to recognize its effects? Is such protest devoid of any effect when faced with the will of the majority? But is this not the same as saying that the organs may violate the Charter? How can the finality of the resolutions be assured in order to allow them to produce the legal consequences, even minimal, foreseen by the Charter provisions?

The lack of judicial review of UN acts (the advisory function of the International Court of Justice, since it is not binding and especially cannot be requested by the States, cannot serve this purpose) is a negative feature of the UN system, equal at least to the lack of effective means of pressure by the Organization on the States.

The situation is quite different when the question of the legality of a UN resolution is raised before the International Court of Justice (and the same can be said of whatever international tribunal) in a dispute between States. In this case the so-called contentious jurisdiction of the Court is at stake, so that the decision of the Court is obligatory for the parties, and for the parties only (so-called *subjective res judicata*). Within these limits, it is perfectly conceivable that the Court can examine the legality of an UN act, even of an act of the Security Council, if the question is relevant in order to decide the case. The problem has notably been raised before the International Court of Justice in the case entitled *Questions of interpretation and application of the 1971 Montreal Convention arising from the aerial incident at Lockerbie (Libyan Arab Jamahiriya v. United States of America) (1992-2003)- Order on provisional measures*, in ICJ, *Reports*, 1992, para. 38 ff., and *Judgment on preliminary objections, ibid.*, 1998, para. 36 ff. The problem has never been solved, since the agreed settlement of the dispute.

Various attempts have been made in legal doctrine to uphold the idea that United Nations' acts cannot be challenged. Appeal was made to the power that the organs would have to interpret the Charter in a way that is binding on the individual member, that is, of a power which in reality, for reasons we have seen, does not exist (see § 6).

Then, an attempt was made to transfer into the UN system principles that in domestic law, or, rather, in some State legal systems, assure the final nature of the acts of certain public organs, such legislative or administrative organs. However, it has been easy to retort, keeping in mind the scarse capability of the United Nations to assert its authority over the Member States that an analogy between the UN organs and State organs does not seem to be the most appropriate.

For a detailed criticism of these views, which were expressed mainly over the question of the expenses for UNEF (established by the General Assembly in 1956) and ONUC (on this, see § 86), see CONFORTI, *Le rôle de l'accord* cit, p. 230 fff.

In our view, a realistic examination of the functioning of the United Nations necessarily leads to the conclusion that the principles which ensure the unchallengibility and the finality of the acts are more or less those of traditional international law. Only the principle of *agreement* and its corollaries are able, in the present situation, to carry out a function of this kind. In the last analysis, the legitimacy of an act cannot be challenged by a State when this State has acquiesced to it, that is, when it has either implicitly or explicitly accepted the act.

The UN practice offers many cases of challenges to the legitimacy of the acts. The so-called legal challenge in fact represents the usual line of defense by a Government when it wants to oppose a given resolution. It is possible to find in the practice, more specifically in the practice of the two main organs, the General Assembly and the Security Council, unwritten rules that specify the significance of acquiescence, setting the limits beyond which the challenge is no longer admissible as well as the relationships between the challenge and the expression of the vote. In ascertaining these unwritten rules, a distinction must be done between the cases when the "challenging" State is not a member of the organ from which the act is issued and the cases when indeed it is a member.

With regard to the first case, the practice is in the sense that a State is acquiescent if it does not proceed to challenge an act as soon as it is given the possibility to do so. For example, it may happen that a Government, party to a dispute, or interested in a situation brought to the attention of the Security Council, participates in Council meetings without the right to vote. In this case, it will have to make known its reservations on the legitimacy of the resolution during the discussion or in any case not after the time when the act is adopted. The high number of examples in the practice conforming to this procedure and especially the care with which the Governments request that their reservation be included in the records of the organ's meetings are testimony to the necessity of this procedure and the existence of the above-mentioned rule on the timeliness of a challenge. When, on the contrary, there has not been participation in the discussion, the reservation may be formulated when the Organization asks the Member State to specify its position regarding the resolution. This usually occurs when the text of the resolution is communicated by the Secretary-General.

For the earliest practice concerning challenges by a non Member State of an organ during discussion or when the act was issued, see CONFORTI, *Le role de l'accord,* cit., p. 237 ff. For the more recent practice, cf., for example, the reservations, on procedure and on the merits, put forward by the Libyan Government against res. no. 731 of January 23, 1992 (see § 54) and no. 748 of March 31, 1992 (see § 55 *bis*) of the Security Council. These resolutions adopted measures against Libya for terrorist acts against PAN AM flight 103 and UTA flight 772 (for the text of the reservations, see, respectively, S/PV.3033 and S/PV. 3063. In S/PV.3033 there also appear the reservations of Sudan and of the representative of the Arab League against the first resolution).

With regard to the second case, which concerns Governments that are members of the organ, the problem arises of the relations between challenges and the expression of the vote.

It cannot be said that a reservation regarding the legality of an act is always implicit in a negative vote since a negative vote may be cast for political or other reasons. On the contrary, acquiescence is avoided only when the challenge is made in a statement *expressed before or immediately after the vote* (expression of the vote). The practice goes in this direction. On the one hand, there are many examples of reservations that accompany a contrary vote, and also here the insistence with which the Governments express them during the discussion stage and claim that they be inserted in the records is certain evidence of their necessity. On the other hand, there are no cases of a negative vote that is not accompanied by an explicit reservation concerning the illegitimacy of the act which has been followed by the attempt of a State to refuse the possible effects of the resolution.

For the earliest practice, see CONFORTI, *Le role de l'accord,* cit., p. 239 ff. For the more recent one, cf., with regard to General Assembly resolutions and as examples: GAOR, 40th sess., 1985, Pl. meet, doc. A/40/PV.116 (reservations of the Iranian Government on the "validity" of General Assembly resolutions on the human rights situation in Iran); GAOR, 41st sess., 1986, Pl. meet., doc. A/41/PV.55 and 56 (reservations of the German Democratic Republic and of other States, identical to the ones expressed in previous years, against res. no. 41/33 on Afghanistan, considered as contrary to Article 2, para. 7 of the Charter); GAOR, 41st. sess., 5th Comm., doc. A/C5/41/SR 20 (identical protests by Afghanistan); GAOR, 41st sess. Pl. mect., doc. A/4/PV.53 (reservations of the United States on the competence of the General Assembly to be concerned with implementation of the judgement of the International Court of Justice of June 27, 1986 in the United States-Nicaragua case); GAOR, 47th sess., 1992, Pl. meet., doc. A/47/PV.70 (reservation of the United States against res. no. 47/19 condemning the U.S. embargo on Cuba). With regard to the Security Council, cf., for example, the reservations advanced by Cuba, at that time a member of the organ, against res. no. 687 of April 3, 1991 (see § 55 *bis*), and specifically against the parts of the resolution on the setting of the boundary between Iraq and Kuwait and the compensation owed by the former for its aggression against the latter; these parts were considered by Cuba as not in accordance with the United Nations Charter (for the Cuban statements, see S/PV.2981).

If a reservation must be explicitly stated in the event of a negative vote, it may be considered implicit in deliberate non-participation in a vote. Such non-participation has, in fact always been understood as the maximum expression of the non-acceptance of a decision owing to its illegitimacy. Cf., among the many cases, GAOR, 2nd sess., 1st Comm., 94th meet., p. 305 and Pl. meet., 111th meet., p. 823 ff., 112th meet., p. 839 ff. and p. 859 (non-participation of the Socialist States in the vote on res. no. 112-II of November 14, 1947 on the independence of Korea, held to be illegal because it was taken without the intervention of the representatives of North Korea in the discussion and therefore contrary to the doctrine of self-determination sanctioned by the Charter); GAOR, 5th sess. Pl. meet., 330th meet., no. 37 ff., 64 ff., 69 ff., 85 ff., and 101 ff. (*idem* for res. no. 500-V of May 18, 1951 on the embargo against China and North Korea, denounced as invalid owing to the Assembly's lack of competence to recommend measures for maintenance of the peace); SCOR, 16th year (1961) 971st meet. (non-participation of Nationalist China in the vote for the admission of Outer Mongolia which was held not to be independent); GAOR, 16th sess., Pl. meet., 1121st meet., no. 615 ff. (non-participation of Great Britain and Portugal in the vote on resolution no. 1747-XVI of February 28, 1962 relating to the independence of the *people* of Southern Rhodesia, for the resolution's being contrary to Article 2, para. 7, of the Charter); GAOR, 16th sess., Pl. meet., 1088th meet., no. 33 (identical behaviour of Portugal for the same reasons, against a resolution on Angola, res. no. 1742-XVI of January 30, 2962). See also the cases of non-participation of Communist China, after its entry in the UN in 1971, in resolutions of the Security Council on military peacekeeping actions, which we have noted at § 25

Also a State which abstains may avoid the effects of acquiescence by expressing its reservation of a legal nature (as in the case of a negative vote) during the discussion stage or during expression of the vote.

A contrary view, which holds that abstention always implies recognition of the legitimacy of the act, seemed to have been held, although in terms that do not make this interpretation certain, by the International Court of Justice in the often cited 1962 opinion on the expenses of the United Nations in the Middle East and in the Congo. Among the various arguments it adopted against the refusal by the Member States to contribute to expenses for the UN emergency force (UNEF) in the Suez crisis (see § 85), the Court also noted incidentally that the Assembly resolutions establishing UNEF were all adopted without any negative votes (cf., ICJ, *Reports*, 1962, p. 170 f.). It thus gave no weight to the fact that several Governments (precisely those that later were to insist in their refusal) abstained from the vote grounding their abstention exactly in the Assembly's lack of competence to intervene with an international force in the Suez (see § 63). In that it was an incidental and very marginal passage in the opinion, it is not clear whether the Court held that abstention, in implying a position of non-opposition to the act, is equivalent to acquiescence. This opinion could in any case be rejected as contrary to a number of unambiguous expressions in the practice. Aside from the UNEF case, abstention accompanied by a reservation regarding the legitimacy of the act can be found, for example, in two Security Council resolutions, respectively, no. 27 of August 1, 1947 and no. 63 of December 24, 1948 on Indonesia's war of independence. In this case the reservations and abstentions came from Belgium, France and Great Britain, and were based on the limit of domestic jurisdiction under Article 2, para. 7 (cf. SCOR, 2nd year, 171-173rd meet. and 3rd year, 229th meet.). The same can be said of the case of the appointment of a mediator in Palestine in 1948: when the Security Council decided in its session of July 15, 1948 to provide the mediator with a certain number of armed guards, the Soviet Union, abstaining, denounced the relative resolution as contrary to Article 43 of the Charter (cf. SCOR, 3rd year, 388th meet., p. 64 ff.). Lastly, reservations of a legal nature were put forward as reason for abstaining during the Assembly discussions on the problem of expenses for dredging the Suez Canal in 1957 (cf. GAOR, 12th sess., Pl. meet., 730th meet., no. 1 ff.), in the Security Council regarding the admission of new members (for example, the reservations of the USSR and the United States in 1961 with regard to the admission, respectively, of Mauritania and of Outer Mongolia: cf. SCOR, 16th year, 971st meet.), again in the Assembly on the restitution of cultural property to the State of origin (cf. the statements of the United Kingdom, in 1989, relating to res. no. 44/18, in GAOR, 44th sess., Pl. meet., doc. A/44/PV.45), and, again in the Security Council, with regard to the parts of res. no. 687 of April 3, 1991 concerning the setting of the boundary between Iraq and Kuwait and compensation owed by Iraq (cf. the statements of Yemen, in S/PV.2981), as well as with regard to res. no. 748 of March 31, 1992 on the measures against Libya (cf. the statements of Capo Verde in S/PV.3063) and so on.

Lastly, acquiescence is to be presumed in the case of a favorable vote. This is, however, a simple assumption and thus subject to evidence to the contrary. Actually, it is not unusual that a State, although voting in favor, expresses reservation on *a part* of the decision being voted upon, the part it intends to disassociate from, or it states that it will follow a *certain interpretation* of the act, and reject any interpretation that is different and, in particular, the one that seems to be held by the majority of members in the organ. Such conduct has found fertile ground, especially in the General Assembly, following the spreading of the practice of approval by consensus (see § 33). In fact, it could be said that this way of voting, which otherwise would not be different from a unanimous vote, and would not deserve a special latin name, is characterized by the fact that it is a convenient loophole for making a decision appear to be supported by all but at the same time allows the States to challenge the act and be disassociated from its effects. This is why the practice of consensus does not deserve an entirely favorable judgement.

One of the most important cases of resolutions approved by consensus but accompanied by various reservations of a large number of States was that on the Declaration and Program of action for the establishment of a new international economic order, adopted by the General Assembly during the sixth special session in 1974 (res. no. 3201 S-VI and 3202 S-VI of May 16, 1974). The reservations, concerning certain parts of the two resolutions, and the way of interpreting them, can be drawn from reports of the plenary sessions (cf. doc. A/PV 2229-A/PV 2231). Another case is that of the General Assembly resolutions requesting the creation of a "peace zone" in the South Atlantic, resolutions adopted with the affirmative votes of the United States and France, but with the reservations of both States not to apply them in the part contrary to the principle of the freedom of navigation on the high seas (cf., for example, the statements of the two States in GAOR, 44th sess., 1989, Pl. meet., doc. A/44PV.55). For other cases of challenges put forward at the same time as a favorable vote, see CONFORTI, *La funzione*, cit, p. 29 f.

When a State has validly challenged the legitimacy of a resolution, when, more generally, acquiescence cannot be attributed to it, its challenge usually reaches its purpose, that is, refusal of the effects of the act and the extraneousness of the State with regard to the act itself. When these are recommendations, the State may avoid even the minimal consequences they produce, and in particular the duty to explain the reasons for conduct not in keeping with the conduct recommended. In the case of binding decisions or of resolutions that constitute the conditions for binding decisions, challenges will involve the rejection of the obligations that derive from the decisions. In turn, the denouncing of the illegality of organizational decisions, that is, decisions establishing organs or providing for the election of members, shall have as a consequence non-cooperation with the organ, non-participation in the proceedings, non-recognition of the acts issued by the organ, the refusal to recognize the legal existence of the organ. Only as far as resolutions that affect the structure of the organization as a whole are concerned, such as resolutions regarding admission and, more generally, membership of the State in the Organization, the consequences of the challenge of legality by a State are likely to be mitigated. A State which challenges the regularity of the presence (or of the expulsion) of another State in the UN may protest, may temporarily suspend its collaboration with the Organization (remember the Soviet Union's temporary abandonment of the main organs between January and June 1950, as a protest against the presence of the Government of Formosa in the UN: see § 19), but in the end it will have no alternative to acquiescence other than that of withdrawal from the Organization.

For the relevant practice see, again, CONFORTI, *Le role de l'accord*, cit., p. 253 ff.

ANALYTICAL INDEX

(the numbers refer to paragraphs)

LEGAL ASPECTS OF INTERNATIONAL ORGANIZATION

1. S. Rosenne: *Procedure in the International Court.* A Commentary on the 1978 Rules of the International Court of Justice. 1983   ISBN 90-247-3045-7
2. T.O. Elias: *The International Court of Justice and Some Contemporary Problems.* Essays on International Law. 1983   ISBN 90-247-2791-X
3. I. Hussain: *Dissenting and Separate Opinions at the World Court.* 1984
                    ISBN 90-247-2920-3
4. J.B. Elkind: *Non-Appearance before the International Court of Justice.* Functional and Comparative Analysis. 1984   ISBN 90-247-2921-1
5. E. Osieke: *Constitutional Law and Practice in the International Labour Organisation.* 1985
                    ISBN 90-247-2985-8
6. O. Long: *Law and Its Limitations in the GATT Multilateral Trade System.* 1985
                    ISBN 90-247-3189-5; Pb: 0-86010-959-3
7. E. McWhinney: *The International Court of Justice and the Western Tradition of International Law.* The Paul Martin Lectures in International Relations and Law. 1987
                    ISBN 90-247-3524-6
8. R. Sonnenfeld: *Resolutions of the United Nations Security Council.* 1988
                    ISBN-90-247-3567-X
9. T.D. Gill: *Litigation Strategy at the International Court.* A Case Study of the Nicaragua versus United States Dispute. 1989   ISBN 0-7923-0332-6
10. S. Rosenne: *The World Court.* What It is and how It works. 4th revised ed. Prepared with the assistance of T.D. Gill. 1989 *For the 5th revised ed., see below Volume 16*
11. V. Gowlland-Debbas: *Collective Responses to Illegal Acts in International Law.* United Nations Action in the Question of Southern Rhodesia. 1990   ISBN 0-7923-0811-5
12. Y. Beigbeder: *The Role and Status of International Humanitarian Volunteers and Organizations.* The Right and Duty to Humanitarian Assistance. 1991
                    ISBN 0-7923-1190-6
13. A.B. Avanessian: *The Iran-United States Claims Tribunal in Action.* 1993 (also published in *International Arbitration Law Library*)   ISBN 1-85333-902-4
14. R. Szafarz: *The Compulsory Jurisdiction of the International Court of Justice.* 1993
                    ISBN 0-7923-1989-3
15. Y.Z. Blum: *Eroding the United Nations Charter.* 1993   ISBN 0-7923-2069-7
16. S. Rosenne: *The World Court.* What It is and how It works. 5th revised ed. 1994
                    ISBN 0-7923-2861-2
17. P.H.F. Bekker: *The Legal Position of Intergovernmental Organizations.* A Functional Necessity Analysis of Their Legal Status and Immunities. 1994 ISBN 0-7923-2904-X
18. S.A. Voitovich: *International Economic Organizations in the International Legal Process.* 1994   ISBN 0-7923-2766-7
19. S.A. Alexandrov: *Reservations in Unilateral Declarations Accepting the Compulsory Jurisdiction of the International Court of Justice.* 1995   ISBN 0-7923-3145-1
20. M. Hirsch: *The Responsibility of International Organizations Toward Third Parties.* Some Basic Principles. 1995   ISBN 0-7923-3286-5
21. A.S. Muller: *International Organizations and their Host States.* Aspects of their Legal Relationship. 1995   ISBN 90-411-0080-6
22. T. Kanninen: *Leadership and Reform.* The Secretary-General and the UN Financial Crisis of the late 1980s.   1995 ISBN 90-411-0102-0

23. C. Tomuschat (Ed.): *The United Nations at Age Fifty.* A Legal Perspective. 1995
ISBN 90-411-0145-4

24. R. Frid: *The Relations Between the EC and International Organizations.* Legal Theory and Practice. 1995
ISBN 90-411-0155-1

25. M.M. Martin Martinez: *National Sovereignty and International Organizations.* 1996
ISBN 90-411-0200-0

26. M. Pomerance: *The United States and the World Court as a 'Supreme Court of the Nations':* *Dreams, Illusions and Disillusion.* 1996
ISBN 90-411-0204-3

27. E. Denters: *Law and Policy of IMF Conditionality.* 1996
ISBN 90-411-0211-6

28. P. van Dijck and G. Faber (Eds.): *Challenges to the New World Trade Organization.* 1996
ISBN 90-411-0236-1

29. C. Peck and R.S. Lee (Eds.): *Increasing the Effectiveness of the International Court of Justice.* Proceedings of the ICJ/UNITAR Colloquium to Celebrate the 50th Anniversary of the Court. 1997
ISBN 90-411-0306-6

30. B. Conforti: *The Law and Practice of the United Nations.* 1996
ISBN 90-411-0233-7

31. N.L. Wallace-Bruce: *The Settlement of International Disputes.* The Contribution of Australia and New Zealand. 1998
ISBN 90-411-0567-0

32. B. Fassbender: *UN Security Council Reform and the Right of Veto.* A Constitutional Perspective. 1998
ISBN 90-411-0592-1

33. R.A. Wessel: *The European Union's Foreign and Security Policy.* A Legal Institutional Perspective. 1999
ISBN 90-411-1265-0

34. A.D. Efraim: *Sovereign (In)equality in International Organizations.* 2000
ISBN 90-411-1310-X

35. P. van Dijck and G. Faber (eds.) *The External Economic Dimension of the European Union.* 2000
ISBN 90-411-1383-5

36. B. Conforti: *The Law and Practice of the United Nations.* Second Revised Edition. 2000
ISBN 90-411-1414-9

37. N.M. Blokker and H.G. Schermers (eds.): *Proliferation of International Organizations.* Legal Issues. 2001
ISBN 90-411-1535-8

38. K.G.Bühler: *State Succession and Membership in International Organizations.* Legal Theories *versus* Political Pragmatism. 2001
ISBN 90-411-1553-6

39. E. Riesenhuber: *The International Monetary Fund under Constraint.* Legitimacy of its Crisis Management. 2001
ISBN 90-411-1577-3

40. Mohammed Sameh M. Amr: *Role of the International Court of Justice as the Principal Judicial Organ of the United Nations.* 2003
ISBN 90-411-2026-2

41. Terry Gill (ed.): *Rosenne's The World Court.* What It Is and How It Works. 6th revised edition. 2003
ISBN 90-04-13633-9

42. B. Conforti: *The Law and Practice of the United Nations.* Third Revised Edition. 2005
ISBN 90-04-14308-4

MARTINUS NIJHOFF PUBLISHERS – LEIDEN / BOSTON